BIG
BOOK OF
Scrap
Quilts

COMPILED AND EDITED BY

L. Amanda Owens
and Patricia Wilens

Oxmoor
House®

Portions of this book were previously published
in the following volumes: *Quick Quilts from Your Scrap
Bag, Scrap Quilts Fast and Fun, Great American Quilts
2001* and *2002, Relax and Quilt,* and *Quick and Easy
Scrap Quilts.*

ISBN: 0-8487-3062-3
Printed in the United States of America
First Printing 2005

Editor in Chief: Nancy Fitzpatrick Wyatt
Executive Editor: Katherine M. Eakin
Art Director: Cynthia Rose Cooper
Copy Chief: Allison Long Lowery

Big Book of Scrap Quilts
Editor: L. Amanda Owens
Senior Designer: Melissa Jones Clark
Editorial Assistants: Shannon Friedmann, Terri Laschober
Illustrator: Kelly Davis
Senior Photographer: John O'Hagan
Photo Stylists: Katie Stoddard, Linda B. Wright
Publishing Systems Administrator: Rick Tucker
Director of Production: Laura Lockhart
Production Manager: Greg A. Amason
Production Assistant: Faye Porter Bonner
Contributing Editor: Patricia Wilens
Contributing Copy Editor: Susan S. Cheatham
Editorial Intern: Mary Catherine Shamblin

Cover: *Jenny's Flower Garden* (page 116)

To order additional publications,
call 800-765-6400.

For more books to enrich your life, visit
www.oxmoorhouse.com

FOR THE

I t's no secret that quiltmakers adore fabric.
We may say that piecing is our favorite part—or
even appliquéing or hand quilting. But I'm
convinced that **many of us make quilts simply
because we *love* fabric.** The textures, colors, and
patterns are utterly enchanting.

**The theory is that using up leftovers from past
projects makes a scrap quilt frugal. In truth, it's
a wonderful excuse to own more fabric. As my
friend Marti Michell says, "A scrap is any piece of**

LOVE OF FABRIC

fabric I haven't used yet—even if that 'scrap' is 5 yards long!" A jumble of pretty prints, perky plaids, exotic batiks, and basic solids generates a heartwarming exuberance that more sedate quilts cannot achieve.

Perhaps that's why the only antique quilt I own is *Baby Baskets,* with little blocks framed by a red check fabric that I find irresistibly cheerful. I often wonder about the person who made it, somewhere in the Midwest between 1885 and 1900. Was she a young girl in Nebraska or a grandmother from Kansas? **Are the plaid fabrics cut from family clothing? Are the blocks small because she didn't have many scraps or because she just liked them that way?**

Sometimes I imagine that I know all about this woman because of what we share. I can tell she wasn't much for hand quilting—something we definitely have in common. Also, we both like to sew, love quilts, and are charmed by bright red plaids. **We are sisters down through the ages because of our love of fabric.**

Baby Baskets (page 177)

It wasn't usual in days gone by for women to sign their quilts. Today's quiltmakers are more assertive, often including a patch citing who made it, when, where, and why—a legacy for the future.

When you make an eye-catching quilt from this book, you become a part of that rich legacy. These quilts provide a creative opportunity to express classic designs through the beautiful array of fabric available today. New tools and time-saving techniques for cutting and piecing add ease to that mix.

Don't try too hard to coordinate fabric or your scrap quilt may lose the spontaneity that invigorates it. Try putting ready-to-sew scraps in pillowcases or large envelopes—one each for light, medium, and dark values. Then reach in and grab whatever you touch. Vow to use any color or print you pull out, no matter what. You'll probably put together fabric you wouldn't usually pair—and that's part of the fun.

Discover up-to-date methods and complete instructions in "Step-by-Step Guide to Quiltmaking" (page 297), as well as informative PinPoints tip boxes sprinkled throughout the book. But most of all, enjoy playing with your beloved stash of fabric.

Patricia Wilens

Contributing Editor

TABLE OF CONTENTS

SCRAP QUILTS

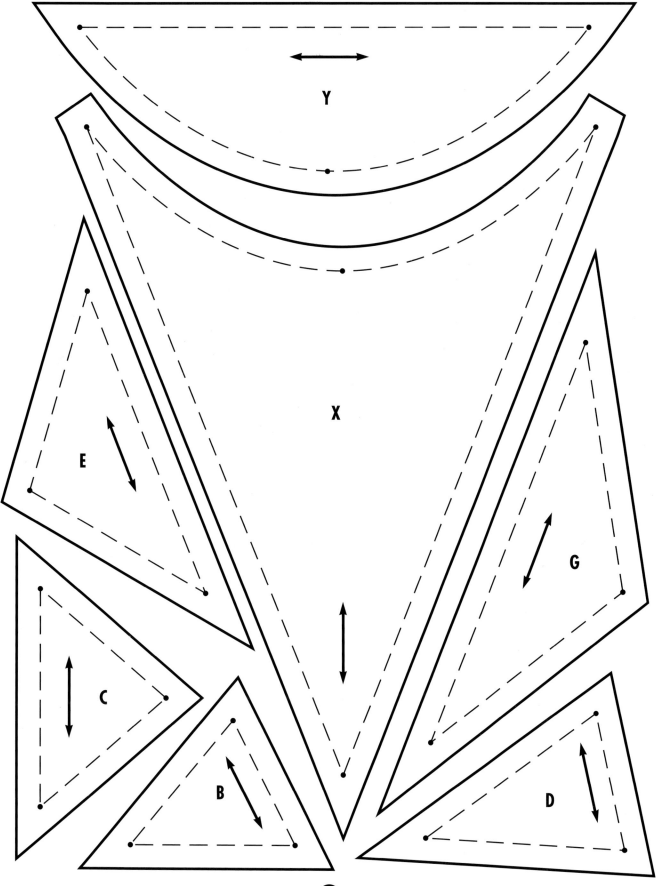

VINTAGE SCOTTIES

Quilt by Sonja Palmer of Plymouth, Minnesota

Scottish terriers were very popular during Franklin D. Roosevelt's presidency, thanks to well-known presidential pet Fala. A gift from a cousin, Fala came to the White House in 1940. He greeted many visiting dignitaries and traveled with FDR around the world. You can use real feedsack material for this quilt or choose reproduction prints.

Finished Size
Quilt: 17¾" x 21¼"
Blocks: 15 (3¼" x 4¼")

Materials
19 (3½" x 4½") scraps for
    appliqué *
4 (2") squares for ball stripes
⅛ yard *each* 4 prints for borders
½ yard muslin
⅛ yard *each* 2 binding fabrics
1 (21" x 25") piece for backing
Black embroidery floss
Paper-backed fusible web (optional)
* *Note:* See page 307 for tips on cutting pieces for appliqué.

12

Cutting

Measurements include ¼" seam allowances, except for appliqué pieces. For hand appliqué, add a scant seam allowance. If fusing, fuse web to wrong side of fabric following manufacturer's instructions and cut out shapes in finished sizes.
From assorted scrap fabrics
• 15 Scotties.
• 4 balls.
From 2" squares
• 4 ball stripes.
From each of 2 border fabrics
• 1 (1¼"-wide) strip.
From each remaining border fabric
• 1 (1½"-wide) strip for borders.
From muslin
• 2 (3¾"-wide) strips. From these, cut 15 (3¾" x 4¾") rectangles for appliqué background.
• 1 (3"-wide) strip. From this, cut 4 (3") squares for border corners.
• 2 (1¼"-wide) strips for borders.
From each binding fabric
• 2 (2" x 23") strips.

Block Assembly

1. Hand-appliqué a Scottie to each muslin rectangle, using 2 strands of floss for blanket stitching. Or fuse Scotties in place; then blanket-stitch. Add a French knot for each dog's eye. (See *Stitch Diagrams* below.)
2. Appliqué a stripe onto each ball. In quilt shown, ball stripes were appliquéd using traditional appliqué with matching thread.
3. Blanket-stitch each ball onto a muslin square.

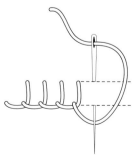

Blanket-Stitch Diagram

Quilt Assembly

1. Referring to photo, join Scottie blocks into 5 horizontal rows of 3 blocks each. Join rows.
2. Join 1 wide and 1 narrow border strip to sides of a muslin border strip to make a strip set. Press. From this, cut 2 (16¾") strips. Join borders to quilt sides with wider border at outside edge.
3. Join remaining border strips in same manner; press. From this strip set, cut 2 (13¼") borders. Join 1 ball block to each end of these borders. Sew borders to top and bottom edges of quilt.

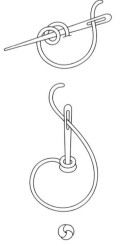

French-Knot Diagram

Quilting and Finishing

1. Layer backing, batting, and quilt top; baste. Quilt as desired. Quilt shown has outline-quilting around dogs and balls and a cable pattern quilted in borders.
2. With wrong sides facing and raw edges aligned, fold each binding strip in half lengthwise and press. Sew 1 pair of strips to quilt sides; trim even with top and bottom edges of quilt. Sew second pair of binding strips to top and bottom edges. Tuck ends under ¼" at corners and secure binding on back of quilt.

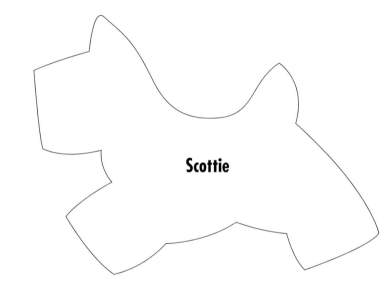

Scottie

Note: Patterns are finished size and do not include seam allowances.

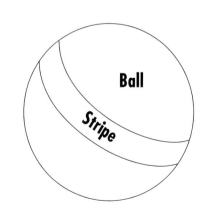

Ball

Stripe

CUPS & SAUCERS

Quilt by Sissy Graves Towers of Rainbow City, Alabama

When sorting scraps by color, most fabric-lovers find one color group stacked higher than others. Use this inclination to combine your favorite colors of fabrics with simple patchwork and basic appliqué to create a collection of saucy teacups based on a popular 1930s pattern.

Finished Size
Quilt: 74½" x 98"
Blocks: 77 (6¾" x 7")
This quilt fits a full-size bed.

Materials
77 (5" x 7") scraps for appliqué
3½ yards muslin
3¾ yards blue setting fabric (includes binding)
5¾ yards backing fabric

Cutting
Make templates of patterns on page 16. Pieces A and G can be rotary-cut, if desired. See page 307 for tips on cutting pieces with templates for appliqué and patchwork. Cut all strips on cross-wise grain.
From muslin
- 13 (3½"-wide) strips. From these, cut 77 (3½" x 7¼") A pieces. (If prewashed fabric is not a full 44" wide, you will need 2 additional strips to cut A pieces.)
- 12 (1½"-wide) strips. From these, cut 77 *each* of E and F.
- 154 (2" x 7¼") G pieces.

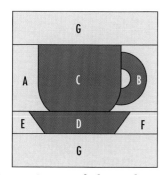

Cups & Saucers Block—Make 77.

From each *scrap fabric*
- 1 each of patterns B and C, adding seam allowances. Prepare pieces for appliqué by turning under curved edges. Do not turn under straight edges, which will be overlapped or finished in seams.
- 1 of Pattern D.

From setting fabric
- 77 (7¼" x 7½") setting blocks.

Block Assembly

1. Position B and C on A, aligning straight edges of A and C. Place curve of handle (B) about ¾" from right edge of A. (Cup overlaps ends of handle.) When satisfied with position, appliqué B and C in place (Block Assembly Diagram).
2. Sew E and F to D as shown to complete saucer section. Press seam allowances toward D.
3. Join saucer section to bottom of teacup section.
4. Sew Gs to top and bottom edges.
5. Make 77 blocks.

Size Variations

	Twin	Queen	King
Finished size	61" x 91"	88" x 98"	95" x 105"
Number of blocks	59	91	105
Number of set blocks	58	91	105
Blocks set	9 x 13	13 x 14	14 x 15
Yardage Required			
5" x 7" scraps	59	91	105
Muslin	2½ yards	4 yards	4⅝ yards
Setting fabric	2⅞ yards	4 yards	4¾ yards
Backing fabric	5½ yards	2⅝ yards (108" wide)	3⅛ yards (108" wide)

Quilt Assembly

1. For Row 1, lay out 6 blocks and 5 setting blocks in a row, alternating blocks as shown (Row Assembly Diagram). For Row 2, lay out 5 blocks and 6 setting blocks.
2. Referring to the photo at left, lay out blocks in 14 rows, alternating rows 1 and 2. Arrange blocks to achieve a nice balance of color and value. When satisfied with the placement, join the blocks in each row.
3. Referring to the photo, join the rows.

Quilting and Finishing

1. Mark quilting design on quilt top as desired. On quilt shown, patchwork is outline-quilted and a purchased stencil design is quilted in each setting block.
2. Layer backing, batting, and quilt top. Then baste together. Quilt as desired.
3. Make 10 yards of bias or straight-grain binding. Bind the quilt edges.

continued

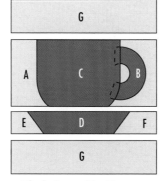

Block Assembly Diagram

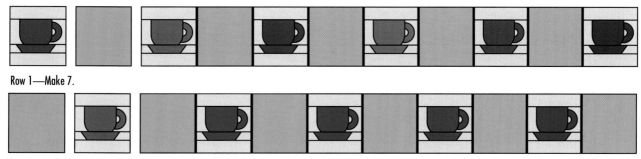

Row 1—Make 7.

Row 2—Make 7.

Row Assembly Diagram

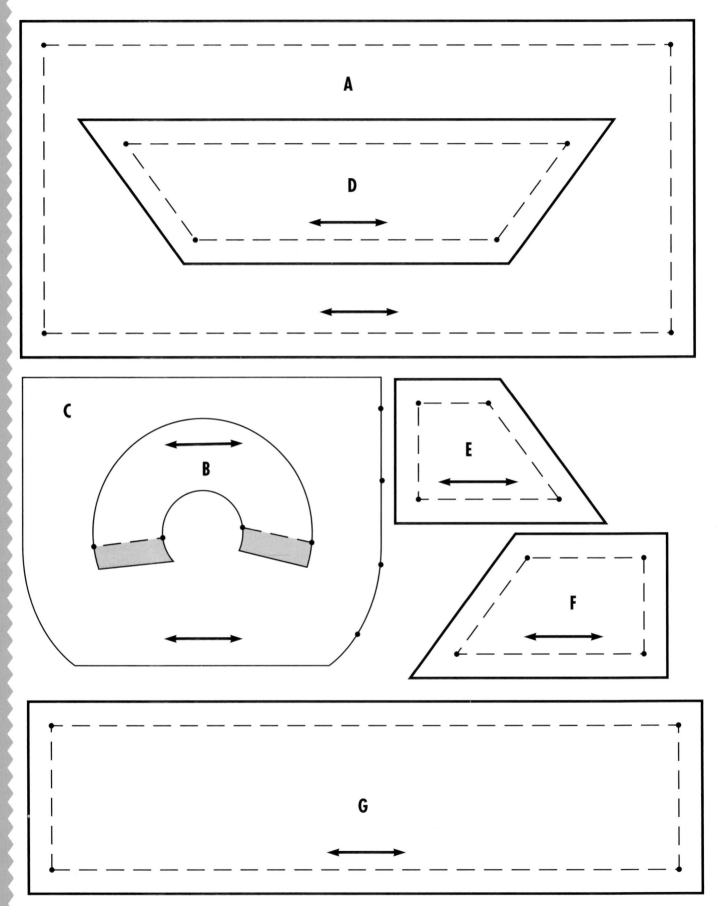

A

D

C

B

E

F

G

WILD STARS

A Sawtooth Star block is about as traditional as it gets, but Jan Wildman transforms the ordinary with fabric and a plan. She used splashy florals, novelty prints, and versatile tone-on-tones and textures. The easy-to-make star gets extra jazz from checkerboard sashing and borders. Jan machine-quilted wiggly lines and circles in asymmetrical repeats.

Rotary cutting and quick-piecing techniques make this an ideal project for beginners or quilters in a hurry.

Finished Size

Quilt: 77" x 87"
Blocks: 42 (8" x 8")

Materials

42 (9" x 22") fat eighths light print scrap fabrics *
42 fat eighths dark print scrap fabrics *
1¼ yards white fabric
4¼ yards dark purple border fabric (includes binding)
5¼ yards backing fabric
* *Note:* Yardage allows for 1 star and 1 background from each fabric.

Cutting

Instructions are for rotary cutting and quick piecing. Cut pieces in order listed to make best use of yardage. When possible, pieces are listed in order needed, so you don't have to cut everything all at once.
From each *scrap fabric*
• 1 (1½" x 22") strip for checkerboard border.
• 1 (2½" x 22") strip. From this, cut 4 (2½") C squares.
• 1 (4½") D square.
• 4 (2½" x 4½") A pieces.
• 8 (2½") B squares.
From white
• 54 (1½" x 22") strips for checkerboard sashing.

continued

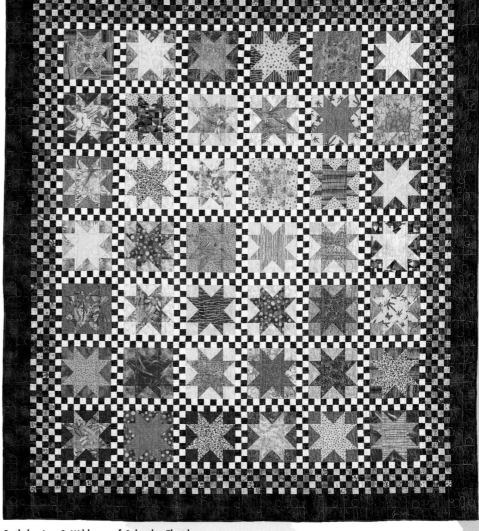

Quilt by Jan C. Wildman of Orlando, Florida

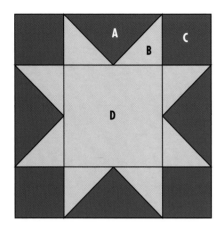

Sawtooth Star Block—Make 42.

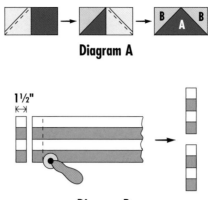

Diagram A

Diagram B

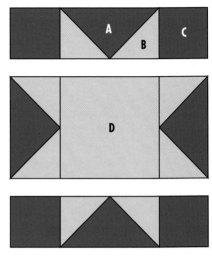

Block Assembly Diagram

From purple
- 4 (5" x 81") lengthwise strips for outer border. Use 81"-long remnant for next cut.
- 54 (1½" x 22") strips for checkerboard sashing.
- 40 (1½" x 22") strips for checkerboard border.
- 1 (30") square for binding.

Block Assembly

1. For each block, choose 4 A pieces and 4 C squares of same fabric, as well as 8 B squares and 1 D of a coordinating fabric.
2. See page 304 for step-by-step instructions on diagonal-corner quick-piecing technique. Using that method, sew B squares to corners of each A piece as shown (Diagram A). Press.
3. Lay out all units in rows (Block Assembly Diagram). Join units in each row. Press seam allowances toward Cs and D. Join rows to complete block.
4. Make 42 blocks.

Quilt Assembly

1. Using 1½" x 22" strips, join 2 purple and 2 white strips (Diagram B). Make 27 strip sets. Press seam allowances toward purple.
2. Cut 14 (1½"-wide) segments from each strip set to get a total of 378 segments.

3. Join 2 segments end to end to make each sashing unit, alternating white and purple fabrics. Make 84 (8-square) sashing units. Press joining seam allowances toward purple.
4. Lay out blocks in 7 horizontal rows, with 6 blocks in each row (Row Assembly Diagram). Place 1 sashing unit at both ends of each row.
5. Join 2 sashing units side by side, turning 1 unit to alternate white and purple fabrics (Row Assembly Diagram). Make 35 double-sashing units, 5 for each row. Add double units to layout between blocks in each row.
6. Join the blocks and sashing in each row.
7. Referring to photo on page 17, join remaining sashing units in 14 horizontal rows with 15 segments in each row. Press joining seam allowances toward purple.
8. Sew 1 sashing row to top of first block row and 1 sashing row to bottom edge of last block row, matching seam lines where row meets vertical sashing unit. Press.

9. Join remaining rows in horizontal pairs. Join all rows, alternating sashing rows and block rows.

Borders

1. Make 20 strip sets as before, using 2 (1½" x 22") strips each of purple and assorted scrap fabrics (Diagram B). Press all seam allowances toward purple. You'll have about 40 strips left over; save these for another project.
2. Cut 14 (1½"-wide) segments from each strip set for a total of 276 (and 4 extra) segments.
3. Join 78 segments for each side border, alternating purple and scrap fabrics. Before you press these joining seams, lay each border against quilt edge to determine which border edge aligns so that fabric colors alternate correctly against checkerboard sashing. Mark this inside edge of border with a pin. Press seam allowances toward segments with a purple square at inside edge.

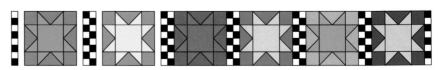

Row Assembly Diagram—Make 7.

4. Sew the assembled borders to the quilt sides.
5. Join 60 strip-set segments in a row for top border. Identify inside edge and press seam allowances; then sew border to top edge of quilt. Repeat for bottom border.
6. Measure length of quilt through middle of pieced top. Trim 2 outer border strips to match quilt length. Sew borders to quilt sides, easing to fit as needed. Press seam allowances toward borders.
7. Measure width of quilt through middle, including side borders. Trim remaining borders to match width. Sew borders to top and bottom edges of quilt, easing to fit as needed. Press seam allowances toward borders.

Quilting and Finishing

1. Layer the backing, batting, and quilt top.
2. Quilt as desired. Quilt shown is machine-quilted with a random pattern of circles and wiggly lines.
3. Make 9½ yards of bias or straight-grain binding from reserved fabric. Bind the quilt edges.

Color Variations

Your star quilt can be wild or not so wild in different ways. Here are some possibilities to inspire you.

RAIL FENCE

Quilt by Rhonda Richards of Birmingham, Alabama; quilted by Sharon Wilson of Montgomery, Alabama

Rhonda Richards is one of many Americans who celebrate their patriotism in quilts. "I had a lot of Americana prints, so Rail Fence was a natural—it was easy to strip-piece them all together," says Rhonda. Rail Fence is a quick and easy quilt that uses lots of scraps in any three-color scheme.

Finished Size
Quilt: 102" x 102"
Blocks: 400 (4½" x 4½")

Materials
100 (2" x 22") red print strips
100 (2" x 22") cream print strips
100 (2" x 22") blue print strips
1¼ yards navy solid fabric for inner border and binding
3 yards stripe border fabric
3 yards 108"-wide backing fabric

Cutting
From navy
• 9 (2" x 42") strips for inner border.
• 10 (2¼" x 42") strips for binding.
From border fabric
• 4 (5"-wide) lengthwise strips.

Block Assembly
1. Join 1 strip each of red, cream, and blue into a strip set (Diagram A). Make 100 strip sets. Press seam allowances away from cream strip.

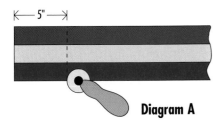

Diagram A

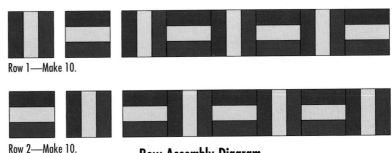

Row 1—Make 10.

Row 2—Make 10.

Row Assembly Diagram

2. Cut 4 (5"-wide) segments from each strip set to get 400 Rail Fence blocks.

Quilt Assembly

1. Lay out blocks in 20 horizontal rows, with 20 blocks in each row (Row Assembly Diagram). For Row 1 and all odd-numbered rows, turn first block vertically with red strip on left. Make 10 odd rows. For Row 2 and all even-numbered rows, turn first block horizontally, with red strip at top. Make 10 even rows. In all rows, press seam allowances toward vertical blocks.
2. Join rows, alternating odd and even (Quilt Assembly Diagram).

Borders

1. Cut 1 navy border strip into 4 equal pieces. Join 1 quarter piece and 2 full strips end to end to make a border for each quilt side.
2. Measure quilt from top to bottom through middle of quilt. Trim 2 border strips to matching length. Sew strips to quilt sides. Press seam allowances toward borders.
3. Measure width of quilt through middle. Trim 2 remaining borders to fit and sew to top and bottom.
4. Measure, trim, and add stripe borders to quilt in same manner.

Quilting and Finishing

1. Mark desired quilting designs on quilt top. Quilt shown has machine quilting on the patchwork and stipple quilting in borders.
2. Layer backing, batting, and quilt top; baste. Quilt as desired.
3. Join binding strips to make 11½ yards of continuous straight-grain binding. Bind quilt edges.

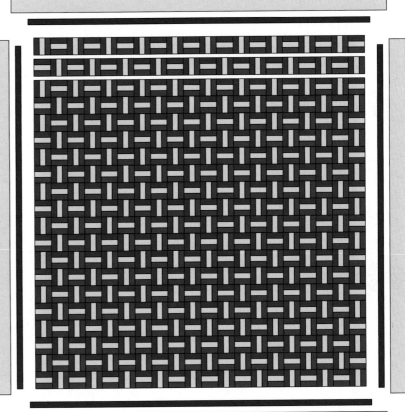

Quilt Assembly Diagram

Size Variations

The quilt shown fits a king-size bed. However, this pattern is easily adapted to fit any bed. Use the chart below as a starting point.

	Wall/Crib	Twin	Double	Queen
Finished size	34½" x 43½"	66" x 93"	79½" x 93"	84" x 102"
Number of blocks	35	216	270	320
Blocks set	5 x 7	12 x 18	15 x 18	16 x 20

QUEEN'S JEWELS

Quilt by Winnie Fleming of Friendswood, Texas;
machine-quilted by Barb Sawyer of Friendswood, Texas

This gem of a quilt is fast, easy, and *sew* much fun. Just cut and stitch strips of jewel-tone fabrics; then cut prepieced units that you can quickly assemble into blocks. If you prefer a homespun look, imagine this design in assorted plaids and earthy prints. The historic name of this block is Night and Day.

Finished Size

Quilt: 61½" x 77½"
Blocks: 12 (14½" x 14½")

Materials

2 yards white-on-white print
2 yards black
96 (2" x 18") scrap strips for blocks *
112 (2½") squares for borders *
4 yards backing fabric
* *Note:* These pieces can be cut from 12 fat quarters, if desired.

Cutting

Instructions are for rotary cutting and strip piecing. For traditional cutting and piecing, use patterns on page 25. Cut all strips on crosswise grain except as noted.
From white
• 6 (2½"-wide) strips for borders.
• 48 (2" x 18") strips for blocks.
From black
• 4 (5" x 72") lengthwise strips for outer borders.
• 2 (2¾" x 72") lengthwise strips for inner side borders.
• 2 (3½" x 72") lengthwise strips for inner end borders.
• 4 (2½" x 72") lengthwise strips for straight-grain binding.

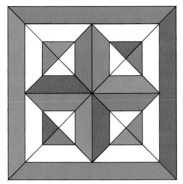

Night and Day Block—Make 12.

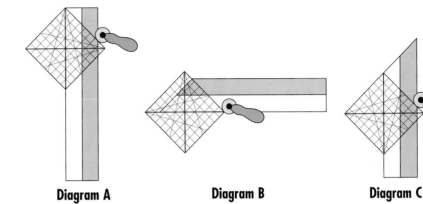

Diagram A   **Diagram B**   **Diagram C**

Block Assembly

1. Join each 2" x 18" white strip to a matching strip of scrap fabric, making 1 (3½"-wide) strip set. Press seam allowances toward scrap fabric.

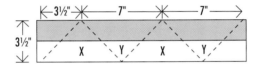

Diagram D

Diagram E

2. Use a square ruler that has a 45° line. Match line with white edge at 1 end of strip set (Diagram A). Trim corner as shown.

3. Turn cutting mat to position cut edge to your left (or right, if you're left-handed). With 45° line on edge of white fabric, slide ruler up to align its edge with top corner (Diagram B). Cut triangle.

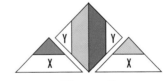

Diagram F

4. Turn the strip again as shown (Diagram C), aligning ruler with corner and white edge of strip set to cut next triangle. Continue cutting the triangles in this manner, turning strip or mat as needed to align the ruler.

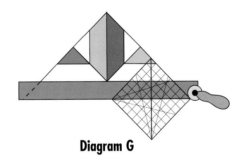

Diagram G

5. From each strip set, cut 2 X triangles with colored tips and 2 Y triangles with white tips (Diagram D) to get 96 of each. To make the selection of triangles random, put Xs and Ys in separate bags or pillowcases; then reach in blind to select triangles as you make each block.

6. Each block has 4 sections. For each section, select 2 X triangles, 2 Ys, and 1 (2" x 18") scrap strip.

7. Join 2 Ys to make a square (Diagram E). Add Xs to sides of square to make a large triangle (Diagram F).

8. Matching centers, sew strip to bottom edge of triangle, letting strip extend at both ends. Press seam allowance toward bottom strip. Align edge of ruler with edge of triangle, matching 45° line with bottom (Diagram G). Trim strip ends at matching angle.

9. Join sections in pairs (Block Assembly Diagram); then join pairs to complete block. Make 12 blocks.

continued

Block Assembly Diagram

Quilt Assembly

1. Lay out blocks in 4 horizontal rows, with 3 blocks in each row. Arrange blocks to achieve a pleasing balance of color and contrast.
2. Join blocks in each row. Then join rows.

Flying Geese Border

Use diagonal-corner technique to make Flying Geese units (see page 304). This method is faster and easier for most people than cutting and sewing triangles.

1. From 2½"-wide white strips, cut 52 (2½" x 4½") pieces.
2. Use 2½" scrap squares to sew corners onto each rectangle (Diagram H). Make 52 Flying Geese units.

Diagram H

3. Referring to photo, join 15 Flying Geese units in a row for each side border. Join 11 units each for top and bottom borders. Sew 1 remaining scrap square to ends of each border.

Borders

1. Measure quilt from top to bottom through middle of quilt. Trim 2¾"-wide black strips to matching length. Sew strips to quilt sides.
2. Measure width of quilt through middle. Trim 3½"-wide black borders to fit; sew to top and bottom edges.
3. Pin Flying Geese borders to sides, matching centers and ends. Sew borders to quilt sides, easing to fit as necessary. Repeat for top and bottom borders.
4. Cut 2 (5") squares from remaining white fabric. Cut squares in half diagonally to get 4 triangles. With right sides facing, center

1 triangle at each corner (Diagram I). Stitch through all layers. Press triangle to right side and check to see that it aligns with border correctly. (Triangles are oversize; trim

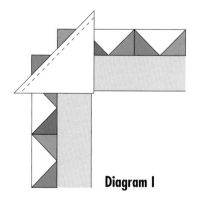

Diagram I

as needed.) Cut excess fabric from seam allowances.

5. Repeat steps 1 and 2 to sew outer borders to quilt top.

Quilting and Finishing

1. Mark quilting designs on quilt top as desired. Quilt shown is machine-quilted in an allover design, with hearts and cables quilted in borders.
2. Layer backing, batting, and quilt top; baste. Quilt as desired.
3. Join remaining black strips end to end to make 8 yards of continuous straight-grain binding. Bind quilt edges.

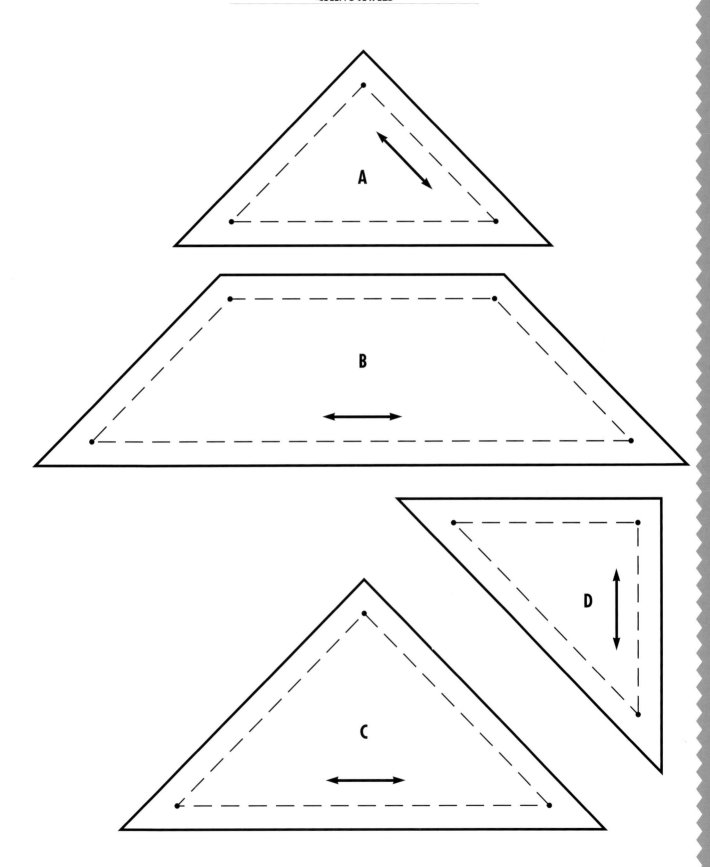

DIZZY GEESE

Quilt by Joan K. Streck of Overland Park, Kansas

"I always come away from a workshop with at least one new idea," says Joan Streck. A class on design and use of the traditional Flying Geese motif gave Joan the idea for Dizzy Geese. "I had an old pattern called Tiled Wedding Ring that I wanted to use in a new way," Joan recalls. She redrew the design with a star inside a ring of flying geese and squared off the block with a corner triangle. This is Joan's first attempt at designing a quilt "from scratch." In addition to designing the block, she added pieced sashing to create small stars between blocks.

Finished Size
Quilt: 74½" x 93"
Blocks: 12 (17" x 17")

Materials
8¾ yards cream tone-on-tone print (includes binding)
15 (18" x 22") fat quarters or scraps (mostly solids, plaids, and stripes)
⅛ yard tan print
5⅝ yards backing fabric

Dizzy Geese Block—Make 12.

Cutting

Instructions are for rotary cutting and quick piecing, except as noted. Make templates for patterns C, D, and H on page 28. Cut all strips on crosswise grain except as noted. Cut pieces in order listed to get best use of yardage.

From cream
- Set aside 2⅝ yards for borders and binding.
- 13 (2¾"-wide) strips. From these, cut 48 (2¾") B squares and 104 of Pattern H.
- 3 (4"-wide) strips. From these, cut 48 of Pattern D.
- 42 (2"-wide) strips. From these, cut 576 (2") E squares and 176 (2" x 3½") F pieces.
- 3 (4⅛"-wide) strips. From these, cut 26 (4⅛") squares. Cut each square in half diagonally to get 52 G triangles.
- 8 (6"-wide) strips. From these, cut 26 (6") squares. Cut squares in half diagonally to get 52 I triangles.
- 1 (17½"-wide) strip. From this, cut 17 (2" x 17½") sashing strips.
- 24 (1¼") K squares.

From scrap fabrics
- 12 (5") A squares.
- 12 same-fabric sets of 4 of Pattern C and 4 of Pattern C reversed (1 set for each block).
- 48 (2" x 21") strips. From these, cut 288 (2" x 3½") F rectangles.
- 32 (2"-wide) strips. From these, cut 352 (2") E squares.

From tan
- 6 (2") J squares.
- 48 (1¼") K squares.

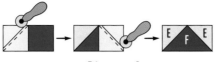

Diagram A

Block Assembly

1. For each block, select 1 A, 4 B squares, 4 Ds, and 1 set of C and C rev. triangles.
2. See instructions on page 304 for diagonal-corner quick-piecing technique. Following those instructions, sew 1 B square to each corner of A square. Press seam allowances toward A.
3. Sew C and C rev. triangles to sides of each D (Block Assembly Diagram). Press seam allowances toward D. Make 4 C/D units.
4. Select 24 scrap F rectangles. Use diagonal-corner technique to sew 1 cream E to each corner of each F to make a Flying Geese unit (Diagram A). Press seam allowances toward Es. Join 3 geese units in a row. Make 4 geese rows.
5. Sew 1 geese row to D edge of each C/D unit. Press seam allowances toward D.
6. Make 4 more geese rows for corners, this time using a scant ¼" seam allowance. Sew H pieces to both ends of each row (Block Assembly Diagram). Press seam allowances

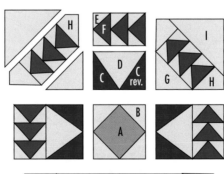

Block Assembly Diagram

Diagram B

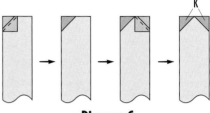

Diagram C

toward H. Then sew G and I triangles to opposite sides of unit as shown. Press seam allowances toward G and I. (Corner unit should measure 6¾", including seam allowances. It may be necessary to adjust H seams to square up block.) Make 4 corner units.

7. Lay out units in 3 horizontal rows as shown (Block Assembly Diagram). Join units in rows; then join rows to complete block.
8. Make 12 blocks.

Quilt Assembly

1. Using diagonal-corner technique, sew 1 cream K square to each corner of each J square (Diagram B). In same manner, sew tan K squares to 1 end of each sashing strip (Diagram C). Set aside 10 strips; then sew remaining tan squares to opposite end of remaining 7 sashing strips.
2. Lay out 2 rows of 3 blocks each, inserting sashing between blocks (Row Assembly Diagram). For Row 1, use sashing with 1 sewn end. For Row 2, use sashing with 2 sewn ends. Between the block rows, lay out 1 Sashing Row as shown. When satisfied with placement, join units in each row. Repeat to make bottom half of quilt.

continued

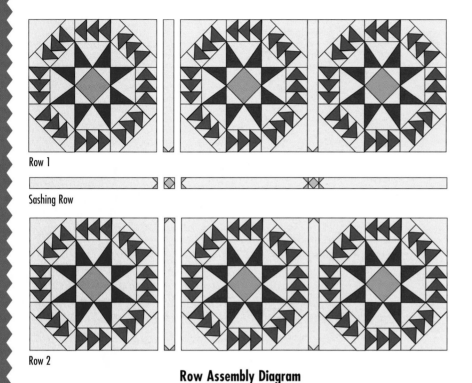

Row 1

Sashing Row

Row 2

Row Assembly Diagram

3. Referring to photo at right, lay out rows to verify placement. Join the rows to complete quilt center.

Borders

1. Use scrap E squares and cream Fs to make 176 Flying Geese units for borders.
2. From fabric reserved for borders, cut 4 (3¾"-wide) lengths for inner border and 4 (4½"-wide) lengths for outer border. Save remainder for binding.
3. Measure quilt length through middle of pieced top. Trim 2 inner border strips to match length. Measure width of pieced top through middle and trim remaining inner border strips to match width.
4. For each side border, sew 46 geese end to end. Match length of geese row with precut side border. (You have enough geese

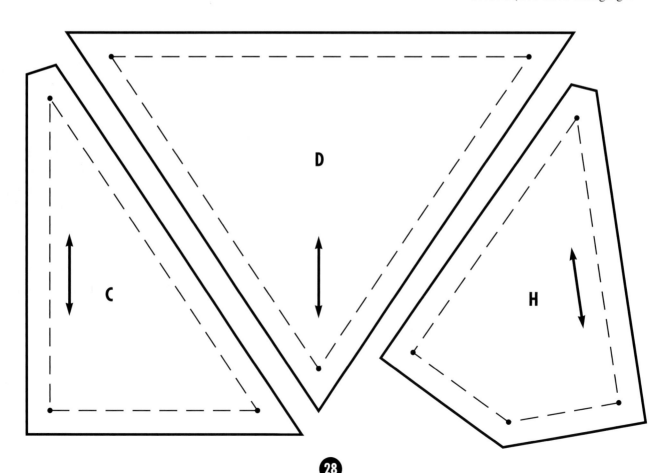

units to add 1 more if needed to match border length.) Sew geese rows to side borders, referring to photo for correct position of each row. (Note that on left border, geese fly south; on right border, they fly north.) Ease geese to fit borders as needed. Then sew joined borders to quilt sides, easing to fit quilt top. Press all seam allowances toward cream border.

5. Join 34 geese end to end for top border. Match length to precut top border, adding 1 more geese unit if needed. Sew the geese to the top border, with the geese flying west. Repeat for the bottom border, positioning the geese flying east.

6. Join 3 geese units with G, H, and I pieces to make each corner unit as before. Referring to photo, sew corners to ends of top and bottom borders.

7. Sew borders to top and bottom edges of quilt top.

8. Measure length of quilt through middle as before. Trim 2 outer border strips to match length. Sew these to quilt sides, easing to fit as needed. Repeat for top and bottom borders. Press the seam allowances toward the outer borders.

Quilting and Finishing

1. Mark quilt top with desired quilting design. Quilt shown is outline-quilted with a cable quilted in each cream border.

2. Layer backing, batting, and quilt top. Baste. Quilt as desired.

3. Make 9½ yards of continuous straight-grain binding from remaining cream fabric. Bind quilt edges.

Size Variations

The quilt shown fits a full-size bed. To make a 93"-square quilt for a queen- or king-size bed, you can add another vertical row of blocks and sashing strips. You'll need:
- 10½ yards background fabric
- At least 20 fat quarters scrap fabrics

Yardage and instructions for solid borders do not change. For the larger quilt, make 16 blocks, 24 sashing strips, and 184 flying geese units for the pieced border.

RELATIVE COMFORT

Quilt by Mary L. Hackett of Carterville, Illinois

Mary Hackett is happy to snub convention when it suits her. So she celebrates this quilt's irregularities instead of trying to hide them.

Mary chose pastels for the cross pieces to contrast with the bright squares and triangles. She placed the brights so that each circle blends into the next. She also designed a half-block to avoid cutting off the circles at the quilt's edges. Hand and machine quilting was done with black thread and variegated pearl cotton.

Finished Size
Quilt: 72½" x 82½"
Blocks: 42 (7½" x 7½")

Materials
21 (9" x 14") light scrap fabrics
19 (9" x 22") fat eighths dark scrap fabrics
¾ yard gold fabric
1½ yards light yellow fabric
2¾ yards black fabric
5¼ yards backing fabric

Cutting
Make templates of patterns A–C, E, and F on page 32. Cut all strips on crosswise grain. Cut pieces in order listed to get best use of yardage. When possible, pieces are listed in order needed, so you don't have to cut everything all at once.
From light scrap fabrics
• 42 sets of 4 Bs (2 sets from each fabric).
From each dark scrap fabric
• 7 (3") sashing squares (127 total).
• 14 of Pattern C (254 total).
From gold
• 4 (3"-wide) strips. From these, cut 56 (3") sashing squares.
• 4 (2¼"-wide) strips. From these, cut 72 of Pattern A (2¼" squares).
From light yellow
• 16 (3"-wide) strips. From these, cut 224 (3") sashing squares.

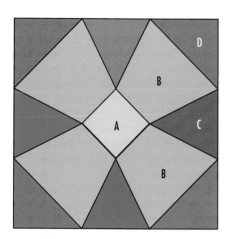

Maltese Cross Block — Make 42.

From black
- 1 (30") square for binding.
- 7 (3⅜"-wide) strips. From these, cut 84 (3⅜") squares. Cut each square in half diagonally to get 168 D triangles.
- 56 of Pattern E.
- 30 of Pattern F and 30 of Pattern F reversed.
- 2 (2⅛") squares. Cut each square in half diagonally to get 4 G triangles for corner blocks.

Block Assembly

1. For each block, choose 1 A square, 1 set of 4 matching B pieces, and 4 D triangles. (Don't worry about C pieces yet.)
2. Sew 1 B piece to each edge of A square, starting and stopping each seam ¼" from each corner of A

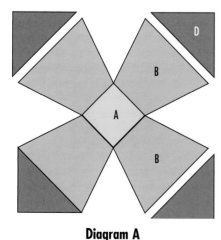

Diagram A

square (Diagram A). Press seam allowances toward Bs.
3. Sew 1 D triangle to end of each B piece as shown. Press seam allowances toward Ds.
4. Make 42 Maltese Cross blocks without Cs.

Quilt Assembly

1. Referring to photo, lay out 7 horizontal rows, with 6 blocks in each row.
2. Sew light yellow squares to opposite sides of each gold square. Press seam allowances toward gold. Add 56 (3-square) units to layout in horizontal rows between block rows, leaving spaces for colored squares.
3. Place colored squares and C pieces in layout. In quilt shown, "circles" are color-coordinated by placing a colored square between 2 Cs of similar color.
4. When satisfied with placement, set Cs into each block (Diagram B). Press seam allowances toward Bs. Complete 42 blocks, returning each finished block to layout.
5. For sashing units between blocks, sew 1 light yellow square to 2 opposite sides of colored square. Press seam allowances toward colored squares.
6. Assemble each block row, alternating sashing units and blocks as shown in photo.

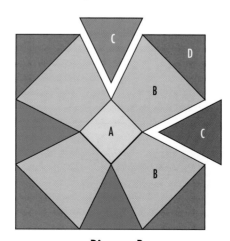

Diagram B

Half-Block — Make 26.

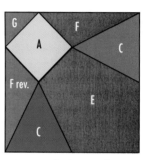

Corner Block — Make 4.

7. Complete sashing rows, joining colored squares between yellow 3-square units. Press seam allowances toward colored squares. Return all units to layout.
8. For each half-block, join Es to 2 adjacent sides of A square. Sew F and F rev. to remaining sides (Half-Block Diagram). Set in selected Cs. Add half-blocks to ends of block rows and add half-block border rows at top and bottom of layout.
9. For each corner block, sew 1 E to 1 edge of A and 1 G triangle to opposite edge (Corner Block Diagram). Sew F and F rev. pieces to remaining sides of A. Set in selected Cs. Add corner blocks to ends of top and bottom border rows.
10. When satisfied with layout, join all horizontal block rows and sashing rows, including half-block border rows. Return assembled rows to layout to verify correct position.
11. Join all rows.

continued

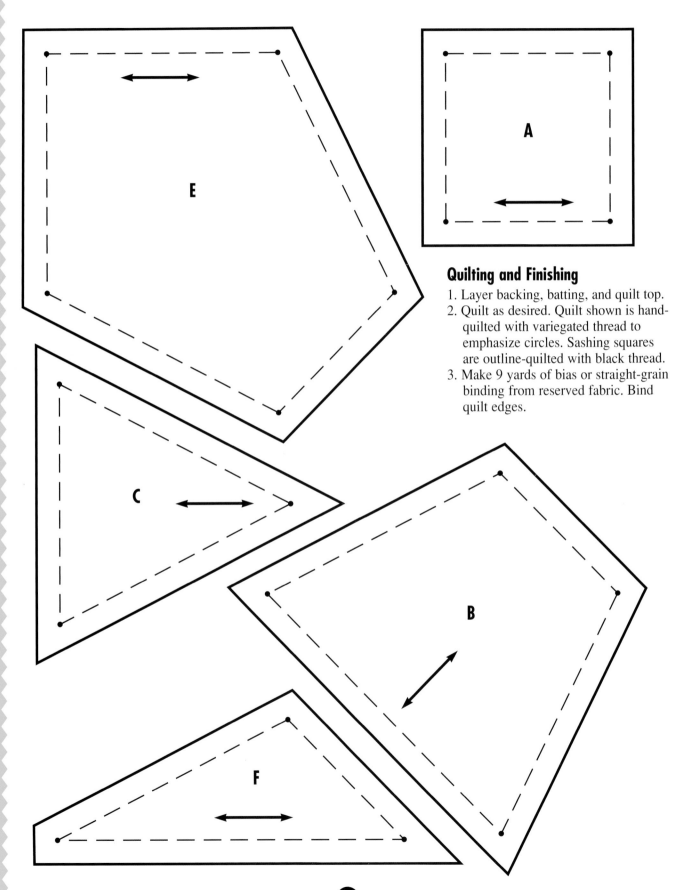

A

E

Quilting and Finishing
1. Layer backing, batting, and quilt top.
2. Quilt as desired. Quilt shown is hand-quilted with variegated thread to emphasize circles. Sashing squares are outline-quilted with black thread.
3. Make 9 yards of bias or straight-grain binding from reserved fabric. Bind quilt edges.

C

B

F

DIAMOND JUBILEE

A charm quilt's patches are all the same shape and size, but no two are cut from the same fabric. Even if some fabrics repeat here, this quilt has charm to spare. Pieced stars hide amid the profusion of colors, but you can use high-contrast fabrics to bring them out. This design is ideal for quilters who enjoy the challenge of sewing set-in seams.

Finished Size

Quilt: 82" x 91"
Blocks: 18 (15¾" x 18")

Materials

240 (2½" x 4½") dark scraps
488 (2½" x 4½") medium scraps
248 (2½" x 4½") light scraps
3 yards border fabric
⅞ yard binding fabric
5½ yards backing fabric

continued

Quilt by Annette Anderson of Ferndale, Washington

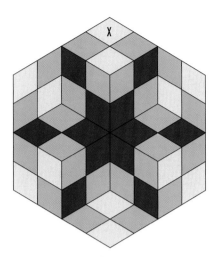

X

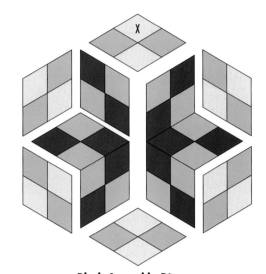

Block Assembly Diagram

Unit 1—Make 120.

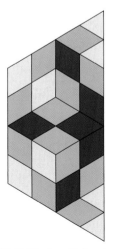 is Unit 2 diagram

Unit 2—Make 124.

Star Block—Make 18.

Cutting

Instructions are for traditional piecing. The scrappy nature of this quilt makes quick piecing inappropriate. Make templates for patterns X, Y, and Z on page 38. (Pattern Z is same as Y without seam allowance on short leg of triangle.)

From dark scrap fabrics
• 240 of Pattern X.

From medium scrap fabrics
• 488 of Pattern X.

From light scrap fabrics
• 248 of Pattern X.

Block Assembly

1. Select 4 diamond Xs—2 dark and 2 medium—for Unit 1. Mark seam allowance on wrong side of each diamond. Join diamonds in dark/medium pairs as shown (Diagram A); then join pairs to complete unit. Make 120 of Unit 1.

2. Make Unit 2 in same manner, using 2 medium diamond Xs and 2 light diamond Xs as shown. Make 124 of Unit 2.

3. For each block, select 6 each of units 1 and 2. Join 3 of Unit 1 as shown to make half-stars, sewing only from dot to dot of marked seam allowance (Block Assembly Diagram). Be sure to leave ¼" unstitched at both ends of each seam. (See "Sewing a Set-in Seam," page 36.)

4. Stitch the center seam to complete the star.

5. Set in 6 of Unit 2 around star to complete block.

6. Make 18 star blocks.

7. For a half-block, join 3 of Unit 1 in a half-star as before. Set in 2 of Unit 2 as shown (Half-Block Assembly Diagram). Then sew 2 more of Unit 2 to remaining edges of half-star; trim these units even with unstitched edge of star as shown. Make 4 half-blocks.

Diagram A

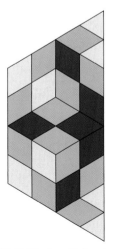

Half-Block—Make 4.

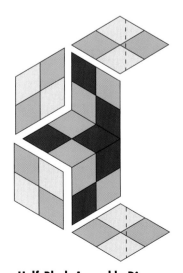

Half-Block Assembly Diagram

34

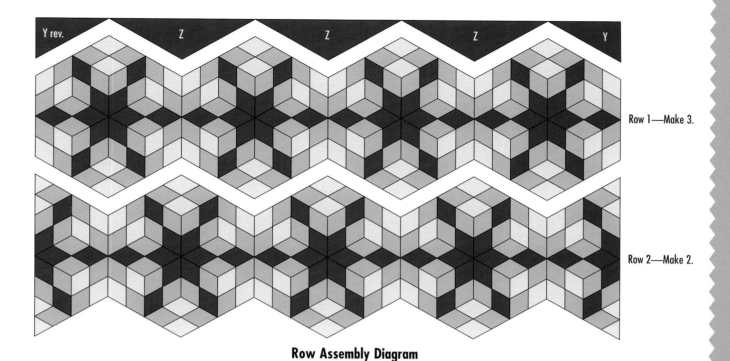

Row 1—Make 3.

Row 2—Make 2.

Row Assembly Diagram

Quilt Assembly

1. For Row 1, join 4 blocks as shown (Row Assembly Diagram). Do not sew beyond the marked seam lines, leaving seam allowances free for setting in. Make 3 of Row 1.
2. In same manner as above, join 3 blocks and 2 half-blocks for Row 2 as shown. Make 2 of Row 2.

3. Referring to photo of quilt on page 37, join rows in 1-2-1-2-1 sequence, carefully sewing set-in seams.
4. Cut 2 (8"-wide) crosswise grain strips of border fabric. From these, cut 2 Y, 2 Y rev., and 6 Z (Diagram B).
5. Sew Y and Y rev. pieces to corners (Row Assembly Diagram). Set in Z pieces as shown.

Borders

1. From remaining border fabric, cut 4 (9½" x 86") lengthwise strips.
2. Measure quilt from top to bottom through middle; trim 2 borders to match length. Sew to quilt sides.
3. Measure quilt from side to side through middle. Trim remaining borders to match width. Sew borders to top and bottom edges.

continued

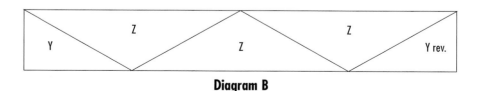

Diagram B

Quilting and Finishing

1. Mark quilting design on quilt top as desired. Quilt shown has straight-line quilting through the center of each X diamond (Quilting Diagram).
2. Layer the backing, batting, and quilt top. Then baste together. Quilt as desired.
3. Make 10 yards of bias or straight-grain binding. Bind the quilt edges.

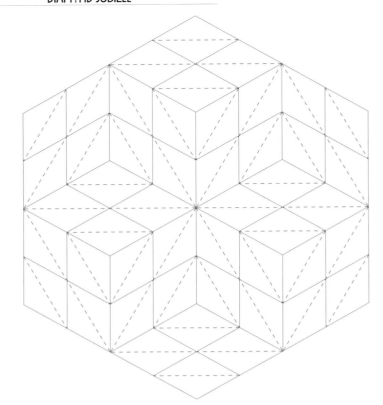

Quilting Diagram

pinpoints

Sewing a Set-in Seam

Setting patchwork pieces into an angled opening requires more than the usual accuracy in sewing. The following methods are helpful in this process. This example shows an 8-pointed diamond star, but the principles apply to other set-in shapes, too.

1. Mark corner points of seam line on each piece, using ruler or window template. Use these matching points to align pieces when pinning. Join pieces that form angled opening, sewing from corner point to corner point. Backstitch at beginning and end of seam, leaving seam allowances open at both ends. To set piece into opening, begin by pinning 1 side in place, using corner points as guide. Sew pinned seam between points, starting at outer edge and stopping at corner dot. Backstitch.

2. With right sides together, realign fabric to pin adjacent side of set-in piece to opposite side of opening. Begin sewing at inside corner dot. Stitch and backstitch, making sure stitches don't pass dot and go into seam allowance. Stitch to outside edge. Press seam allowances open or to 1 side, as you prefer.

continued

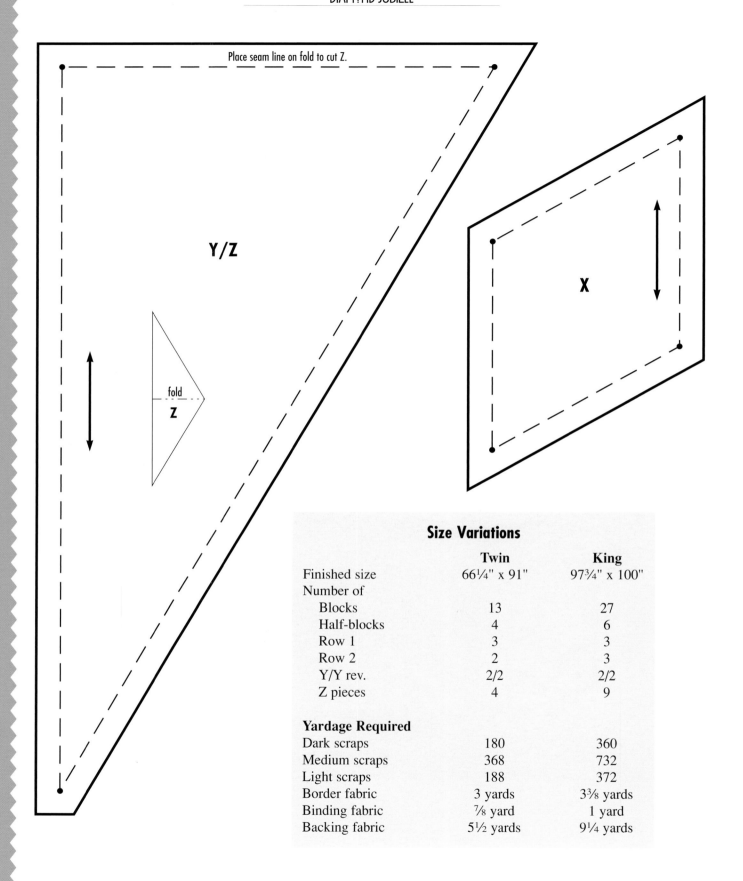

Place seam line on fold to cut Z.

Y/Z

fold

Z

X

Size Variations

	Twin	King
Finished size	66¼" x 91"	97¾" x 100"
Number of		
Blocks	13	27
Half-blocks	4	6
Row 1	3	3
Row 2	2	3
Y/Y rev.	2/2	2/2
Z pieces	4	9
Yardage Required		
Dark scraps	180	360
Medium scraps	368	732
Light scraps	188	372
Border fabric	3 yards	3⅜ yards
Binding fabric	⅞ yard	1 yard
Backing fabric	5½ yards	9¼ yards

PERSUASION

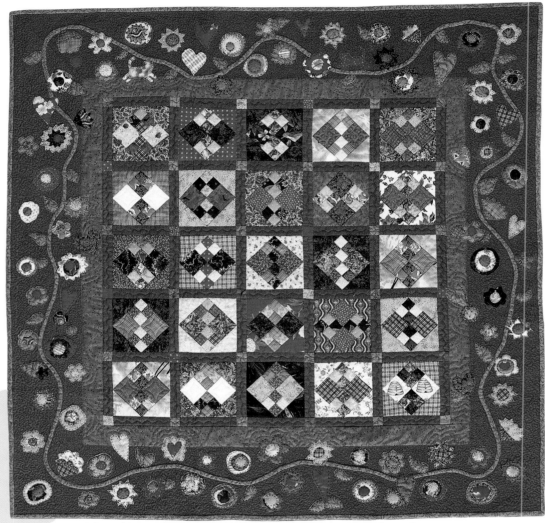

Quilt by Patricia Wilens of Birmingham, Alabama; machine-quilted by Lynn Witzenburg of Des Moines, Iowa

When you dare to stray from tradition, go all out! This wall hanging starts with basic four-patch blocks, but the border throws caution to the wind. We call it "free-form appliqué"—no patterns, no seam allowances, no rules at all. Have fun creating all manner of doodads to make your border unique. Such easy sewing makes appliquéing a joy.

Finished Size
Quilt: 52" x 52"
Blocks: 25 (5¾" x 5¾")

Materials
1⅝ yards teal
1 yard green (includes binding)
½ yard red
24 (or more) 8" x 10" assorted scraps for piecing and appliqué
3 yards backing fabric
⅜"-wide bias pressing bar
Black and white embroidery floss or pearl cotton

Cutting
Cut strips on crosswise grain except teal border strips. Cut in order listed. Add remnants to scrap fabrics for blocks and border appliqué.
From teal
• 4 (6¾" x 56") lengthwise strips.
• 60 (1½" x 6¼") sashing strips.
From green
• 20" square for bias vine.
• 5 (2½"-wide) strips for binding.
From red
• 4 (2½"-wide) strips for inner border.

continued

39

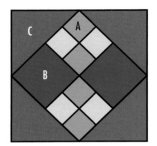

Improved Four-Patch Block—Make 25.

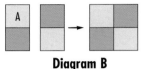

Diagram A

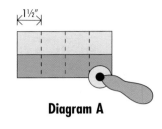

Diagram B

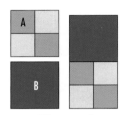

Diagram C

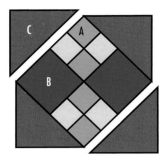

Block Assembly Diagram

Block Assembly

1. Cut 1 (1½" x 6") strip from each of 2 scrap fabrics. Join strips in a strip set (Diagram A). Press seam allowances toward darker fabric.
2. Cut strip set into 4 (1½"-wide) A segments as shown.
3. Join segments in pairs to make 2 four-patch units (Diagram B).
4. From another scrap, cut 2 (2½") B squares. Join these with four-patches to complete center unit (Diagram C).
5. Cut 2 (3¾") squares of another color fabric. Cut each square in half diagonally to get 4 C triangles.
6. Center C triangles on 2 opposite sides of center unit, leaving triangle "ears" on each side (Block Assembly Diagram). Press seam allowances toward triangles. Then sew triangles to remaining sides to complete block.
7. Make 25 Improved Four-Patch blocks in this same manner, using scraps as desired. Set aside remaining scraps for appliqué.

Quilt Assembly

1. Lay out 6 rows of sashing strips as shown (Row Assembly Diagram). From assorted scraps, cut 36 (1½") sashing squares. Fill in sashing squares between sashing strips and at row ends as shown.
2. Lay out blocks in 5 rows of 5 blocks each, placing remaining sashing strips between blocks and at row ends as shown. Rearrange blocks to get a nice balance of fabrics, colors, and value.
3. When satisfied with placement of all units, join blocks and sashing strips in each block row. Join sashing strips and squares in each sashing row.
4. Join the rows.

Borders

1. Measure quilt from top to bottom through middle of pieced top. Trim 2 red border strips to match length. Sew these to quilt sides. Press seam allowances toward borders.
2. Measure quilt from side to side through middle of quilt. Trim remaining red borders to match quilt width. Sew trimmed borders to top and bottom edges of quilt. Press seam allowances toward borders.
3. Sew teal border strips to quilt edges and miter corners.

Appliqué

1. Cut 5¼ yards of 1¼"-wide continuous bias from 20" green square. (See page 176 for instructions on preparing bias for appliqué.) Sew and press a continuous length of ⅜"-wide bias for vine.
2. Starting at center of any side, pin vine on teal border in meandering wiggle. Use matching thread to hand-appliqué vine in place. Don't worry about finishing bias ends—these will be covered with doodads later.
3. From scraps, cut assorted leaves, flowers, and other shapes for appliqué. We've provided some patterns to get you started, but it's more fun to cut pieces freehand. On quilt shown, no 2 pieces are alike and hearts are asymmetrical because they were cut freestyle.

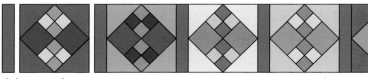

Block Row—Make 5.

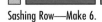

Sashing Row—Make 6.

Row Assembly Diagram

Some doodads are just circles. For method shown, do not add seam allowances. For traditional hand appliqué, add seam allowances and prepare pieces for appliqué as described on page 307.

4. Pin appliqués on border as desired. Layer pieces on top of each other for added interest. Position a doodad appropriately to cover ends of vine.

5. Use floss or pearl cotton and a small, even utility stitch to topstitch pieces in place. Add embroidery stitches—such as French knots—if desired.

Quilting and Finishing

1. Mark quilting design on quilt top as desired. On quilt shown, blocks are outline-quilted, and a small squiggle is quilted in sashing. Border background is stipple-quilted with echo quilting around doodads.

2. Layer backing, batting, and quilt top; baste. Quilt as desired.

3. Make 6 yards of continuous bias or straight-grain binding. Bind quilt edges.

STARS OF YESTERDAY

Quilt by Kristi Hammer of Yuma, Arizona

Inspired by an antique quilt, Kristi Hammer used reproduction fabrics to make these pink and brown Union Star blocks. Kristi changed the value placement in each block to make the piecing a challenge. She selected a pink-and-brown print for the border that ties it all together. Our instructions call for equal amounts of pink and brown (ranging from pale pink and barely tan to almost red and deep chocolate), but you can use as many fabrics as you like or more of one color than another if you prefer.

Finished Size

Quilt: 70" x 84"
Blocks: 20 (12" x 12")

Materials

1 (14" x 22") piece *each* 10 pink prints and 10 brown prints (includes binding)
1 (9" x 16") piece *each* 20 light shirting prints for block backgrounds
1¾ yards light tan for sashing
2⅛ yards border fabric
4¼ yards 45"-wide backing fabric or 2⅛ yards 90"-wide backing

Cutting

Instructions are for rotary cutting and quick piecing. Cut all strips on crosswise grain except as noted. For traditional cutting and piecing, use patterns on page 44. Cut pieces in order listed to get best use of yardage.

From each *pink and brown print*
• 1 (2½" x 22") strip for binding. *
• 1 (8") square for D triangle-squares.
• 3 (5¼") squares. Cut each square in quarters diagonally to get 12 B triangles.
• 1 (4½") A square.
• 4 (2½") C squares.

Pieces are for 20 blocks. Mix and match fabrics as desired.

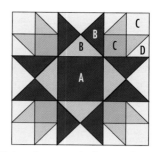

Union Square Block—Make 20.

From each *background fabric*
- 1 (8") square for D triangle-squares.
- 1 (5¼") square. Cut square in quarters diagonally to get 4 B triangles.
- 4 (2½") C squares.

From sashing fabric
- 6 (2½" x 60") lengthwise strips.
- 13 (2½" x 28") strips. From these, cut 25 (2½" x 12½") sashing strips.

From border fabric
- 4 (6½" x 75") lengthwise strips. *
* *Note:* Use remaining border fabric for straight-grain binding, if desired.

Block Assembly

1. On wrong side of each 8" square of background fabric, mark a 2-square by 2-square grid of 2⅞" squares, leaving a 1" margin on all sides (Diagram A). Draw diagonal lines through squares as shown.
2. With right sides facing, match each marked piece with 1 (8") square of pink or brown fabric. Stitch ¼" seam on both sides of diagonal lines. (Red line shows first continuous stitching path; blue line shows second path.) Press. Cut on all drawn lines to get 8 D triangle-squares.

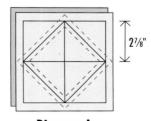

Diagram A

3. For each block, select 4 Bs, 4 Cs, and 8 D triangle-squares from same background fabric; from pink and brown prints, choose 1 A square, 4 B triangles of 1 print and 8 Bs of another print, and 4 C squares.
4. For each corner unit, join 1 print C square, a background C square, and 2 D triangle-squares as shown (Diagram B). Make 4 corner units. Press seam allowances toward Cs.
5. For each triangle unit, join B triangles in pairs as shown (Diagram C). Press seam allowances toward same fabric in each pair. Join pairs to complete unit. Make 4 triangle units.
6. Lay out 4 corner units, 4 triangle units, and 1 A square in 3 rows as shown (Block Assembly Diagram). Position triangle units with background fabric at outside edge and corner units with background C square in outside corner.
7. Sew triangle units to opposite sides of A square. Sew corner units to remaining triangle units as shown. Press seam allowances toward triangle units.
8. Join rows to complete block.
9. Make 20 blocks, varying fabrics and value placement as desired.

Quilt Assembly

1. Referring to photo, lay out blocks in 5 horizontal rows, with 4 blocks in each row. Lay 12½" sashing strips between blocks and at row ends. Move blocks around to get a nice balance of color and value.

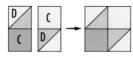

Diagram B

Diagram C

2. When satisfied with block placement, join blocks and sashing strips in each row. Press seam allowances toward sashing.
3. Lay out rows again, placing 60" sashing strips between rows. Join rows and sashing, trimming sashing strips to fit.

Border

1. Measure length of quilt through middle. Trim 2 border strips to match. Stitch to quilt sides, easing to fit as needed. Press seam allowances toward borders.
2. Measure width of quilt through middle of quilt top and trim remaining borders to fit. Sew border; strips to top and bottom edges of quilt, easing to fit.

Quilting and Finishing

1. Mark quilt top with desired quilting design. On quilt shown, blocks are outline-quilted. Create your own design for sashings and border or look for commercial stencils to fit those areas.
2. Layer backing, batting, and quilt top. Baste. Quilt as desired.
3. For pieced binding as shown, sew 15 (2½" x 22") strips end to end to get 8¾ yards of continuous straight-grain binding. If you prefer, you can make continuous bias or straight-grain binding from a single fabric. Bind quilt edges.

continued

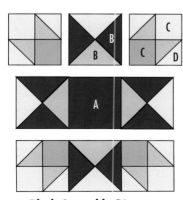

Block Assembly Diagram

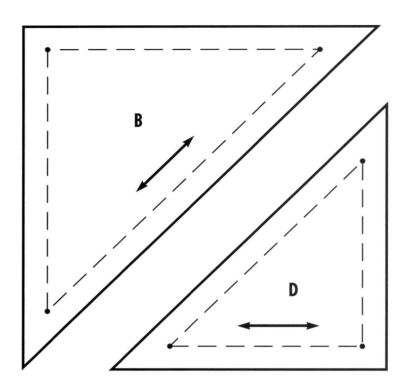

Size Variations

The quilt shown fits a twin-size bed. Use this chart as a starting point to adapt the design for a larger bed. These sizes use the same strip widths for sashings and borders.

Double/Queen
Finished size: 84" x 84"
Number of blocks: 25
Blocks set: 5 x 5

King
Finished size: 98" x 98"
Number of blocks: 36
Blocks set: 6 x 6

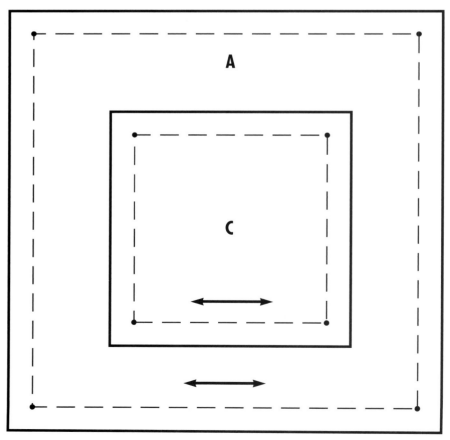

DOUBLE T

T Blocks were a symbol of the Temperance movement, an effort by some nineteenth-century women to abolish alcohol. Diane Burdin was attracted to the pattern after seeing an antique quilt. She varied the placement of light and dark fabrics, making "maverick" blocks that keep the pattern interesting.

Finished Size
Quilt: 66" x 81¾"
Blocks: 20 (12¾" x 12¾")

Materials
15 (9" x 22") fat eighths assorted
   solid fabrics
20 fat eighths assorted print fabrics
⅜ yard orange for sashing squares
1¾ yards brown print for sashing
¾ yard binding fabric
5 yards backing fabric

Cutting
Cut all strips on crosswise grain.
Several blocks in this quilt have
1 odd piece or 1 odd T in them.
Instructions are given for matching
blocks, but mix them if you like.
From assorted solids
• 80 (2" x 5") A rectangles in sets
   of 4.*
• 160 (2½") B squares in sets of 8. *
* *Note:* Each block uses 4 A pieces
and 8 Bs of matching fabric.
From each assorted print
• 8 (2" x 5") A rectangles.
• 1 (5") square (C).
• 1 (7⅝") square. Cut squares
   in quarters diagonally to get
   4 D triangles.
• 2 (4⅛") squares. Cut squares in
   half diagonally to get 4 E triangles.
From orange
• 3 (3½"-wide) strips. From these,
   cut 30 (3½") squares for sashing.
From brown print
• 17 (3½"-wide) strips. From these,
   cut 49 (3½" x 13¼") sashings.

continued

Quilt by Diane J. Burdin of Batavia, Illinois

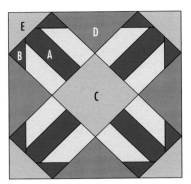

Double T Block—Make 20.

Block Assembly

1. For each block, choose 8 print A pieces and 4 solid As. Join 2 print pieces to both sides of 1 solid A to make a square (T Unit Diagram). Make 4 A units.

T Unit Diagram

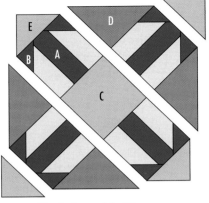

Block Assembly Diagram

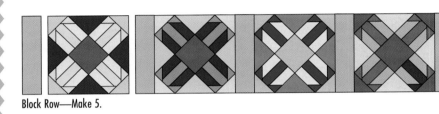

Block Row—Make 5.

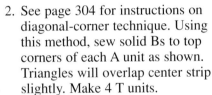

Sashing Row—Make 6.

Row Assembly Diagram

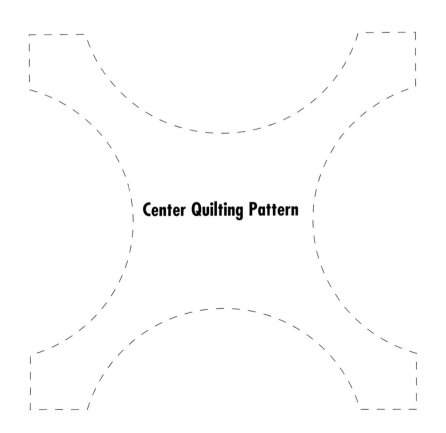

Center Quilting Pattern

2. See page 304 for instructions on diagonal-corner technique. Using this method, sew solid Bs to top corners of each A unit as shown. Triangles will overlap center strip slightly. Make 4 T units.
3. Lay out 4 T units, 1 C, 4 Ds, and 4 Es (Block Assembly Diagram). Join units in diagonal rows as shown. Then join rows to complete block.
4. Make 20 T blocks.

Quilt Assembly

1. Lay out blocks in 5 horizontal rows, with 4 blocks and 5 sashing strips in each row (Row Assembly Diagram). Make 5 block rows.
2. Join 5 sashing squares and 4 sashing strips into a row. Make 6 sashing rows.
3. Referring to photo on page 45, alternate sashing rows and block rows. Join rows to complete top.

Quilting and Finishing

1. Mark quilting designs on quilt top as desired. On quilt shown, patchwork is quilted in-the-ditch. Quilting pattern for C square is at left. Create your own quilting design for sashing strips or look for a commercial stencil that fits that area.
2. Layer backing, batting, and quilt top; baste. Quilt as desired.
3. Make 8½ yards of continuous bias or straight-grain binding. Bind quilt edges.

Working with Bias Edges

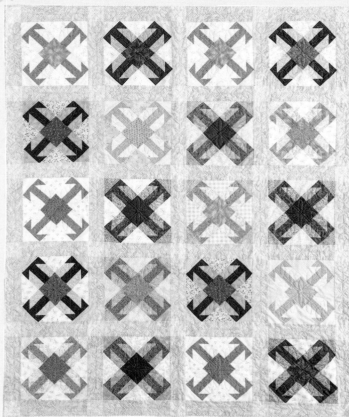

Rhonda Richards, whose quilts are featured on pages 20 and 230, made a version of Double T in pastels—and came up with a helpful tip.

Some of Rhonda's blocks were a little wobbly in the center (Photo A).

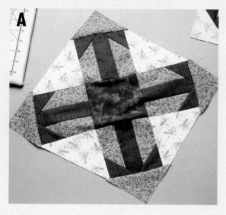

Rather than lying flat, the center square raised off the table a bit. Rhonda realized she wasn't handling the D pieces carefully. Those triangles are cut on the bias on two sides and can stretch during sewing and pressing. When this happens, the block won't lie flat.

To fix the problem, Rhonda pinned each corner of the block to a ruled ironing surface (Photo B). This ensures that you don't stretch your block beyond the size it's supposed to be. Then she sprayed enough starch on the block to make it damp (Photo C). If you don't like starch, mist your block with water. With your iron set on "steam," gently press the block flat and to size (Photo D). Begin in the center and slowly move outward to press the block flat. The steam reshapes the block and redistributes the roomy areas so that the block will lie flat (Photo E).

Use this trick with care: If you get carried away, you'll stretch the block out of shape and make it too big. But with a little careful pressing, you can repair minor mistakes.

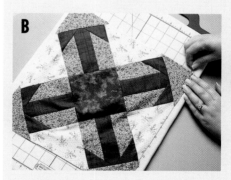

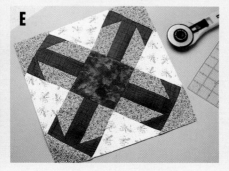

BIRDS IN THE AIR

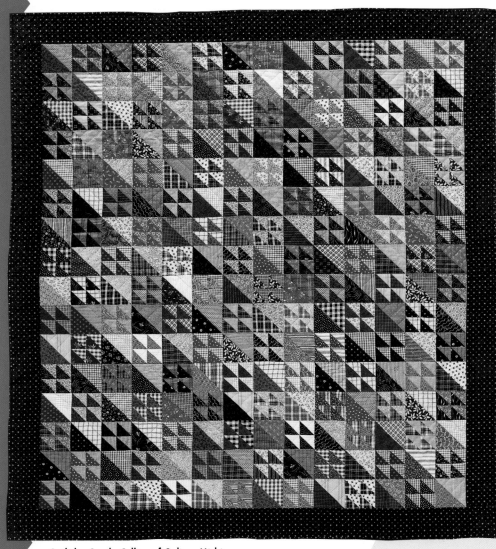

Quilt by Carole Collins of Galien, Michigan

Quick-pieced triangle-squares make this a fun quilt to assemble over a long weekend. Enjoy raiding your scrap bag and mixing it up.

Finished Size

Quilt: 64" x 72"
Blocks: 56 (8" x 8")

Materials

56 (5") squares dark scraps
56 (5") squares medium/light scraps
112 (5" x 7¾") dark scraps
112 (5" x 7¾") medium/light scraps
3 yards border/binding fabric
4 yards backing fabric

Unit A Assembly

1. On wrong side of each light 5" square, draw a diagonal line through center (Unit A Diagram).
2. With right sides facing, match each marked square with 1 dark square. Stitch on both sides of diagonal line as shown.
3. Cut on drawn line to separate 2 triangle-squares. Press seam allowances toward dark fabric.
4. Make 112 of Unit A (2 for each block), varying fabric combinations as desired.

Unit B Assembly

See page 306 for illustrated step-by-step instructions for sewing quick-pieced triangle-squares.

1. On wrong side of each light 5" x 7¾" piece, mark a 1-square by 2-square grid of 2⅞" squares as shown (Unit B Diagram).
2. Stitch grid as shown. Press. Cut on all drawn lines to get 4 matching triangle-squares. Press seam allowances toward dark fabrics.
3. Join 4 matching triangle-squares as shown to make 112 of Unit B (2 for each block).

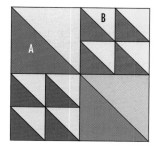

Birds in the Air Block—Make 56.

Block Assembly

1. Select 2 each of units A and B.
2. Lay out units in 2 rows (Block Assembly Diagram), positioning each unit with dark half of triangle-squares at bottom as shown. Join units in 2 rows. Press joining seam allowances toward Unit A in each row.
3. Join rows to complete block.
4. Make 56 blocks.

Quilt Assembly

Lay out blocks in 8 horizontal rows, with 7 blocks in each row. When satisfied with placement, join blocks in each row. For ease of assembly, press joining seam allowances in 1 direction in even-numbered rows and in the opposite direction in odd-numbered rows. Then join rows.

Borders

1. Measure length of quilt through middle of pieced top. From border fabric, cut 2 (4½"-wide) border strips to match quilt length. Stitch borders to quilt sides, easing to fit as needed. Press seam allowances toward borders.
2. Measure width of quilt through middle of quilt, including side borders. Cut 2 (4½"-wide) border strips to match quilt width. Sew borders to top and bottom edges of quilt, easing to fit as needed. Press seam allowances toward borders.

Quilting and Finishing

1. Mark the pieced quilt top with the desired quilting design. The quilt shown has hand-quilted diagonal lines through each Unit A and outline-quilting in the Unit B triangles.
2. Layer backing, batting, and quilt top with backing seams parallel to top and bottom edges of quilt. Baste. Quilt as desired.
3. Make 8 yards of continuous bias or straight-grain binding. Bind quilt edges.

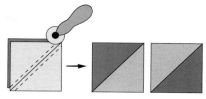

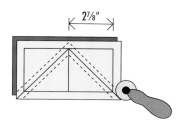

Unit A—Make 112.

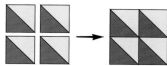

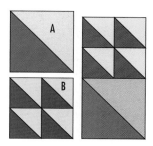

Unit B—Make 112.

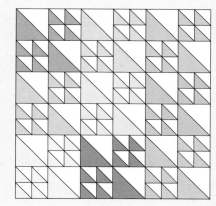

Block Assembly Diagram

Color Variations

Quilt birds of a different feather, if you like. Just imagine exotic green parrots, sassy red cardinals, or an aviary of pastel canaries or lovebirds.

CROSSED CANOES

Quilt by Lynn Williams of Snohomish, Washington

Two color combinations (blue and yellow, red and green) progress from light to dark across the surface of this wall hanging. Making this quilt is a great way to use up scraps in specific color families. The quilt also poses the challenge of sorting and rating fabrics by value as well as color.

Finished Size

Quilt: 42" x 42"
Blocks: 25 (6" x 6")

Materials

25 (4½" x 12") light/medium scraps
25 (4½" x 12") dark/medium scraps
¼ yard solid border fabric
⅝ yard print border fabric
⅝ yard binding fabric
1½ yards backing fabric

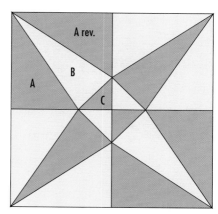

Crossed Canoes Block—Make 25.

Positive-Negative Diagram

Cutting

Make templates for A, B, and C from patterns on page 52.

Sort fabrics by value. In this quilt, blue/yellow blocks alternate with red/green blocks, each block becoming progressively darker in value. For a coordinated color scheme like this, pair lightest fabric of each color with lightest fabric of coordinating color and continue matching fabrics of similar value until darkest fabrics are paired. If colors are varied, pair fabrics of different colors but similar value and intensity. If you prefer,

limit your fabrics to 2 high-contrast colors to get a positive-negative look (Positive-Negative Diagram). Select fabric pairs for 25 blocks.

From each *fabric*
- 2 A triangles.
- 2 A reversed triangles.
- 2 B triangles.
- 2 C triangles.

Block Assembly

1. Sew A and A rev. of 1 fabric to sides of each opposite fabric B as shown (Block Assembly Diagram).

continued

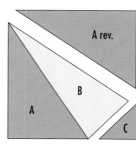
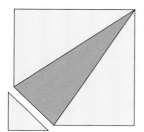
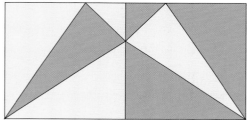

Block Assembly Diagram

Size Variations

	Twin	Full/Queen	King
Finished size	66" x 96"	84" x 96"	96" x 96"
Number of blocks	126	168	196
Blocks set	9 x 14	12 x 14	14 x 14
Yardage Required			
Light/medium scraps	126	168	196
Medium/dark scraps	126	168	196
Solid border fabric	⅜ yard	⅜ yard	⅜ yard
Print border fabric	2½ yards	2½ yards	2⅞ yards
Binding fabric	⅞ yard	⅞ yard	1 yard
Backing fabric	5¾ yards	5¾ yards	8¾ yards

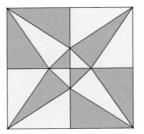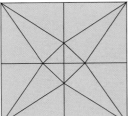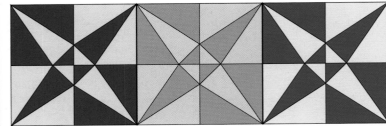

Row Assembly Diagram

Press all seam allowances toward same fabric.

2. Sew Cs of opposite fabric to bottom edge of each B to complete quadrant.
3. Join quadrants in pairs as shown and then join halves to complete block.
4. Make 25 Crossed Canoes blocks.

Quilt Assembly

1. Lay out blocks in 5 horizontal rows of 5 blocks each (Row Assembly Diagram). Start with lightest blocks at the left corner of Row 1 and darkest blocks at right corner of Row 5. Rearrange blocks as desired to achieve a pleasing balance of color and value.
2. When satisfied with layout, join blocks in each row.
3. Join the rows.

Borders

1. From solid border fabric, cut 4 (1½"-wide) crosswise strips. Measure quilt from top to bottom through middle and trim 2 borders to match length. Sew borders to quilt sides.
2. Measure quilt from side to side through middle. Trim remaining borders to match quilt width. Sew borders to top and bottom edges of quilt.
3. From print border fabric, cut 4 (5¼"-wide) crosswise strips. Sew these to quilt in same manner as for inner border.

Quilting and Finishing

1. Mark quilting design on pieced top as desired. Quilt shown is outline-quilted.
2. Layer backing, batting, and quilt top. Baste. Quilt as desired.
3. Make 5 yards of bias or straight-grain binding. Bind quilt edges.

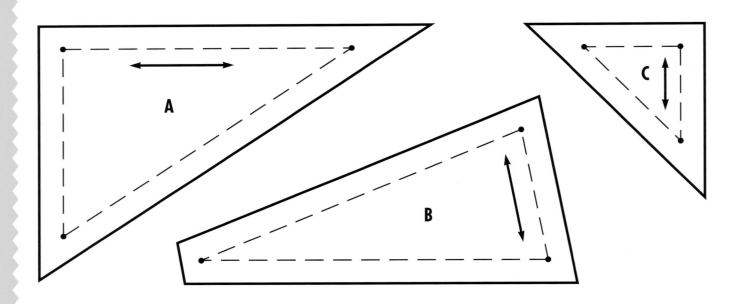

SPARKS: JULY

This tipped star block is an example of the unexpected colorplay Rebecca Rohrkaste invests in her quilts. She first made some of these blocks during a quilting weekend with friends and then put them aside for more than a year. When she pulled them out again, Rebecca eliminated some blocks, made some new ones, and reworked others to get the effect she wanted. Working on the quilt over a Fourth of July weekend, Rebecca thought the blocks "look like fireworks or hot summer stars." She gave the quilt its name because of this illusion.

Finished Size
Quilt: 60" x 72"
Blocks: 30 (12" x 12")

Materials
30 (11" x 22") pieces purple, gold, and orange prints
30 (10" x 16") dark prints
4 yards backing fabric
¾ yard purple binding fabric

Cutting
Make templates of patterns B, C, D, and E on page 55.
From each *11" x 22" print*
• 1 (5") A square.
• 4 each of patterns B, C, and D.
From each *dark print*
• 4 of Pattern E.

continued

Quilt by Rebecca Rohrkaste of Berkeley, California

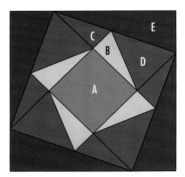

Tipped Star Block*—Make 30.
* Quilt historians identify this block as Delaware Cross Patch, first published as a Nancy Cabot pattern in the 1930s.

Block Assembly

1. For each block, select 4 sets of matching C and D pieces, 1 A square, 4 Bs, and 4 E pieces. B and E pieces can match or not.
2. Sew 1 C/D set to each B piece (Block Assembly Diagram). Press seam allowances away from B.

3. Start with any B/C/D unit. With right sides of A and B facing, match wide (D) end of unit with A square. Stitch a partial seam, stopping about halfway down B.
4. Working counterclockwise around block, add remaining B/C/D units to A square.
5. After last unit is sewn, complete first unit's seam. Press seam allowances toward A.
6. Add E pieces to corners to complete block. Press seam allowances toward Es.
7. Make 30 blocks.

Quilt Assembly

1. Referring to photo on page 53, lay out blocks in 6 horizontal rows, with 5 blocks in each row.
2. When satisfied with block placement, join blocks in each row.
3. Join rows.

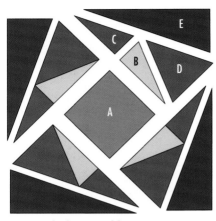

Block Assembly Diagram

Quilting and Finishing

1. Mark quilting designs on pieced top as desired. Quilt shown is quilted in-the-ditch.
2. Layer backing, batting, and quilt top. Baste. Quilt as desired.
3. Make 7½ yards of straight-grain or bias binding. Bind quilt edges.

Size Variations

The quilt shown fits a twin-size bed. However, the pattern is easily adapted to fit any bed. Use this chart as a starting point. You can add a border to make the quilt a bit larger.

Double
Finished size: 72" x 96"
Number of blocks: 48
Blocks set: 6 x 8

Queen
Finished size: 84" x 96"
Number of blocks: 56
Blocks set: 7 x 8

King
Finished size: 108" x 108"
Number of blocks: 81
Blocks set: 9 x 9

Color Variations

Celebrate with all-American Tipped Star blocks. Or choose fabrics with quiet personalities to make a cool galaxy of stars.

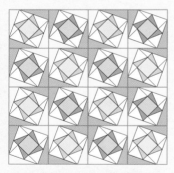
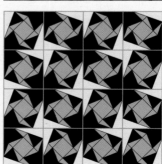

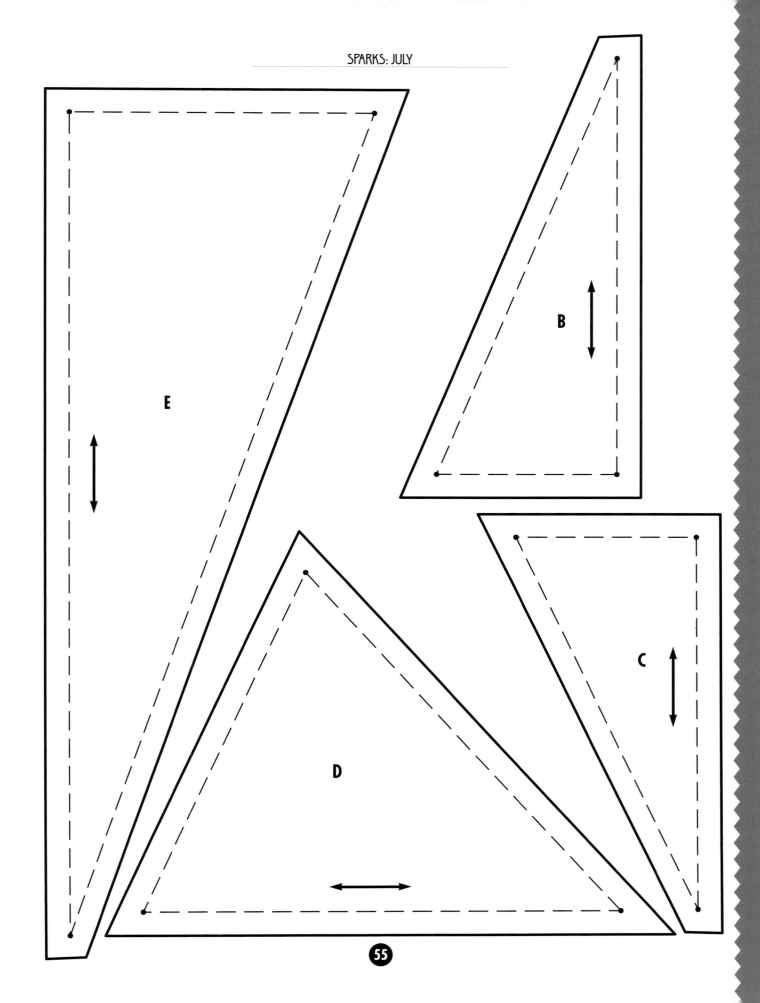

E

B

C

D

TREE OF LIFE

Quilt by Gerry Sweem of Reseda, California

Early American quilters often set blocks pointing to the quilt's middle rather than marching along in an upright position. This antique set along with reproduction fabrics and an abundance of triangles makes this design a classic. Sawtooth borders frame a pieced border embellished with appliquéd oak leaves.

Finished Size
Quilt: 75" x 75"
Blocks: 22 (10" x 10")

Materials
7¾ yards cream miniprint or muslin
6 (¼-yard) pieces or scraps for leaf appliqués and tree trunks
25 (¼-yard) pieces or scraps for triangles
11 (4⅞") squares for tree base
⅞ yard binding fabric
5 yards backing fabric

Cutting
Instructions are for quick piecing. For traditional cutting and piecing, use patterns A, B, C, D, and F on pages 60 and 61. Pattern for leaf is on page 60. Cut the pieces in order listed (large pieces first and then small pieces from leftovers).
From cream
• 4 (15½") squares. Cut each square in quarters diagonally to get 12 G setting triangles.
• 2 (13½") squares. Cut each square in half diagonally to get 4 Z triangles.
• 5 (12½") squares. Cut each square in quarters diagonally to get 20 X triangles.

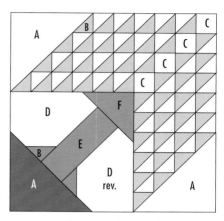

Tree of Life Block—Make 22.

- 4 (11¼") squares. Cut each square in quarters diagonally to get 16 Y triangles.
- 3 (10½") setting squares.
- 2 (8") squares. Cut each square in half diagonally to get 4 H triangles.
- 43 (7") squares for sawtooth border triangle-square grids.
- 74 (6" x 9½") for block and mountain border triangle-square grids.
- 22 (4⅞") squares. Cut each square in half diagonally to get 44 A triangles.
- 22 of Pattern D and 22 of Pattern D rev.
- 3 (1½"-wide) crosswise grain strips. From these, cut 88 (1½") C squares.

From each leaf/trunk fabric
- 2 of Leaf Pattern. (Cut 4 leaves with long stems and 8 with short stems as indicated on pattern.)
- 2 (4" x 10") rectangles. Set aside 1 rectangle. From remaining rectangle, cut 2 (2" x 4⅜") E pieces, 1 (3⅜") square, and 2 (1⅞") squares. Cut squares in half diagonally to get 2 F triangles and 4 B triangles. Sort 22 sets of matching trunk pieces, 1 for each block.

From scrap fabrics
- 43 (7") squares for sawtooth border triangle-square grids.

- 74 (6" x 9½") for block and mountain border triangle-square grids.
- 98 (1⅞") squares. Cut each square in half to get 196 B triangles.

Block Assembly

See page 306 for illustrated step-by-step instructions for stitching triangle-square grids. Refer to Block Assembly Diagram throughout.

1. On wrong side of each 6" x 9½" cream rectangle, draw a 2-square by 4-square grid of 1⅞" squares (Diagram A), leaving border of about 1" on all sides. Draw diagonal lines through each marked square as shown. With right sides facing and raw edges aligned, match each cream rectangle with scrap rectangle of same size.

2. Stitch each grid as shown. (Red lines on diagram show first path around grid, sewing into margin around grid and pivoting at corners; blue lines show second path.) When stitching is complete on both sides of diagonal lines, press. Cut on drawn lines to get 16 scrap/cream triangle-squares from each grid. Stitch 55 grids to get 880 triangle-squares, 40 for each block. (Set aside 19 grids for mountain border.)

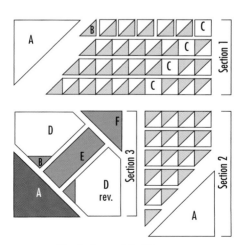

Block Assembly Diagram

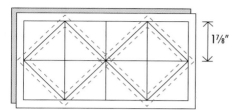

Diagram A

3. Cut each ground triangle in half diagonally to get 22 A triangles, 1 for each block.

4. For each block, select 40 triangle-squares, 8 scrap B triangles, 4 C squares, 2 cream A triangles, 1 set of trunk pieces (2 Bs, 1 E, 1F), 1 ground A triangle, and 1 each of D and D rev.

5. For Section 1, arrange triangle-squares, C squares, and B triangles in 4 horizontal rows (Block Assembly Diagram). Position triangle-squares as shown, changing position on opposite sides of C squares. When satisfied with placement, join units in each row. Press; then join rows. Add cream A triangle as shown to complete Section 1. Press seam allowance toward A.

6. For Section 2, arrange triangle-squares and B triangles in rows as shown. Join units in each row. Press; then join rows. Add cream A triangle to complete Section 2. Press seam allowance toward A.

7. For Section 3, sew trunk B triangles to short edges of D and D rev. pieces as shown. Press seam allowances toward Ds.

8. Sew D/B units to opposite sides of E. Press seams toward E.

9. Join A and F triangles to trunk unit corners to complete Section 3. Press seams toward triangles.

10. Join sections 2 and 3. Press. Join Section 1 to complete block.

11. Make 22 Tree of Life blocks.

continued

Quilt Assembly

1. Lay out blocks, setting squares, G setting triangles, and H corner triangles in 7 diagonal rows (Quilt Assembly Diagram). Position tree blocks as shown or as desired.
2. When satisfied with placement, join blocks and triangles in rows.
3. Join rows. Add remaining corner triangles to first and last rows as shown. Press seams. Assembled quilt top should measure approximately 57" square.

Sawtooth Border

1. On wrong side of each 7" cream square, draw a 2-square by 2-square grid of 2⅜" squares (Diagram B). Draw diagonal lines through each marked square as shown. With right sides facing and raw edges aligned, match each cream square with scrap square of same size.
2. Stitch each grid as shown. (Red lines on diagram show first path around grid, sewing into margin around grid and pivoting at corners; blue lines show second path.) When stitching is complete on both sides of diagonal lines, press. Cut on drawn lines to get 8 scrap/cream triangle-squares

Quilt Assembly Diagram

from each grid. Stitch 19 grids to get 148 triangle-squares for first border. (Set aside remaining grids and triangle-squares for outer border.)
3. Referring to photo on page 56, join 37 triangle-squares in a row for each quilt side.
4. Join triangle-square row to opposite sides of quilt, easing to fit as needed.
5. From scrap fabric, cut 4 (1⅞") squares for border corners. Sew

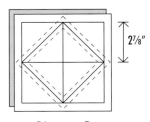

Diagram B

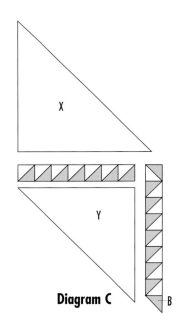

Diagram C

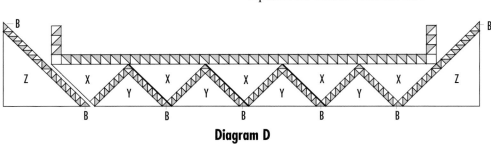

Diagram D

1 square onto each end of both remaining rows. Sew rows to remaining quilt sides, easing to fit as needed.

Mountain Border

1. Mark and sew remaining 6" x 9½" triangle-square grids (see Block Assembly, Step 1, and Diagram A on page 57). Cut out 304 triangle-squares.
2. Join 7 triangle-squares in a row (Diagram C). Sew this strip to 1 short leg of 1 Y triangle. Press seam allowance toward Y.
3. Join 8 more triangle-squares in a row, turning first triangle-square in different direction as shown. Add 1 B triangle at row end. Sew row to remaining short leg of Y triangle. Press seam allowance toward Y.
4. Sew 1 X triangle to top edge of Y unit. Make 16 X/Y units.
5. Join 4 X/Y units for each border, sewing left edge of X triangle to right edge of preceding Y unit (Diagram D). Add 1 more X triangle to right end of each row.
6. Sew 1 assembled border to each quilt side.
7. To finish corners, join remaining triangle-squares and B triangles in 4 rows as shown (left corner, Diagram D), sewing 16 triangle-squares and 2 Bs in each row. Stitch rows across corners.
8. Stitch Z triangles onto each corner to square up quilt top (Diagram D).
9. Use remaining 7"-square grids to stitch and cut out 196 triangle-squares for outer sawtooth border.
10. Make 2 rows of 48 triangle-squares each. Stitch rows to 2 opposite sides of quilt. Join remaining triangle squares in 2 rows of 50 and sew these to remaining quilt sides.
11. Referring to photo on page 56, appliqué leaves on Z triangles. Center 1 long-stemmed leaf at each corner; then overlap a short-stemmed leaf on each side.

continued

½
Feathered
Wreath
Quilting Pattern

Quilting and Finishing

1. Mark quilting designs on quilt top as desired. On quilt shown, triangle-squares are outline-quilted. The pattern for feathered wreaths quilted in setting pieces is on page 59; the pattern for mountain border triangles is on opposite page. See page 310 for tips on making your own quilting stencil.
2. Layer backing, batting, and quilt top; baste. Quilt as marked or as desired.
3. Make 8½ yards of continuous straight-grain or bias binding. Bind quilt edges.

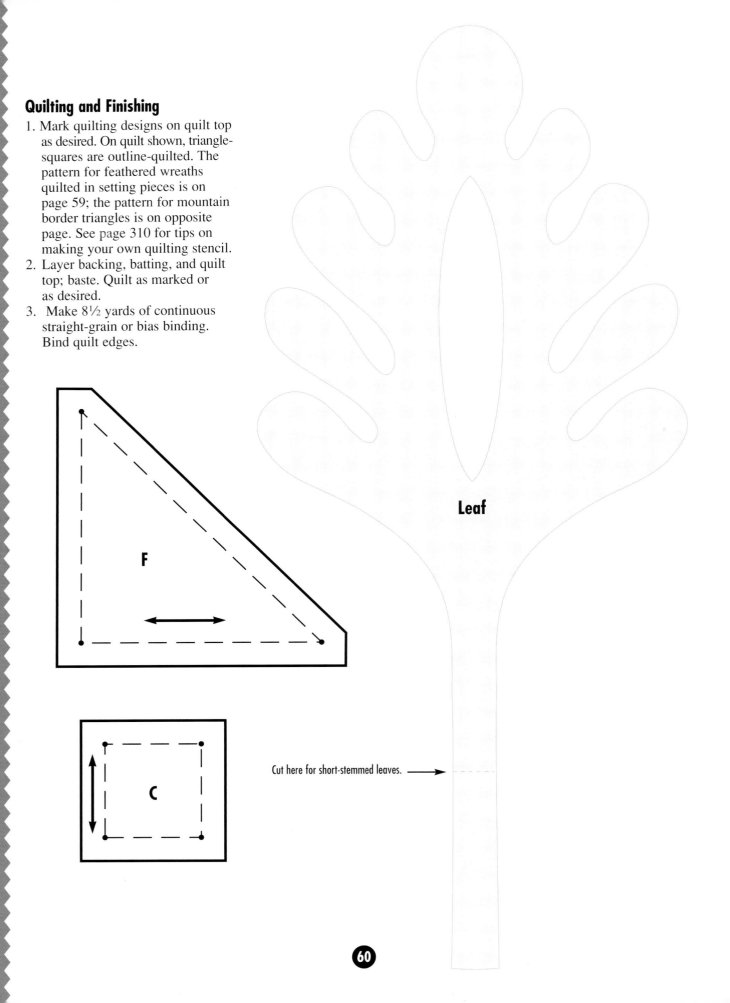

F

C

Leaf

Cut here for short-stemmed leaves. ⟶

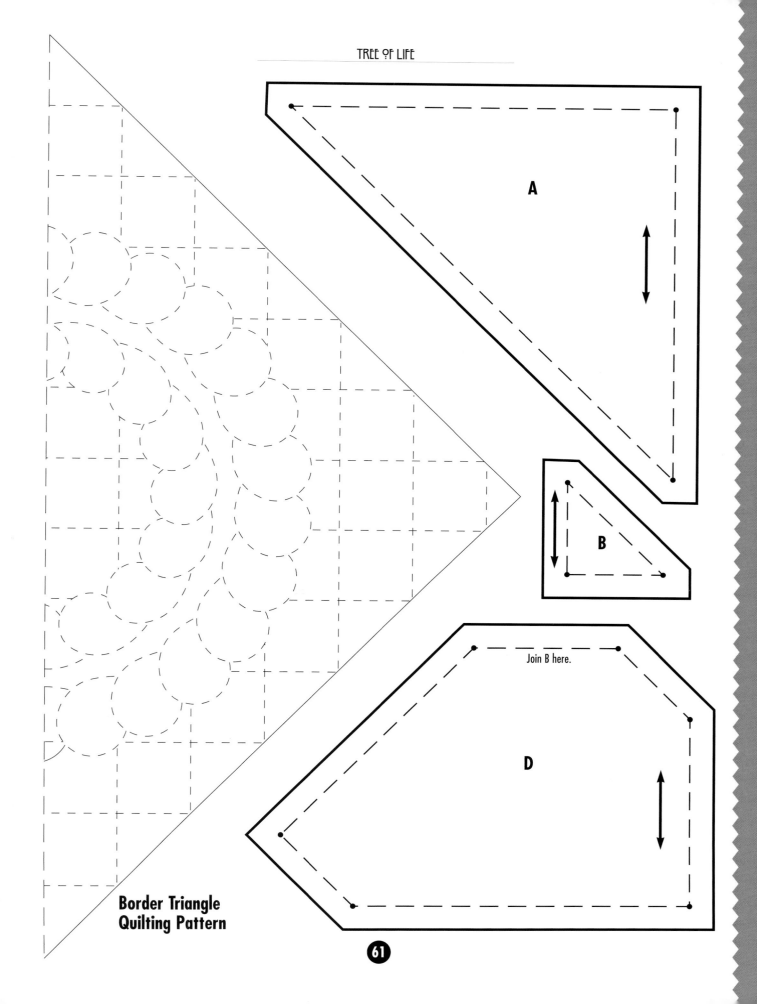

A

B

Join B here.

D

**Border Triangle
Quilting Pattern**

WINDING WAYS

Quilt by Tish Fiet of Jackson, Mississippi

Tish Fiet has a closet dedicated to her fabric collection. Her love of fabric is evident in this quilt, which features about 60 different fabrics.

The points and curved seams of this pattern make it a challenge. This interesting design is particularly appropriate for hand piecing.

Finished Size
Quilt: 66" x 79"
Blocks: 99 (5¾" x 5¾")

Materials
17 (18" x 22") fat quarters light scrap fabrics
17 fat quarters dark scrap fabrics
⅝ yard turquoise accent fabric
3 yards border fabric (includes binding)
4 yards backing fabric

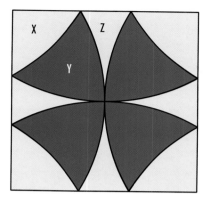

Winding Ways Block 1—Make 50.

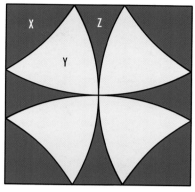

Winding Ways Block 2—Make 49.

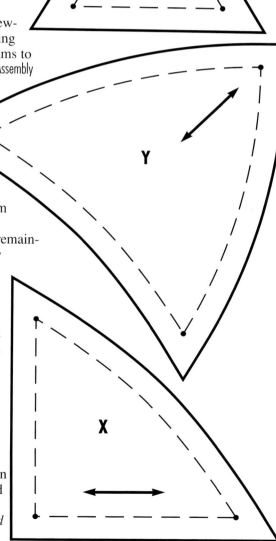

Cutting

Cut all strips on crosswise grain except as noted. Make templates of patterns X, Y, and Z. Use a 1/16"-diameter hole punch (see box on page 67) to make corner dots in templates as indicated on patterns. Cut pieces in order listed to get best use of yardage.

From light scrap fabrics
• 49 sets of 4 Y pieces.
• 50 sets of 4 X pieces and 4 Z pieces.

From dark scrap fabrics
• 50 sets of 4 Y pieces.
• 49 sets of 4 X pieces and 4 Z pieces.

From turquoise
• 8 (1½"-wide) crosswise strips for inner border.
• 7 (1"-wide) crosswise strips for binding accent flange.

From border fabric
• 4 (6¼" x 68") lengthwise strips.
• 1 (32") square for binding.

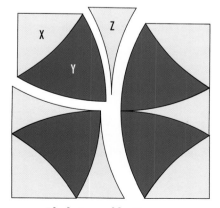

Block Assembly Diagram

Block Assembly

1. For each Block 1, choose 1 set of dark Y pieces and matching sets of light X and Z pieces.

2. See page 114 for tips on sewing a curved seam. Matching corner dots, piece X/Y seams to make 4 corner units (Block Assembly Diagram). Press seam allowances toward Ys.

3. Sew 1 Z piece to 1 side of a corner unit; then join another corner unit to opposite side of Z to make a half-block as shown. Press seam allowances toward Ys.

4. Sew Zs to both sides of 1 remaining corner unit. Press. Sew remaining Z to last corner unit as shown. Join both corner units to make second half-block.

5. Carefully sew curved seam to join block halves. Press.

6. Make 50 of Block 1. Use light Ys and dark X and Z pieces to make 49 of Block 2 in same manner.

Quilt Assembly

1. Lay out blocks in 11 horizontal rows, with 9 blocks in each row. Start Row 1 (and all odd-numbered rows)
continued

Color Variations

If cool colors aren't your thing, you can make a Winding Ways quilt that's hot stuff using bright, warm colors. Or take a softer approach with pastels.

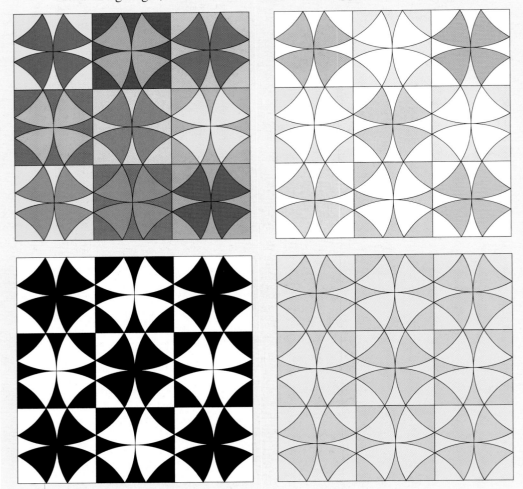

with Block 1 and alternate blocks 1 and 2 across row. Start Row 2 (and all even-numbered rows) with a Block 2 and alternate blocks across row.

2. When satisfied with placement of blocks, join blocks in each row. Press all joining seam allowances toward Block 2s. Then join rows.

Borders

1. Join 2 accent fabric strips end to end to make a border strip for each side of quilt.

2. Measure length of quilt top through middle of pieced top. Trim 2 border strips to match quilt length.

Sew borders to quilt sides, easing to fit as needed. Press seam allowances toward borders.

3. Measure width of quilt top through middle, including side borders. Trim remaining borders to match width. Sew borders to top and bottom edges of quilt, easing to fit as needed. Press seam allowances toward borders.

4. Repeat steps 2 and 3 to join outer borders to quilt.

5. Join 2 flange strips end to end. With wrong sides facing, press pieced strip in half lengthwise. Matching raw edges, baste strip to outer border along 1 side of

quilt. Repeat for opposite side. For top and bottom edges, piece remaining flange strips to fit. Fold and press each strip; then baste to quilt edges.

Quilting and Finishing

1. Mark the top with the desired quilting design. Quilt shown is outline-quilted.

2. Layer backing, batting, and quilt top. Baste. Backing seams will be parallel to top and bottom edges of quilt. Quilt as desired.

3. Make 8⅛ yards of bias or straight-grain binding from reserved fabric. Bind quilt edges.

SUNFLOWER SAYONARA

Every block in this sunny quilt is red, yellow, and green, but scrap fabrics make each block dramatically different. The blocks, made as going-away gifts by Terri Shinn's guild friends, combine piecing and appliqué. Terri's quilt tops off the color scheme with a coordinating border fabric of bold zigzag stripes. The strong color updates this adaptation of a 1930s pattern.

Finished Size

Quilt: 77" x 87"
Blocks: 42 (10" x 10")

Materials

42 (11") red squares
42 (10" x 18") green scraps
42 (10") yellow squares
42 (3½" x 6") brown/black
    scraps
¾ yard fabric for middle border
2⅜ yards fabric for outer border
1 yard binding fabric
5½ yards backing fabric

continued

Quilt by Terri Shinn of Snohomish, Washington, from friendship blocks made by the Anchorage (Alaska) Log Cabin Quilters; quilted by Tammy Christman

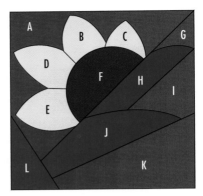

Sunflower Block — Make 42.

Cutting

Make templates of patterns B–L on pages 68 and 69. Use a $\frac{1}{16}$"-diameter hole punch or large needle to punch corner dots in templates as indicated on patterns. Mark dots on wrong side of each appliqué piece for matching. Before cutting, read "Borders" and decide whether you prefer diagonal-corner quick-piecing technique or traditional piecing for flying geese. Instructions are for rotary cutting. For traditional cutting, use patterns M and N on page 68 to make templates.

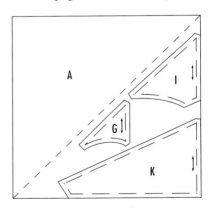

Diagram A

From each *red square*
• 2 triangles (Diagram A). Set aside 1 triangle for piece A. From second triangle, cut 1 each of G, I, and K as shown.

From each *green scrap*
• 1 (7" x 10") for border.
• 1 each of patterns H, J, and L.
• 56 (3" x 5½") pieces or 56 of Pattern M for border triangle units.

From each *yellow square*
• 1 (3½" x 10") piece for border.
• 1 each of patterns B, C, D, and E.
• 104 (3") squares or 104 of Pattern N for border triangle units.

From each *black/brown scrap*
• 1 of Pattern F.

Block Assembly

1. Select pieces for 1 block. Turn under seam allowances on pieces B, C, D, and F except those that will be overlapped by another piece or stitched into seam. Pin pieces onto A, referring to photo on page 70 and diagrams for placement. Align raw edge of F with diagonal edge of A triangle;

Block Assembly Diagram

position points of B, D, and E a scant ½" from perpendicular edges of triangle.

2. When satisfied with placement, appliqué pieces in place in alphabetical order, overlapping pieces as shown on pattern. Press appliquéd triangle.

3. Matching dots, pin G to H. Join curved edges of G and H (Block Assembly Diagram), piecing by hand or machine. (See page 114 for tips on piecing curved seams.) If you have trouble piecing curved seam, you can turn under seam allowance on H and appliqué edge onto G. Press seam allowance toward G.

4. Stitch I to bottom edge of H as shown. Press seam allowance toward I.

5. Piece or appliqué curved edge of J to bottom of H/I, matching dots. Press seam allowance toward J.

6. Stitch K to the bottom edge of I/J. Press the seam allowance toward K.

7. Join stem section to appliquéd triangle, aligning sections at top right corner of block. (Triangle A is longer than stem section.) Press seam allowance toward A.

Size Variations

	Twin	Queen	King
Finished size	67" x 87"	87" x 97"	97" x 97"
Number of blocks	35	56	64
Blocks set	5 x 7	7 x 8	8 x 8
Number of Flying Geese	44	56	60
Yardage Required			
Red scraps	35	56	64
Green scraps	35	56	64
Yellow scraps	35	56	64
Brown/black scraps	35	56	64
Middle border fabric	¾ yard	¾ yard	¾ yard
Outer border fabric	2⅜ yards	2⅝ yards	2⅞ yards
Binding fabric	1 yard	1 yard	1 yard
Backing fabric	5½ yards	8 yards	9 yards

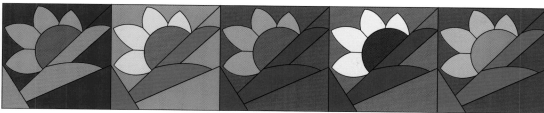

Row Assembly Diagram

8. Align ruler with raw edge of J/K at bottom left corner of block. With ruler in position, use a rotary cutter to trim corner of A triangle.
9. Sew L to A/J/K corner to complete block. Press seam allowance toward L.
10. Make 42 Sunflower blocks in this manner.

Quilt Assembly

1. Lay out 7 horizontal rows, with 6 blocks in each row (Row Assembly Diagram). Rearrange blocks as desired to achieve a pleasing balance of color and value. When satisfied with placement, join blocks in each row.
2. Join rows, referring to photo on page 70.

Borders

1. Referring to page 304, use the diagonal-corner technique to sew 2 yellow squares to 1 green rectangle (Diagram B). Or sew N triangles to M triangle traditionally as shown. Make 48 flying geese.
2. Add 1 triangle corner to 1 corner only of remaining 8 M pieces, sewing 4 left corners and 4 right corners as shown (Diagram C).
3. Referring to photo on page 70, join 13 flying geese end to end

in a row for each side border. In same manner, join 11 flying geese in a row for each border at top and bottom of quilt. Add 1 corner unit to both ends of each row.
4. Sew the borders to the quilt edges, easing to fit as needed. Miter the border corners.

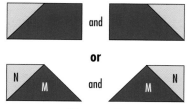

Diagram C

5. For middle border, cut 8 (2½"-wide) crosswise strips. Join 2 strips end to end to make each border.
6. Measure quilt from top to bottom through middle. Trim 2 middle borders to match length. Sew border strips to quilt sides.
7. Measure quilt from side to side through middle. Trim remaining middle borders to match quilt width. Sew borders to top and bottom edges of quilt.

8. From outer border fabric, cut 4 (4½"-wide) lengthwise border strips. Measure quilt, trim, and sew outer borders as for middle borders.

Quilting and Finishing

1. Mark quilting design on quilt top as desired. Quilt shown is outline-quilted with details quilted on appliqué pieces as shown on patterns.
2. Layer backing, batting, and quilt top. Baste. Quilt as desired.
3. Make 9⅜ yards of straight-grain or bias binding. Bind quilt edges.

continued

Hole-Punch Source

Marking corners of seam lines helps you align patchwork to sew challenging curved seams. If you make a small hole in your template, you can mark the back of patchwork pieces. When matching pieces, insert a pin through both holes to align seam lines.

A source for a ¹⁄₁₆"-diameter hole punch is Paper Wishes; 888-300-3406; www.paper wishes.com. Click on "Paper-crafting Supplies" and select "Punches & Cutters." Then scroll down to McGill ¹⁄₁₆" craft punch.

Note: Information valid as of July 2005

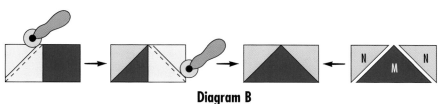

Diagram B

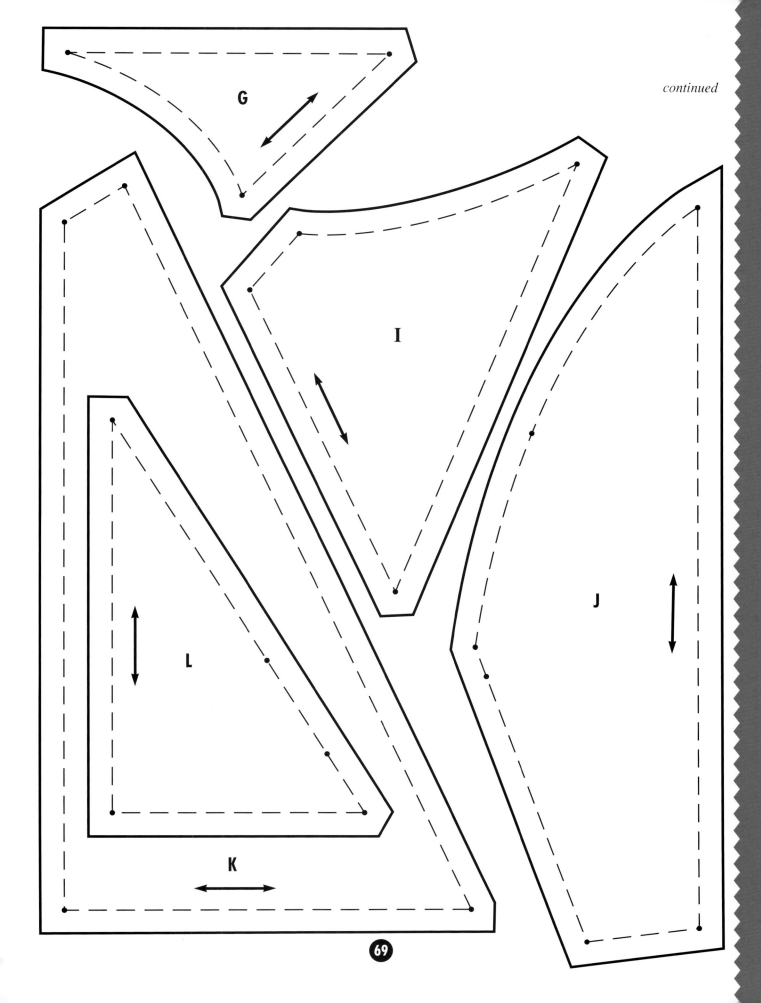

continued

G

I

L

K

J

Color Variations

If the bright, bold colors of Terri Shinn's quilt are not quite your style, just imagine a field of sunflowers in a color scheme that suits you. To get your creative juices started, we've illustrated a couple of suggestions. At left is a soft, pastel version; at right is the look of earth tones.

BASKET OF FLOWERS

Quick-piecing techniques make easy work of this basket block. In pretty pastels or bold colors, there are few blocks that are more favored by scrap-lovers. This quilt takes the cake with a fabulous Log Cabin border. The combination of blocks creates a modern-day scrap classic.

Finished Size

Quilt: 71" x 85"
Blocks: 17 (10" x 10") Basket blocks
32 (10" x 10") Log Cabin blocks

Materials

4½ yards white or muslin
17 (¼-yard) pieces pastel prints
¾ yard binding fabric
5¼ yards backing fabric

Cutting

Instructions are for quick-piecing. See page 306 for step-by-step instructions for triangle-square grids. (For a scrappier look, cut single triangles to piece by hand.) Cut pieces in order listed to get most efficient use of yardage. Cut all strips on crosswise grain.

From white
- 6 (15½") squares. Cut each square in quarters diagonally to get 22 setting triangles (and 2 extra).
- 4 (8"-wide) strips. From these, cut 16 (8" x 10½") pieces for triangle-square grids. Use waste from previous cut to get 1 more 8" x 10½" piece for a total of 17 pieces.
- 40 (1½"-wide) strips for Log Cabin blocks.
- 2 (6½"-wide) strips. From these, cut 34 (2½" x 6½") C pieces.
- 9 (4⅞") squares. Cut each square in half diagonally to get 17 D triangles (and 1 extra).
- 26 (2⅞") squares. Cut each square in half diagonally to get 51 A triangles (and 1 extra).

continued

Quilt by Kitty Sorgen of Newbury Park, California, for her granddaughter, Rachel Hildreth; machine-quilted by Marilyn Peterson

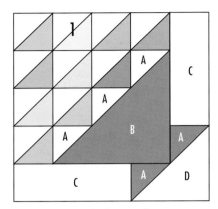

Basket Block—Make 17.

From each *pastel print*
- 1 (8" x 10½") piece for triangle-square grids.
- 1 (7") square. Cut square in half diagonally to get 1 B triangle. From remaining triangle, cut 1 (2⅞") square. Cut this square in half diagonally to get 2 A triangles.
- 6 (1½" x 25½") strips for Log Cabin blocks.

Basket Block Assembly

1. On wrong side of each white square, draw a 2-square by 3-square grid of 2⅞" squares (Diagram A). Draw diagonal lines through squares as shown. With right sides facing, match each white square with a print fabric.
2. Stitch each grid as shown. (Red lines on diagram show first path around grid, sewing into margin around grid and pivoting at corners; blue lines show second path.) When you have completed

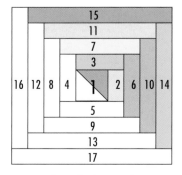

Log Cabin Block—Make 32.

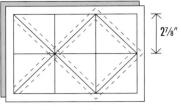

Diagram A

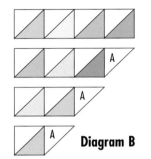

Diagram B

stitching on both sides of diagonal lines, press.
3. Cut on all lines to get 12 triangle-squares from each grid. Stitch 17 grids to get 204 triangle-squares: 10 for each Basket block, 1 for each Log Cabin block, and 2 extra.
4. For each Basket block, select 10 triangle-squares and 3 white A triangles. Arrange squares and triangles in 4 horizontal rows as shown (Diagram B). Check position of triangle-squares, placing white and print fabrics as shown. When satisfied with placement, join units in each row. Press; then join rows.
5. To complete block, select 1 B triangle and 2 matching A triangles, as well as 2 Cs and 1 D.
6. Sew B triangle to diagonal edge of triangle-square unit (Basket Block Assembly Diagram). Press seam allowance toward B.
7. Join 1 A triangle to 1 end of each C piece. Position triangles as shown to get 2 mirror-image units. Press seam allowances toward C.
8. Sew A/C units to block sides as shown. Press seam allowances toward A/C units.
9. Add D triangle to complete block. Press seam allowance toward D.
10. Make 17 Basket blocks.

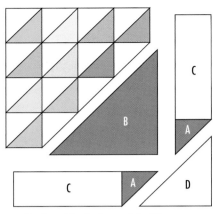

Basket Block Assembly Diagram

Log Cabin Block Assembly

It is not necessary to cut individual pieces for logs with this stitch-and-flip method.

1. For each block, start with 1 triangle-square. Select a print strip for first log. With right sides facing, match strip to print side of triangle-square as shown (Diagram C). Be sure triangle-square is positioned correctly; then stitch. Trim log even with bottom of square. Press seam allowance toward log.
2. Position sewn unit with new log at bottom. With right sides facing, match 1 new print strip to side of unit as shown (Diagram D); stitch. Trim strip even with center square. Press seam allowance toward new log.
3. Turn block to position new log at bottom. With right sides facing, match 1 white strip to right edge

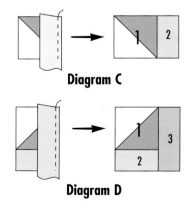

Diagram C

Diagram D

and stitch (Diagram E). Trim log even with block as before and press seam allowance toward new log.

4. Turn unit so newest log is at bottom. With right sides facing, match 1 white strip to right edge of block and stitch (Diagram F). Trim log even with block and press.

5. Continue adding logs in this manner until you have 4 logs on each side of center triangle-square (Log Cabin Block Diagram). Always press seam allowances toward newest log; then rotate unit to put new log at top before you add next strip.

6. Make 32 Log Cabin blocks.

Quilt Assembly

1. Lay out Basket blocks in 5 diagonal rows as shown (Quilt Assembly Diagram). Arrange blocks to get a nice balance of color and value.

2. Add Log Cabin blocks and setting triangles to row ends as shown. Check to be sure each Log Cabin block is positioned correctly.

3. When satisfied with placement, join blocks and setting triangles in each row. You will have 4 setting triangles left over for corner units. Join rows.

4. Join remaining setting triangles to make 2 corner units as shown. Sew corners in place.

5. See page 307 for tips on cutting pieces for appliqué. Make templates for flower patterns E, F,

and G. From scraps, cut 4 each of F and G; cut 4 pairs of E leaves.

6. Center F pieces over diagonal seam between Log Cabin blocks at each corner. Pin F and G pieces in place; then tuck E leaves under F. When satisfied with placement, appliqué pieces in place.

Quilting and Finishing

1. Mark quilting design on quilt top as desired. Quilt shown is machine-quilted with a large feather pattern over Log Cabin border.

2. Layer backing, batting, and quilt top. Baste. Quilt as desired.

3. Make 9 yards of continuous bias or straight-grain binding. Bind quilt edges.

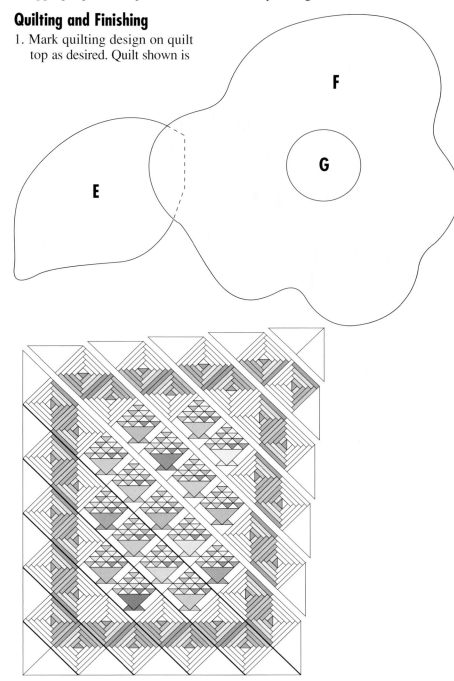

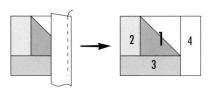

Diagram E

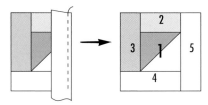

Diagram F

Quilt Assembly Diagram

FANTASY FISH

Quilt by Roxanne Elliott of Trussville, Alabama; machine-quilted by Lynn Witzenburg of Des Moines, Iowa

This quick-pieced quilt turns any room into a tropical paradise. Use one of today's popular mottled fabrics to provide a watery background for scrap-fabric fish. Choose jewel-tone fabrics, such as shown here; if you prefer, select soft pastels or crayon colors (see box on page 76).

Finished Size
Quilt: 72½" x 86"
Blocks: 9 (13½" x 18") Block 1
     30 (4½" x 6") Block 2

Materials
3⅜ yards water fabric
2⅛ yards outer border fabric
½ yard inner border fabric
14 (⅛-yard) pieces or scraps for fish
1 yard binding fabric
5½ yards backing fabric

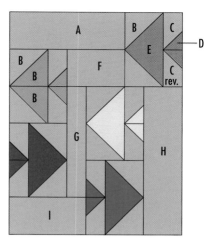

Block 1—Make 9.

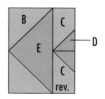

Block 2—Make 30.

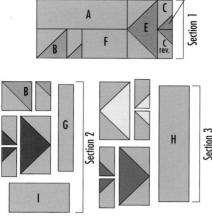

Block 1 Assembly Diagram

Cutting

Instructions are for rotary cutting and quick piecing. Cut all strips on cross-wise grain except as noted. For traditional cutting and piecing, use patterns on pages 77–79. Cut pieces in order listed to get best use of yardage.

From water fabric
- 27 (3½"-wide) strips. From these, cut:
  —9 (3½" x 12½") H pieces.
  —9 (3½" x 9½") A pieces.
  —150 (3½") B squares.
  —9 (3½" x 6½") I pieces.
  —9 (3½" x 5") F pieces.
  —150 (2" x 3½") C pieces.
- 1 (14"-wide) strip. From this, cut:
  —1 (12½" x 14") Y piece.
  —4 (6½" x 14") X pieces.
- 3 (2"-wide) strips. From these, cut:
  —9 (2" x 9½") G pieces.
  —2 (2" x 6½") Z pieces.

From outer border fabric
- 4 (9" x 75") lengthwise strips. Add remaining fabric to scraps for fish, if desired. Leftover fabric is enough for 13 Es and 26 matching Ds.

From inner border fabric
- 8 (2"-wide) strips.

*From scrap fabrics *
- 66 (3½" x 6½") E pieces.
- 18 (3½") B squares.
- 150 (2") D squares.

* *Note:* Cut scrap fabrics in sets: 2 Bs and 2 Ds make 1 fish, or 1 E and 2 Ds make 1 fish.

Block Assembly

Refer to Block 1 Assembly Diagram.
1. For each block, select 4 E/D sets of scrap fabrics and 1 B/D set. From water fabric, select 10 Bs; 10 Cs; and 1 each of A, F, G, H, and I.
2. On wrong side of 1 B water square, draw a diagonal line from corner to corner. With right sides facing, match 1 marked water square with each scrap B square. Stitch on drawn line (Diagram A). Trim excess fabric from corner, leaving a ¼" seam allowance from seam line. Press open.
3. See tips on quick-piecing diagonal-corners on page 304. Use this technique to sew B corners to each E piece (Diagram B) and D corners to each C (Diagram C). Be sure to sew 5 C/D units with seam angling right and 5 units with seam angling left as shown.
4. For Section 1, join 1 B/B square with 1 C/D unit and 1 piece F. Sew 1 piece A to top of row.

Press seam allowances toward A. Then sew B/E unit to end of row. Join 2 C/D units end to end to make fish tail as shown (Diagram D); join tail to B/E unit.
5. For Section 2, join remaining B square with its C/D unit. Join 2 C/D units; then join tail to 1 B/E fish. Sew B unit to top of B/E fish. Then sew piece G to right side as shown. Complete section with piece I at bottom.
6. For Section 3, assemble C/D tails and join to 2 B/E fish. Join fish as shown. Complete section with piece H at right side.
7. Join sections 2 and 3; then sew Section 1 at top to complete block. Press.
8. Make 9 of Block 1, varying scrap fabrics as desired.
9. Use remaining B, C, D, and E pieces to make 30 of Block 2 (Diagram D).

continued

Diagram A

Diagram B

Diagram C

Diagram D

Quilt Assembly

1. Lay out large blocks in 3 vertical rows of 3 blocks each (Quilt Assembly Diagram). If desired, turn blocks upside down here and there to vary fish placement. Add X and Y pieces to rows as shown.
2. When satisfied with placement, join blocks and setting pieces in each row. Then join rows.

Borders

1. Measure width of quilt through middle of pieced top. Trim 2 inner border strips to this measurement. Stitch border strips to top and bottom edges of quilt.
2. Sew 2 remaining inner border strips end to end for each side border. Measure length of quilt through middle and trim side borders to this length. Sew border strips to sides, easing to fit.
3. Select 15 of Block 2 for each side border. Join blocks side by side, inserting a Z piece somewhere in each row as shown (Quilt Assembly Diagram). Sew borders to quilt sides. (To allow for piecing variations, Zs can be omitted or more can be added to make the border fit the quilt.)

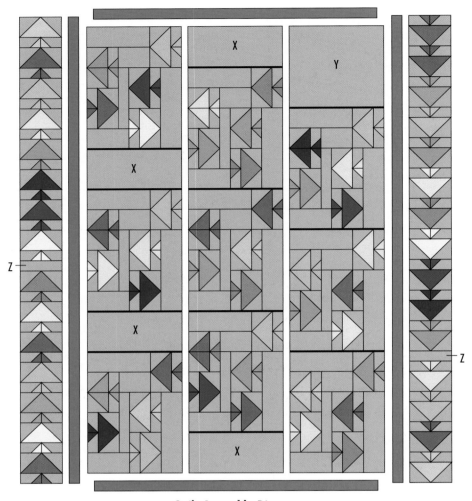

Quilt Assembly Diagram

Color Variations

Make a splash with fish of a different color. Here, check out alternatives that float pale fish peacefully cruising along in a calm sea and bright fish boldly jumping out at you.

Pastel Alternate Color Scheme

Primary Alternate Color Scheme

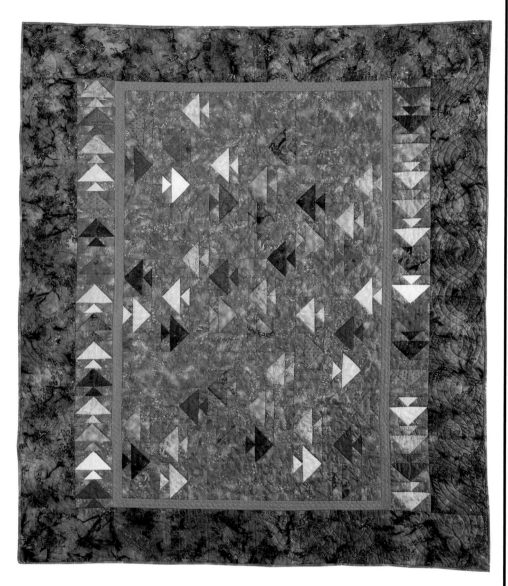

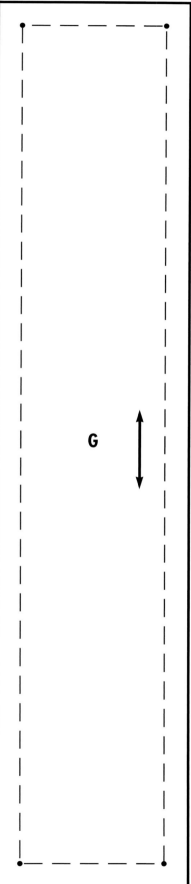

G

4. Measure the length of the quilt through the middle of the pieced top and trim 2 outer border strips to match the quilt length. Sew the borders to the quilt sides.

5. Measure quilt width through middle; trim remaining outer border strips to match quilt width. Sew the borders to top and bottom edges.

Quilting and Finishing

1. Mark the pieced top with the desired quilting design. The quilt shown is machine-quilted with repeated wavy lines quilted across the "ocean" and the inner border. A commercial stencil was used to mark the cable in the outer border.

2. Layer the backing, the batting, and the quilt top, and baste them together. Then quilt as desired.

3. Make 9¼ yards of continuous straight-grain or bias binding. Bind the quilt edges.

continued

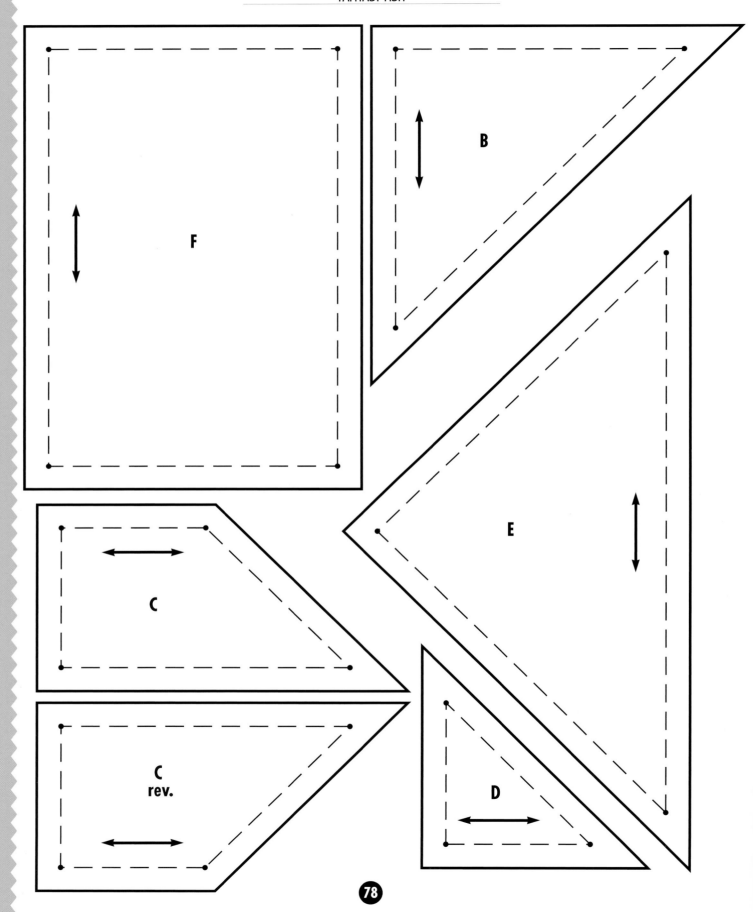

For Pattern H, draw a 3½" x 12½" rectangle.

H

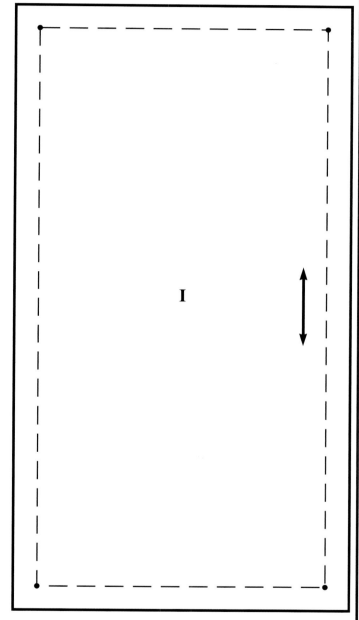

I

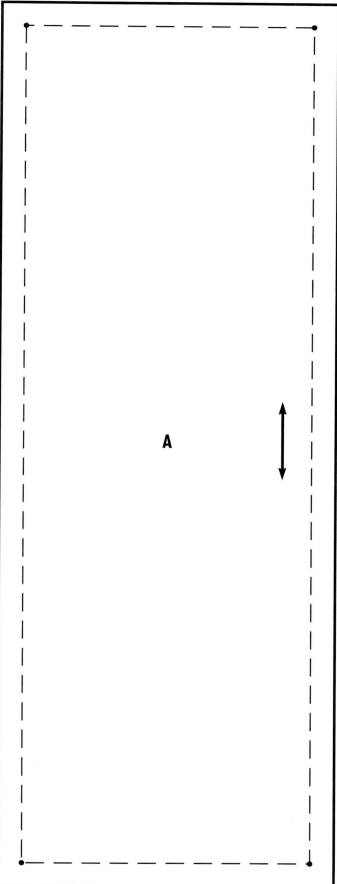

A

CROSSROADS TO JERICHO

Quilt by Joan Ross of Fairhope, Alabama

Nine squares in a tic-tac-toe formation is one of patchwork's basic building blocks—the versatile nine-patch. This variation turns the nine-patch on point so that the muslin squares connect in continuous chains across the quilt.

This sparkling quilt combines bright tone-on-tone prints with muslin, but it's fun to dream up other color schemes. Think about mixed pastels with a purple chain or scraps of blue with a yellow chain. The possibilities are as varied as your scraps.

Finished Size

Quilt: 84" x 92"
Blocks: 72 (8½" x 8½")

Materials

⅜ yard *each* of 18 print fabrics
2¼ yards muslin
¾ yard binding fabric
2½ yards 108"-wide backing fabric

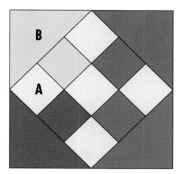

Crossroads to Jericho Block — Make 72.

Cutting

Instructions are for rotary cutting. For traditional cutting, use patterns on page 82.

From each *print*

- 3 (2½") crosswise strips, 1 for strip piecing the nine-patch and 2 for outer border pieces.
- 8 (5⅛") squares. Cut each square in half diagonally to get 16 B triangles.

From muslin

- 31 (2½"-wide) crosswise strips. Set aside 8 strips for inner border.

Block Assembly

1. For Strip Set 1, join 1 strip of print fabric and 2 muslin strips as shown (Strip Set 1 Diagram). Press seam allowances toward print strip. Make 9 of Strip Set 1.
2. For Strip Set 2, join 2 strips of print fabric and 1 muslin strip as shown (Strip Set 2 Diagram). Press seam allowances toward print strips. Make 5 of Strip Set 2.
3. From each strip set, rotary-cut 16 (2½"-wide) segments as shown to get a total of 144 Strip Set 1 segments and 72 Strip Set 2 segments (and 8 extra).
4. For each block, select 2 Strip Set 1 segments and 1 Strip Set 2 segment. Join segments to form a nine-patch (Nine-Patch Diagram). Make 72 nine-patches.

5. Select a nine-patch for the first block. Find 1 B triangle to match each print fabric. Sew 1 triangle to each of 2 opposite sides of nine-patch, matching fabrics as shown (Block Assembly Diagram). Press seam allowances toward triangles. Add triangles to remaining sides to complete block.
6. Make 72 blocks.

Quilt Assembly

1. Lay out blocks in 9 rows of 8 blocks each. Arrange blocks to get a pleasing balance of color and value. When satisfied with placement, join blocks in each row (Row Assembly Diagram).
2. Referring to photo, join rows.

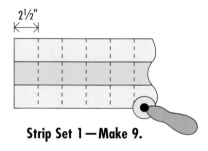

Strip Set 1 — Make 9.

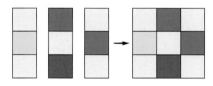

Nine-Patch Diagram

Borders

1. Join 2 muslin strips end to end for each inner border.
2. Measure quilt from top to bottom through middle. Trim 2 borders to match. Sew to quilt sides.
3. Measure quilt from side to side through middle. Trim remaining borders to match quilt width. Sew borders to top and bottom edges.
4. For outer border, cut 176 (2½" x 6½") Cs from remaining strips of print fabric. Referring to photo, join 46 Cs in a row for each side border and 42 Cs each for top and bottom borders. Referring to page 309, sew borders to quilt and miter corners.

continued

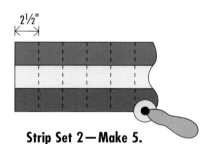

Strip Set 2 — Make 5.

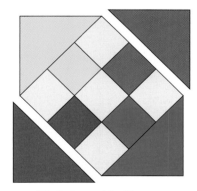

Block Assembly Diagram

Row Assembly Diagram

Quilting and Finishing

1. Mark quilting design on quilt top as desired. The quilt shown is machine-quilted with outline quilting in blocks, stipple quilting in inner border, and wide cable in outer border.
2. Layer backing, batting, and quilt top. Baste. Quilt as desired.
3. Make 10 yards of bias or straight-grain binding. Bind quilt edges.

Size Variations

	Twin	Full	King
Finished size	66" x 92"	76" x 92"	100" x 100"
Number of blocks	54	63	100
Blocks set	6 x 9	7 x 9	10 x 10
Number of			
Strip Set 1	7	8	12½
Strip Set 2	3½	4	6½
C pieces	158	168	200

Yardage Required

	Twin	Full	King
⅜-yard print fabrics	14	16	26
Muslin	2 yards	2 yards	2⅞ yards
Binding fabric	¾ yard	¾ yard	⅞ yard
108"-wide backing fabric	2 yards	2⅜ yards	3 yards

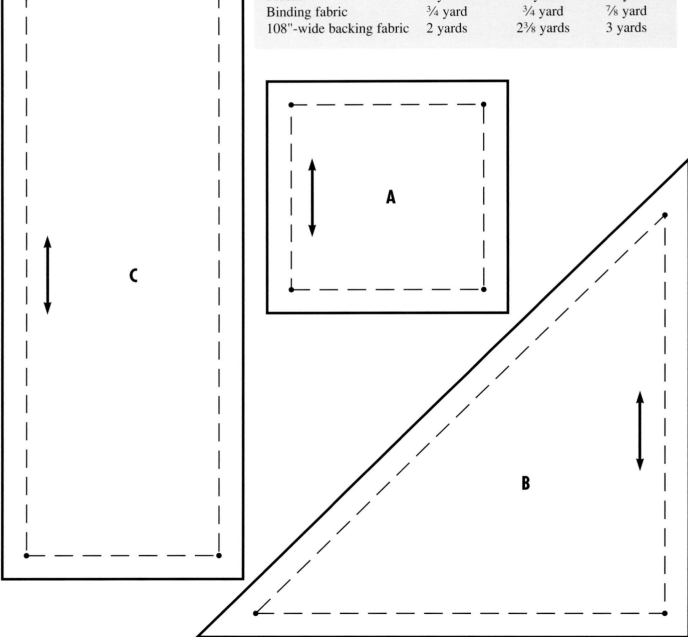

WILDFLOWERS

Here's a recipe for success: Mix one basic leaf shape and a basket of scrap fabrics. Appliqué thoroughly, add a pinch of embroidery, and—voilà!—you have a garden that will last a lifetime. The simplest of appliqué brings life to any reproduction of this Depression-era quilt, which still blooms with old-fashioned sweetness.

Finished Size

Quilt: 61" x 75"
Blocks: 48 (7" x 7")

Materials

48 (2" x 3½") green scraps
240 (2" x 3½") assorted scraps
¾ yard inner border fabric
3¾ yards background fabric
¾ yard binding fabric
4 yards backing fabric
Green embroidery floss

continued

Antique quilt owned by Patricia Cox of Minneapolis, Minnesota

Wildflower Block—Make 48.

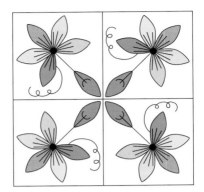

Four-Block Diagram

Cutting

Instructions are for hand appliqué. Make a template of Pattern A on page 85 and see page 307 for tips on cutting appliqué pieces.

From each green scrap
• 1 of Pattern A.

From each assorted scrap
• 5 of Pattern A.

From background fabric
• 4 (8" x 63") lengthwise strips for outer borders.
• 48 (7½") squares.

Block Assembly

1. Fold each background square in half diagonally and then crease to establish the diagonal center line.
2. Center 1 square over pattern on page 85, aligning edges and centering crease with stem embroidery line. Lightly trace outline of block on fabric.

3. Turn under seam allowances on A pieces. Referring to pattern, pin pieces in place. Petals will overlap slightly at center of flower. When satisfied with the position of the pinned pieces, appliqué them in place.
4. Use 2 strands of green embroidery floss to work the stem and the vine in backstitches. Cover ends of petals at center with satin stitches (see Stitch Diagrams on page 85).
5. Appliqué and then embroider 48 blocks.

Quilt Assembly

1. For ease of assembly, join blocks in groups of 4 so that green leaves meet at center (Four-Block Diagram). Make 12 four-block units.
2. Referring to photo on page 83, lay out four-block units in 4

horizontal rows with 3 units in each row (Row Assembly Diagram). Arrange units in rows to achieve pleasing balance of color and contrast.
3. Join units in each row. Join rows.

Borders

1. Cut 8 (2½"-wide) crosswise strips from fabric for inner border. Join 2 strips end to end to make each border strip.
2. Measure pieced top from top to bottom through middle. Trim 2 borders to match length. Sew border strips to quilt sides.
3. Measure quilt from side to side through middle. Trim remaining inner borders to match quilt width. Sew borders to top and bottom edges.
4. Measure quilt, trim, and sew outer borders in same manner.

Quilting and Finishing

1. Mark quilting design on quilt top as desired. On quilt shown, flowers and blocks are outline-quilted and 1"-wide diagonal cross-hatching is quilted in borders.
2. Layer backing, batting, and quilt top. Backing seams will run parallel to top and bottom edges. Baste. Quilt as desired.
3. Make 8 yards of 2½"-wide bias or straight-grain binding. Bind quilt edges.

Row Assembly Diagram

Satin stitch: Starting at top of circle, bring needle up on 1 side and insert it on opposite side. Carry the thread behind the work to repeat, stitching from 1 side to the other. Keep all stitches parallel, smooth, and close together.

Satin-Stitch Diagram

Backstitch: Working from right to left or top to bottom, bring needle up on drawn guideline. Take a stitch backward and bring needle up an equal distance ahead of first hole made by thread. Repeat, taking needle back to end of previous stitch.

Backstitch Diagram

continued

Color Variations

Stretch your imagination to create a new block with these patterns.

Here's our suggestion for a Wild-flowers quilt that's a little different. Standing up straight, the same flower fits a block approximately 5½" x 9" (finished size).

Your choice of color scheme makes your quilt unique. Consider bright flowers on a dark background or pale blooms on mottled blue for the look of water lilies.

So many possibilities—not enough time!

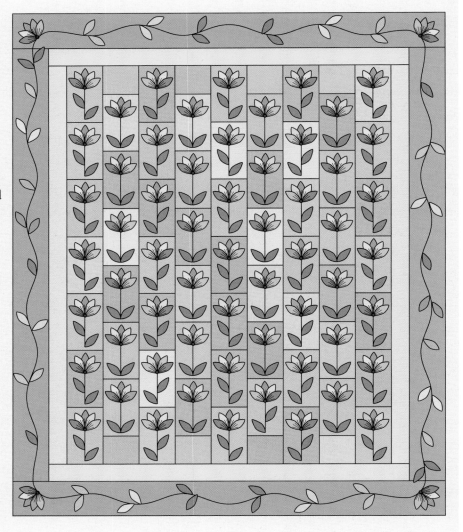

Size Variations

	Full	Queen	King
Finished size	75" x 89"	89" x 103"	103" x 103"
Number of blocks	80	120	144
Blocks set	8 x 10	10 x 12	12 x 12
Yardage Required			
Assorted scraps	400	600	720
Green scraps	80	120	144
Inner border fabric	¾ yard	¾ yard	¾ yard
Background fabric	5¼ yards	7⅛ yards	8¼ yards
Binding fabric	⅞ yard	1 yard	1 yard
Backing fabric	4¾ yards	8¼ yards	9¼ yards

BEDDING DOWN

Winter is serious business in Alaska, where quilts must be especially warm and cozy. A cheerful assortment of handsome plaid fabrics makes Kristina Bell's quilt a classic example that warms the soul as well as hands and feet. What looks like an allover pattern is really 20 blocks of a pieced design called Barrister's Block.

Finished Size

Quilt: 74" x 90"
Blocks: 20 (16" x 16")

Materials

40 (6⅞") squares light/medium plaid fabrics
40 (6⅞") squares medium/dark plaid fabrics
20 (9½" x 18") white-on-white scraps or 1⅝ yards of 1 fabric
20 (7" x 18") pieces of dark solid fabrics
½ yard fabric for inner border
2½ yards fabric for outer border
⅞ yard binding fabric
5½ yards backing fabric

continued

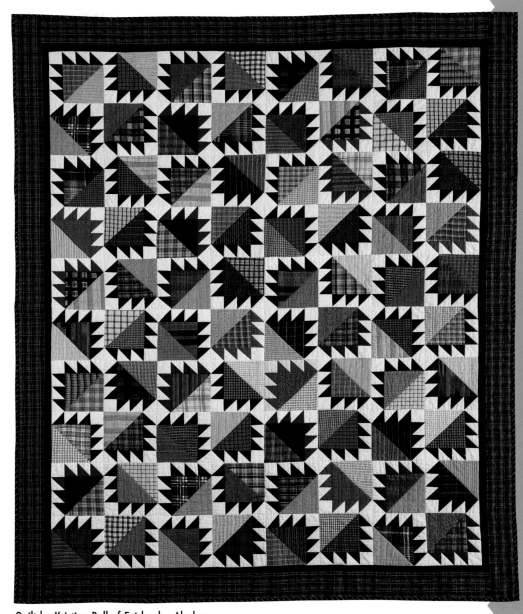

Quilt by Kristina Bell of Fairbanks, Alaska

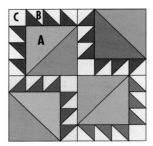

Barrister's Block—Make 20.

Block Assembly

Instructions are for rotary cutting and quick piecing. Before cutting, read block instructions and decide whether you prefer quick piecing or traditional piecing. For traditional cutting, use patterns on page 89.

The Barrister's Block has 4 quadrants, each a different combination of fabrics.

1. On wrong side of a light/medium plaid square, draw a diagonal line from corner to corner. With right sides facing, match marked square with a dark fabric. Sewing a ¼" seam allowance, stitch through both layers on *both sides* of line (Diagram A).

2. Cut along drawn line to get 2 triangle-squares. Make a total of 80 triangle-squares. Press seam allowances toward darker fabrics.

3. From each white-on-white fabric, cut a 2½" x 18" strip. From this, cut 4 (2½") C squares.

4. On wrong side of each 7" x 18" piece of white-on-white fabric, draw a 2-square by 6-square grid of 2⅞" squares (Diagram B). Mark diagonal lines through centers of squares as shown.

5. With right sides facing, match each marked piece with 1 solid fabric. Stitch on both sides of diagonal lines, pivoting at each grid corners as shown. (Red lines on diagram show continuous stitching line; blue lines show second stitching line.) Press stitching. Cut on all drawn lines to get 24 triangle-squares from each grid. Press seam allowances toward dark fabric.

6. Sort out 80 sets of small triangle-squares, 6 for each quadrant. Match each set with 1 plaid triangle-square and 1 C square.

7. Join small triangle-squares in 2 rows of 3 squares each, sewing light side of 1 square to dark side of next square (Diagram C). Press seams toward dark fabric.

8. Position plaid triangle-square with dark side on left as shown; sew 1 row of small triangle-squares to right side of large square. Sew C square to dark end of remaining row; sew this row to top of plaid square as shown. In this manner, make 80 units.

9. Select 4 units for each block. Referring to Barrister's Block Diagram for positioning, join units in pairs; then join pairs to complete block. Make 20 blocks.

Quilt Assembly

1. Lay out blocks in 5 horizontal rows, with 4 blocks in each row (Row Assembly Diagram). Arrange blocks as desired to achieve a pleasing balance of color and value.

2. When satisfied with placement, join blocks in each row.

3. Join rows as shown in photo on page 87.

Borders

1. For inner border, cut 8 (1½"-wide) crosswise strips. Join 2 strips end to end to make each border.

2. Measure quilt from top to bottom through middle of pieced top. Trim side borders to match length. Then sew borders to quilt sides.

3. Measure quilt from side to side through middle. Trim remaining borders to match. Sew borders to top and bottom edges of quilt.

4. For outer border, cut 4 (4½"-wide) lengthwise strips. Measure quilt, trim, and sew outer borders as for inner border.

Diagram A

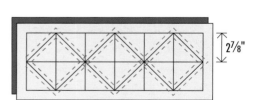

Diagram B

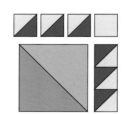

Diagram C

Row Assembly Diagram

Size Variations

	Queen	King
Finished size	90" x 90"	106" x 106"
Number of blocks	25	36
Blocks set	5 x 5	6 x 6

Yardage Required

Light/medium squares	50	72
Medium/dark squares	50	72
White-on-white fabrics	25 or 2 yards	36 or 2½ yards
Solid fabrics	25	36
Inner border fabric	½ yard	⅝ yard
Outer border fabric	2¾ yards	3⅛ yards
Binding fabric	⅞ yard	1 yard
Backing fabric	8¼ yards	9⅜ yards

Quilting and Finishing

1. Mark quilting design on pieced top as desired. On quilt shown, quilting follows lines in plaid fabrics.
2. Layer backing, batting, and quilt top. Backing seams will parallel top and bottom edges of quilt. Then baste them together. Quilt as desired.
3. Make 9½ yards of bias or straight-grain binding. Bind quilt edges.

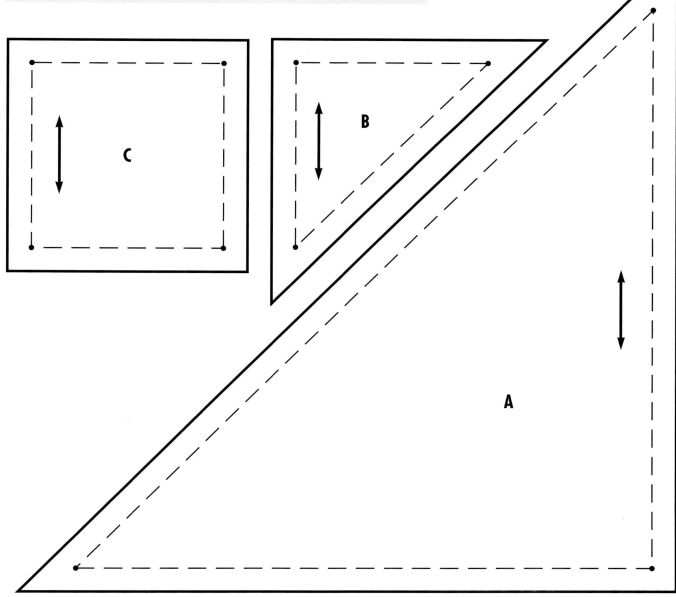

SUMMER BASKETS

Quilt by Tracey M. Brookshier of Capitola, California; machine-quilted by Laura Lee Fritz of Napa, California

Tracey Brookshier likes bold, bright, way-out-there, in-your-face *color*.

"My favorite part of quilting is choosing all the fabrics to go into a quilt," Tracey says, "and my favorite quilts have lots of different fabrics."

The fabrics in *Summer Baskets* all coordinate with the colors in the sumptuous border fabric, which appears as a unifying element in the center of each basket.

Finished Size

Quilt: 85¾" x 100"
Blocks: 50 (10" x 10")

Materials

2¾ yards print border fabric
1½ yards coordinating fabric
    for setting triangles
⅜ yard inner border fabric
50 (7" x 13") basket fabrics *
49 (6" x 21") tone-on-tone prints for
    block backgrounds *
1 yard binding fabric
2⅝ yards 108"-wide backing
* *Note:* You can substitute 17 fat quarters for baskets and another 17 fat quarters for block backgrounds.

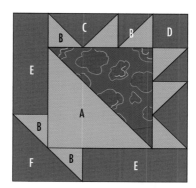

Basket Block—Make 50.

Cutting

Instructions are for rotary cutting and quick piecing. For traditional cutting and piecing, use patterns below and on page 94. Cut all strips on crosswise grain except as noted.

From border fabric

• 4 (6¾" x 90") lengthwise strips for outer border.

• 25 (6⅞") squares. Cut each square in half diagonally to get 50 A triangles.

From setting fabric

• 5 (15½") squares. Cut each square in quarters diagonally to get 18 setting triangles (and 2 extra).

• 2 (8") squares. Cut each square in half diagonally to get 4 corner triangles.

From each basket fabric

• 1 (6⅞") square. Cut square in half to get 1 A triangle. Discard extra triangle or use for another block.

• 2 (2⅞") squares. Cut 1 square in half to get 2 B triangles. Save second square for triangle-squares.

• 4 (2½") squares for B piecing.

From binding fabric

• 1 (32") square for bias binding. Add remainder to block background fabrics.

From each background fabric

• 1 (5") square. Cut square in half diagonally to get 1 F triangle. Discard extra triangle or use for another block.

• 1 (2⅞") square for B triangle-squares.

• 2 (2½" x 6½") E pieces.

• 2 (2½" x 4½") C pieces.

• 1 (2½") D square.

Block Assembly

1. For each block, select 1 set of A and B basket pieces; 1 set of B, C, D, E, and F background pieces; and 1 border print A triangle (Block Assembly Diagram). Join A triangles; press seam allowances toward basket fabric.

2. Lightly mark a diagonal line on wrong side of 1 (2⅞") B square of basket fabric. With right sides facing, match this with same-size square of background fabric. Stitch ¼" seam on both sides of line (Diagram A). Press. Cut apart on the drawn line to get 2 B triangle-squares.

3. See page 304 for instructions on diagonal-corners technique. Use this method to sew 2½" squares to corners of each C rectangle (Diagram B).

4. Sew B triangles to ends of each E piece, making sure triangles point in opposite directions as shown.

5. Lay out units (Block Assembly Diagram). Join 1 B triangle-square to end of B/C unit at top of block. Sew combined unit to top edge of A square.

6. Join D, B triangle-square, and B/C unit. Sew combined unit to right side of block.

7. Sew B/E strips to left and bottom edges as shown. Then sew F triangle to bottom left corner to complete block. Make 50 blocks.

continued

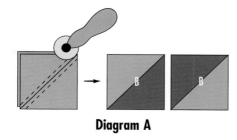

Diagram A

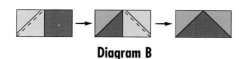

Diagram B

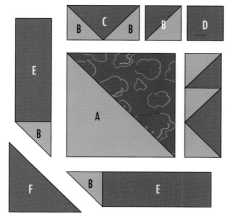

Block Assembly Diagram

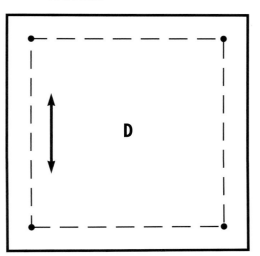

D

Quilt Assembly

1. Lay out blocks in 10 diagonal rows (Quilt Assembly Diagram). Move blocks as desired around to achieve a nice balance of color and fabrics. When satisfied with block placement, end rows with setting triangles as shown. Join blocks and triangles in each row.
2. Join rows to complete quilt center. Sew corner triangles in place as shown.

Borders

1. Cut 8 (1½"-wide) strips of inner border fabric. Sew 2 strips end to end for each border.
2. Measure length of quilt through middle of pieced top. Trim 2 border strips to match length. Sew these to quilt sides, easing to fit as needed. Press seam allowances toward borders. Repeat for top and bottom borders.
3. Add outer border strips in the same manner.

Quilting and Finishing

1. Mark the quilting design as desired. The quilt shown is outline-quilted by machine with free-motion quilting (with red thread) adding hearts and curlicues around the baskets.
2. Layer backing, batting, and quilt top. Baste. Quilt as desired.
3. Use remaining binding fabric to make 10½ yards of continuous straight-grain or bias binding. Bind quilt edges.

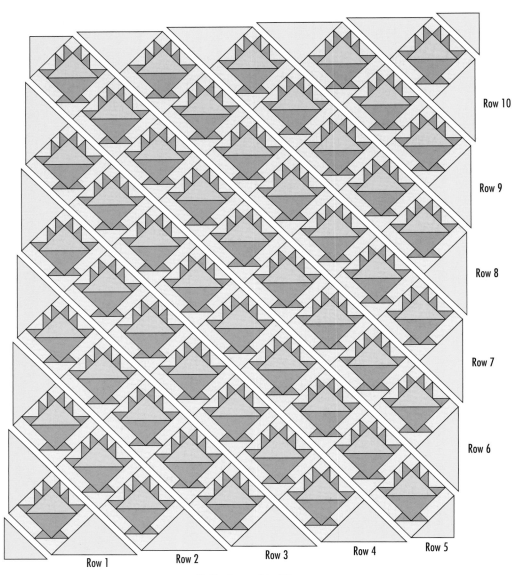

Row 10
Row 9
Row 8
Row 7
Row 6
Row 5
Row 1
Row 2
Row 3
Row 4

Quilt Assembly Diagram

continued

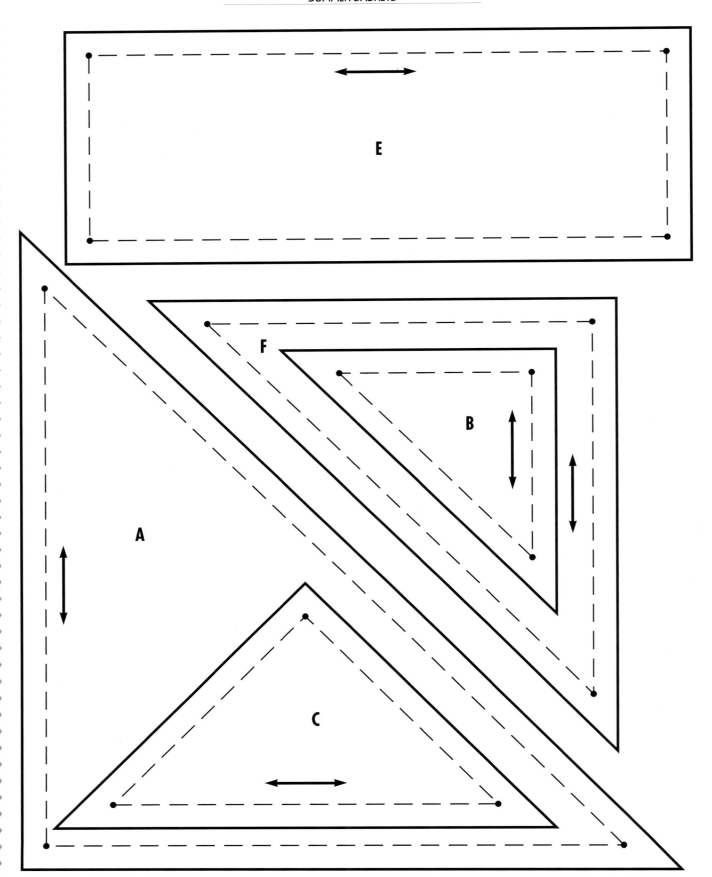

SPIDER WEB

Red stars accent this web of Flying Geese patchwork. Wild Goose Chase blocks and sashing place scrap fabrics against a neutral background. Choose traditional piecing or quick-piecing techniques to make the geese.

Marion Watchinski's quilt is patterned after one made by her husband's great-grandmother at the turn of the twentieth century.

Finished Size

Quilt: 84" x 93"
Blocks: 9 (16" x 16")
Half-blocks: 12 (8½" x 16")

Materials

768 (2⅛") scrap squares *
7½ yards muslin
1¾ yards red fabric
7¾ yards backing fabric
* Note: See page 304 for quick-piecing techniques.

continued

Quilt by Marion Roach Watchinski of Overland Park, Kansas

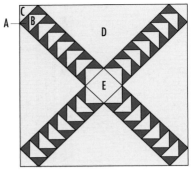

Wild Goose Chase Block—Make 9.

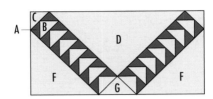

Half-Block—Make 12.

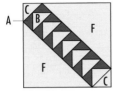

Quarter-Block—Make 4.

Cutting

Before cutting, read "Block Assembly" instructions and decide whether you prefer the diagonal-corner technique or traditional piecing for flying geese. Instructions are for rotary cutting. For traditional cutting, use the patterns on page 100 to make the templates.

From scrap fabrics
- 1,536 (1¾") squares to make geese with diagonal-corner technique or 768 (2⅛") squares for traditional piecing. Cut 2⅛" squares in half diagonally to get 1,536 A triangles.

From muslin
- 2 (5½" x 86") and 2 (3½" x 86") lengthwise strips for outer border.
- 4 (2¼" x 80") lengthwise strips for inner border.
- 4 (9" x 15½") for triangle-squares.
- 12 (13¾") squares. Cut each square in quarters diagonally to get 48 D triangles.
- 18 (7⅛") squares. Cut each square in half diagonally to get 36 F triangles.
- 3 (4¾") squares. Cut each square in quarters diagonally to get 12 G triangles.

- 720 (1¾" x 3") pieces to make geese with diagonal-corner technique or 180 (3¾") squares for traditional piecing. Cut 3¾" squares in quarters diagonally to get 720 B triangles for geese.
- 16 (3¾") squares. Cut squares in quarters diagonally to get 64 B triangles for sashing.
- 9 (3") E squares.
- 36 (2⅝") squares. Cut each square in half diagonally to get 72 C triangles.
- 24 (3") H squares for diagonal-corner technique or 24 (2¼") H squares for traditional piecing.

From red
- 4 (9" x 15½") for triangle-squares.
- 8 (1¾"-wide) crosswise strips. From these, cut 128 I diamonds. Mark seam allowances on wrong side of each diamond.

Block Assembly

1. Referring to page 304, use the diagonal-corner technique to sew 2 A squares to 1 B rectangle (Diagram A). Or sew A triangles to B triangle traditionally as shown. Make 720 flying geese. Set aside 272 geese for sashing.

2. Join 7 geese in a row (Diagram B). Add 1 C triangle to left end of row as shown. Press seam allowances toward C. Make 64 geese units.

Diagram B

3. Select 4 geese units, 4 D triangles, and 1 E square for each block. Sew triangles to sides of 2 geese units as shown (Block Assembly Diagram). Press seam allowances toward triangles. Sew remaining geese units to opposite sides of

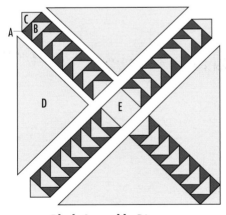

Block Assembly Diagram

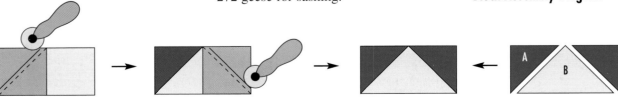

Diagram A

Sashing Unit—Make 24.

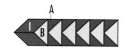

Half-Sashing Unit—Make 16.

E square. Press seam allowances toward square. Join units as shown to complete block. Make 9 blocks.

4. For each half-block, select 2 geese units, 2 F triangles, and 1 each of triangles D and G. Sew G triangle to end of 1 geese unit as shown (Half-Block Assembly Diagram). Sew F triangle to side of same unit. Join D and F triangles to second unit as shown. Press seam allowances toward triangles. Join halves to complete half-block. Make 12 half-blocks.

Sashing Assembly

1. Use diagonal-corner technique to sew 4 A corners on each H square (Diagram C). Or sew A triangles to H square traditionally as shown.
2. Select 8 geese, 4 I diamonds, 2 B triangles, and 1 H unit. Join 4 geese in a row as shown (Sashing Assembly Diagram). Make 2 geese units.
3. Join the diamonds in pairs as shown. Referring to page 36, set

B triangle into each pair. Sew 1 diamond unit to the end of each geese unit.

4. Join units in a row to complete sashing. Make 24 sashing units.
5. For the half-sashing, join a pair of diamonds and then set in 1 B triangle as before. Join 5 flying geese in a row. Make 16 half-sashing units.

continued

Diagram C

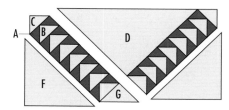

Half-Block Assembly Diagram

Sashing Assembly Diagram

5. For quarter-block, sew F triangles to sides of geese unit as shown (Quarter-Block Assembly Diagram). Sew C triangles to ends of geese unit. Press seam allowances toward triangles. Make 4 quarter-blocks.

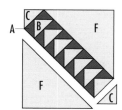

Quarter-Block Assembly Diagram

Size Variations

	Twin	King
Finished size	65½" x 93"	102½" x 111½"
Number of		
Blocks	6	16
Half-blocks	10	16
Quarter-blocks	4	4
Sashing units	17	40
Half-sashing units	14	20
Triangle-squares	52	76
Blocks set	2 x 3	4 x 4

Yardage Required

2⅛" scrap squares	576	1,200
Muslin	6 yards	10¾ yards
Red fabric	1¾ yards	2¼ yards
Backing fabric	5⅝ yards	9½ yards

Row 1—Make 2.

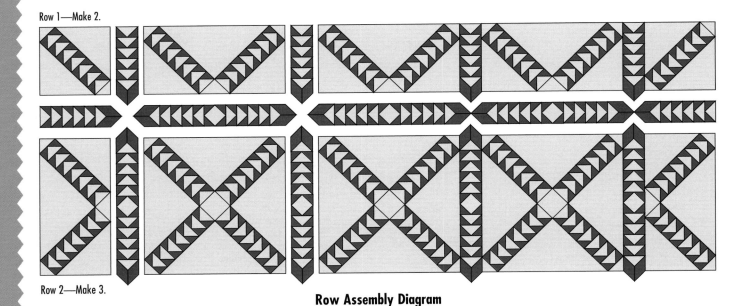

Row 2—Make 3.

Row Assembly Diagram

Quilt Assembly

Joining these rows requires careful pinning and precise sewing. See page 36 for information on sewing set-in seams. Throughout assembly, refer to the photo at right and Row Assembly Diagram.

1. For Row 1, join 3 half-blocks, 2 quarter-blocks, and 4 half-sashing units in a row as shown. Stop stitching at the marked point ¼" from the ends of the diamonds. Diamond points will extend at the bottom of row. Make 2 of Row 1.

2. For Row 2, join 3 blocks, 2 half-blocks, and 4 sashing units in a row as shown. Start and stop each seam at marked point on diamonds. Diamonds will extend beyond top and bottom of row. Make 3 of Row 2.

3. To join Row 1 to Row 2, select 3 sashing units and 2 half-sashing units. Sew long sides of sashing units to blocks, stopping at marked points on diamonds and leaving star points unstitched for now.

4. At each star center, fold back 2 adjacent pairs of diamonds to keep them out of the way. Stitch the mitered seam connecting the opposite pair of diamonds (Diagram D). Start stitching at the block corner and sew to the end of the diamond points as indicated by the arrow. Press the seam allowance open. Stitch the opposite pair in same manner. Then stitch the center seam of star.

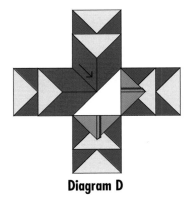

Diagram D

5. Join remaining Row 2 units in this manner. Referring to the photo at right, end with second Row 1.

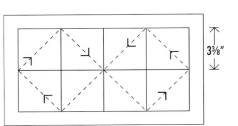

Diagram E

Borders

1. Measure pieced top through middle. Trim 2¼"-wide muslin strips to correct length. Sew border strips to quilt edges with square corners.

2. See page 306 for instructions on quick-piecing triangle-squares. On wrong side of each 9" x 15½" muslin piece, draw a 2-square x 4-square grid of 3⅜" squares (Diagram E). With right sides together, pair each muslin piece with 1 matching red fabric and stitch together. Start in center of 1 side and follow arrows around, pivoting at corners, to stitch entire grid without having to remove fabric from sewing machine. Cut triangle-squares

apart on drawn lines and press. Make 62 triangle-squares. (For traditional piecing, cut 62 J triangles from both muslin and red fabrics.)

3. Join 31 triangle-squares for the top border. Sew the border to the top edge of the quilt, easing to fit as needed. Repeat for the bottom border.

4. Measure the quilt from the top to the bottom through the middle of the pieced top. Trim 3½"-wide muslin strips to correct length. Sew border strips to quilt sides. Then trim 5½"-wide muslin borders to match quilt's width and sew these to top and bottom edges of quilt.

Quilting and Finishing

1. Mark desired quilting design on pieced top. Quilt shown has 1"-square cross-hatching in muslin areas and outline quilting inside star points.

2. Layer the backing, batting, and quilt top. Backing seams are parallel to the top and bottom edges. Then baste them together. Quilt as desired.

3. Use the remaining red fabric to make 10⅛ yards of bias or straight-grain binding. Bind the quilt edges.

continued

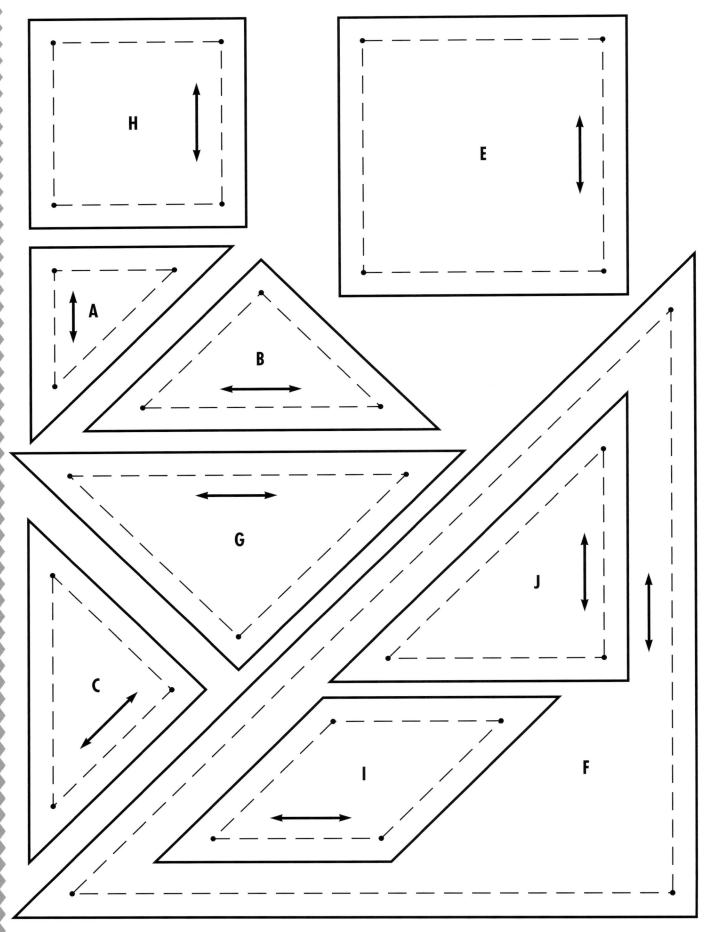

RE-VISION

ew of us are lucky enough to have the number of reproduction fabrics that Linda Anderson owns. She won this collection of fabrics at a quilt show. This quilt is Linda's interpretation of the many scrap quilts her grandmother made for Lutheran missions. There are nearly 100 fabrics in Linda's quilt—our instructions call for at least 25, which still gives plenty of variety.

Finished Size

Quilt: 83" x 83"
Blocks: 41 (9" x 9")

Materials

¼ yard *each* of 25 print fabrics
5½ yards white or muslin
2½ yards 90"-wide backing fabric

continued

Quilt by Linda Anderson of Fresno, California

Cutting

Instructions are for rotary cutting and quick piecing. Cut all strips crosswise except border strips as noted. Cut pieces in order listed.

From each *scrap fabric*

- 2 (1½"-wide) strips. From these, cut 5 (1½" x 8") pieces for strip sets 1 and 2, 3 (1½" x 11") pieces for Strip Set 4, and 5 (1½" x 2½") F pieces.
- 1 (3"-wide) strip. From this, cut 9 (3") squares for prairie points, 1 (2½" x 13") piece for Strip Set 3, and 2 (1½" x 2½") F pieces (7 F pieces are extras).

From all remaining scrap fabrics

- 1 (1½"-wide) strip from each of 9 fabrics. From each of these, cut 3 (1½" x 11") pieces for Strip Set 4.
- 4 (2⅜") squares from each of 4 fabrics. Cut each square in half diagonally to get 8 Z triangles of each fabric for pinwheel blocks.

From white

- 1 (2⅜-yard) length. From this, cut 4 (6" x 85") lengthwise strips for borders. From remainder, cut 100 (1½" x 8") pieces for strip sets 1 and 2.
- 9 (3½"-wide) strips. From these, cut 100 (3½") B squares.
- 2 (5½"-wide) strips. From these, cut 16 (5½") C squares.
- 25 (1½"-wide) strips. From these, cut 32 (1½" x 10½") G strips, 32 (1½" x 9½") E strips, 32 (1½" x 7½") D strips, and 4 (1½" x 12½") H strips.
- 4 (11") squares. Cut each square in quarters diagonally to get 16 X setting triangles.
- 2 (7⅜") squares. Cut each square in half diagonally to get 4 Y corner triangles.

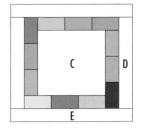

Block 1—Make 25.

Block 1 Assembly

1. Stitch 1 (1½" x 8") white strip between 2 strips of same print to make Strip Set 1 (Strip Set 1 Diagram). Make 2 of Strip Set 1. Stitch 1 strip of same print between 2 white strips to make 1 Strip Set 2 (Strip Set 2 Diagram). Press all seam allowances toward print fabric.
2. Cut 5 (1½"-wide) segments from each strip set.
3. Join 2 Strip Set 1 segments and 1 Strip Set 2 segment to make a nine-patch unit (Diagram A). Using all cut segments, you can make 5 nine-patch units of same fabric combination.
4. Repeat with remaining 1½" x 8" strips to get a total of 125 nine-patch units.
5. For each block, select 5 assorted nine-patches and 4 B squares. Join squares in horizontal rows (Block Diagram); then join rows to complete block.
6. Make 25 of Block 1.

Block 2—Make 16.

Block 2 Assembly

1. Join any 3 (2½" x 13") strips (Strip Set 3 Diagram). Make 8 of Strip Set 3, varying fabrics. You will have 1 (2½" x 13") strip left over.
2. From each strip set, cut 8 (1½"-wide) segments to get a total of 64 segments, 4 for each block.
3. With right sides facing, match 1 segment to 1 C square, aligning segment top with square corner. Stitch, stopping at least 2" from square corner and leaving end unsewn (Diagram B). Press seam allowances toward colored strip.
4. Sew second segment to top edge of combined units as shown. Press seam allowances toward print fabrics. Add third and fourth segments in same manner. Then go back and finish first seam, stitching over last segment.

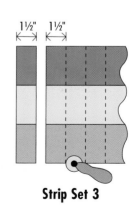

Strip Set 3

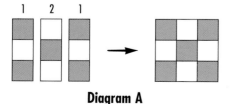

Diagram A

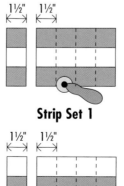

Strip Set 1

Strip Set 2

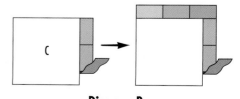

Diagram B

5. Sew D strips to 2 sides of block. Press seam allowances toward Ds. Then stitch E strips to remaining sides to complete block.

6. Make 16 of Block 2.

Side and Corner Blocks Assembly

1. For each side block, select 1 X triangle, 9 F pieces, and 2 Gs. Join 4 Fs in a row; then stitch row to 1 side of triangle (Side Block Diagram). Press seam allowances

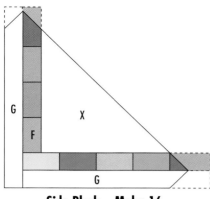

Side Block—Make 16.

toward pieced row. Join remaining 5 Fs in row and stitch row to second side of triangle. Last brick in each row extends past triangle (these are trimmed later).

2. Sew 1 G strip to triangle side as shown. Press seam allowance toward pieced row. Stitch second G to adjacent triangle side in same manner to complete block.

3. Make 16 side blocks.

continued

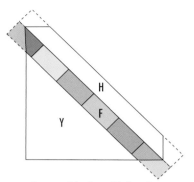

Corner Block—Make 4.

4. For each corner block, select 1 Y triangle, 6 F pieces, and 1 H strip. Join Fs in a row (Corner Block Diagram); then sew row to diagonal edge of triangle. Handle triangle carefully as this edge is bias and can stretch if you're not careful. Join H strip to pieced row. Press seam allowances toward pieced row. Make 4 corner blocks.

Quilt Assembly

1. Lay out blocks in 9 diagonal rows as shown (Quilt Assembly Diagram). Start and end each row with Block 1 and alternate blocks as shown. When satisfied with block placement, join blocks in each row.
2. Add side blocks to row ends.
3. Join rows, mitering seams where side blocks meet.
4. Add corner blocks at each corner of quilt.
5. Trim ends of pieced print strips even with X and Y triangles.

Borders

1. Select 2 (1½" x 11") strips of same print fabric and 1 strip of another fabric. Join strips as shown (Strip Set 4 Diagram). Press all seam allowances toward top strip. Make 34 of Strip Set 4.
2. Cut 4 (2½"-wide) segments from each strip set to get a total of 136 segments for border.
3. Referring to photo on page 103, join 34 segments in a vertical row for each side border. Turn adjacent segments to offset seam

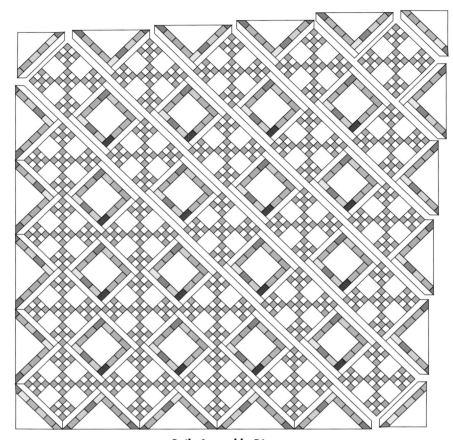

Quilt Assembly Diagram

allowances. Stitch rows to quilt sides, easing to fit as needed.
4. Join 2 horizontal rows with 34 segments in each row. Set aside.
5. For each pinwheel block, select 4 Z triangles each of 2 fabrics. Join pairs of contrasting triangles to make 4 triangle-squares. Join squares in rows; then join rows to complete block (Pinwheel Block Diagram). Make 2 pinwheel blocks with same fabric combination; then make 2 more blocks of second fabric combination.

6. Stitch pinwheel blocks to both ends of each pieced border. Stitch borders to top and bottom edges of quilt, easing to fit as needed.
7. Measure length of pieced top through middle. Trim 2 white border strips to match length. Stitch border strips to quilt sides. Press seam allowances toward borders.
8. Measure width of pieced top through middle, including side borders. Trim remaining white borders to match quilt width. Sew to top and bottom edges of quilt, easing to fit as needed.

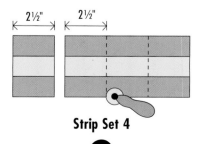

Strip Set 4

Pinwheel Block Diagram

Quilting and Finishing

1. Mark quilt top with desired quilting design. Blocks of quilt shown are machine-quilted in-the-ditch and other areas are utility-quilted by hand. Pattern for heart-and-wave motif stitched in X triangles is on this page. Same heart is quilted in each B square; wavy lines are quilted in D, E, G, and H strips, as well as in white border. Linda also added tying in pieced border because her grandmother usually tied her quilts.

2. Layer backing, batting, and quilt top. Baste. Quilt as desired.

3. Fold 56 (3") squares in half (Diagram C) and in half again (Diagram D). Press. Pin prairie points to 1 side edge of quilt top, aligning raw edges and overlapping points as needed to fit edge of quilt (Diagram E). Baste. Repeat on each remaining side.

4. Fold backing of quilt away from edges; pin or baste to hold backing temporarily in place. Using a ¼" seam, stitch around edges of quilt through prairie points, quilt top, and batting.

5. Trim batting close to stitching. Press prairie points out. Remove pins or basting from backing. Turn under ¼" on each edge of backing and slipstitch backing in place behind prairie points.

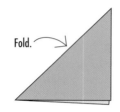

Fold.

Diagram C

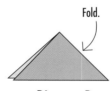

Fold.

Diagram D

Diagram E

Heart-and-Wave Quilting Pattern

HONEYBEE

Quilt by Connie J. Nordstrom of Farmington, New Mexico

This block offers the chance to learn two quiltmaking techniques: mitering corners and hand appliquéing. The border surrounds center squares featuring large-scale prints. The simple leaf shape is a basic component of classic appliqué.

Finished Size
Quilt: 87" x 99"
Blocks: 42 (10¾" x 10¾")

Materials
42 (5¾") squares large print fabrics
42 (10" x 14") coordinating small print fabrics
4¼ yards muslin
2⅝ yards tan fabric for sashing and inner border
⅛ yard brown for sashing squares
3 yards print border fabric *
1 yard binding fabric
3 yards 104"-wide backing fabric
* *Note:* Yardage is for lengthwise strips. If you need to cut crosswise strips in order to accommodate border print, buy at least 2 yards.

Cutting
Make a template of leaf pattern on facing page. Cut pieces in order listed to make best use of yardage. Cut all strips on crosswise grain except as noted. When possible, pieces are listed in order needed, so you don't have to cut everything all at once.
From each small print
• 12 of Leaf Pattern.
From muslin
• 13 (11¼"-wide) strips. From these, cut 168 (3¼"x 11¼") strips.
From tan
• 4 (2½" x 87") lengthwise strips for inner border.
• 71 (2¼" x 11¼") sashing strips.
From brown
• 30 (2¼") sashing squares.
From outer border fabric
• 4 (6" x 106") lengthwise strips or 12 (6" x 43") crosswise strips.

Honeybee Block—Make 42.

Block Assembly

1. For each block, choose 4 muslin strips, 1 (5¾") center square, and 1 set of 12 leaves.
2. Fold each muslin strip in half and crease to mark center. Mark center on each edge of square in same manner. Matching center points, stitch 1 muslin strip to each side of square, starting and stopping each seam ¼" from edge of square. Miter corners. Block should be 11¼" square.
3. Turn under seam allowance on each leaf. Center 1 leaf over each mitered seam, with bottom point of leaf slightly above corner of center square. Pin 1 leaf on each side of each corner leaf. When satisfied with placement, appliqué leaves in place to complete block.
4. Make 42 blocks.

Quilt Assembly

1. Lay out blocks in 7 horizontal rows of 6 blocks each. Place sashing strips between the blocks. Arrange blocks to achieve a pleasing balance of color and pattern.
2. When satisfied with placement of blocks, join blocks and sashing in each row. Press seam allowances toward sashing strips.
3. Lay out block rows. Between rows, lay out remaining sashing strips and sashing squares in horizontal rows, with 6 strips and 5 squares alternating in each row. Join units in each sashing row. Press seam allowances toward sashing.
4. Join all the rows.

Borders

1. Measure length of quilt through middle of pieced top. Trim 2 inner border strips to match the quilt length.
2. Sew borders to quilt sides, easing to fit as needed. Press seam allowances toward borders.
3. Measure width of quilt through middle, including side borders. Trim remaining inner borders to match width. Sew borders to top and bottom edges of quilt, easing to fit as needed. Press.
4. Mark center on each edge of quilt and on each outer border strip. Matching centers, sew borders to quilt, starting and stopping each seam ¼" from corner. Miter border corners.

Quilting and Finishing

1. Layer the backing, batting, and quilt top.
2. Quilt as desired. The quilt shown is outline-quilted with echo-quilting around appliqués and clamshell pattern quilted in sashing. Fleur-de-lis Quilting Pattern for block center is below.
3. Make 10⅝ yards of bias or straight-grain binding from reserved strips. Bind quilt edges.

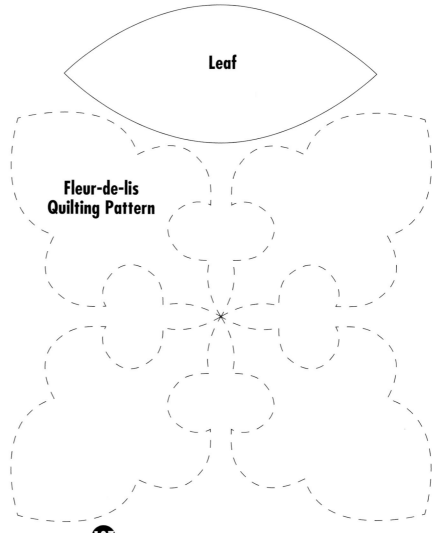

Leaf

Fleur-de-lis Quilting Pattern

SPOOLS

Quilt by Carole Collins of Galien, Michigan

Q uiltmakers have a passion for sewing paraphernalia, so we honor our crafting heritage with this easy-to-sew traditional block. Old-fashioned wooden spools are now much prized by antique collectors. In pioneer days, a homemaker wrapped her homespun thread and yarn on these spools to keep them clean and tangle free until the next weaving day.

Finished Size

Quilt: 66" x 78"
Blocks: 143 (6" x 6")

Materials

½ yard *each* of 7 light prints
72 (6" x 17") medium/dark fabrics or equivalent scraps
¾ yard binding fabric
4 yards backing fabric

Cutting

Instructions are for rotary cutting and quick piecing. For traditional techniques, make templates of patterns on page 110.
From each *light fabric*
• 7 (2½"-wide) crosswise strips. From these, cut 42 (2½" x 6½") B rectangles to get a total of 286 Bs (and 8 extra), 2 for each block.
From each *medium/dark fabric*
• 2 (2½" x 17") strips. (*Note:* For traditional cutting, use templates instead of cutting strips.) From each strip, cut 4 (2½") A squares and 1 (2½" x 6½") C rectangle.

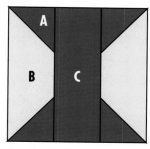

Spools Block—Make 143.

Block Assembly

1. For each block, select 4 As and 1 C of same fabric; then select 2 matching Bs. Referring to page 304, use the diagonal-corner technique to sew 2 A squares to each B rectangle (Diagram A). Or sew A triangles to B traditionally. Make 2 A/B units for each block. Press the seam allowances toward the triangles.
2. Join A/B units to sides of C as shown (Block Assembly Diagram). Press seam allowances toward C.
3. Make 143 Spools blocks.

Quilt Assembly

1. Lay out 11 blocks in a horizontal row. Turn alternating blocks on their sides as shown (Row Assembly Diagram). Odd-numbered rows start and end with upright blocks. Even-numbered rows start and end with turned blocks. Lay out 13 rows.
2. Rearrange blocks to achieve a pleasing balance of color and value. When satisfied with placement, join blocks in each row.
3. Referring to photo, join rows.

Quilting and Finishing

1. Mark quilting design as desired. Quilt has diagonal lines quilted on each block, spaced ¾" apart.
2. Layer backing, batting, and quilt top. Backing seams will run parallel to top and bottom edges of quilt. Baste. Quilt as desired.
3. Make 9 yards of bias or straight-grain binding. Bind quilt edges.

continued

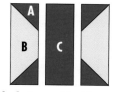

Block Assembly Diagram

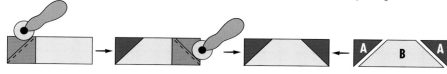

Diagram A

Row 1—Make 7.

Row 2—Make 6.

Row Assembly Diagram

Size Variations

	Full	Queen	King
Finished size	78" x 90"	90" x 102"	102" x 102"
Number of blocks	195	255	289
Blocks set	13 x 15	15 x 17	17 x 17
Yardage Required			
Light ½ yards	10	12	14
Dark scraps	98	128	145
Binding fabric	⅞ yard	1 yard	1 yard
Backing fabric	2¾ yards	2¾ yards	3 yards
	(90" wide)	(108" wide)	(108" wide)

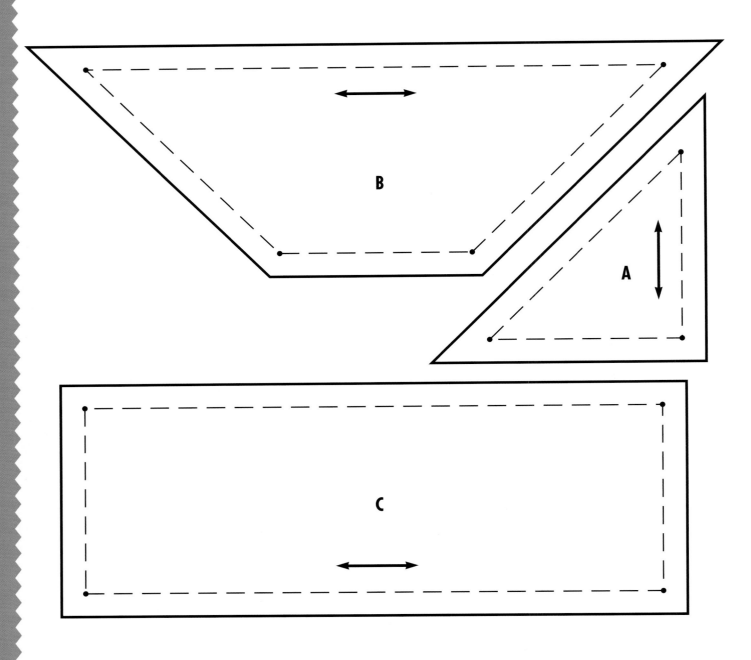

DEVIL ON THE RUN

Quilt by Nancy Wagner Graves of Manhattan, Kansas

Curved seams aren't *sew* difficult. A little practice will leave you wondering what the fuss was about. The basic unit of this patchwork is a curve-seamed two-patch that appears in traditional Drunkard's Path designs. A Devil's Puzzle variation inspired the name of this quilt, hand-pieced on-the-go by Nancy Graves. Contrasting piping, sewn in with the binding, adds a nice finishing touch.

Finished Size

Quilt: 84" x 102"
Blocks: 20 (18" x 18")
Partial Blocks: 18 (6" x 18")

Materials

952 (3½") scrap squares
6¾ yards background fabric
⅞ yard binding fabric
3⅛ yards 90"-wide backing fabric
10¾ yards ⅛"-diameter cording (optional)
1/16"-diameter hole punch (optional; see page 67 for source information)

continued

Unit 1—Make 360.

Unit 2—Make 552.

Corner Block—Make 4.

Devil's Puzzle Block—Make 20.

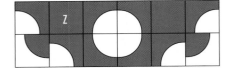

Partial Block—Make 18.

Cutting

Make templates of patterns X, Y, and Z on page 113. Mark matching dots on templates as shown on patterns X and Y. Use $1/16$"-diameter hole punch to make corner dots. There are excellent ready-made templates available for Drunkard's Path patchwork. Look for them at quilt shops or in mail-order catalogs.

From scrap fabrics
• 360 of Pattern X.
• 552 of Pattern Y.
• 40 Z squares.

Note: Mark dots on wrong side of each X and Y piece.

From background fabric
• 12" x 42" for piping.
• 552 of Pattern X.
• 360 of Pattern Y.

Note: Mark dots on all X and Y pieces.

Block Assembly

1. Referring to page 114, choose the desired method for sewing the curved seam. Make 360 of Unit 1 as shown, using scrap Xs and background Ys. Then make 552 of Unit 2, using background Xs and scrap Ys.

2. For each block, select 16 of Unit 1 and 20 of Unit 2. Arrange units in 6 horizontal rows (Block Assembly Diagram).

When satisfied with placement, join units in each row. Then join rows to complete block. Make 20 blocks.

3. For each partial block, select 2 of Unit 1, 8 of Unit 2, and 2 Z squares. Arrange units in 2 horizontal rows (Partial Block Diagram). Join units in each row; then join rows to complete partial block. Make 18 partial blocks.

4. For corner block, select 1 of Unit 1, 2 of Unit 2, and 1 Z square. Join units in 2 rows as shown (Corner Block Diagram); then join rows to complete corner block. Make 4 corner blocks.

Block Assembly Diagram

Size Variations

	Crib	Twin	King
Finished size	42" x 42"	66" x 84"	102" x 102"
Number of			
Blocks	4	12	25
Partial blocks	8	14	20
Corner blocks	4	4	4
Blocks set	2 x 2	3 x 4	5 x 5
Yardage Required			
Scrap squares	256	616	1,156
Background fabric	$2\frac{1}{4}$ yards	$5\frac{1}{2}$ yards	$9\frac{3}{4}$ yards
Binding fabric	$5/8$ yard	$7/8$ yard	1 yard
Backing fabric	$1\frac{3}{8}$ yards	$2\frac{1}{8}$ yards (90" wide)	$3\frac{1}{8}$ yards (120" wide)

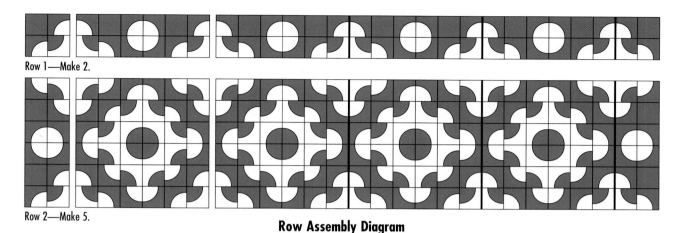

Row 1—Make 2.

Row 2—Make 5.

Row Assembly Diagram

Quilt Assembly

1. For Row 1, join 2 corner blocks and 4 partial blocks as shown (Row Assembly Diagram). Make 2 of Row 1.
2. For Row 2, join 4 blocks and 2 partial blocks as shown. Make 5 of Row 2.
3. Referring to photo on page 115, join 5 of Row 2. Join Row 1s to top and bottom edges of quilt.

Quilting and Finishing

1. Mark desired quilting design on quilt top. Quilt shown is outline-quilted, with a curved diamond (Diamond Quilting Pattern) quilted in each four-patch of background fabric.
2. Layer the backing, batting, and quilt top. Baste. Quilt as desired.
3. Cut 10 (1"-wide) crosswise strips from remaining background fabric. Sew strips end to end to make a continuous strip for piping. Cover cording with strip, leaving ⅜" seam allowance.
4. Matching raw edges, pin piping around quilt top edge. Clip piping seam allowance at quilt corners.
5. Make 10¾ yards of bias or straight-grain binding. Piping is sewn into binding seam as you go.
   continued

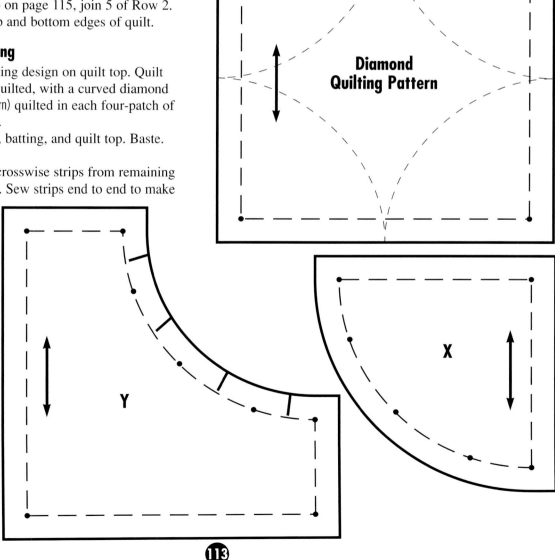

Z

Diamond Quilting Pattern

Y

X

pinpoints

Piecing a Curved Seam

Piecing curves doesn't have to be difficult. It just requires a little extra care to ensure a smooth, accurate seam. Try making a few practice units, using the methods described below, to see which technique you prefer.

Machine Piecing

1. On each Y piece, make small clips between dots as shown on pattern. (Be careful not to cut into seam line. Clips let seam allowance spread so that curved edges will match for piecing.)
2. With right sides facing, match 1 X and 1 Y. Pin curved edges together, matching dots (Diagram A). Let Y piece gather as necessary but make it as smooth as possible at curved edge.
3. With Y piece on top, machine-stitch curved seam. Start at 1 end and carefully stitch around curve, smoothing creases away from seam as you sew (Diagram B). Remove each pin before you stitch over it.
4. Press seam allowance toward Y. Steam out puckers in seam.

Hand Piecing

1. Clip and pin pieces as described for machine piecing.
2. Make a knot in end of sewing thread. Bring up needle to start stitching at first dot.
3. Use small running stitch to carefully sew from dot to dot (Diagram B). Remove pins as you go.
4. At last dot, knot off thread.
5. Press seam allowance toward Y.

Appliquéing

This method takes more time but produces a smooth, perfect curve on each seam.

1. Make pressing template for piece X. Use heat-resistant, translucent plastic (available at quilting shops or from mail-order sources) or lightweight aluminum (such as the bottom of a disposable pie pan—a good excuse to buy and eat a yummy ready-to-bake pie!). Cut pressing template so that it includes seam allowances on straight edges but *does not* include seam allowance along curve (Diagram C).
2. Place fabric piece X facedown on ironing board. Spray curved edge with water or spray starch. Place pressing template on fabric, aligning straight edges (Diagram D). Use tip of iron to press curved seam allowance back over template edge. (If using aluminum template, keep your fingers away from the iron—metal will become hot at pressed edge.) When seam allowance is dry, remove template.
3. Aligning straight edges, pin X to Y (Diagram E).
4. Sew curved edge with a machine topstitch (Diagram F) or hand-blindstitch (Diagram G), using thread that matches X.

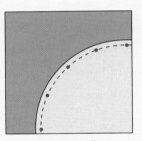

Diagram A

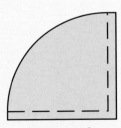

Diagram B

Diagram C

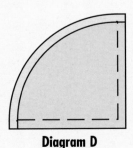

Diagram D

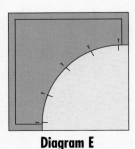

Diagram E

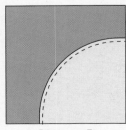

Diagram F

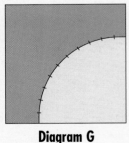

Diagram G

JENNY'S FLOWER GARDEN

Quilt by Elaine M. Nielson of Seward, Nebraska

This classic Irish Chain quilt was made by two women, kindred spirits a generation apart.

The top was hand-pieced by Elizabeth Jenny Cobb (1872–1947) of St. Joseph, Missouri. Jenny's cousin kept the top until 1991, when it was rescued from the trash by Elaine Nielson's aunt. Elaine was happy to complete Jenny's quilt.

She says, "Though our lives didn't overlap, we share the love of piecing and color and quilts."

Finished Size

Quilt: 82" x 82"
Blocks: 49 (10½" x 10½")

Materials

17 (18" x 22") fat quarters print scrap fabrics
1 (9" x 22") fat eighth yellow fabric
1 yard pink solid fabric (includes binding)
1 yard green solid fabric
3¼ yards muslin
5 yards 44"-wide backing fabric or 2½ yards 90"-wide fabric

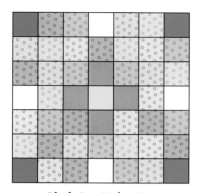

Block 1—Make 25.

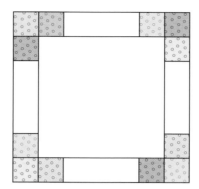

Block 2—Make 24.

Cutting

Instructions are for rotary cutting and quick piecing. Cut all strips on crosswise grain. Cut pieces in order listed to get best use of yardage.

From scrap fabrics
• 150 (2" x 22") strips.

From yellow
• 3 (2" x 22") strips.

From pink
• 11 (2" x 22") strips.
• 8 (2½" x 42") strips for straight-grain binding.

From green
• 25 (2" x 22") strips.

From muslin
• 37 (2" x 22") strips.
• 10 (5" x 22") strips.
• 5 (8" x 42") strips. From these, cut 24 (8") squares for Block 2.

Block Assembly

In Strip Set Diagrams, muslin, pink, yellow, and green fabrics are shown in required positions. All other fabrics are scrap fabrics of any color.

1. For Strip Set 1, select 2 green strips, 1 muslin strip, and 4 scrap strips. Join strips as shown (Strip Set 1 Diagram). Make 5 of Strip Set 1, using different scrap fabrics in each set. Press seam allowances toward center (muslin) strip.

2. Rotary-cut 10 (2"-wide) segments from each of Strip Set 1 to get 50 segments for Block 1.

3. Join 7 scrap strips for each Strip Set 2 (Strip Set 2 Diagram). Press seam allowances toward center strip.

Rotary-cut 50 (2"-wide) segments for Block 1.

4. For Strip Set 3, select 1 pink strip and 6 scrap strips. Make 5 of Strip Set 2 as shown (Strip Set 3 Diagram). Press seam allowances toward center (pink) strip. Cut 50 (2"-wide) segments for Block 1.

5. For Strip Set 4, select 2 pink strips, 1 yellow strip, 2 muslin strips, and 2 scrap strips. Make 3 strip sets as shown (Strip Set 4 Diagram). Press seam allowances toward center (yellow) strip. Cut 25 (2"-wide) segments for Block 1.

6. Select any 2 segments from each of strip sets 1, 2, and 3; choose

1 Strip Set 4 segment. Join 7 segments as shown (Block 1 Assembly Diagram), turning them as needed to get opposing seam allowances in adjacent rows. Make 25 of Block 1.

7. For Strip Set 5, sew 2 scrap strips to opposite sides of 1 (5"-wide) muslin strip as shown (Strip Set 5 Diagram, page 118). Make 5 of Strip Set 5. Press seam allowances toward center (muslin) strip. Cut 48 (2"-wide) segments for Block 2.

8. For Strip Set 6, select 4 scrap strips and 1 (5"-wide) muslin strip. Make 5 of Strip Set 6 as shown (Strip Set 6 Diagram, page 118). Press
continued

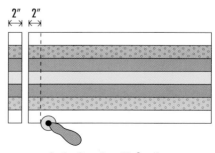

Block 1 Assembly Diagram

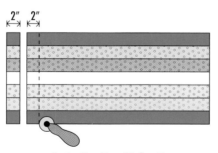

Strip Set 1—Make 5.

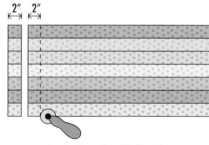

Strip Set 2—Make 5.

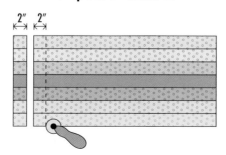

Strip Set 3—Make 5.

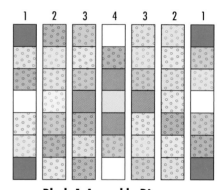

Strip Set 4—Make 3.

seam allowances toward center (muslin) strip. Cut 48 (2"-wide) segments for Block 2.

9. For each Block 2, select 1 (8") muslin square and 2 segments from each of strip sets 5 and 6. Join Set 5 segments to square as shown (Block 2 Assembly Diagram). Then add Set 6 segments to complete block. Make 24 of Block 2.

Quilt Assembly

1. Lay out blocks in 7 horizontal rows (Row Assembly Diagram). Start rows 1, 3, 5, and 7 with Block 1 and alternate blocks as shown. Start rows 2, 4, and 6 with Block 2.
2. When satisfied with placement of blocks, join blocks in each row. Press seam allowances toward Block 2.
3. Join block rows.

Borders

1. For Strip Set 7, join 2 muslin strips, 1 green strip, and 2 scrap strips. Make 13 of Strip Set 7

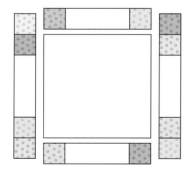

Block 2 Assembly Diagram

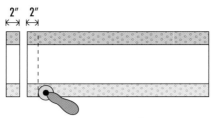

Strip Set 5—Make 5.

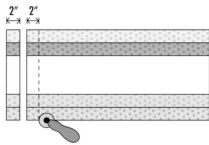

Strip Set 6—Make 5.

(Strip Set 7 Diagram). Press seam allowances toward center (green) strip. From these, rotary-cut 128 (2"-wide) segments for borders.

2. Join 32 segments in a row for each border (Border Diagram). Match seam lines carefully, stepping down each adjacent segment so that top muslin square is opposite first scrap square of previous segment. Press borders.
3. Use acrylic ruler and rotary cutter to trim muslin squares along both sides of pieced border strip. Be sure to leave ¼" seam allowance. (If you prefer, you can sew border seams first and then trim excess fabric from seam.)
4. Sew borders to edges of quilt, easing to fit as needed. Press.

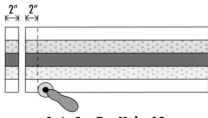

Strip Set 7—Make 13.

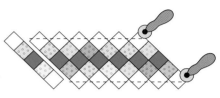

Border Diagram

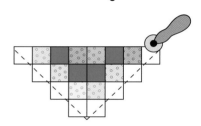

Corner Unit—Make 4.

5. For 1 corner unit, cut 4 (2") green squares, 8 (2") muslin squares, and 8 (2") squares of scrap fabrics. Join squares in rows (Corner Unit Diagram). Then join rows to complete unit. Make 4 corner units.
6. Sew straight edge of 1 corner unit to each corner of quilt. Trim muslin squares on each side, leaving ¼" seam allowance.

Quilting and Finishing

1. Mark quilt top with desired quilting design. Quilt shown is outline-quilted, and large roses are quilted in center of each Block 2. To find appropriate quilting design for Block 2, look for stencil design, such as feathered wreath or flower, that has diameter of about 6".
2. Layer backing, batting, and quilt top. Baste. Quilt as desired.
3. Make 9⅜ yards of straight-grain binding from reserved pink strips. Bind quilt edges.

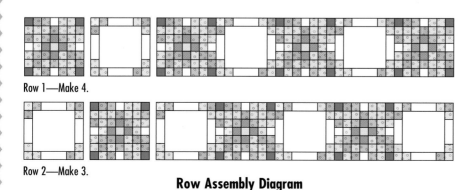

Row 1—Make 4.

Row 2—Make 3.

Row Assembly Diagram

COURTHOUSE STEPS

Appearances are deceiving in this striking quilt. The design looks like a complex assembly of Japanese lanterns, but it is really easy to make. Can you find the block? Here's a hint: Each black square is the *center* of one block. You'll want a mix of large-, medium-, and small-scale prints as well as varied colors to make a quilt with interesting texture.

Finished Size

Quilt: 79" x 89½"
Blocks: 42 (10½" x 10½")

Materials

3 (1" x 42") strips *each* of 84 print fabrics
Assorted scraps for appliqué
27" square green fabric for vine
¼ yard blue fabric for bird appliqués
3 yards black solid fabric
5½ yards backing fabric
½"-wide bias pressing bar

continued

Quilt by Marion Roach Watchinski of Overland Park, Kansas

Plan Ahead

This block is easy to sew, but it takes planning to achieve the overall design. Use the Planning Diagram at right to map out your quilt so that you can enjoy sewing without worrying about what goes where. Make several photocopies to try different arrangements.

Sort your fabrics into color groups; then get a colored marker to match each group. For example, say you have four yellow fabrics. The diagram shows that each block is visually divided into quadrants. Choose any quadrant, on any block, and color it yellow. Then color the *adjacent* quadrant in the *adjacent* block. Repeat 3 times, spacing 4 yellow "lanterns" randomly around the quilt. When you color a quadrant on the outside edge, choose a second quadrant on another edge. Repeat with each color until you've positioned each fabric.

Use the diagram as a guide as you sew the blocks, matching fabrics in neighboring quadrants. It doesn't matter which fabric you use in any position as long as adjacent quadrants match.

Block Assembly

For this stitch-and-cut method, it is not necessary to make templates for the "steps."

1. From black fabric, cut 2 (2"-wide) crosswise strips. From these, cut 42 (2") A squares.
2. Select 4 sets of fabric strips for Block 1A. Strips are sewn in numerical order as shown on Courthouse Steps Block Diagram. For first step, with right sides together, match fabric strip to 1 side of square and stitch (Diagram A). Trim the strip even with bottom of square. Press seam allowance toward step.
3. Repeat with second fabric on opposite side of square (Diagram B).

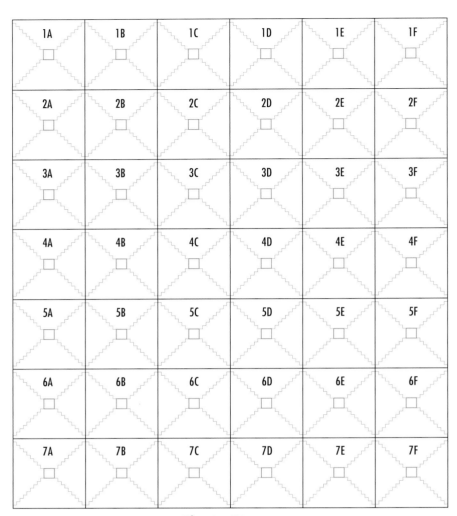

Planning Diagram

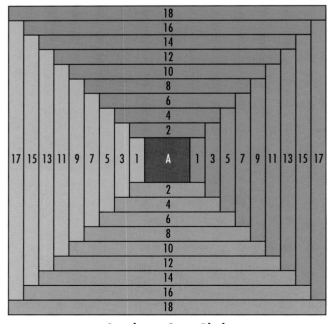

Courthouse Steps Block

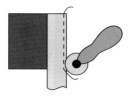

Diagram A

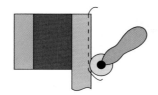

Diagram B

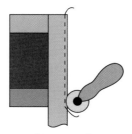

Diagram C

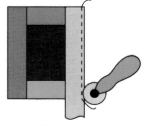

Diagram D

4. Referring to Planning Diagram, turn block so that sewn steps are at top and bottom of square. With right sides facing, match next fabric strip to square edge and stitch (Diagram C). Trim strip even with bottom step and press. (Throughout block assembly, always press seam allowances toward newest step.)

5. Turn unit so that last step is at left. With right sides facing, match fourth fabric strip to remaining edge of square and stitch (Diagram D). Trim strip and press.

6. Continue adding steps in this manner until you have nine steps on all sides of center square (Courthouse Steps Block Diagram). Completed block will measure approximately 11" square.

7. In this manner, make 42 Courthouse Steps blocks.

Quilt Assembly

Throughout assembly, refer to Planning Diagram to keep fabrics positioned correctly.

1. Lay out 7 rows, with 6 blocks in each row. Check position of fabrics. When satisfied with placement, join blocks in each row.

2. Lay out rows in order. Check placement of blocks again; then join rows in numerical order to assemble quilt.

Border

1. Cut 4 (8½" x 94") strips of black fabric. See page 309 for tips on sewing a mitered border corner. Measure quilt and trim border strips as needed. Sew strips to quilt and miter corners.

2. Use green fabric to make 9¾ yards of 1½"-wide continuous bias. From this, cut 4 (88"-long) strips for appliqué.

3. See page 176 for tips on bias appliqué. Fold, stitch, and press bias strips with pressing bar. Prepared vines should be ½" wide.

4. On seam line of 1 border strip, place pins at both corners and center. Midway between center and each corner, place 2 more pins on *outside edge* of border.

5. Fold 1 bias strip in half to find center. Pin center of vine at center of border, ¾" above seam. Working out from center, pin vine in place, curving bias up toward next pin and down again toward corner pin. Edge of vine should be ¾" above or below a marked point. Pin ends of vine at mitered seam but don't trim excess until flowers and leaves are in place.

6. Repeat vine placement on remaining 3 borders.

7. Make templates of appliqué patterns on pages 123 and 124. Cut 4 B flowers, 4 C leaves, and 4 birds from scrap fabrics and prepare pieces for appliqué. Referring to photo on page 122, pin Bs and Cs in place at corners, covering ends of vine. Pin 1 bird at center of each strip, with its feet about ½" above vine.

continued

Size Variations			
	Twin	**Queen**	**King**
Finished size	68½" x 89½"	89½" x 100"	100" x 100"
Number of blocks	35	56	64
Blocks set	5 x 7	7 x 8	8 x 8
Yardage Required			
Sets of scrap strips for blocks	70	112	176
Black fabric	3 yards	3⅜ yards	3⅜ yards
Backing fabric	5½ yards	8¼ yards	9¼ yards

From red border print
- 8 (1¼"-wide) strips for inner border.

From cream print
- 8 (1¾"-wide) strips for middle border.

From black-on-red print
- 33" square for binding.
- 2 (5" x 88") and 2 (5" x 99") lengthwise strips for outer border.
- 1 (18" x 99") and 2 (40" x 99") lengthwise strips for backing.

Block Assembly

Refer to Block Assembly Diagram throughout.

1. For each Sawtooth Star block, select 1 A square, 4 Bs, 8 C squares, and 4 D squares. (Fabrics can match or vary, as desired.)
2. Use diagonal-corners technique (page 304) to join 2 Cs to each B (Diagram A). Make 4 B/C units for each block.
3. Join units in 3 horizontal rows as shown. Join rows to complete block. Make 93 blocks.
4. For each Double Star block, select 1 E, 4 Fs, 8 Gs, 4 Hs, 4 Bs, 8 Cs, and 4 Ds.
5. Use diagonal-corners method to make 4 B/C units and 4 F/G units. Join E, F/G, and H units to make block center in same manner as Sawtooth Star; then add B/C units and Ds to complete block. Make 7 blocks (Double Star Block Diagram).

Quilt Assembly

Refer to Quilt Assembly Diagram throughout.

1. Lay out blocks in 10 rows, with 10 blocks in each row. Place Double Star blocks as desired.
2. Join blocks in each row. Then join rows.

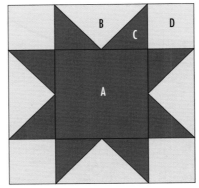

Sawtooth Star Block—Make 93.

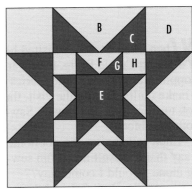

Double Star Block—Make 7.

  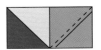 

Diagram A

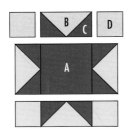

Block Assembly Diagram

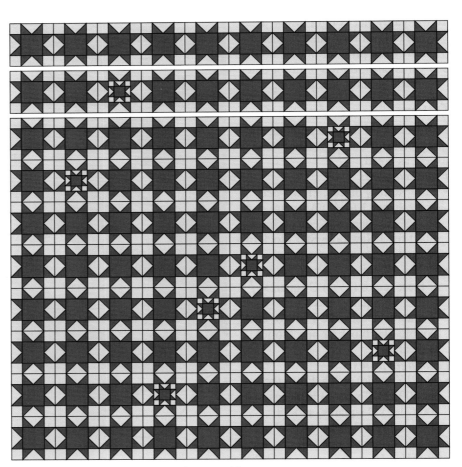

Quilt Assembly Diagram

Borders

1. Join 2 red print strips end to end to assemble each border.
2. Measuring through middle of quilt, measure quilt from top to bottom. Trim 2 borders to match length. Sew strips to quilt sides.
3. Measure width of quilt. Trim 2 borders to fit and sew to top and bottom edges.
4. Repeat steps 1, 2, and 3 to assemble and sew cream middle border strips to quilt top.
5. Add black-on-red print border in same manner.

Quilting and Finishing

1. Mark quilting designs on quilt top as desired. Quilt shown is outline-quilted by machine, with an X stitched across each A and D square. A simple cable is hand-quilted in borders.
2. Layer backing, batting, and quilt top; baste. Quilt as marked or as desired.
3. Make 10⅝ yards of continuous bias or straight-grain binding from remaining black-on-red print. Bind quilt edges.

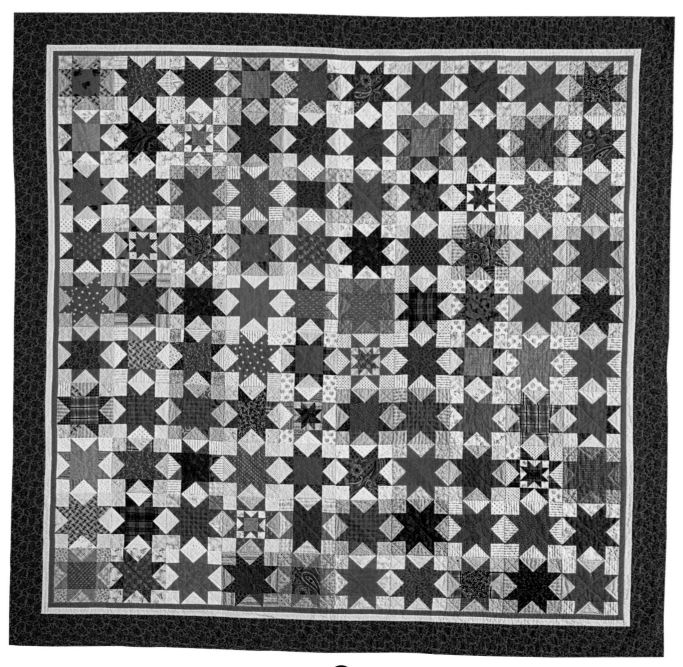

AFRICAN KING

Quilt by Elayne D. Vognild of Crossville, Tennessee

A quilt pictured in a magazine inspired Elayne Vognild to try her hand at a traditional design using nontraditional fabrics. She selected the classic Spider Web block and interpreted it in African-style fabrics.

Finished Size

Quilt: 93" x 108"
Blocks: 42 (12" x 12")

Materials

168 (2" x 30") strips assorted gold, black, orange, and rust fabrics
42 (4⅜" x 8¾") red and gold prints for block corners
32 (3½" x 43") strips assorted black prints and stripes for sashing strips and borders
34 (3½") squares red and gold prints for sashing squares
1 yard black binding fabric
3¼ yards 104"-wide backing

Block Assembly

1. Choose 1 (2"-wide) strip each of light, medium, and dark value; then choose any fourth strip. Join strips in any order (Diagram A). Press seam allowances in 1 direction.

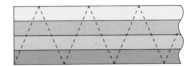

Diagram A

2. Make template of Pattern X. Mark seam lines on template as shown on pattern.
3. Place template on strip set, matching bottom of template with 1 edge of strip set. Cut 1 X triangle. Turn template upside down, aligning its bottom edge with opposite edge of strip set, and cut another X triangle. In this manner, cut 8 X triangles.
4. Join alternating triangles in 4 pairs as shown (Block Assembly Diagram). Join pairs; then join halves. Press all seam allowances in 1 direction.
5. Cut 1 (4⅜" x 8¾") piece into 2 (4⅜") squares. Cut each square in half diagonally to get 4 Y triangles. Sew 1 triangle to each corner of block. Press seam allowances toward X triangles.
6. Make 42 blocks.

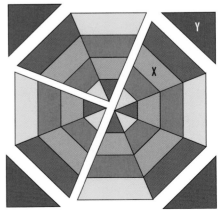

Block Assembly Diagram

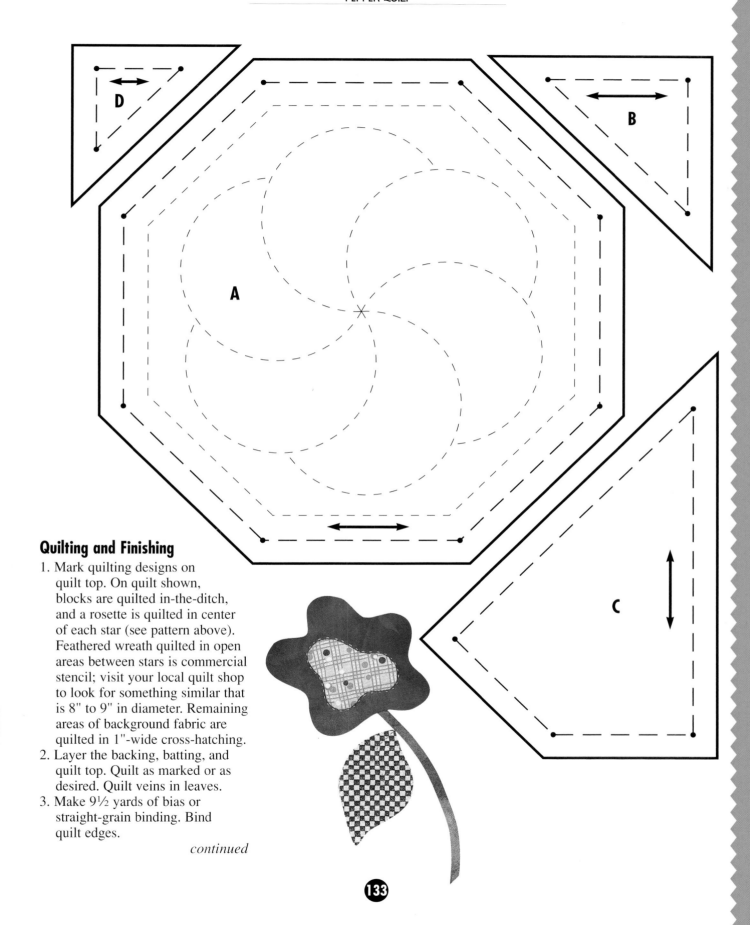

D

B

A

C

Quilting and Finishing

1. Mark quilting designs on quilt top. On quilt shown, blocks are quilted in-the-ditch, and a rosette is quilted in center of each star (see pattern above). Feathered wreath quilted in open areas between stars is commercial stencil; visit your local quilt shop to look for something similar that is 8" to 9" in diameter. Remaining areas of background fabric are quilted in 1"-wide cross-hatching.

2. Layer the backing, batting, and quilt top. Quilt as marked or as desired. Quilt veins in leaves.

3. Make 9½ yards of bias or straight-grain binding. Bind quilt edges.

continued

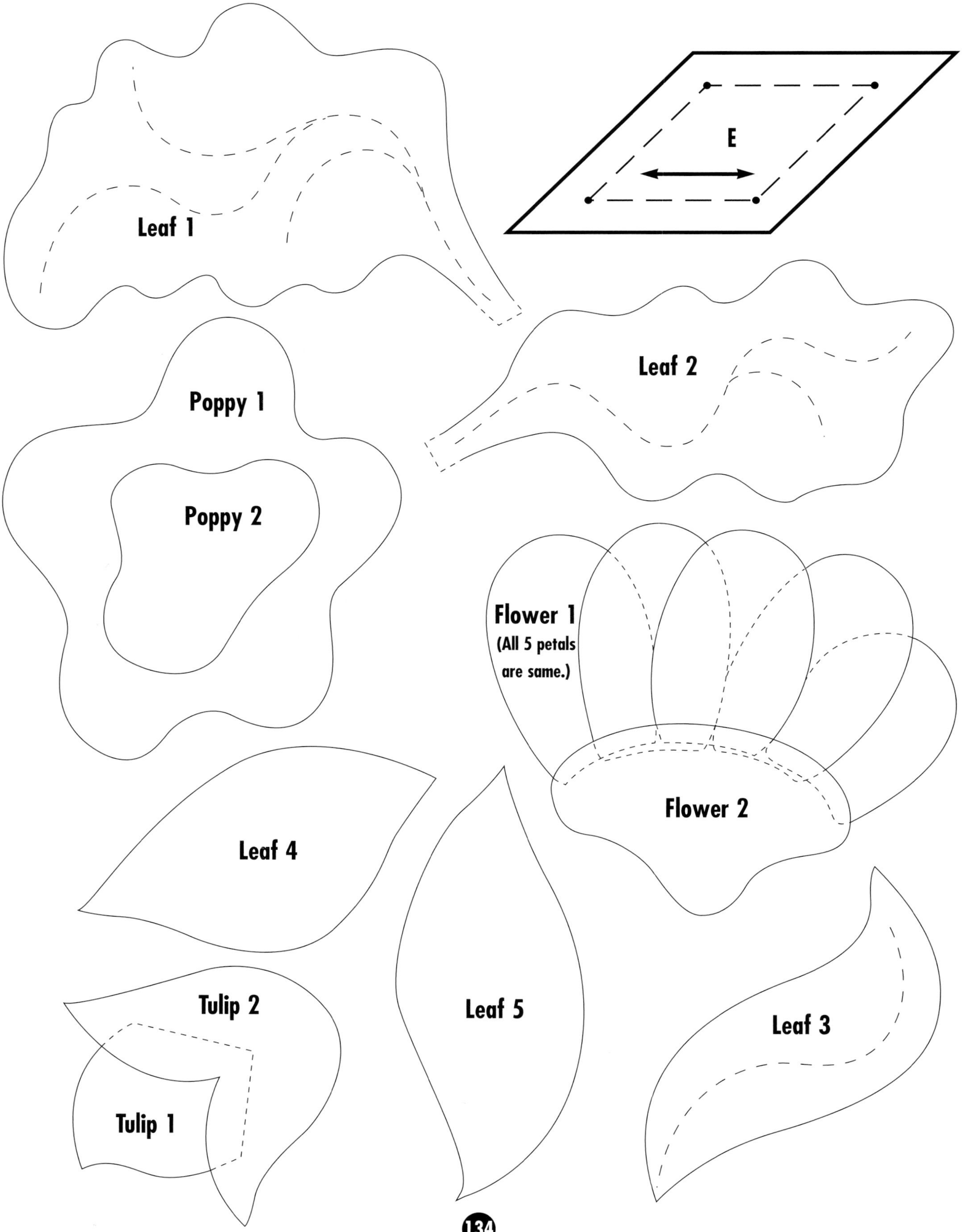

Leaf 1

E

Leaf 2

Poppy 1

Poppy 2

Flower 1
(All 5 petals
are same.)

Flower 2

Leaf 4

Tulip 2

Leaf 5

Leaf 3

Tulip 1

MAPLE STREET RAG

Don't let a riot of fabrics fool you into thinking that this quilt is hard to sew: It's made of simple Maple Leaf blocks. For the windswept leaves, Karen Kratz-Miller uses mostly plaid fabrics in warm autumn colors of gold, orange, and hot pink, highlighted with a bit of summer's green. Stars on the black background fabrics evoke a night sky, while splashes of blue herald the coming day. For a winter's tale of Maple Street, see Karen's cool version of this quilt on page 138.

Finished Size

Quilt: 65" x 85"
Blocks: 48 (10" x 10")

Materials

48 (9" x 22") fat eighths
    autumn-colored fabrics or
    equivalent scraps
48 fat eighths black and blue
    fabrics or equivalent scraps
⅞ yard binding fabric
2 yards 90"-wide backing fabric

continued

Quilt by Karen Kratz-Miller of Cincinnati, Ohio

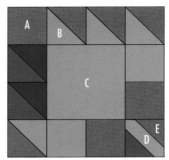

Maple Leaf Block—Make 48.

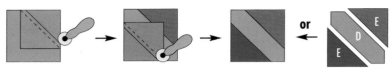

Diagram B

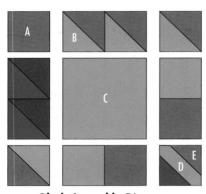

Block Assembly Diagram

Cutting

Instructions are for rotary cutting and quick piecing. See page 306 for directions on quick-pieced triangle-squares and page 304 for diagonal-corner technique. For traditional cutting, use patterns on page 140.

From each colored fabric
- 1 (4½" x 11") piece for B triangle-squares.
- 1 (5½") C square.
- 3 (3") squares for A and D.

From each black or blue fabric
- 1 (4½" x 11") piece for B triangle-squares.
- 3 (3") A squares.
- 2 (2¼") E squares.

From remaining fabrics
- 116 (3") A squares for border.

Block Assembly

1. On wrong side of each 4½" x 11" light fabric, mark a 3-square grid of 3⅜" squares (Diagram A). Mark diagonal lines through centers of squares as shown.
2. With right sides together, match 1 light fabric to 1 dark fabric. Stitch on both sides of diagonal lines, pivoting at corners as shown. Press stitching.

3. Cut on all drawn lines to get 6 triangle-squares. Press seam allowances toward dark fabric.
4. Use diagonal-corner technique to make stem square. Sew 2¼" dark square to top right corner of 3" square of light fabric as shown (Diagram B). Trim seam allowance and press corner to right side. Repeat with another 2¼" dark square in bottom left corner as shown. (For traditional piecing, sew E triangles to opposite sides of D piece as shown.)
5. For each block, select 6 triangle-squares, 1 C square, 2 light A squares, 3 dark A squares, and 1 D/E stem square. Choose units of same fabrics or varied fabrics, as desired. Arrange squares in 3 rows as shown (Block Assembly Diagram). Join squares in rows; then join rows to complete block.
6. Make 48 Maple Leaf blocks.

Quilt Assembly

1. Lay out blocks in 8 horizontal rows, with 6 blocks in each row. In rows 1, 3, 5, and 7, block positions alternate between stem in bottom right corner and stem in top right corner (Row Assembly Diagram). In rows 2, 4, 6, and 8,

block positions alternate between stem in bottom left corner and stem in top left corner as shown.
2. For each border unit, join 4 A squares in a row. Make 16 units. Place 1 unit at both ends of each row as shown.
3. Rearrange blocks and border units as desired to achieve pleasing balance of color and value. When satisfied with placement, join blocks and border units in each row.
4. Join rows as shown in photo on opposite page.
5. For top and bottom borders, assemble 2 rows with 26 A squares in each row. Sew rows to top and bottom edges of quilt.

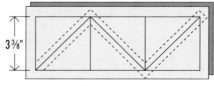

3⅜"

Diagram A

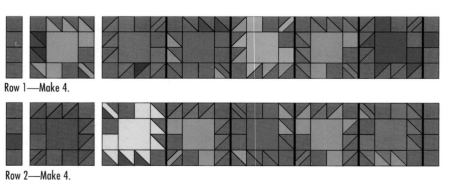

Row 1—Make 4.

Row 2—Make 4.

Row Assembly Diagram

Quilting and Finishing

1. Mark quilting design on pieced top as desired. Quilt shown is quilted in an allover pattern of concentric arcs that is sometimes called the Baptist Fan.
2. Layer backing, batting, and quilt top. Then baste them together. Quilt as desired.
3. Make 8⅝ yards of straight-grain or bias binding. Bind the quilt edges.

Size Variations

	Full	Queen	King
Finished size	75" x 95"	85" x 95"	95" x 95"
Number of blocks	63	72	81
Blocks set	7 x 9	8 x 9	9 x 9
Number of border squares	132	140	148

Yardage Required

	Full	Queen	King
Light fat eighths	63	72	81
Dark fat eighths	63	72	81
Binding fabric	⅞ yard	⅞ yard	1 yard
108"-wide backing fabric	2⅜ yards	2⅝ yards	3 yards

MAPLE STREET BLUES

Quilt by Karen Kratz-Miller of Cincinnati, Ohio

All seasons have unique beauty, and Karen Kratz-Miller catches their colors in her series of Maple Leaf quilts. Compare this frosty version with the heat of *Maple Street Rag* (page 135). Here, white and black background fabrics tell a winter's tale of a snowy night on Maple Street. Cutting big prints into small squares makes the background shimmer like swirling snowflakes.

Finished Size

Quilt: 55" x 55"
Blocks: 25 (10" x 10")

Materials

48 (9" x 22") fat eighths blue fabrics or equivalent scraps
5 fat eighths black-on-white prints or equivalent scraps
10 fat eighths black-and-white prints or equivalent scraps
5 fat eighths white-on-black prints or equivalent scraps
½ yard striped binding fabric
1¾ yards backing fabric

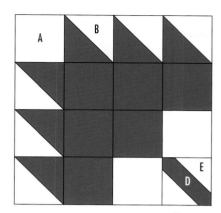 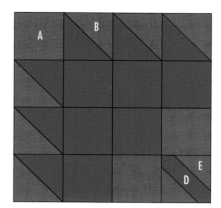

Maple Leaf Block—Make 25.

Cutting

This Maple Leaf block is made in same manner as described on page 136 except that 4 A squares replace square C.

From each *blue fabric*

- 1 (4½" x 11") piece for B triangle-squares.
- 7 (3") squares for A and D.

From each *background fabric*

- 1 (4½" x 11") piece for B triangle-squares.
- 3 (3") A squares.
- 2 (2¼") squares for E.

Note: Save the remaining fabric for making border squares (see "Quilt Assembly").

Making Blocks

Follow the Block Assembly instructions on page 136 to make the triangle-squares and the stem squares. Assemble the squares as shown (Block Assembly Diagram). Make 25 blocks, changing the background colors from mostly white to mostly black.

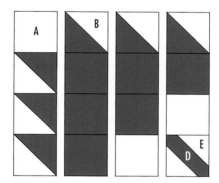

Block Assembly Diagram

Quilt Assembly

1. From remaining background fabric, cut 84 (3") A squares for border. Join 22 white squares and 22 black squares for top and bottom borders. Join remaining squares in four-square units (page 136), making each unit from similar fabrics.
2. Referring to photo, make 5 rows of 5 blocks each (page 136). Add border units to rows. Join rows.
3. Join the top and bottom borders to the quilt.

Quilting and Finishing

1. Mark the quilting design on the pieced top as desired. The quilt shown is machine-quilted with undulating lines to look like wind.
2. Layer backing, batting, and quilt top. Backing seams will parallel top and bottom edges of quilt. Then baste them together. Quilt as desired.
3. Make 6⅜ yards of straight-grain binding. Then bind the quilt edges.

continued

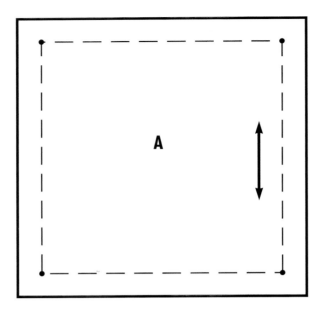

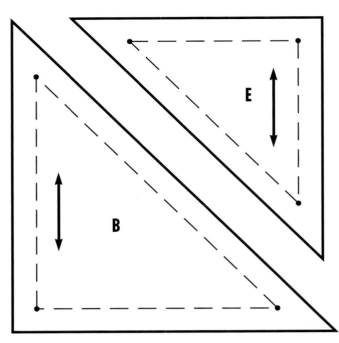

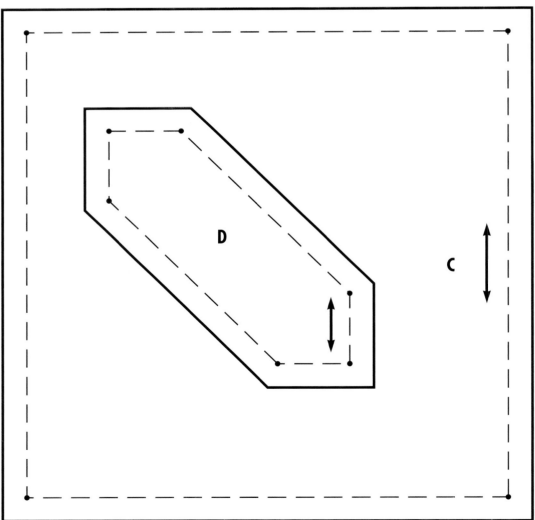

CORN & BEANS

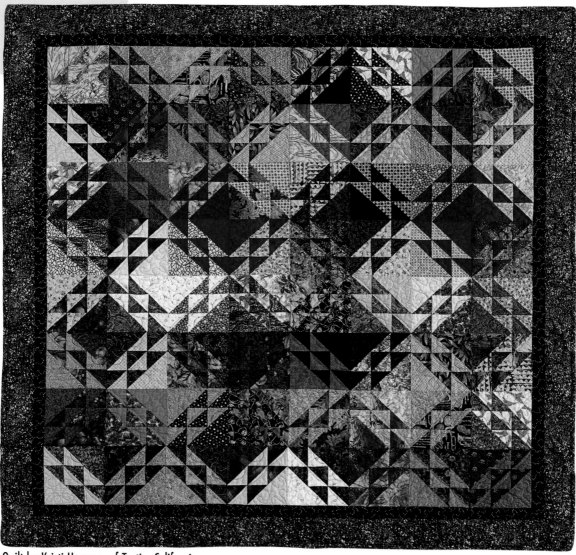

Quilt by Kristi Hammer of Tustin, California

Kristi Hammer updates an easy-to-sew block of triangles by adding scraps to the recipe. Instead of using one fabric in each block, she places a different fabric of the same color family in each quadrant of the block. The interplay of light, medium, and dark values makes this quilt a shimmering interpretation of a time-honored favorite.

Finished Size
Quilt: 56" x 56"
Blocks: 16 (12" x 12")

Materials
32 (6" x 14") light/medium fabrics
    or equivalent scraps
32 (6" x 14") medium/dark fabrics
    or equivalent scraps *
⅜ yard fabric for inner border
1¾ yards fabric for outer border
    and binding
3⅜ yards backing fabric
* *Note:* Divide fabrics into 8 color groups, with 4 fabrics in each.
continued

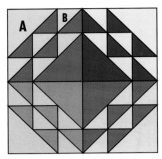

Corn & Beans Block—Make 16.

Block Assembly

Instructions are for rotary cutting. For traditional cutting, use patterns on opposite page.

1. From each scrap fabric, cut 1 (4⅞") square and 5 (2⅞") squares. Cut large square in half diagonally to get 2 A triangles. Cut smaller squares in half diagonally to get 10 B triangles. Divide triangles into 2 equal sets, 1 for each of 2 blocks.
2. For each block, select 4 sets of medium/dark triangles from same color family. Pair each with a light/medium set. (Treat mediums as either light or dark, depending on value of companion fabric.) Each pair makes 1 quadrant.
3. Work on 1 quadrant of block at a time. Begin with B triangles. Join 3 light/dark pairs into triangle-squares as shown in top left corner of Block Assembly Diagram. Press seam allowances toward dark fabric.
4. Join remaining B triangles to triangle-squares, making 3 horizontal rows as shown (bottom left corner of diagram). Join rows to complete center unit of quadrant (bottom right corner of diagram).
5. Sew light and dark A triangles to opposite sides of unit as shown.
6. Repeat steps 3–5 to complete 4 quadrants for each block.
7. Position quadrants as shown, with light A triangles at outside corners. Join the adjacent units to make 2 halves of block. Press the seam

allowances in opposite directions. Join halves to complete block.
8. Make 16 blocks.

Quilt Assembly

1. Lay out blocks in 4 horizontal rows of 4 blocks each. When satisfied with placement, join blocks in each row (Row Assembly Diagram).
2. Referring to photo on page 141, join rows.

Borders

1. Cut 8 (1½"-wide) crosswise strips for inner border. Join 2 strips end to end for each border.
2. Measure quilt from top to bottom and trim 2 borders to match length. Sew borders to quilt sides.
3. Measure quilt from side to side and trim remaining borders to match quilt width. Sew borders to top and bottom edges of quilt.
4. Cut 4 (3½"-wide) lengthwise outer border strips. Measure quilt; then trim and sew borders to quilt as for inner border.

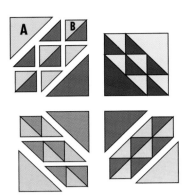

Block Assembly Diagram

Quilting and Finishing

1. Mark the quilting design on the pieced top as desired. The quilt shown is machine-quilted in an allover pattern, featuring a leaf border design.
2. Layer the backing, the batting, and the pieced top (see page 312). Then baste them together. Quilt as desired.
3. Use remaining border fabric to make 6½ yards of bias or straight-grain binding. Bind quilt edges.

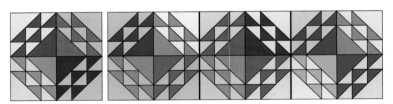

Row Assembly Diagram

Size Variations

	Twin	Full	Queen	King
Finished size	68" x 92"	80" x 92"	92" x 104"	104" x 104"
Number of blocks	35	42	56	64
Blocks set	5 x 7	6 x 7	7 x 8	8 x 8
Yardage Required				
Dark scraps	18	21	28	32
Light scraps	18	21	28	32
Inner border fabric	½ yard	½ yard	½ yard	½ yard
Outer border fabric	2⅝ yards	2⅝ yards	3 yards	3 yards
Backing fabric	5¾ yards	5¾ yards	8½ yards	9½ yards

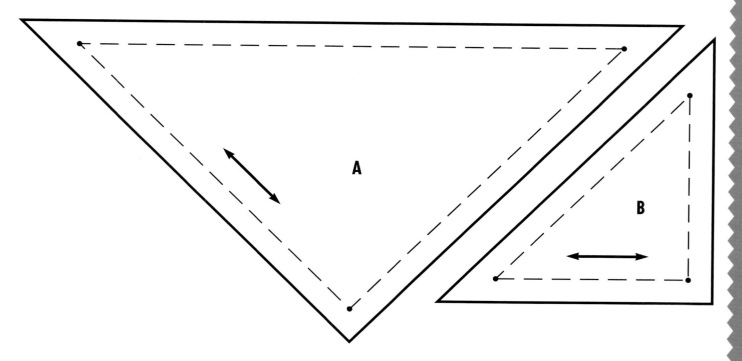

A

B

Color Variations

If the earth tones of Kristi's quilt (see the illustration below) are not your style, just imagine a color scheme that suits you better. To give you some ideas, we offer a few dynamic suggestions.

Black & White

Monochromatic

Amish Traditions

Sea & Sky

STAR QUILT

Quilt by Linda Gibson of Cumming, Iowa

This star block is not an old pattern, but Linda Gibson gave it the look of an antique with her choice of subdued colors and fabric prints. If you can't figure out where the block is in this quilt, here's a hint: The dark stars are formed by the block corners.

Finished Size
Quilt: 91" x 104"
Blocks: 42 (13" x 13")

Materials
8 (1-yard) pieces beige prints
14 (¼-yard) pieces light-colored prints
14 (¼-yard) pieces medium-colored prints
20 (⅜-yard) pieces very dark prints
8¼ yards backing fabric

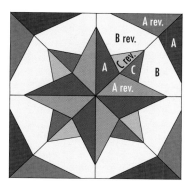

Star Block—Make 42.

Cutting

Cut all strips on crosswise grain. Make templates of patterns A, B, C, and D on page 147. Cut pieces in order listed to get best use of yardage.
From beige prints
• 21 (8"-wide) strips. From these, cut 168 of Pattern B and 168 of Pattern B reversed. Set aside 42 matched sets of 8 (4 B, 4 B reversed) for blocks.
• 56 of Pattern D for border units.
From each light-colored print
• 3 (2½"-wide) strips. From these, cut 168 of Pattern A and 168 of Pattern C. Set aside 42 matched sets of 4 for blocks.
From each medium-colored print
• 3 (2½"-wide) strips. From these, cut 168 of Pattern A reversed and 168 of Pattern C reversed. Set aside 42 matched sets of 4.
From very dark prints
• 27 (6½"-wide) strips. From these, cut 224 of Pattern A and 224 of Pattern A reversed.
• 224 (4") squares for prairie points.

Block Assembly

1. For each block, select matched sets of 4 light print As and 4 medium print As rev. for center star. Then choose a matched set of 4 Bs and 4 Bs rev. for beige background and matched sets of 4 Cs and 4 Cs rev. for small star points. Finally, choose 4 dark As and 4 dark As rev., mixing fabrics as desired.

2. Sew each C to a B and each C rev. to a B rev. as shown (Block Assembly Diagram). Press the seam allowances toward Bs. Then add A and A rev. pieces to each unit to get 8 triangular sections. Then press the seam allowances toward As.
3. Join 2 sections as shown to get 4 square quadrants. Join quadrants to complete block.
4. Make 42 star blocks.
5. For each border block, select 1 dark A, 1 dark A rev., and 1 D. Stitch each A to edge of D as shown (Diagram A); then stitch mitered seam to join A pieces. Make 56 border blocks.

continued

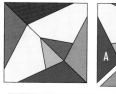

Block Assembly Diagram

Diagram A

Quilt Assembly

1. Lay out star blocks in 7 horizontal rows, with 6 blocks in each row (Quilt Assembly Diagram). Add 2 border blocks with Ds adjacent at ends of each row as shown.
2. For top border row, lay out 14 border blocks, rotating as shown. Repeat for bottom border row.
3. Arrange blocks to get pleasing balance of color and value. When satisfied with block placement, join blocks in each row.
4. Join rows.

Quilting and Finishing

1. Mark quilt top with desired quilting design. On quilt shown, A and C pieces are quilted in-the-ditch; dark stars are quilted $3/8$" and 1" inside seam lines with contrasting thread. Designs quilted in B and D pieces are shown on patterns.
2. Layer backing, batting, and quilt top. Baste. Quilt as desired.
3. Fold 59 dark squares in half (Diagram B) and in half again (Diagram C). Press. Pin prairie points to 1 side edge of quilt top, aligning raw edges and overlapping points as needed to fit the edge of quilt (Diagram D). Baste. Repeat on opposite side.
4. Fold, press, and pin 53 prairie points in same manner for each top and bottom border.
5. Fold backing of quilt away from edges; pin or baste to hold backing temporarily in place. Using a $1/4$" seam, stitch around edges of quilt through prairie points, quilt top, and batting.
6. Trim batting close to stitching. Press prairie points out. Remove pins or basting from backing. Turn under $1/4$" on each edge of backing and slipstitch backing in place behind prairie points.

Quilt Assembly Diagram

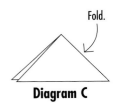

Diagram B

Fold.

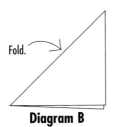

Diagram C

Fold.

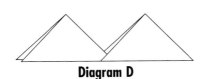

Diagram D

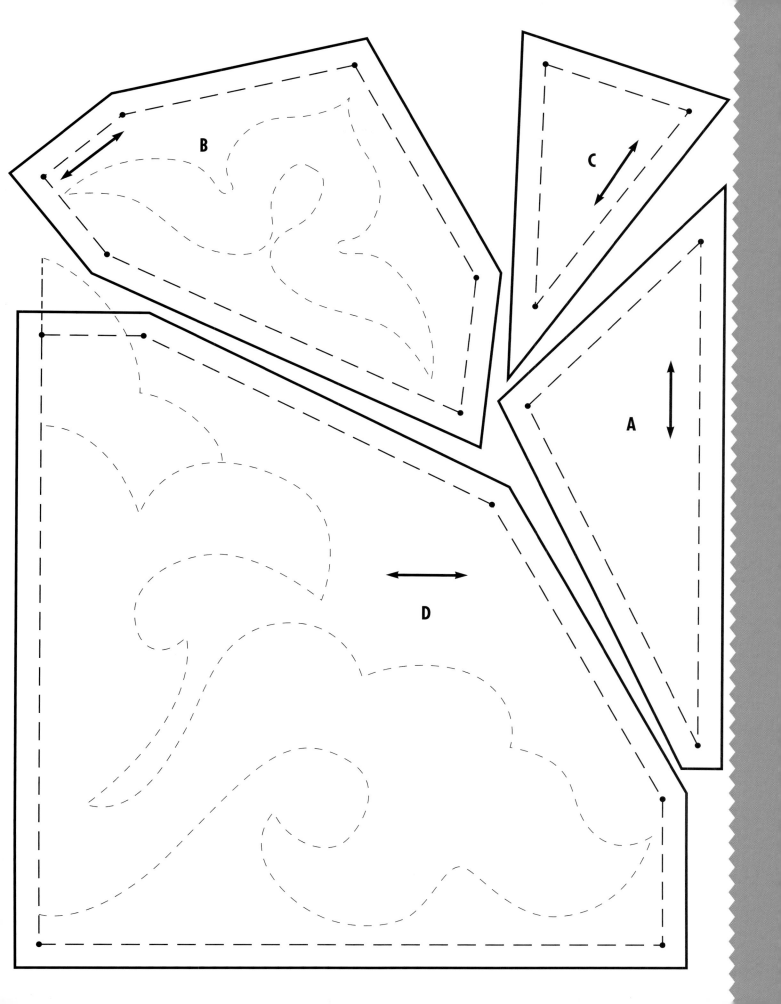

B

C

A

D

BOW TIE MEDALLION

Quilt pieced by Jane Strickland of Tamaroa, Illinois;
quilted by Dorothy Yakabovich, Felecita Kellerman, Carol Przygoda,
Rigina Heisner, Barb Forys, Carol Porter, Mary Ann Bathon, and Irene Bathon

Combine two sizes of Bow Tie blocks to make this striking king-sized quilt. The diagonal-corners technique makes the blocks quick and easy to stitch.

Finished Size
Quilt: 99" x 99"
Blocks: 140 (6" x 6") Block 1
        56 (6" x 6") Block 2

Materials
35 (9" x 15") scraps bright prints
28 (7" x 9") scraps bright prints
6 yards tan print
1⅝ yards black (includes binding)
3 yards 90"-wide backing fabric

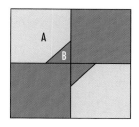

Block 1—Make 140.

Block 1 Assembly Diagram

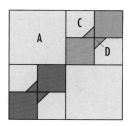

Block 2—Make 56.

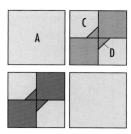

Block 2 Assembly Diagram

Cutting

Instructions are for rotary cutting and quick piecing. Cut strips on crosswise grain except as noted.

From each 9" x 15" scrap
- 8 (3½") A squares.
- 8 (1¾") B squares.

From each 7" x 9" scrap
- 8 (2") C squares.
- 8 (1⅛") D squares.

From tan
- 10 (6½"-wide) strips for pieced borders or 4 (6½" x 105") lengthwise strips. (If cutting lengthwise, use leftover to cut A squares.)
- 33 (3½"-wide) strips. From these, cut 392 (3½") A squares.
- 11 (2"-wide) strips. From these, cut 224 (2") C squares.

From black
- 1 yard for binding.
- 8 (2"-wide) strips for borders.

Block Assembly

1. See page 304 for instructions on diagonal-corners technique. With right sides facing, match 1 B square to 1 corner of 1 tan A square (Diagram A). Stitch diagonally from corner to corner of B square. Trim the excess fabric ¼" from

seam. Make 2 A/B units, using matching fabrics.
2. Join 2 A/B units and 2 matching print A squares to complete block (Block 1 Assembly Diagram). Make 140 of Block 1.
3. Use diagonal-corners method to sew each print D square to a corner of a tan C square.
4. Matching print fabrics, join 2 C/D units and 2 C squares to make block. Make 112 small blocks.
5. Join 2 C/D units and 2 tan As to complete block (Block 2 Assembly Diagram). Make 56 of Block 2.

Quilt Assembly

1. Join blocks in quarter sections. Start by laying out 7 of Block 1 in a horizontal row, turning blocks as shown (Partial Quilt Assembly Diagram). For remaining 6 rows, alternate Block 1 and Block 2 as shown in each row.

continued

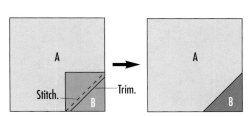

Diagram A

Partial Quilt Assembly Diagram

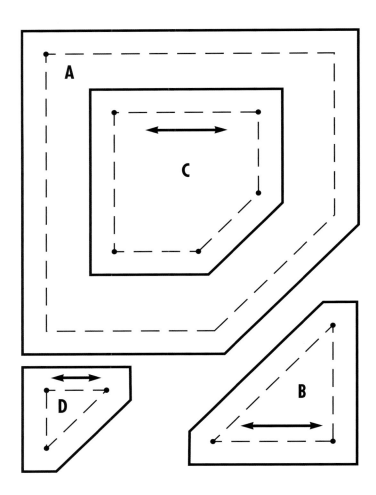

2. When satisfied with block placement, join blocks in each row. Then join rows.
3. Make 4 quarter sections.
4. Referring to photo on page 148, join 2 sections for top half of quilt and 2 sections for bottom half, rotating sections as shown. Join halves to complete center quilt top.

Borders

1. Join 2 black strips end to end to make a border for each quilt side.
2. Measure length through middle of top. Trim 2 border strips to this measurement. Sew strips to sides, easing to fit. Press seam allowances toward borders.
3. Measure width through middle; trim remaining border strips to this measurement. Sew strips to top and bottom edges of quilt.
4. Repeat steps 2 and 3 to join tan border strips to each side of quilt.

Quilting and Finishing

1. Mark quilt top with desired quilting design. Quilt shown is outline-quilted and has diagonal lines quilted in borders.
2. Layer backing, batting, and quilt top. Baste. Quilt as desired.
3. Make 11¼ yards of continuous bias or straight-grain binding. Bind quilt edges.

Color and Set Variations

The possible combinations of large and small Bow Tie blocks are as varied as the color and fabric choices a scrap-lover can imagine. To get those creative juices flowing, consider these suggestions for other quilts you can make with this versatile pair of blocks.

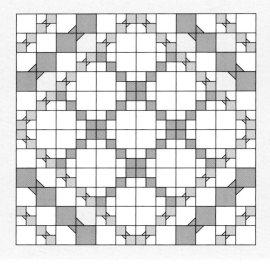

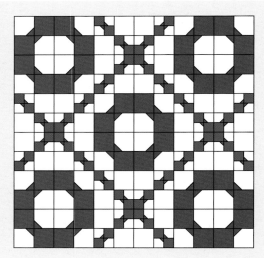

BASKETS OF LIBERTY

Marvelous fabrics give these baskets real flower power. The fabrics are made by Liberty of London (a British manufacturer of quality cottons), hence the name Beverly Leasure gives her quilt. Pick a bouquet of prints for a fabulously floral quilt all your own.

Finished Size

Quilt: 66" x 87"
Blocks: 35 (9" x 9")
This quilt fits a twin-size bed. Because of the pieced border, size variations are not recommended for this quilt.

Materials

35 (9" x 22") fat eighths print fabrics or equivalent scraps
1¼ yards light print fabric for sashing squares and pieced border
2⅝ yards dark print fabric
2 yards muslin
5½ yards backing fabric

continued

Quilt by Beverly A. Leasure of Dunedin, Florida

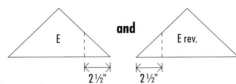

and

E   E rev.

2½"   2½"

Diagram A

Cutting

Instructions are for rotary cutting. For traditional cutting, use patterns on page 154.

From each *print*

- 3 (4¼") squares. Cut squares in quarters diagonally to get 12 A triangles.
- 4 (2⅜") squares. Cut squares in half diagonally to get 8 B triangles.

Note: Set aside remaining print fabric for borders.

From light print

- 24 (2¼") F squares for sashing.

From dark print

- 4 (3"-wide) and 4 (2"-wide) lengthwise strips for borders.
- 58 (2¼" x 9½") strips for sashing.

From muslin

- 9 (7¼") squares. Cut squares in quarters diagonally to get 35 C triangles (and 1 extra).
- 35 (5⅜") squares. Cut squares in half diagonally to get 70 D triangles.
- 35 (5⅜") squares. Cut squares in half diagonally to get 70 E triangles. Trim 2½" from longest edge of each triangle (Diagram A). Be sure to cut 35 triangles on right side (E) and 35 triangles on left side (E reversed).

Block Assembly

1. For each block, select 6 A triangles and 4 B triangles of light-value fabric and matching set of medium- or dark-value fabric. From muslin triangles, select 1 C, 2 Ds, and 1 each of E and E rev.
2. Join B triangles in 4 light-dark pairs as shown (Block Assembly Diagram). To make basket handle, join 2 pairs to make 2 diagonal rows as shown. Sew rows to short sides of C triangle. Press seam allowances toward C.
3. Sew light A triangle to the top of handle section. Press seam allowance toward A.
4. Sew Ds to sides of unit as shown to complete top half of block.
5. For bottom half, join light and dark A triangles in 3 rows as shown. Join to make triangle.
6. Sew light A triangles to ends of E and E rev. as shown. Sew units to sides of large triangle to complete bottom half of block.
7. Join halves to complete block.
8. Make 35 basket blocks.

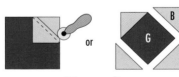

Diagram B

Quilt Assembly

1. Lay out the blocks in 7 horizontal rows of 5 blocks each. Join the blocks in each row, sewing 1 sashing strip between the blocks as shown (Row Assembly Diagram).
2. For each sashing row, join 5 sashing strips and 4 F squares as shown. Press the seam allowances toward the sashing. Then make 6 sashing rows.
3. Join the rows as shown in the photo on page 151, alternating the block rows and the sashing rows.

Borders

1. Measure the quilt from the top to the bottom through the middle of the pieced top and trim 2 inner border strips to match the length. Sew the borders to the quilt sides.
2. Measure quilt from side to side through middle and trim remaining inner borders to match quilt width. Sew borders to top and bottom edges of quilt.
3. See page 304 to decide if you prefer diagonal-corner quick-piecing technique or traditional piecing for middle border. For quick piecing, cut 376 (2") squares from remaining light print fabric and 94 (3½") squares from print scraps, cutting 2 or 3 squares from each fabric. For traditional cutting, use templates B and G (see page 154).

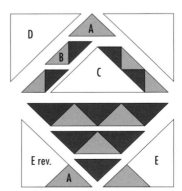

Block Assembly Diagram

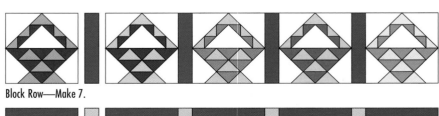

Block Row—Make 7.

Sashing Row—Make 6.

Row Assembly Diagram

4. Use diagonal-corner technique to sew 4 light corners on each G square (Diagram B). Or sew B triangles to G square traditionally as shown. Assembled unit should be 3½" square. Make 94 units.

5. For each side border, join 26 units in a row. Sew borders to quilt sides, easing quilt to fit as needed.

6. Join 21 units in each row for top and bottom borders. Sew borders to top and bottom edges of quilt.

7. Measure the quilt; then trim and sew the outer borders to the quilt as for inner borders.

Quilting and Finishing

1. Mark quilting design as desired. Quilt has outline quilting and cross-hatching in D triangles. See page 154 for feather motif in C triangles.

2. For prairie points, cut 202 (2¾") H squares from remaining scraps. See below to add prairie point edging. If prairie points are not desired, see page 315 for tips on binding quilt traditionally when quilting is complete.

3. Layer backing, batting, and quilt top. Baste. Quilt as desired.

4. Blindstitch backing (see below).

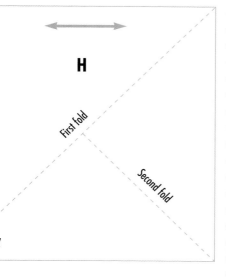

H

First fold

Second fold

continued

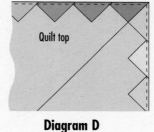

pinpoints

Fold.

Fold.

Diagram A   **Diagram B**

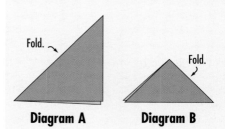

Diagram C

Quilt top

Diagram D

Edging with Prairie Points

Adding an edging of prairie points is a popular and attractive way to finish a quilt. Making the points is as simple as folding squares.

This type of edging does not use standard binding. Instead, the backing edges are turned under and blindstitched in place by hand. This may be a less sturdy finish than a machine-stitched binding, so reserve prairie-point edgings for quilts that will not experience a lot of wear.

To be able to turn the backing under, be sure the quilting stops at least ½" from the edge of the quilt top.

1. With wrong sides together, fold each fabric square in half diagonally (Diagram A). Press.

2. Fold each triangle in half again to make a smaller triangle (Diagram B). Press.

3. Arrange prairie points on right side of quilt, aligning raw edges of triangles and quilt top. Triangles will overlap, with each fitting between folds of its neighbor (Diagram C). Space prairie points evenly along each side. For *Baskets of Liberty,* position 57 points on each side and 44 points at top and bottom edges.

4. When satisfied with placement of prairie points, topstitch in place ¼" from raw edge (Diagram D).

5. Layer quilt with batting and backing. Quilt as desired.

6. Trim backing fabric even with quilt top. Trim batting ¼" shorter than quilt top on all sides.

7. Turn points so that they face out from quilt top, turning under raw edge of quilt top. Press lightly.

8. Turn under ¼" on all sides of backing fabric. Blindstitch folded edge of backing to back of prairie-point edging (Diagram E).

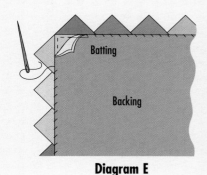

Batting

Backing

Diagram E

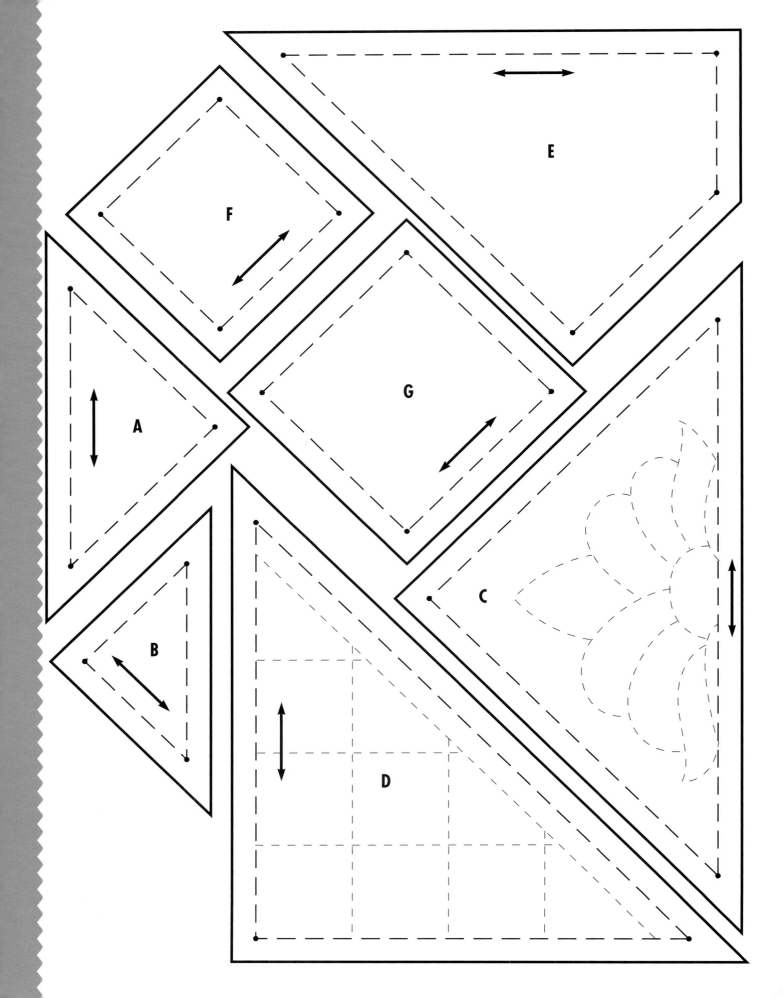

E

F

A

G

B

C

D

STARBURST

Antique quilt owned by Patricia Cox of Minneapolis, Minnesota

The nineteenth-century quilter who made this charming quilt didn't have the benefit of an acrylic ruler with neatly marked 60° angles to guide her cutting. To follow in her footsteps, you can use traditional cutting and sewing methods. Or you can rotary-cut and strip-piece with today's handy tools and techniques. Either way, you'll make a quilt you can be proud of.

Finished Size
Quilt: 60" x 78½"
Blocks: 28 (9¾" x 11¼")

Materials
10 (18" x 22") fat quarters blue fabrics or equivalent scraps
5 fat quarters white fabrics or equivalent scraps
½ yard tan fabric
⅛ yard red fabric
3½ yards tone-on-tone pink fabric
¾ yard inner border fabric
¾ yard binding fabric
3¾ yards backing fabric

continued

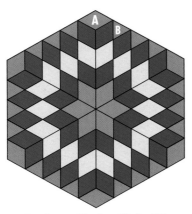

Starburst Block—Make 28.

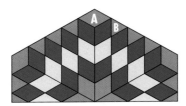

Half-Block—Make 4.

Cutting

Instructions are for rotary cutting and quick piecing. Before cutting, read block instructions and decide if you prefer quick piecing or traditional piecing. For traditional cutting, use patterns on page 158. Cut all strips on crosswise grain except as noted.

From blue fabrics
• 135 (1½" x 18") strips.

From white fabrics
• 68 (1½" x 18") strips.

From tan
• 68 (1½" x 18") strips.

From red
• 3 (1½" x 18") strips.

From pink
• 14 (1¾"-wide) strips. From these, cut 544 B triangles. To rotary-cut triangles, align 60° ruler marking with bottom of strip to make first cut (Diagram A). To make second cut,

Diagram A

Diagram B

Diagram C

Diagram D

align second 60° marking with bottom of strip and edge of ruler with top corner of strip (Diagram B). To cut next triangle, realign ruler to first 60° marking (Diagram C). Continue cutting triangles, alternating alignment of ruler with each cut.

• 4 (3½" x 76") lengthwise strips for borders.
• 7 (5⅝" x 28") strips. From these, cut 54 C triangles.
• 1 (6⅛"-wide) strip. From this, cut 6 (3⅝" x 6⅛") rectangles. Cut 3 rectangles in half diagonally to get 6 D triangles (Diagram D). Cut 3 remaining rectangles in other direction to get 6 Ds reversed. Referring to pattern on page 158, trim ¾" from tip of each triangle.
• 12 (1½" x 28") strips. From these, cut 180 A diamonds.

Size Variations

	Full/Queen	King
Finished size	80" x 101"	99" x 101"
Number of blocks	53	68
Half blocks	6	8
Strip Set 1	42	53
Strip Set 2	43	55
Strip Set 3	43	55
Blocks set	7 x 8	9 x 8
Number of pieces to cut		
Blue A	330	424
Pink A	336	432
Pink B	1,014	1,304
Pink C	104	134
Pink D	16	20
Yardage Required		
Blue fat quarters	18	23
White fat quarters	10	12
Tan fat quarters	3	4
Red fat quarters	1	1
Pink fabric	4½ yards	5⅝ yards
Inner border fabric	¾ yard	1⅛ yards
Binding fabric	¾ yard	⅞ yard
108"-wide backing fabric	2½ yards	3 yards

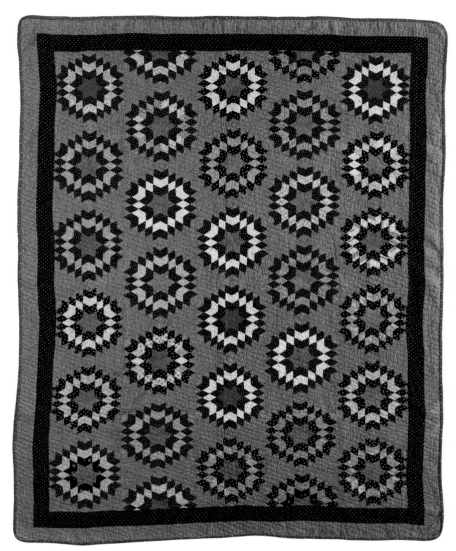

Strip Set 1—Make 22.

Strip Set 2—Make 23.

Strip Set 3—Make 23.

Block Assembly

1. Referring to Strip Set Diagrams, join blue and white strips to make 22 of Strip Set 1 and 23 of Strip Set 2 as shown. Make 20 of Strip Set 3 as shown with tan fabric and 3 of Strip Set 3 with red fabric. Press all seam allowances toward blue.

2. Place 1 strip set on cutting mat. Position ruler with 60° marking aligned with bottom edge of strip set as shown (Diagram E). Make this first cut to remove selvage and establish a 60° angle.

3. Turn cutting mat to position cut edge to your left. Position ruler with line marking 1½" on cut edge; cut 1 (1½"-wide) diagonal strip (Diagram F). Cut 8 (1½"-wide) segments from each strip set. Keep separate stacks of segments from sets 1, 2, and 3.

4. Sew 1 B triangle to bottom of each segment of strip sets 1 and 2 (Diagram G).

5. Use technique for cutting strip sets to rotary-cut 184 A diamonds from remaining blue strips. Sew Bs to 1 edge of each blue A diamond (Diagram G).

6. For each block, select 6 A/B units and 6 segments *each* of strip sets 1, 2, and 3. (Strip Set 3 units should have same fabric for center

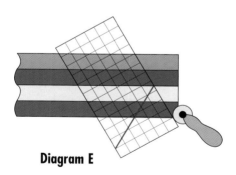

Diagram E

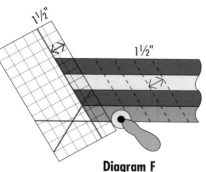

Diagram F

star, but remaining units can vary if you want to mix blue fabrics.) Join units to make 6 sections (Diagram G). Press seam allowances toward strip set segments 1 and 3.

continued

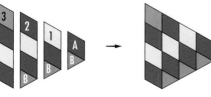

Diagram G

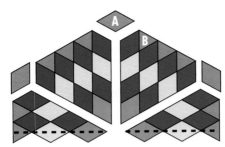

Block Assembly Diagram

7. Join 3 sections; then join block halves as shown (Block Assembly Diagram).
8. Set in pink A diamonds at corners to complete block. (See page 36 for tips on sewing set-in seams.)
9. For half-block, make 2 sections and 2 partial sections as shown (Half-Block Assembly Diagram). Partial sections consist of 1 Strip Set 1 segment, 1 Strip Set 3 segment, and 2 extra B triangles. Join sections and set in 2 A diamonds to complete half-block. Dotted line in diagram indicates seam line for

Half-Block Assembly Diagram

quilt assembly; excess fabric will then be trimmed from the seam allowance.
10. Make 28 Starburst blocks and 4 half-blocks.

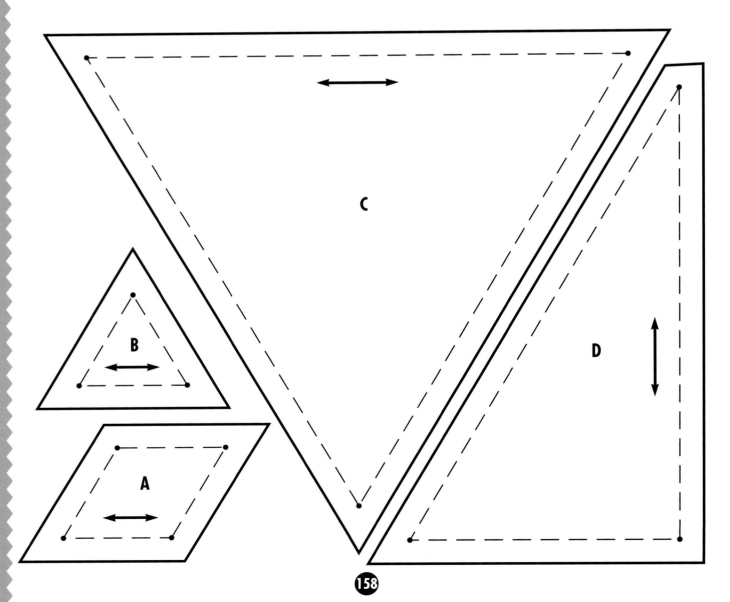

Quilt Assembly

1. For Row 1, lay out 6 blocks in a vertical row, with 1 pink A diamond at the top of each block. Fill spaces between blocks with Cs (Row Assembly Diagram). Sew Ds and Ds rev. to first and last blocks in row as shown. When satisfied with position of blocks, sew Cs to opposite edges of each block. Press seam allowances toward triangles. Join block/triangle units to complete row. Make 3 of Row 1.

2. For Row 2, lay out 5 blocks and 2 half-blocks, placing Cs between the blocks as shown. Sew Cs to each block and press the seam allowances toward the triangles. Then join the block/triangle units to complete the row. Make 2 of Row 2.

3. Referring to Row Assembly Diagram and photo on page 157, join rows.

Borders

1. Cut 8 (3"-wide) crosswise strips for inner border. Sew 2 strips end to end to make 1 border strip for each side.

2. Measure quilt from top to bottom through middle of pieced top and trim 2 borders to match length. Sew borders to quilt sides.

3. Measure quilt from side to side through middle and trim remaining borders to match quilt width. Sew borders to top and bottom edges of quilt.

4. Measure the quilt length and trim 2 outer strips to match as before. Sew borders to quilt sides. Measure quilt width and trim remaining strips to match; sew borders to top and bottom edges of quilt.

Row Assembly Diagram

Quilting and Finishing

1. Mark quilting design on quilt top as desired. The quilt shown has diagonal lines, spaced ½" apart, quilted across quilt surface.

2. Layer backing, batting, and quilt top. Backing seams will parallel top and bottom edges of quilt. Baste. Quilt as desired.

3. Make 8 yards of bias or straight-grain binding. Bind quilt edges.

PINK LEMONADE

Quilt by Shelby Sawyer Morris of Cartersville, Georgia

Lemonade is refreshing on hot summer days in the South, where Shelby Morris lives. Inspired by the floral border fabric, Shelby quick-pieced Shoo-fly blocks in pastel colors that reminded her of sweet summertime pleasures.

Finished Size
Quilt: 64" x 80"
Blocks: 48 (6" x 6")

Materials
½ yard *each* 5 light prints
¼ yard *each* 7 dark prints
¼ yard *each* 2 pink prints for frames
¾ yard medium pink floral for frames and inner border
1½ yards dark blue print for frames, middle border, and binding
2½ yards yellow floral border fabric
2 yards 90"-wide backing fabric

Cutting

Instructions are for rotary cutting and quick piecing. Cut all strips on crosswise grain except as noted. Cut pieces in order listed to get best use of yardage.

From light prints
- 7 (2⅞"-wide) strips. From these, cut 96 (2⅞") squares. Cut squares in half diagonally to get 192 A triangles, 4 for each block.
- 12 (2½"-wide) strips. From these, cut 192 (2½") B squares, 4 for each block.
- 16 (1½"-wide) strips (3 of each print). From these, cut 40 (8½"-long) strips and 40 (6½"-long) strips for 20 frames, 4 matching strips for each block.

From dark prints
- 7 (2⅞"-wide) strips. From these, cut 96 (2⅞") squares. Cut squares in half diagonally to get 192 A triangles, 4 for each block.
- 7 (2½"-wide) strips. From these, cut 48 (2½") B squares, 1 for each block center.

From medium pink floral
- 6 (2½"-wide) strips for inner border. Add remaining fabric to pink prints for frames.

From 3 pink prints for frames
- 11 (1½"-wide) strips. From these, cut 28 (8½"-long) strips and 28 (6½"-long) strips for 14 frames, 4 matching strips for each block.

From dark blue print
- 7 (1½"-wide) strips for middle border.
- 11 (1½"-wide) strips. From these, cut 30 (8½"-long) strips and 30 (6½"-long) strips for 15 frames, 4 matching strips for each block.
- 8 (2½"-wide) strips for binding.

From yellow floral
- 4 (5½" x 72") lengthwise strips for outer border.

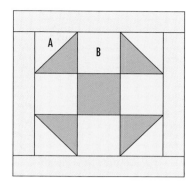

Shoo-fly Block—Make 48.

Block Assembly

1. For each block, select 4 A triangles and 4 B squares from same light fabric. Then choose 4 A triangles and 1 B square from same dark fabric.
2. Join light and dark triangles to make a triangle-square (Block Assembly Diagram).
3. Arrange triangle-squares and B squares in rows as shown. Join units in each row; then join rows. Press seam allowances toward light fabric Bs.
4. Select set of 4 frame strips. Sew 6½" strips to block sides. Press seam allowances toward strips. Then add 8½" strips to top and bottom edges to complete block.
5. Make 48 blocks, choosing light and dark combinations at random.

Quilt Assembly

1. Lay out blocks in 8 horizontal rows, with 6 blocks in each row. Rotate blocks so that frame seams won't meet and make a lump (Frame Diagram).
2. When satisfied with block placement, join blocks in each row.
3. Join rows to complete quilt center.
4. Piece pink floral border strips to make 2 (66"-long) borders and 2 (54"-long) borders.
5. Measure length of quilt through middle of pieced top. Trim longer strips to match quilt length. Stitch borders to quilt sides.

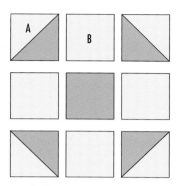

Block Assembly Diagram

6. Measure width of quilt through middle of pieced top. Trim remaining pink strips to match quilt width. Sew borders to top and bottom edges of quilt.
7. Add dark blue middle border and yellow floral outer border in same manner.

Quilting and Finishing

1. Mark the pieced quilt top with desired quilting design. Quilt shown is hand-quilted in a Baptist Fan pattern.
2. Layer backing, batting, and quilt top. Baste together. Then quilt as desired.
3. Join dark blue strips to make 9 yards of continuous straight-grain binding. Then bind the quilt edges.

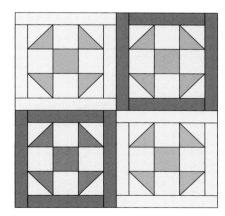

Frame Diagram

ODD FELLOWS MARCH

Quilt by Susan Marie Stewart of Buena Vista, Colorado

Patterns within patterns emerge when these blocks come together. Big stars and squares-within-squares appear that aren't suggested when you see the original block. (The block is also known as Crosses and Losses or Double X.) Susan Stewart used a plethora of plaids to make these blocks, surrounded by a flock of flying geese units in the borders.

Finished Size
Quilt: 82½" x 90½"
Blocks: 56 (8" x 8")

Materials
5½ yards muslin
1¾ yards 60"-wide red plaid for
    bias inner border (or 1½ yards
    45"-wide for pieced border)
½ yard green for middle border
2⅜ yards brown check for outer
    border
25 (12" x 13") plaids for blocks
8 (7" x 13") plaids for Goose Chase
4 (4½") squares red for border corners
⅞ yard brown plaid for outer border
    corners and binding
2¾ yards 90"-wide backing fabric
8 buttons (optional)

Cutting
Instructions are for rotary cutting and quick piecing. For traditional cutting and piecing, use patterns on page 165. Cut all strips on crosswise grain except as noted. Cut pieces in order listed to get best use of yardage.
From muslin
- 7 (13"-wide) strips. From these, cut 38 (7" x 13") pieces for block triangle-squares and pieced border.
- 15 (2⅞"-wide) strips. From these, cut 112 (2⅞") squares. Cut squares in half diagonally to get 224 A triangles (4 for each block).
- 13 (2½"-wide) strips. From these and scraps, cut 224 (2½") B squares (4 for each block).
From red plaid
- 4 (4½" x 76") bias strips from corner to corner for first border.
- 1 (12" x 13") piece for blocks.
- 1 (7" x 13") for border.
From brown check
- 4 (4½" x 85") lengthwise strips for outer border.
- 2 (12" x 13") pieces for blocks.
- 1 (7" x 13") for border.
From each 12" x 13" plaid (including red and brown pieces above)
- 1 (7" x 13") piece for block triangle-squares.
- 2 (4⅞") squares. Cut each square in half diagonally to get 4 C triangles (2 for each block).
From brown plaid
- 1 (30") square for binding.
- 4 (4½") squares for outer border corners.

Block Assembly
1. On wrong side of 1 (7" x 13") piece muslin, draw a 2-square by 4-square grid of 2⅞" squares, leaving a ⅝" margin on all sides (Diagram A). Draw diagonal lines through each square as shown.
2. With right sides facing, match marked muslin piece with 1 (7" x 13") plaid piece. Stitch ¼" seam on both sides of diagonal lines.

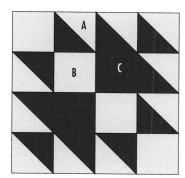

Odd Fellows March Block—Make 56.

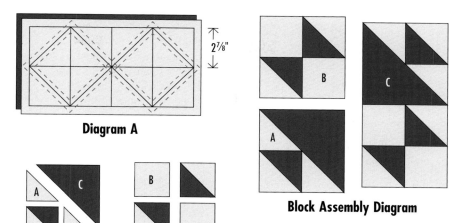

Diagram A

2⅞"

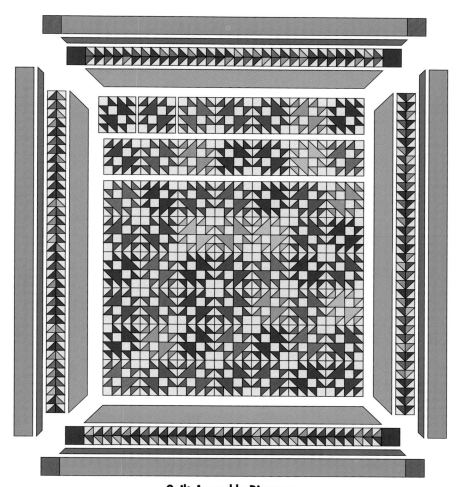

Block Assembly Diagram

Diagram B   **Diagram C**

(Red lines on diagram show first continuous stitching path; blue lines show second path.) Press.

3. Cut on all drawn lines to get 16 triangle-squares.

4. Stitch 28 triangle-square grids to get 56 sets of 6 triangle-squares for each block. Set aside 112 remaining triangle-squares for Goose Chase border.

5. For each block, select 6 triangle-squares and 2 C triangles of same fabric, as well as 4 A triangles and B squares.

6. Sew 1 A triangle to both dark sides of 1 triangle-square (Diagram B). Press seam allowances toward A triangles. Add C triangle to complete A/C unit. Make 2 A/C units for each block.

7. Sew B squares to dark sides of remaining triangle-squares (Diagram C). Press seam allowances toward Bs. Join 2 to complete B unit. Make 2 B units for each block.

8. Join A/C units and B units in 2 rows (Block Assembly Diagram). Join rows to complete block.

9. Make 56 blocks.

Quilt Assembly

1. Lay out blocks in 8 horizontal rows, with 7 blocks in each row. Turn adjacent blocks as shown (Quilt Assembly Diagram).

2. When satisfied with block placement, join blocks in each row.

3. Join the rows.

continued

Quilt Assembly Diagram

Diagram D

Borders

1. Sew 1 red plaid border to each quilt side, mitering corners. Press seam allowances toward borders.
2. Mark triangle-square grid on 10 remaining 7" x 13" muslin pieces. Pair each with 1 plaid piece; stitch grids as before to get 160 more triangle-squares. With reserved units, you should have 272.
3. Join triangle-squares in pairs to make 136 Goose Chase units (Diagram D).
4. Join 36 units in row for each side border (Quilt Assembly Diagram, page 163). Sew borders to quilt sides, easing to fit as needed.
5. For top and bottom borders, join remaining units in 2 (32-unit) rows. Add 1 (4½") red plaid square to ends of both strips. Sew borders to top and bottom edges of quilt, easing to fit as needed.
6. Cut 8 (1¾"-wide) strips of green fabric. Join 2 strips end to end for each border. Center 1 border on each edge of quilt and stitch. Miter border corners.
7. Measure length and width through middle of the top. Trim 2 brown check borders to match length and 2 borders to match width. Sew longer borders to quilt sides, easing to fit as needed. Press seam allowances toward borders.
8. Stitch brown squares to ends of remaining borders. Press seam allowances toward borders. Sew borders to top and bottom edges, easing to fit as needed.

Quilting and Finishing

1. Mark quilt top with desired quilting design. On quilt shown, blocks and Goose Chase border are outline-quilted, with echo quilting in muslin triangles. A Variable Star is quilted in B squares where 4 blocks meet and in border corner squares. Pattern for Celtic Chain quilted in bias plaid border is on opposite page.
2. Layer backing, batting, and quilt top. Baste. Quilt as desired.
3. Make 10 yards of continuous bias or straight-grain binding. Bind quilt edges.
4. Add buttons to border corners, if desired.

Color Variations

Every odd fellow (or woman) has to march to the beat of his own band. This quilt is just as much fun in glowing jewel tones, soft pastels, or stark monochromatics.

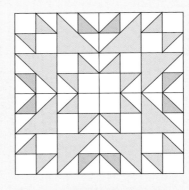

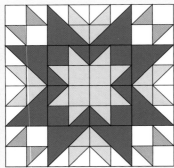

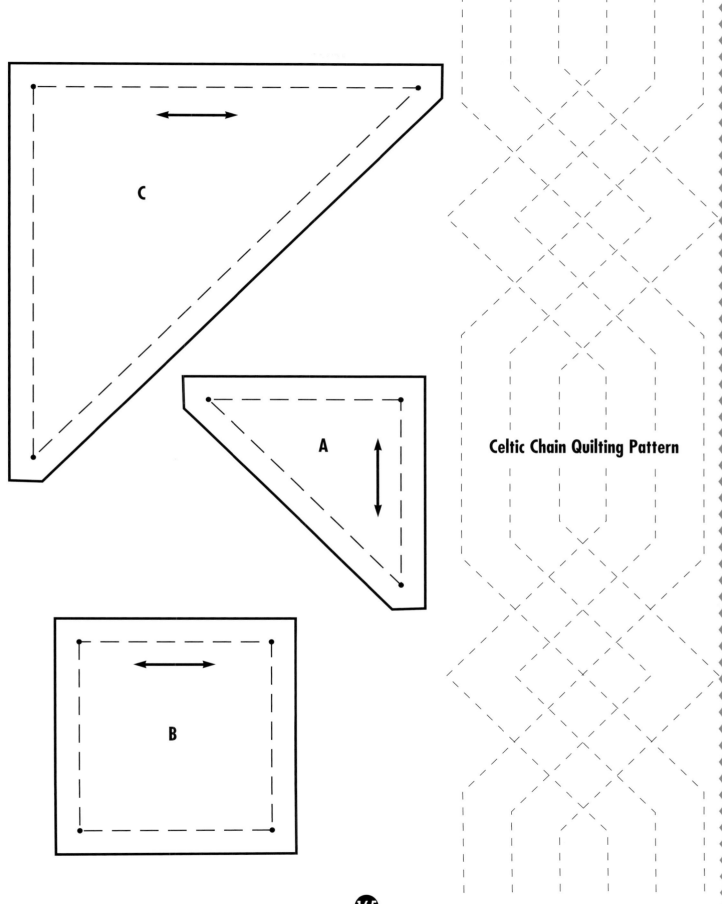

C

A

B

Celtic Chain Quilting Pattern

WILD GOOSE CHASE

Quilt by Carole Collins of Galien, Michigan

Antique scrap quilts fascinate Carole Collins, who loves making reproductions of her favorite patterns. In pioneer days, fabric was too precious a commodity for quiltmakers to worry whether prints coordinated. Carole's quilt captures that exuberant love of fabric, blending prints, plaids, and stripes in a joyous mix that guarantees satisfaction in any color scheme.

Finished Size
Quilt: 75" x 90"
Blocks: 30 (15" x 15")

Materials
30 (11¼") squares red prints
15 (¼-yard) pieces navy and/or gold prints and plaids
15 (¼-yard) pieces light shirting prints and plaids
⅞ yard binding fabric
5½ yards backing fabric

Cutting
Instructions are for rotary cutting and quick piecing. Cut all strips on crosswise grain. Cut pieces in order listed to get best use of yardage.
From each *navy/gold print*
• 2 (4"-wide) strips. From these, cut 2 (4") E squares and 24 (2¼" x 4") B pieces.
• 8 (3") D squares.
From each *light shirting print*
• 1 (2⅝"-wide) strip. From this, cut 8 (2⅝") squares. Cut each square in half diagonally to get 16 C triangles.
• 48 (2¼") A squares.

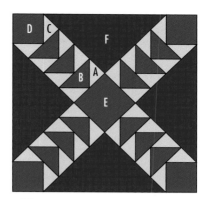

Wild Goose Chase Block—Make 30.

Block Assembly

1. For each block, choose 24 A squares and 8 C triangles of same fabric. Select 12 Bs, 4 D squares, and 1 E of same fabric.
2. With the right sides facing, match the corners of 1 A and 1 B (Diagram A). See page 304 for step-by-step instructions on diagonal-corner quick-piecing technique. Stitch A to B, trim the seam allowance, and press A to the right side. Stitch another A square to the opposite corner of B as shown. Press. Make 12 matching Goose Chase units.
3. Stitch 1 C triangle to 1 side of a D square (Diagram B). Sew a second C triangle to adjacent side as shown. Press seam allowances toward Cs. Make 4 matching corner units.
4. Join 1 corner unit and 3 Goose Chase units in a row as shown (Diagram C). Make 4 pieced units.
5. Choose 1 red fabric square. Cut square in quarters diagonally to get 4 F triangles. Join F triangles to both sides of 2 pieced rows (Block Assembly Diagram). Press seam allowances toward red.
6. Join remaining pieced rows to opposite sides of E square. Press seam allowances toward E.
7. Join the triangle units to the center pieced row to complete the block.

8. Make 30 Wild Goose Chase blocks.

Quilt Assembly

1. Lay out blocks in 6 horizontal rows, with 5 blocks in each row. When satisfied with block placement, join blocks in each row.
2. Join the rows.

Quilting and Finishing

1. Mark quilting design as desired. Quilt is quilted in-the-ditch around each goose, and red triangles are quilted in parallel lines.
2. Layer backing, batting, and quilt top. Baste. Quilt as desired.
3. Make 9⅜ yards of continuous bias or straight-grain binding. Bind quilt edges.

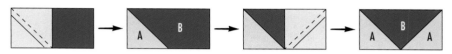

Diagram A

Diagram B

Diagram C

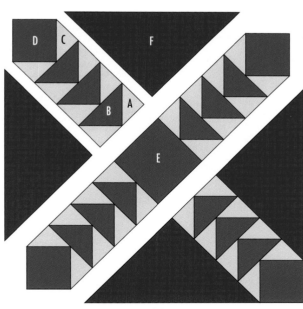

Block Assembly Diagram

PRAIRIE QUEEN

Quilt by Gerry Sweem of Reseda, California

Folksy plaids and peppy stripes make a delightful combination in this cozy quilt. Don't worry about matching plaids and stripes at the seams. Let the lines fall where they may; the mismatched quality adds an element of charm. This variation of the Prairie Queen block is also known as Aunt Vina's Favorite, Cross & Chains, and Richmond.

Finished Size

Quilt: 96½" x 96½"
Blocks: 60 (9" x 9")

Materials

30 (18" x 22") fat quarters light/medium fabrics
30 fat quarters medium/dark fabrics
6 (16¾") squares light/medium fabrics or equivalent scraps
10 (⅛-yard) pieces red fabrics
1 yard binding fabric
3 yards 108"-wide backing fabric

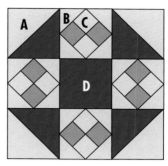

Prairie Queen Block—Make 60.

Cutting

Instructions are for rotary cutting and quick piecing. Before cutting, read block instructions and decide whether you prefer quick piecing or traditional piecing. For traditional cutting, use patterns on page 172.

From each light/medium fabric
• 2 (6" x 10") pieces.
• 2 (1⅝" x 13½") strips.
• 16 (2½") squares. Cut squares in half diagonally to get 32 B triangles.

From remaining light/medium fabric
• 81 (2½") E squares for sashing.

From each medium/dark fabric
• 2 (6" x 10") pieces.
• 2 (3½") D squares.

From remaining medium/dark fabric
• 4 (2½" x 14") strips and 140 (2½" x 9½") strips for sashing.

From red fabrics
• 60 (1⅝" x 13½") strips.

Block Assembly

1. For each block, select 1 (6" x 10") piece, 16 B triangles, and 1 (1⅝") strip of same light fabric. Choose 1 (6" x 10") piece and 1 D square of 1 dark fabric and 1 (1⅝") strip of red. Each fabric will appear in at least 2 blocks, but avoid repeating same combination.

2. On wrong side of 6" x 10" light fabric, mark a 2-square grid of 3⅞" squares (Diagram A). Mark diagonal lines through squares. With right sides facing, match marked fabric with dark fabric piece. Stitch on both sides of diagonal lines. (Red lines show first path of continuous stitching; blue lines show second path.) Press the stitching; then cut on drawn lines to get 4 A triangle-squares. Press seam allowances toward dark fabric.

3. Sewing generous ¼" seam, join 1⅝"-wide strips as shown (Diagram B). Press seam allowance toward red. From this, cut 8 (1⅝"-wide) segments as shown. Again sewing generous ¼" seam, join 2 segments to make four-patch (Diagram C). Make 4 four-patches.

4. Sew B triangles to 2 opposite sides of each four-patch (Diagram D). Press seam allowances toward triangles. Sew 1 B triangle to each remaining side of four-patch.

5. You now have 9 (3½"-square) units for the block: 4 A triangle-squares, 4 B/C four-patches, and 1 dark D square. Arrange units in rows as shown (Block Assembly Diagram), checking to be sure four-patch units are turned to position the red squares as shown. Join units in each row. Press seam allowances toward dark fabrics. Then join rows to complete block.

6. Make 60 Prairie Queen blocks.

continued

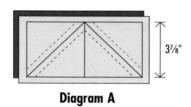

Diagram A

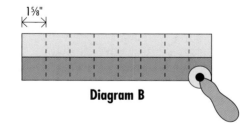

Diagram B

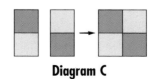

Diagram C

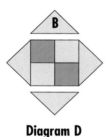

Diagram D

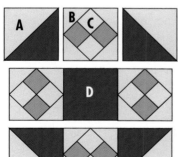

Block Assembly Diagram

Quilt Assembly

1. Cut each 16¾" light-medium square in quarters diagonally to get 24 setting triangles.

2. For Row 1, join 10 blocks with sashing strips between blocks (Quilt Assembly Diagram). For matching sashing row, join 10 sashing strips and 11 E squares end to end as shown. Press seam allowances toward sashing in both rows. Join sashing row to block row; then sew setting triangles to both ends of row as shown.

3. For Row 2, join 8 blocks with sashing strips between blocks as shown. Join 8 sashing strips and 9 sashing squares to make matching sashing row. Join block row and sashing row; then add setting triangles to row ends.

4. Continue joining blocks and sashing in diagonal rows, making rows 1–5 as shown.

5. For Row 6, sew 1 setting triangle to each side of 14" sashing strip, matching bottom edges as shown. Sashing strip will be longer than triangles. Press seam allowances toward sashing. Trim excess sashing at corner, using edge of triangles as cutting guideline (Diagram E).

6. Refer to Quilt Assembly Diagram for half of the quilt. Repeat steps 2–5 above to make a second set of rows.

7. Referring to Quilt Assembly Diagram and photo opposite, join rows 1–6. Repeat to assemble second set of rows 1–6.

8. For center sashing row, join 11 sashing squares and 10 sashing strips end to end as shown. Add 14" sashing strips at each end of row. Press seam allowances toward sashing.

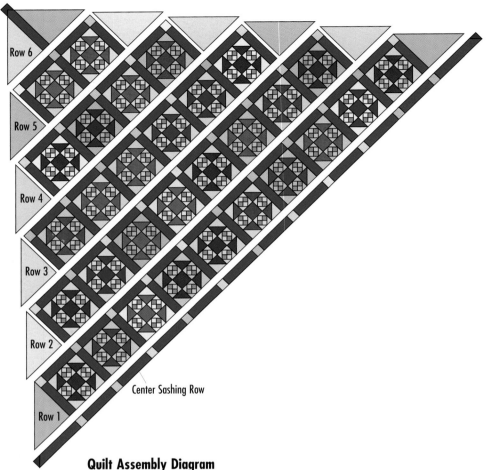

Quilt Assembly Diagram

Row 6
Row 5
Row 4
Row 3
Row 2
Row 1
Center Sashing Row

9. Join the quilt halves to the sides of the center sashing row, matching the seams at the sashing squares. When rows are joined, trim ends of center sashing row at quilt corners.

Quilting and Finishing

1. Mark quilting design on pieced top as desired. Quilt shown has straight lines of quilting, spaced 1⅜" apart, in 1 direction only (Quilting Diagram). Lines go through blocks and sashing strips and extend into setting triangles.

2. Layer backing, batting, and quilt top. Baste. Quilt as desired.

3. Make 11 yards of straight-grain or bias binding. Bind quilt edges.

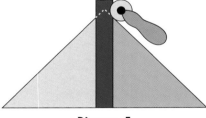

Diagram E

Quilting Diagram

continued

Size Variations

	Twin	Full/Queen
Finished size	65" x 96½"	81" x 96½"
Number of blocks	38	49
Blocks set	4 x 6	5 x 6
9½"-long sashing strips	92	116
Sashing squares	55	68
Setting triangles	20	22

Yardage Required

	Twin	Full/Queen
Light fat quarters	19	25
Dark fat quarters	19	25
16¾" squares	5	6
⅛-yard red pieces	13	17
Binding fabric	⅞ yard	⅞ yard
Backing fabric	6 yards	6 yards

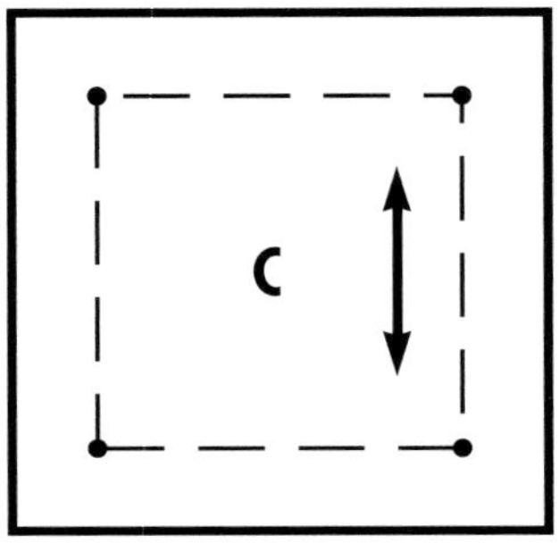

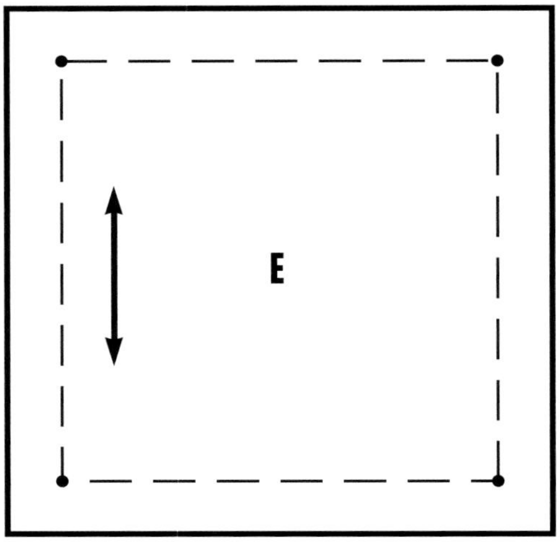

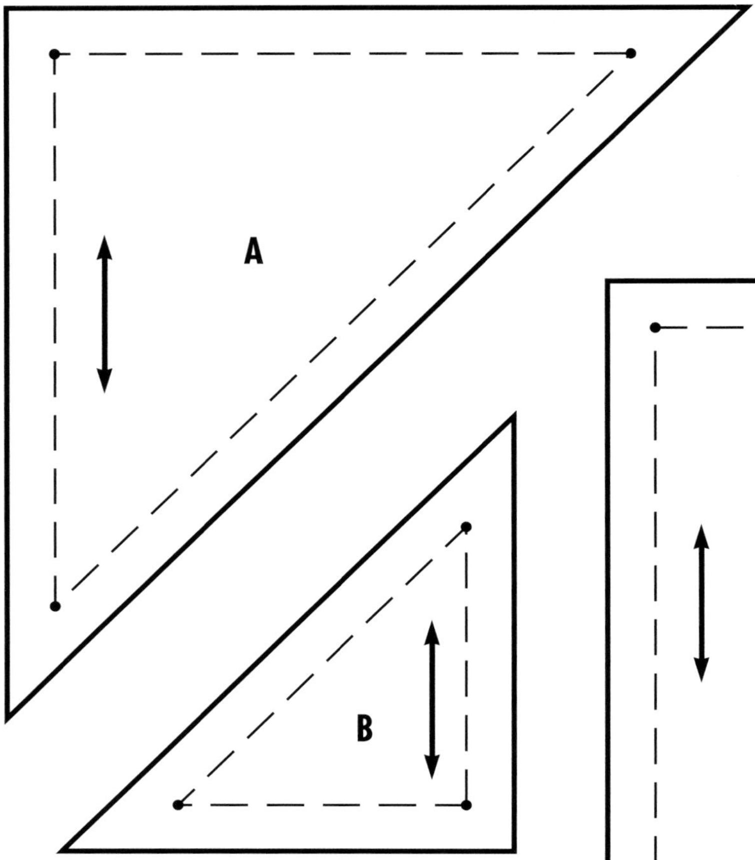

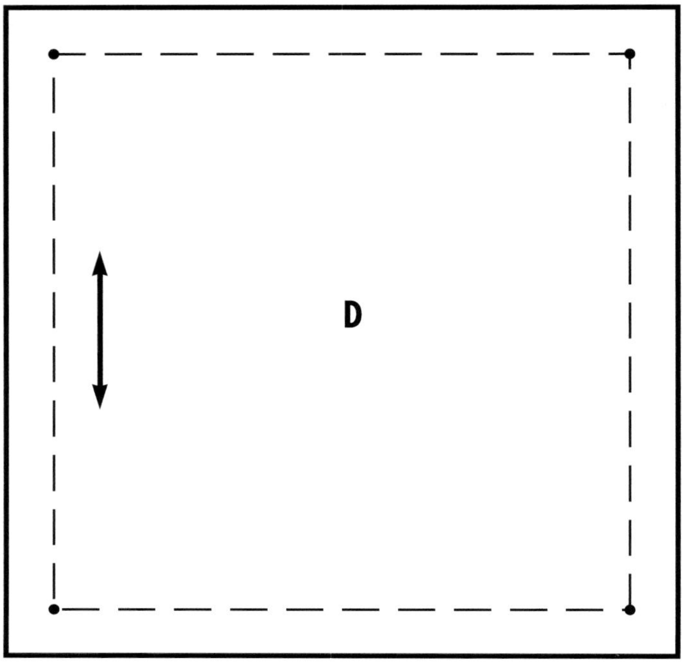

EVENING STAR

Quilt by Darlene C. Christopherson of China Spring, Texas

A beautiful appliquéd border turns this simple wall hanging into a work of art. This is the most basic of appliqué, perfect for a beginner or anyone who loves handwork. The graceful vine surrounds a field of Evening Star blocks. Also known as Sawtooth Star, this block is a patch-work classic, found in some of the earliest existing antique quilts.

Finished Size
Quilt: 41" x 41"
Blocks: 36 (4" x 4")

Materials
72 (3" x 9") scraps of blue, rose, and brown prints
1¾ yards background fabric
⅝ yard brown print for inner border and binding
½ yard blue/brown print fabric for vine
⅛ yard blue fabric for sashing squares
1¼ yards backing fabric
½"-wide bias pressing bar

continued

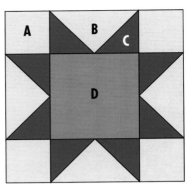

Evening Star Block—Make 36.

Cutting

Instructions are for rotary cutting and quick piecing. For appliqué and traditional cutting and piecing techniques, make templates of patterns on opposite page.

From each of 36 scrap fabrics
• 1 (2½") D square.

From each remaining scrap fabric
• 8 (1½") squares for C star points.

Note: Save remaining scraps for leaves.

From background fabric
• 14 (1½" x 42") strips. From these, cut 144 (1½" x 2½") Bs and 144 (1½") A squares.
• 3 (4½" x 42") strips. From these, cut 84 (1½" x 4½") sashing strips.

From blue
• 49 (1½") A squares for sashing.

From inner border fabric
• 4 (1" x 42") strips. Set aside remaining fabric for straight-grain binding and leaves.

From outer border fabric
• 4 (5" x 42") strips.

Block Assembly

1. Referring to page 304, use the diagonal-corner technique to sew 2 matching C squares to each B (Diagram A). Or sew C triangles to B traditionally. Make 4 B/C units for each block. Press seam allowances toward triangles.
2. For each block, select 4 B/C units, 4 A squares, and 1 D square. Sew

B/C units to sides of D as shown (Block Assembly Diagram). Press seam allowances toward D. Sew A squares to ends of remaining B/C units. Press seam allowances toward squares. Join rows to complete block.
3. Make 36 blocks.

Quilt Assembly

1. For sashing rows, join 6 sashing strips and 7 sashing squares as shown (Row Assembly Diagram). Make 7 sashing rows.
2. Lay out blocks in 6 rows, with 6 blocks in each row, placing sashing between blocks and at row ends. In quilt shown, blocks are placed so that star points of the same color family appear in diagonal rows from top left corner of quilt to bottom right (see photo on page 173). Place sashing rows between block rows.
3. When satisfied with placement of blocks, join blocks in each row.
4. Referring to photo, join blocks rows and sashing rows.

Borders

1. Measure quilt from top to bottom and trim 2 borders to match the length. Sew borders to quilt sides.
2. Measure quilt from side to side and trim remaining borders to match quilt width. Sew borders to top and bottom edges of quilt.
3. Referring to page 309, sew the outer border strips to the quilt and miter the corners.

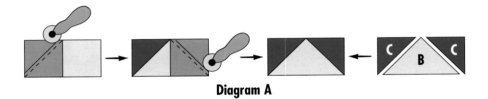

Diagram A

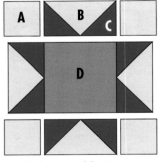

Block Assembly Diagram

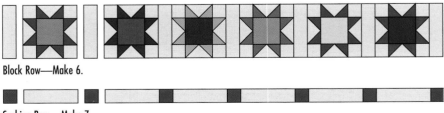

Block Row—Make 6.

Sashing Row—Make 7.

Row Assembly Diagram

4. Make 178" of 1½"-wide contin-uous bias. See page 176 for information on preparing the bias for appliqué.

5. Use pin to mark center of each outer border strip, 1½" from bot-tom edge. To mark high and low placement points for vine, measure 4½"-wide border seg-ments on both sides of center point, marking each spot with pin 1" below the inner border seam or 1½" from bottom edge (Diagram B). Place 7 pins on each border. At each corner, measure 3½" from last pin to mark outer edge of corner curve.

6. Starting at any side, baste pre-pared bias strip onto outer border. Curve bias up and down, match-ing pin placement points and removing pins as you go (Diagram B). Curve bias around corners with bottom of curve at mitered seam. When satisfied with posi-tion of bias, trim excess and over-lap ends as necessary. Appliqué bias vine in place.

7. Cut 260 leaves from the remain-ing scraps. Prepare the leaves for appliqué.

8. Pin about 65 leaves on each bor-der, overlapping the vine as desired. Cover the ends of the bias with 1 or more leaves to hide the overlap. When satisfied with the placement, appliqué the leaves in place.

Quilting and Finishing

1. Mark quilting design as desired. Quilt shown on page 173 has diagonal lines quilted over the quilt surface, spaced ¼" apart.

2. Layer backing, batting, and quilt top. Backing seams run parallel to top and bottom edges of quilt. Baste. Quilt as desired.

3. Make 4¾ yards of straight-grain binding. Bind quilt edges.

continued

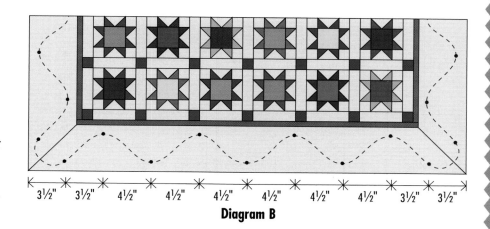

Diagram B

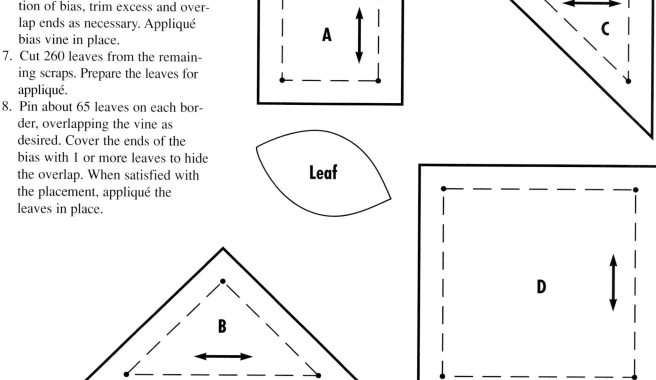

Making Bias Appliqué

Making curvy appliquéd vines and flower stems is easy with fabric strips cut on the bias. Use *bias pressing bars* of metal or heat-resistant plastic to prepare bias strips for appliqué. Available in various widths, bias bars are sold at quilt shops and through mail-order catalogs.

1. Start with fabric square. Instructions state size of square and width of strips to cut. Cut the square in half diagonally to get 2 triangles. See page 315 for instructions on continuous bias. Or cut bias strips, measuring from cut edge of each triangle (Photo A).

2. With wrong sides facing, fold strip in half lengthwise. Stitch ¼" from edges, making narrow tube. Slide tube over pressing bar, centering seam on flat side of bar (Photo B).

3. Press the seam allowance to 1 side or press it open, as you prefer (Photo C). Be careful when handling metal bars—they get hot! Remove bar when pressing is complete. Trim seam allowance if needed.

4. With seam against background fabric, baste or pin bias strip in place (Photo D). A steam iron will help shape strip. Appliqué strip onto background fabric, sewing inside curves first and then outside curves so that bias lies flat.

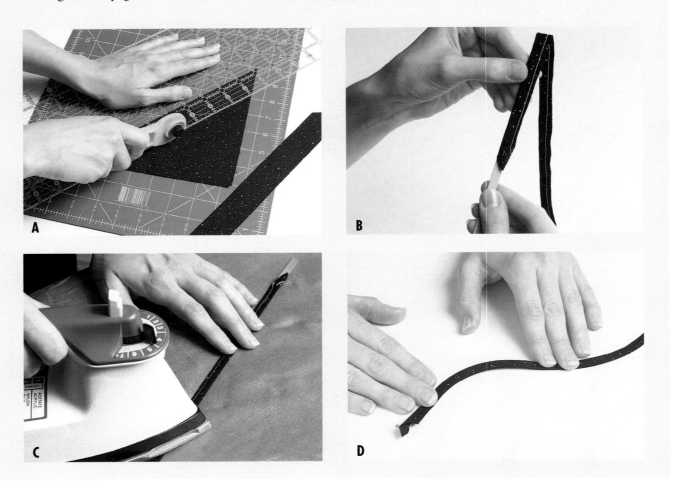

BABY BASKETS

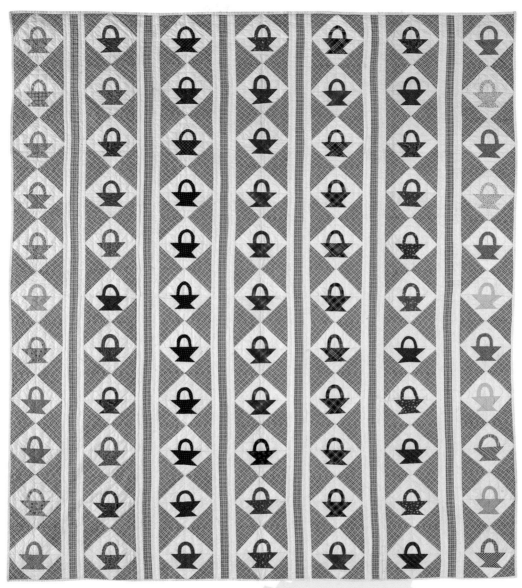

Antique quilt owned by Patricia Wilens of Birmingham, Alabama

This lightweight quilt was made in the late 1800s by someone who had a fine collection of plaids. The red-checked theme fabric is an unusual choice for the period, as is the vertical set. Combine your favorite scraps with an exciting theme fabric to make a contemporary version of this sweet antique.

Finished Size
Quilt: 67" x 77"
Blocks: 77 (7" x 7")

Materials
3½ yards muslin (includes binding)
3 yards red check *
13 (⅛-yard) pieces or scraps
2 yards 90"-wide backing fabric
* *Note:* Block corners are cut on bias in original quilt. But this requires more yardage and adds difficulty of working with bias edges. Yardage is for corners cut on straight of grain.

continued

177

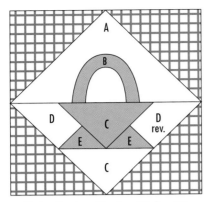

Baby Basket Block—Make 77.

Cutting

Instructions are for both traditional and rotary cutting. Make templates of patterns B and D on opposite page, referring to page 302 for tips on making templates for piecing and for appliqué. Other pieces can be rotary cut.

From muslin

- 12 (1½" x 80") lengthwise strips for sashing.
- 39 (5⅞") squares. Cut each square in half diagonally to get 77 A triangles (and 1 extra).
- 39 (3½") squares. Cut each square in half diagonally to get 77 C triangles (and 1 extra).
- 77 of Pattern D.
- 77 of Pattern D reversed.

From red check

- 6 (1½" x 80") lengthwise strips for sashing.
- 154 (4½") squares. Cut each square in half diagonally to get 308 corner triangles.

From scraps

- 39 (3½") squares. Cut each square in half diagonally to get 77 C triangles (and 1 extra).
- 77 (2⅛") squares. Cut each square in half diagonally to get 154 E triangles.
- 77 of Pattern B. Add seam allowance around template when cutting Bs.

Block Assembly

1. For each block, select 1 each of muslin A, C, D, and D rev. From scraps, select 2 E triangles and 1 each of B handle and C triangle. Scrap fabrics can be uniform in each block like quilt shown or you can mix scraps as desired.
2. Turn under the seam allowance on B curves. Leave the seam allowance unturned at the bottom straight ends.
3. Fold A triangle in half and crease to mark center. Fold B in same manner. Center B on A triangle, matching centers and aligning straight edges (Block Assembly Diagram). Appliqué B onto A. Press.
4. Stitch E triangles onto straight ends of Ds and Ds rev. Press seam allowances toward triangles.
5. Sew D/E units onto short legs of C scrap triangle as shown. Press seam allowances toward C.
6. Join muslin C triangle to bottom of basket unit as shown. Press the seam allowance toward C triangle.
7. Join 2 halves of basket. Press seam allowance toward A triangle.
8. Sew 1 corner triangle to 2 opposite sides of block. Press seam

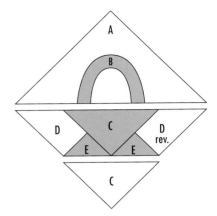

Block Assembly Diagram

allowances toward triangles. Add triangles to remaining opposite corners to complete block.
9. Make 77 basket blocks.

Quilt Assembly

1. Lay out blocks in 7 vertical rows, with 11 blocks in each row. Arrange blocks to achieve pleasing balance of color and value. When satisfied with placement, join blocks in each row.
2. Stitch each check sashing strip between 2 muslin strips. Make 6 muslin/check/muslin sashings. Press seams toward check.
3. Join block rows with sashing

Size Variations			
	Full	**Queen**	**King**
Finished size	77" x 91"	87" x 98"	97" x 98"
Number of blocks	104	124	140
Block rows	8	9	10
Blocks per row	13	14	14
Sashing rows	7	8	9
Yardage Required			
Muslin	4½ yards	5¼ yards	5½ yards
Red check	4½ yards	5½ yards	5¼ yards
⅛ yard pieces	18	21	24
Binding fabric	⅞ yard	1 yard	1 yard
Backing fabric (104" wide)	2⅜ yards	2⅝ yards	3 yards

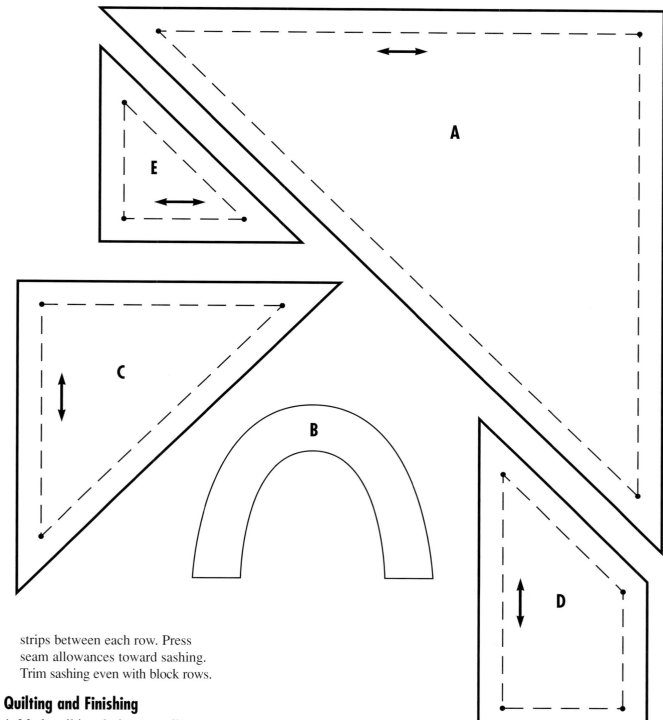

strips between each row. Press
seam allowances toward sashing.
Trim sashing even with block rows.

Quilting and Finishing

1. Mark quilting design on quilt
   top as desired. Quilt shown is
   outline-quilted.
2. Layer backing, batting, and quilt
   top. Baste. Quilt as desired.
3. Make 8¼ yards of straight-grain
   or bias binding from remaining
   muslin. Bind quilt edges.

TULIP GARDEN WEDDING

Quilt by Elsie M. Campbell of Montrose, Pennsylvania

This lovely quilt was born out of a class Elsie Campbell taught on making Double Wedding Ring quilts. She made a small sample for the class, but she liked it so much that she had to make it a full-size quilt. Elsie added red tulips appliqués at the request of a friend so he could make the quilt an anniversary gift for his wife. Elsie's beautiful trapuntoed quilting makes this quilt a real standout.

Finished Size
Quilt: 84" x 84"
Blocks: 88 (4½" x 10") partial rings

Materials
20 (18" x 22") fat quarters of assorted solids fabrics for arcs
½ yard *each* dark red, medium red, and dark green for appliqué
4½ yards mint (includes binding)
4½ yards white or muslin
2½ yards 90"-wide backing fabric
10 yards ¹⁄₁₆"-diameter soft cording for piping
Stuffing for trapunto (optional)

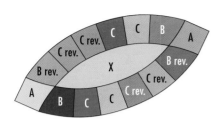

Partial Ring—Make 88.

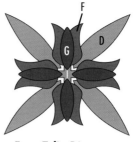

Partial Ring Assembly Diagram

Four-Tulip Diagram

Cutting

Make templates of patterns A, B, C, X, and Y for piecing and patterns D–I for appliqué (pages 184 and 185). Cut pieces in order listed to get best use of yardage.

From each solid fat quarter
- 7 (2½" x 22") strips to get a total of 126 strips. Mixing fabrics together, from these, cut:
  —184 of Pattern A.
  —176 of Pattern B.
  —176 of Pattern B reversed.
  —352 of Pattern C.
  —352 of Pattern C reversed.

From dark green
- 76 of Pattern D (leaf).
- 4 of Pattern E (partial stem).
- 16 of Pattern H (half stem).
- 5 of Pattern I (complete stem).

From dark red
- 56 of Pattern F.

From medium red
- 56 of Pattern G.

From mint
- 1 yard for binding.
- 4 (6½" x 90") lengthwise strips for outer border.
- 48 of Pattern X.
- 16 of Pattern Y.

From white
- 9 (1"-wide) strips for piping.
- 2 (31¾") squares. Cut squares in half diagonally to get 4 Z triangles.
- 4 (8" x 90") lengthwise strips for appliqué border.
- 40 of Pattern X.
- 9 of Pattern Y.

Partial Ring Assembly

1. For each partial ring, join 1 B rev., 2 Cs rev., 2 Cs, 1 B, and 1 A into arc as shown (Partial Ring Assembly Diagram). For second arc, join A, B, 2 Cs, 2 Cs rev., and 1 B rev.
2. Sew both arcs to opposite sides of X piece (Partial Ring Diagram). Stitch seams to join As to B rev. of opposite arc. Press seam allowances away from X.
3. Complete 48 partial rings with green Xs and 40 with white Xs.

Appliqué

1. Center an I piece on a white Y. Pin 4 Fs and 4 Gs in place on each spoke of I stem (Four-Tulip Diagram). Tuck 4 Ds under tulips. When satisfied with placement, appliqué pieces in place. Make 5 four-tulip blocks.
2. Lay out partial rings, four-tulip blocks, remaining Ys, and 4 Z triangles (Quilt Assembly Diagram). Starting at center, join rings to adjacent Ys to form circles as
continued

Quilt Assembly Diagram

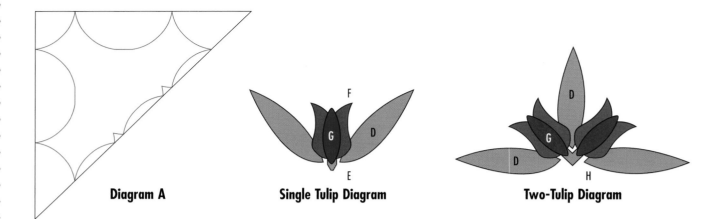

Diagram A **Single Tulip Diagram** **Two-Tulip Diagram**

shown, stitching mitered seams to join adjacent rings. Set in 8 A pieces to outside edge of center unit as shown.

3. Join outer segments surrounding each Z triangle. Appliqué edges of surrounding arcs to each Z triangle (Diagram A).

Borders

1. With right sides facing, layer 2 white border strips (Diagram B). Use acrylic ruler to measure 45° angle and mark sewing line from corner to edge of strips. Stitch through both strips on marked line. Trim excess fabric as shown. Repeat with second pair of strips. Press seam allowances to 1 side or open, as desired (Diagram C).

2. With the right sides facing, layer both sections (Diagram D). Stitch 45°-angle seams as before.

3. Unfold window border and press (Diagram E).

4. Center pieced quilt over window border. Appliqué outer edges of circle segments to white border. (Y template can be used as guide here.)

5. Pin 1 each of E, F, and G at each mitered corner seam. Tuck Ds under tulip as shown (Single Tulip Diagram). Then pin 4 two-tulip units on each outside edge (Two-Tulip Diagram). When satisfied with placement, appliqué each tulip section in place.

6. When your appliqué work is complete, carefully trim any excess white fabric from behind rings, leaving at least ¼" seam allowance.

7. Center 1 green border strip on each edge and stitch borders to quilt, mitering corners.

Quilting and Finishing

1. Mark quilting design as desired. Quilt shown has cross-hatching behind quilted feather plumes, hearts, and lovebirds, which are trapuntoed for added dimension. Design quilting motifs or look for commercial stencils that fit these areas.

2. Layer the backing, batting, and quilt top. Then baste together. Quilt as desired.

3. Join 1"-wide white strips end to end in continuous strip. With wrong sides facing and raw edges together, fold strip over cording. Use zipper foot (or equivalent) to stitch close to cording. With raw edges aligned, baste piping to outer edge of quilt.

4. Make 10 yards of continuous bias or straight-grain binding. Bind quilt edges.

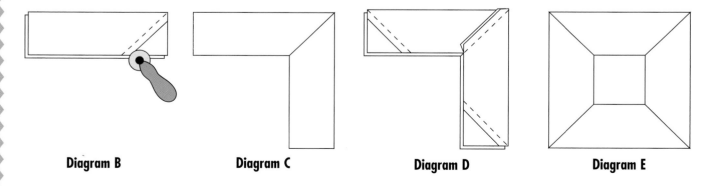

Diagram B **Diagram C** **Diagram D** **Diagram E**

continued

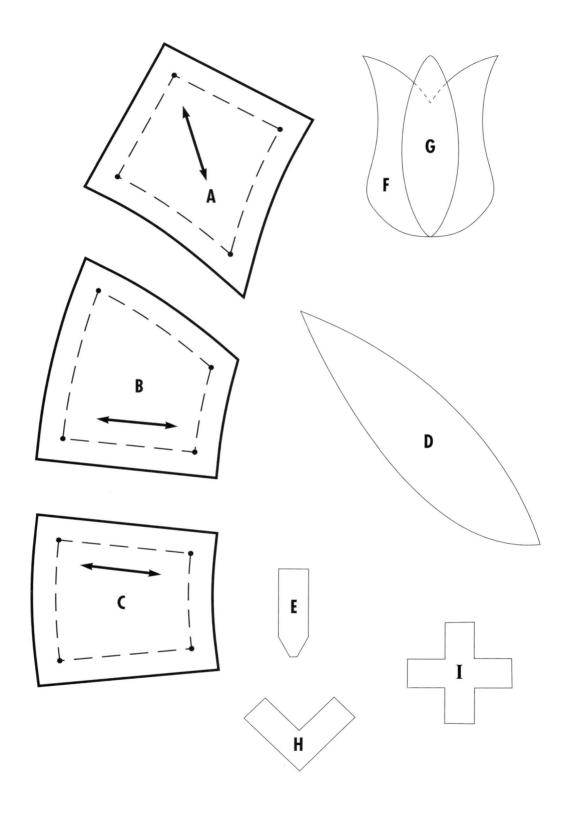

A

B

C

D

E

F

G

H

I

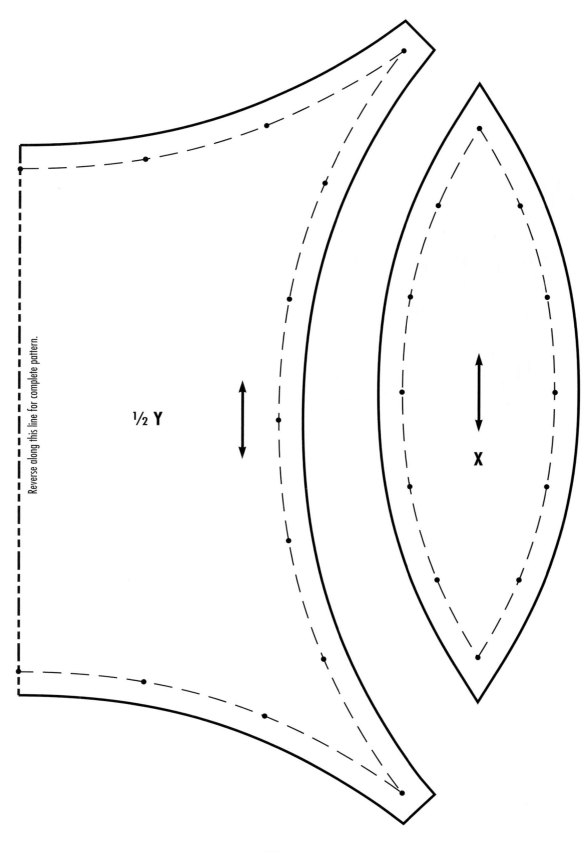

½ **Y**

Reverse along this line for complete pattern.

X

STRING SQUARES

Quilt by Carole Collins of Galien, Michigan

Waste not want not, as the saying goes. String piecing can be a scrap-saver's favorite technique because it helps a quilt-maker use up the narrowest of leftover fabrics. Join strips to create new "fabric" from which pieces are cut. This quilt uses different fabrics and strip widths to get a terrific look. The muted colors are an autumn harvest of pumpkin, cinnamon, maple leaf red, and goldenrod. A mix of print and plaid fabrics balances light, medium, and dark values.

Finished Size
Quilt: 65" x 77"
Blocks: 20 (12¼" x 12¼")

Materials
14 (18" x 22") fat quarters or
    equivalent scraps
¾ yard fabric for inner border
2 yards fabric for outer border
⅞ yard binding fabric
4 yards backing fabric

String Squares Block — Make 20.

Quarter-Block Unit — Make 80.

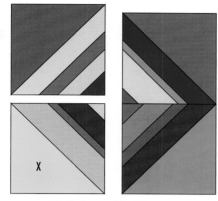

Block Assembly Diagram

Block Assembly

Instructions are for rotary cutting. Cut all strips on crosswise grain. For traditional cutting, use pattern on page 189.

1. From fabric for outer border, cut 4 (6½"-wide) lengthwise strips. Set these aside for border. Then add the remaining fabric to the scraps.

2. From the assorted scraps, cut 40 (7") squares. Cut each square in half diagonally to get 80 X triangles. Then set the triangles aside.

3. From the remaining fabrics, cut 27 strips about 21" long in 4 strip widths: 1¼" wide, 1½" wide, 1¾" wide, and 2" wide. Cut a total of 108 strips. (It's a good idea to cut some strips on the bias. When string-pieced triangles are cut from strip sets, most cut edges will be bias. But if the original cut strip is bias, then the cut edge will be straight grain. Mixing grain direction will reduce the danger of distortion when working with string-pieced triangles.)

4. Select 1 strip of each width. Join these 4 strips lengthwise—in any order you please—to make 1 strip set. The width of the assembled strip set should be 5". (If you use more strips or strips of different widths, make sure the finished strip set is 5" wide, including seam allowances at the outside edges.) Make 27 strip sets, each made up of a different combination of fabrics. Press the seam allowances in each strip set in the same direction.

5. Using acrylic ruler, align 45°-angle marking with bottom of 1 strip set to establish 45° angle. Rotary-cut 3 X triangles from the strip set as shown (Cutting Diagram). Repeat with the remaining strip sets to get a total of 80 string-pieced triangles.

6. Join each string-pieced triangle with solid triangle to get quarter-block unit. Make 80 units as shown. On 40 units, press seam allowances toward solid triangle; on remaining units, press toward pieced triangle.

7. Select 4 quarter-block units for each block. Join the blocks in pairs (Block Assembly Diagram). Then join the pairs to complete the block.

8. Make 20 blocks.

continued

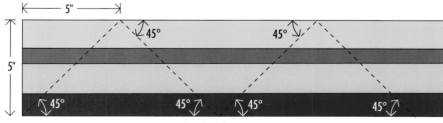

Cutting Diagram

Quilt Assembly

1. For each horizontal row, lay out 4 blocks as shown (Row Assembly Diagram). Lay out 5 rows. Arrange blocks to get pleasing balance of color and value. When satisfied with placement, join blocks in each row.
2. Referring to photo on page 186, join rows.

Borders

1. From inner border fabric, cut 8 (2½"-wide) crosswise strips. Join 2 strips end to end to make each border.
2. Measure the quilt from the top to the bottom through the middle of the pieced top and trim the side borders to match the length. Sew the borders to the quilt sides.
3. Measure the quilt from side to side through the middle of the pieced top and trim the remaining borders to match the quilt width. Sew the borders to the top and bottom edges of the quilt.
4. Repeat steps 2 and 3 to sew outer border to quilt.

Quilting and Finishing

1. Mark quilting design on quilt top as desired. Quilt shown is outline-quilted.
2. Layer backing, batting, and quilt top. Backing seams will parallel top and bottom edges of quilt. Then baste them together. Quilt as desired.
3. Make 8¼ yards of straight-grain or bias binding. Bind the quilt edges.

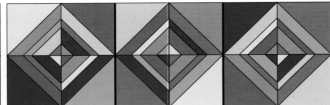

Row Assembly Diagram

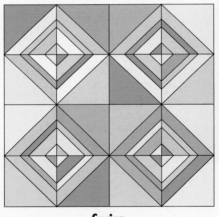

Winter

Color Variations

Carole Collins's quilt artfully displays the colors of autumn. Here are suggestions for *String Squares* in exciting color schemes for winter, spring, and summer.

Spring

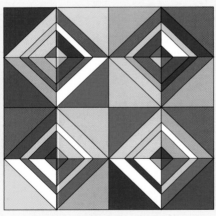

Summer

Size Variations

	Full	Queen	King
Finished size	77" x 89½"	89½" x 102"	102" x 102"
Number of blocks	30	42	49
Blocks set	5 x 6	6 x 7	7 x 7

Yardage Required

	Full	Queen	King
Fat quarters	22	30	37
Inner border fabric	¾ yard	¾ yard	¾ yard
Outer border fabric	2¼ yards	2⅝ yards	3 yards
Binding fabric	⅞ yard	⅞ yard	1 yard
Backing fabric	5½ yards	8¼ yards	9½ yards

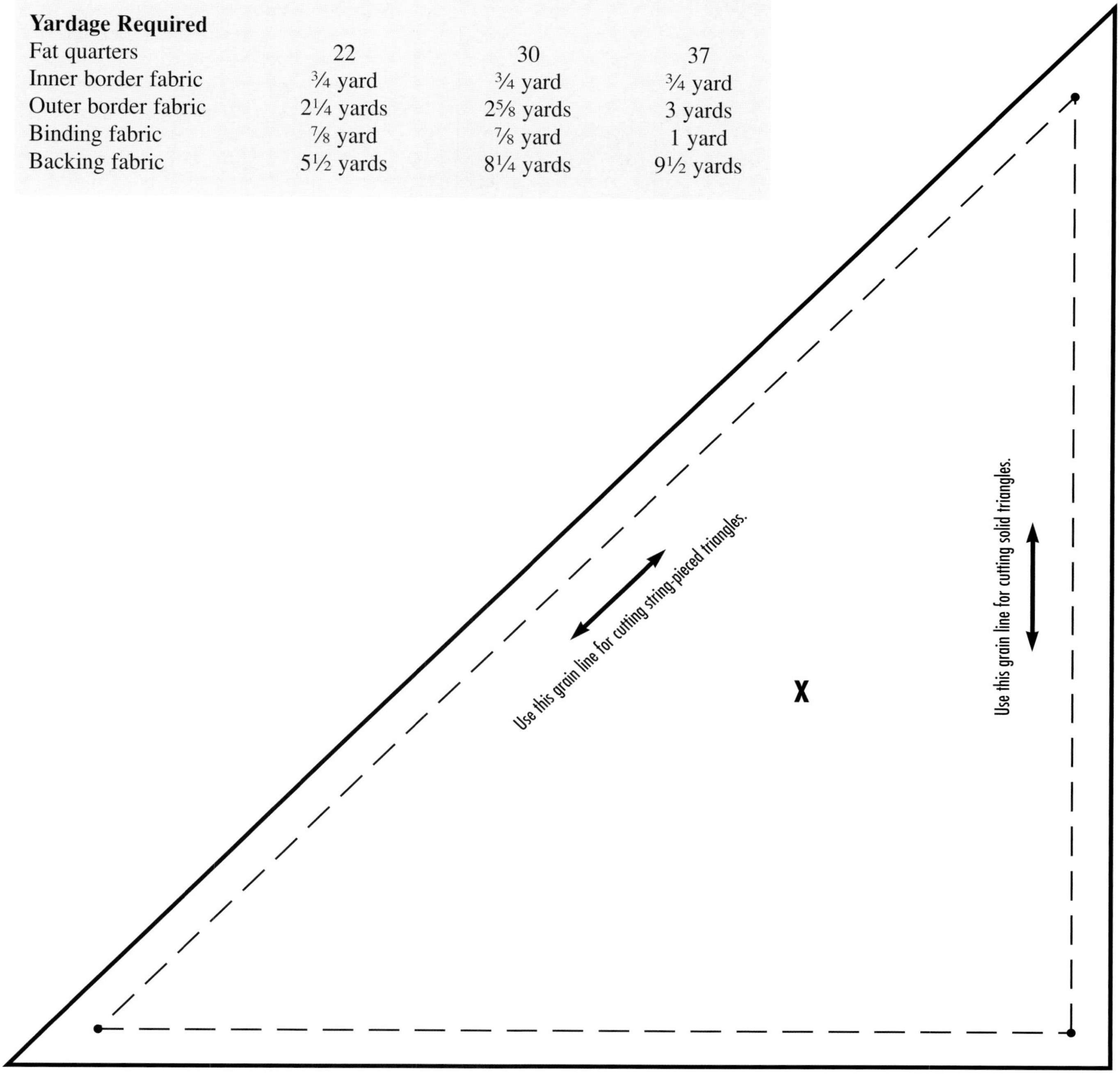

Use this grain line for cutting string-pieced triangles.

Use this grain line for cutting solid triangles.

X

DRESDEN ON THE HALF SHELL

Quilt by Bette Lee Collins of Red Bluff, California

A friend gave Bette Lee Collins a stack of 1930s Dresden Plate blocks. Bette appliquéd the yellow centers and created this scrappy setting and border with authentic 1930s fabrics. "The half-shell (or clamshell) quilting seemed to give the quilt a continuous motion that I liked," says Bette. She combined the block name and the quilting pattern name to title her quilt.

Finished Size
Quilt: 70" x 87"
Blocks: 12 (15" x 15")

Materials
24 (18" x 22") fat quarters assorted prints for blocks and borders (approximately 5 yards total)
⅛ yard green for stems
¼ yard yellow for sashing squares and appliqué
4¾ yards white for background
¾ yard binding fabric
5½ yards backing fabric
¼"-wide bias pressing bars (optional)

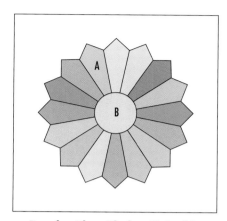

Dresden Plate Block—Make 12.

Cutting

Cut all strips on crosswise grain except as noted. Make templates for patterns A and B, leaf, small circle, small posy, medium posy, and large posy on page 193.

From assorted prints
- 192 As.
- 136 (2½" x 4¼") C rectangles for sashing and borders.
- 74 (2½" x 4½") D rectangles. Be sure to keep C and D rectangles separate. (You might put each group in a labeled zip-top plastic bag until needed.)
- 128 leaves.
- 4 large posies.
- 22 medium posies.
- 18 small posies.

From green plaid
- 4 (⅞"-wide) strips. Fold strips in thirds so they are approximately ¼"-wide and press (use bias bars for pressing, if desired). Cut strips into 14 (9"-long) stems.

From yellow
- 12 Bs.
- 22 small circles for posy centers.
- 6 (2½") sashing squares.

From white
- 2 (7" x 72") lengthwise strips for side borders and 2 (7" x 68") lengthwise strips for top and bottom borders.
- 12 (15½") background squares.

Block Assembly

1. Join 16 A pieces to make circle. Baste under ¼" seam allowance around outer edge.
2. Fold and crease the background squares in half horizontally, vertically, and diagonally to make appliqué guidelines. Pin pieced circle on background square, aligning points of A pieces with creased guidelines.
3. Baste under ¼" seam allowance around edges of B piece. Center B on A circle. Appliqué A and B to background. Make 12 blocks (Dresden Plate Block Diagram).
4. Turn block over. Carefully trim background fabric behind A and B, leaving ¼" seam allowance.

Quilt Assembly

1. Join 4 C pieces to make sashing strip. Make 17 sashing strips.
2. Lay out 4 horizontal rows, with 3 blocks and 2 sashing strips in each row (Quilt Assembly Diagram). Join units in each row. Press seam allowances toward blocks.
3. Join 3 sashing strips and 2 yellow squares to make each sashing row as shown. Make 3 sashing rows.
4. Join block rows and sashing rows to complete quilt center.

continued

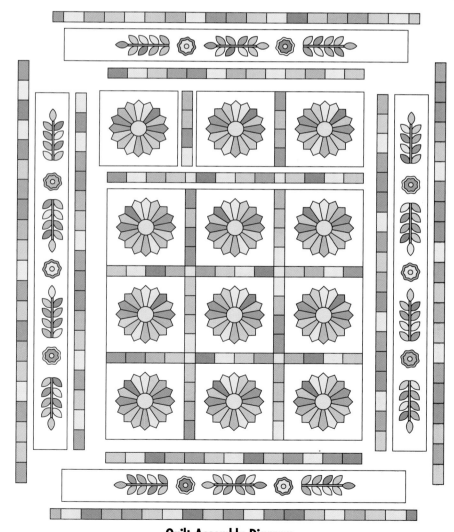

Quilt Assembly Diagram

Borders

1. For top inner border, join 12 C pieces and 1 D piece. Join to top edge of quilt, easing to fit as needed. Repeat for bottom border.

2. For each side border, join 8 C pieces and 10 Ds. Sew borders to quilt sides, easing to fit as needed.

3. Measure length of quilt through middle of pieced top. Trim longer white border strips to match length. Sew these to quilt sides, easing to fit. Press seam

Border Corner Diagram

allowances toward borders. Measure the width of the quilt, and then trim remaining white strips to match width. Sew borders to top and bottom edges of the quilt.

4. At each border corner, appliqué 1 large posy (Border Corner Diagram). Appliqué medium posy on top; then add small circle.

5. Appliqué medium posies at sides of each large posy as shown. Add small posy on top of each medium posy; then add small circle.

6. Center remaining medium posies on white borders in line with sashing strips (Quilt Assembly Diagram, page 191). Appliqué posies in place; then add small posies and small circles on each.

7. Center stems and leaves between medium posies as shown. Note different position of leaves at center top and center bottom. When satisfied with placement, appliqué pieces to borders.

8. For each side border, join 4 C pieces and 17 D pieces. Sew borders to quilt sides, easing to fit.

9. For top border, join 10 C pieces and 9 Ds. Center border at top edge and trim ends to match quilt width. Sew border to top edge of quilt. Repeat for bottom border.

Quilting and Finishing

1. Mark quilting designs on quilt top as desired. Quilt shown is outline-quilted in fans and around appliqué. Blocks are filled with a clamshell design. Appliquéd border is outline-quilted with echo quilting around posies. Outer border has a scallop pattern in each rectangle.

2. Layer backing, batting, and quilt top. Baste. Quilt as desired.

3. Make 9 yards of straight-grain binding. Bind quilt edges.

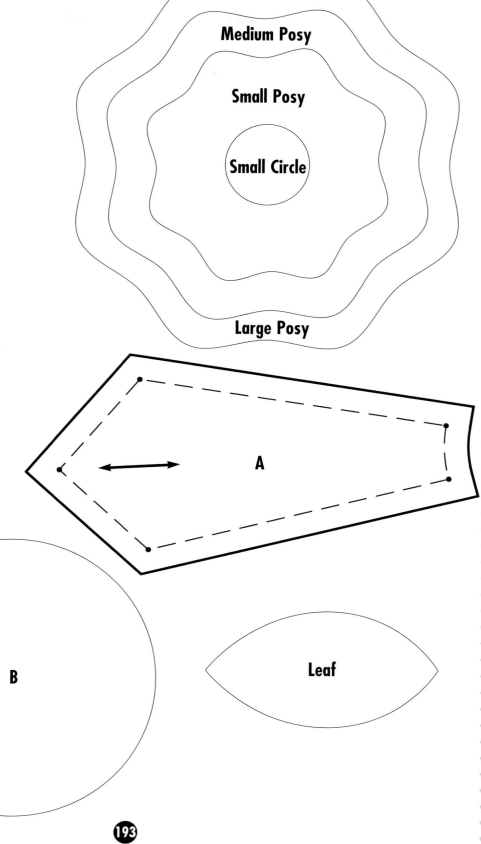

Medium Posy

Small Posy

Small Circle

Large Posy

A

B

Leaf

KALEIDOSCOPE

The careful placement of light and dark fabrics creates the kaleidoscopic effect of this quilt. Surrounded by light fabrics that seem to recede, the dark fabrics advance in bursts of color against halos of light. This quilt is a patchwork of plaids, but you can achieve a similar effect with other fabrics.

Finished Size

Quilt: 51½" x 66"
Blocks: 48 (7¼" x 7¼")

Materials

24 (4½" x 10") dark scraps
48 (4½" x 10") medium/dark scraps
24 (4½" x 10") light scraps
4 (5" x 9") fabrics for border appliqué (optional)
48 (3" x 6") light scraps
2 yards border fabric
¾ yard binding fabric
3⅜ yards backing fabric

Quilt by Peggy Ann Taggart of Whitewater, Wisconsin

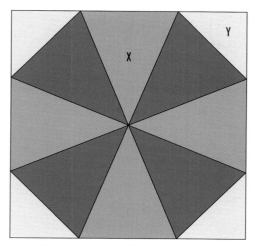

Kaleidoscope Block A—Make 24.

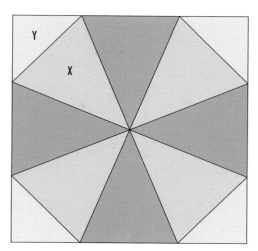

Kaleidoscope Block B—Make 24.

Block Assembly

Two blocks alternate to create the kaleidoscope look of this quilt. Block A uses dark and medium colors that dominate the overall design. Block B uses medium/dark and light colors. Both blocks are assembled in the same manner.

For traditional cutting, make templates of patterns X and Y on page 197.

1. For Block A, select dark fabric and medium fabric. Cut 4 X triangles from each fabric. For rotary cutting, see Cutting Diagram.
2. Join contrasting color triangles in pairs (Block Assembly Diagram).
3. Join 2 pairs of triangles for half-block; join half-blocks. Press seam allowances toward dark triangles.
4. From 1 (3" x 6") light fabric, cut 2 (3") squares. Cut squares in half

diagonally to get 4 Y triangles. Sew 1 Y to end of each dark X to complete block. Make 24 of Block A.
5. Make Block B in same manner. Use 4 X triangles of medium/dark fabric and 4 X triangles of light fabric. Sew Y triangles to ends of light X triangles. Make 24 of Block B.

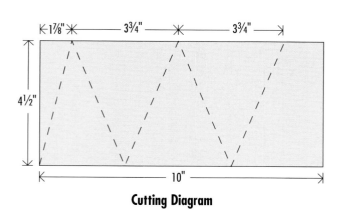

Cutting Diagram

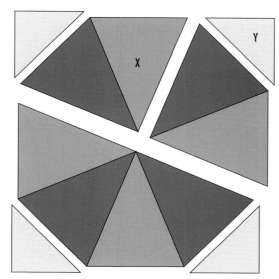

Block Assembly Diagram

continued

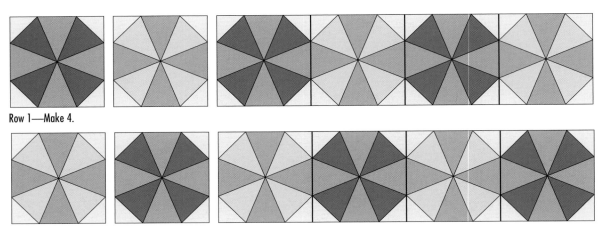

Row 1—Make 4.

Row 2—Make 4.

Row Assembly Diagram

Quilt Assembly

1. Lay out 8 horizontal rows of 6 blocks each, alternating A and B blocks as shown (Row Assembly Diagram). Lay out 4 of Row 1, starting with A block; lay out 4 of Row 2, starting with B block. Rearrange as needed to achieve balance of color and contrast.
2. When satisfied with placement, join blocks in each row.
3. Join rows, alternating rows as shown in photo on page 194.

Border

1. From border fabric, cut 4 (4¼" x 72") lengthwise strips. Measure quilt through middle and trim border strips to fit as needed.
2. For embellishments, cut 8 (1½" x 6½") bias strips from remaining fabrics. Turn under ¼" seam allowances on long sides of each strip and press. Appliqué strips onto borders as desired.
3. Sew borders to quilt and miter the corners (see page 309).

Quilting and Finishing

1. Mark quilting design on pieced top as desired. Quilt shown has outline quilting in patchwork. Straight-line quilting parallels appliquéd embellishments in the borders.
2. Layer backing, batting, and quilt top. Backing seams will parallel top and bottom edges. Baste. Quilt as desired.
3. Make 7 yards of bias or straight-grain binding. Bind quilt edges.

Size Variations

	Twin	Full/Queen	King
Finished size	66" x 95"	80½" x 95"	95" x 95"
Number of			
A Blocks	48	60	72
B Blocks	48	60	72
Blocks set	8 x 12	10 x 12	12 x 12
Yardage Required			
Dark scraps	48	60	72
Medium/dark scraps	96	120	144
Light scraps	48	60	72
3" x 6" light scraps	96	120	144
Border fabric	2¾ yards	2¾ yards	2¾ yards
Binding fabric	⅞ yard	1 yard	1 yard
Backing fabric	5⅜ yards	5⅞ yards	8¾ yards

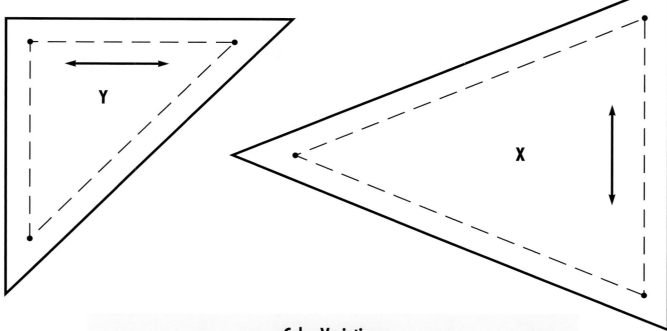

Color Variations

Changing the placement of light and dark fabrics can have as much impact on the effect of this design as the colors you choose.

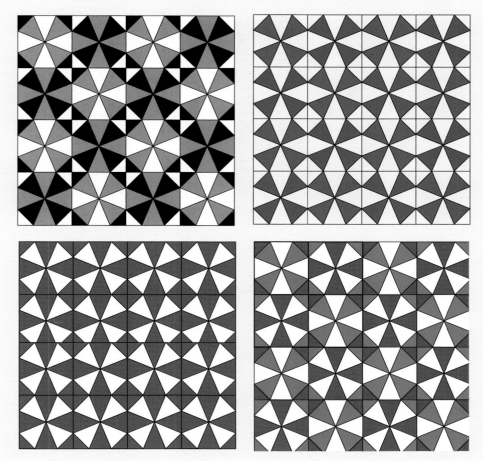

FUNKY CHICKEN

Quilt by Freddy Moran of Orinda, California

The class assignment was to create an original design based on a natural theme. To Freddy Moran's surprise, her imagination hatched this chicken block. "I've no idea how I arrived at this," she says, "but I love the whimsy of it." The blocks make a fun border for Painted Daisy blocks, which Freddy found in Ruth McDowell's book *Symmetry*. When she saw the pattern, Freddy says, "I knew my chickens had found a place to roost."

Finished Size
Quilt: 80" x 86"
Blocks: 40 (5" x 8") chicken blocks
9 (14" x 14") Painted Daisy blocks
28 (6⅛" x 7⅞") daisy quarter-blocks

Materials
2⅜ yards white fabric for border
¾ yard *each* 4 white or beige prints
¾ yard red stripe fabric *
⅝ yard red for chicken combs
¼ yard orange for beak
¼ yard *each* 16 plaids for daisies
¼ yard *each* 2 brown prints
¼ yard *each* 10 prints for chicken backgrounds
¼ yard black-on-white print
20 (4" x 15") scraps for chickens
10 (6") squares gold for chicken feet
⅞ yard binding fabric
2⅝ yards 90"-wide backing fabric
* *Note:* Yardage is for pieced borders. To cut lengthwise borders, you need 2¼ yards.

Cutting

Cut strips on crosswise grain except as noted. Make templates for A–J on pages 202 and 203. Cutting and piecing instructions for other pieces are for rotary cutting and quick piecing. Cut pieces in order listed.

From white fabric
• 4 (4¼" x 84") border strips.
Note: Use remainder for piecing, if desired.

From each white/beige print
• 16 of Pattern A.
• 16 of Pattern C.
• 16 of Pattern D.
• 16 of Pattern G.
• 16 of Pattern I.
• 16 of Pattern F.

From red
• 1 (12"-wide) strip. From this and remaining fabric, cut 10 (6" x 12") pieces for chicken comb triangle-squares.

From orange
• 20 (2⅝") squares. Cut squares in half diagonally to get 40 P triangles.

From each plaid
• 4 of Pattern B.
• 4 of Pattern E.
• 4 of Pattern H.

From brown print 1
• 64 of Pattern J.

From brown print 2
• 25 (2½") L squares.

From each chicken background fabric (Makes 4 blocks.)
• 1 (6" x 12") piece for comb N triangle-squares.
• 1 (6") square for feet N triangle-squares.
• 2 (2⅝") squares. Cut squares in half diagonally to get 4 P triangles, 1 for each block.
• 8 (1½" x 5½") O pieces, 2 for each block.
• 12 (1½") Q squares, 3 for each block.
• 4 (1½") squares for N diagonal-corners, 1 for each block.
• 2 (1½" x 8½") strips for border spacers (cut from only 4 fabrics to get a total of 8).

From black-on-white print
• 16 (2½" x 6⅜") K pieces.
From each chicken scrap (Makes 2 blocks.)
• 2 (3½" x 4½") M pieces, 1 for each block.
• 2 (2½") L squares, 1 for each block.

Painted Daisy Block Assembly

1. For each quarter-block unit, select 1 each of B, E, and H from same fabric (Diagram A). Choose 1 each of pieces A, C, D, F, G, and I, mixing background fabrics as desired.
2. Working in alphabetical order, join pieces in 3 sections as shown. Join each section. Set in 1 J piece to complete quarter-block unit. Make 4 identical

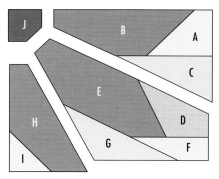

Diagram A

quarter-block units for each daisy, total of 64 units (16 sets of 4).
3. Sew brown L squares to 1 end of each K strip.
4. Lay out units in rows, matching fabrics and rotating units to form daisies (Quilt Assembly Diagram).

continued

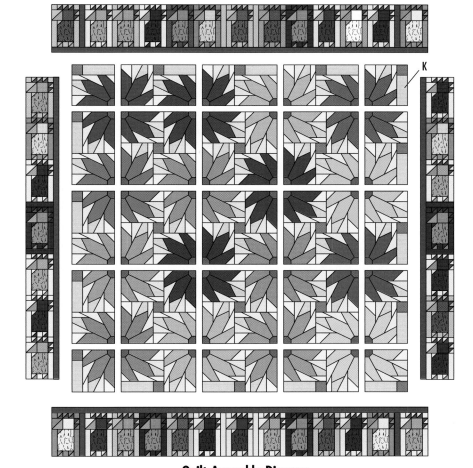

Quilt Assembly Diagram

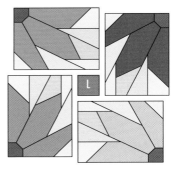

Daisy Block Assembly Diagram

5. Sew 1 K/L unit to 5 quarter-blocks in top row as shown. Press seam allowances toward K/L. Then join units in top row, being sure to check position against diagram. Repeat for bottom row.
6. For second row, join 1 K/L unit to quarter-blocks at each end as shown; then join 2 quarter-blocks to make each end unit.
7. Each Painted Daisy block has 4 quarter-blocks of different fabric sewn around L square. To begin, stitch L to bottom of top left unit (Daisy Block Assembly Diagram), matching corners as shown, but do not complete seam; stop sewing about halfway down length of L. Add top right unit, stitching complete seam. Add bottom right unit in same manner; then join bottom left unit. When all 4 units are sewn to L, complete first unit seam to edge of block.
8. Make 8 more daisy blocks in same manner. Return each completed block to quilt layout to check for correct placement and alignment of matching fabrics in adjacent blocks.
9. When blocks are complete, join blocks and end units in each row.

Chicken Block Assembly

1. On wrong side of each 6" x 12" background piece, draw 2-square by 5-square grid of 1⅞" squares, leaving 1" margin on all sides (Diagram B). Draw diagonal lines through each square as shown.
2. With right sides facing, match each marked piece with 1 (6" x 12") piece of red fabric. Stitch ¼" seam on both sides of diagonal lines. (Red lines on diagram show first continuous stitching path; blue lines show second path.) Press.
3. Cut on all drawn lines to get 20 comb triangle-squares, 5 for each of 4 blocks.
4. On wrong side of each 6" square of background fabric, draw a 2-square by 2-square grid of 1⅞" squares (Diagram C). Draw diagonal lines through each square as shown. With right sides facing, match each marked piece with 1 (6") square of gold fabric. Stitch grid as before. Press. Cut on drawn lines to get 8 triangle-squares for feet, 2 for each of 4 blocks.
5. For each block, select 1 L/M set and 1 orange P triangle. Then choose 5 comb triangle-squares, 2 feet triangle-squares, 1 P triangle, 2 O strips, 3 Q squares, and 1 N diagonal-corner square, all with same background fabric.
6. See tips on diagonal-corner quick-piecing technique on page 304. Follow those instructions to sew N square to 1 corner of M (Chicken Block Assembly Diagram).
7. Join P triangles as shown. Stitch P square to 1 side of L. Join 2

comb triangle-squares as shown and join to opposite side of L. Press seam allowances toward L. (On the quilt shown, some combs are turned this way and that for added charm.)
8. Sew 3 comb triangle-squares and 2 Qs in a row as shown. Press seam allowances toward Qs. Stitch row to top of head unit.
9. Join 1 Q and 2 feet triangle-squares in row. Sew feet to bottom of M. Press seam allowances toward M. Then sew O strips to unit sides as shown. Press seam allowances toward Os.
10. Join head and body units to complete block.
11. Make 40 chicken blocks.

Borders

1. Cut 16 (1½"-wide) strips from red stripe. Join pairs of strips end to end to assemble borders.
2. For each side border, select 7 chicken blocks, including 1 block in each row that matches pair of spacer strips. Sew spacers to top and bottom edges of matching block, trimming strips to fit. Press seam allowances toward spacers.
3. Join 7 blocks in vertical row (Quilt Assembly Diagram), placing spacer block in middle of row.

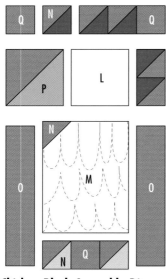

Chicken Block Assembly Diagram

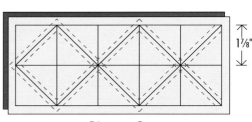

Diagram B

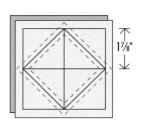

Diagram C

4. Matching centers, sew red border strip to the inside edge of each chicken row. Trim excess fabric from border ends. (Save scraps for top and bottom borders.) Sew borders to quilt sides, easing to fit as needed.

5. For top border, select 13 chicken blocks, including 1 with matching spacer strips. Sew spacers to both sides of block and then join 11 blocks in horizontal row, with spacer block at center (Quilt Assembly Diagram, page 199). From red border scraps, cut 2 (1½" x 8½") pieces and sew 1 piece to each end of the row. Join the remaining chicken blocks to row ends as shown.

6. Matching centers, sew red border strip to inside edge of chicken row. Trim excess fabric from ends of border. Sew border to top edge of quilt, easing to fit as needed.

7. Repeat steps 5 and 6 for bottom border.

8. Sew 2 red borders to quilt sides. Trim excess fabric. Join red borders to top and bottom edges of quilt in same manner.

9. Measure length of quilt through middle of top. Trim 2 white borders to this measurement. Sew border strips to sides, easing to fit. Measure width through middle, including side borders. Trim remaining strips to fit and stitch to top and bottom edges.

Quilting and Finishing

1. Mark pieced top with desired quilting design. On quilt shown, a hexagon pattern is quilted over daisies to look like chicken wire. Chicken blocks have quilted feathers, and more chickens are quilted in white borders. Patterns for hexagon and chicken designs are on page 203. For feathers, mark irregular scallops.

2. Layer backing, batting, and quilt top. Baste. Quilt chicken blocks in-the-ditch. Quilt remainder of quilt as marked or as desired.

3. Make 9½ yards of continuous bias or straight grain binding. Bind quilt edges.

continued

201

J

C

E

H

D

I

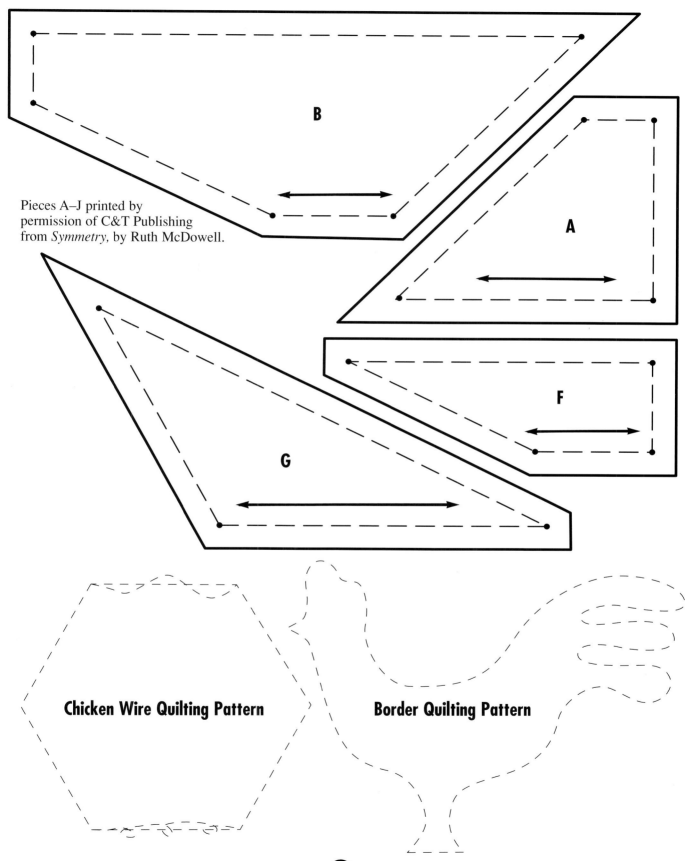

Pieces A–J printed by
permission of C&T Publishing
from *Symmetry,* by Ruth McDowell.

B

A

F

G

Chicken Wire Quilting Pattern

Border Quilting Pattern

SPIRAL FEATHERED STAR

Antique quilt owned by Becky Herdle of Rochester, New York

Lovers of exceptional piecing will find two challenges in these spinning wheels: curved seams and precise, narrow points. Enjoy working with scraps to produce a contemporary version of this 1940s vintage quilt.

Finished Size
Quilt: 69" x 80½"
Blocks: 42 (11½" x 11½")

Materials
5½ yards muslin
42 (¼-yard) print fabrics or scraps
¾ yard binding fabric
4¼ yards backing fabric or 2⅛ yards 90"-wide backing

Cutting
See page 302 for tips on making templates for piecing. Window templates are recommended to mark seam lines on wrong side of each piece. Make templates of patterns A–E on page 206.
From muslin
• 252 of Pattern A.
• 504 of Pattern C.
• 42 of Pattern E.
From scraps
• 252 of Pattern A.
• 504 of Pattern B.
• 168 of Pattern D.

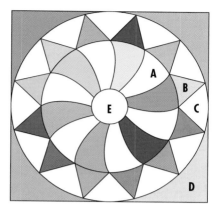

Spiral Feathered Star Block—Make 42.

Diagram A

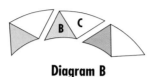

Diagram B

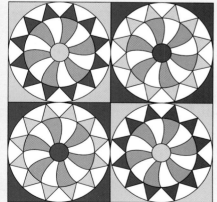

Block Assembly Diagram

Block Assembly

See page 114 for tips on stitching a curved seam. Refer to Block Assembly Diagram throughout.

1. Select 6 scrap A pieces for each block. Sew each piece to 1 muslin A (Diagram A). Press seam allowances toward scraps.
2. Join A pairs to make inner circle.
3. Select 12 each of pieces B and C. Stitch B/C pairs (Diagram B). Press seam allowances toward Cs.
4. Join B/C pairs to make outer circle.
5. With right sides facing, pin A circle to B/C circle. Clip seam allowances if necessary. Stitch circles together. Press.
6. Add 4 Ds to the outside edges of block, carefully following drawn seam line on wrong side of each piece. Press seam allowances toward Ds.
7. Piece or appliqué E over A seam allowances at block center.
8. Make 42 Spiral Feathered Star blocks.

Quilt Assembly

1. Referring to photo, join blocks in 7 horizontal rows of 6 blocks each.
2. Join rows.

Quilting and Finishing

1. Mark quilting design as desired. Quilt shown is outline-quilted.
2. Layer backing, batting, and quilt top. Baste. Quilt as desired.
3. Make 8½ yards of binding. Bind the quilt edges.

continued

Color Variations

These ideas show how the color and value of the fabrics you use create different kinds of swirling stars.

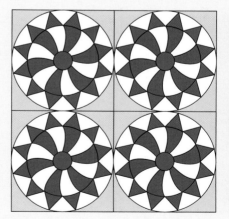

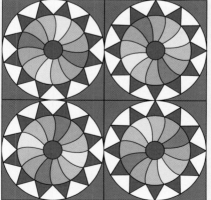

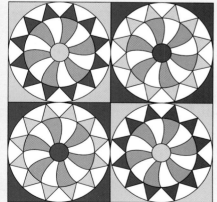

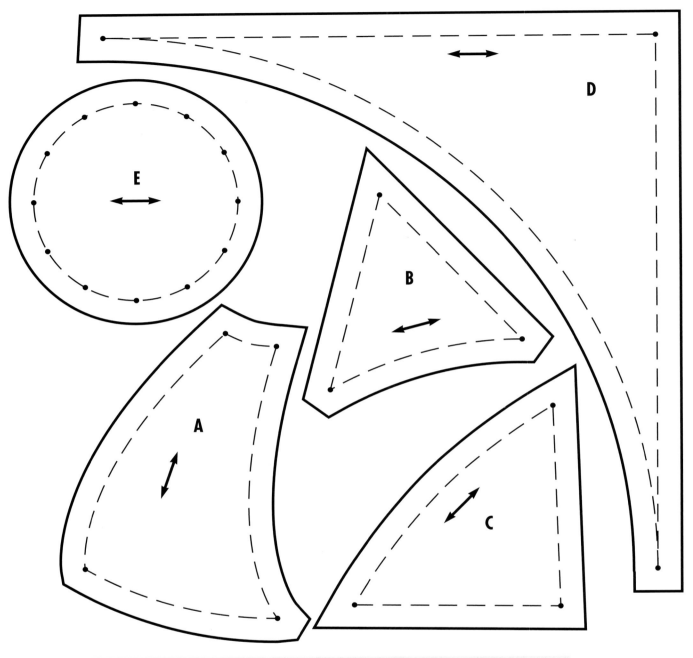

Size Variations

	Full	Queen	King
Finished size	80½" x 92"	92" x 92"	103½" x 103½"
Number of blocks	56	64	81
Blocks set	7 x 8	8 x 8	9 x 9
Yardage Required			
Muslin	6¼ yards	8½ yards	10½ yards
¼-yard pieces	54	60	77
Binding fabric	⅞ yard	⅞ yard	1 yard
108"-wide backing fabric	2½ yards	3 yards	3 yards

SIGNS & SYMBOLS

Fusible appliqué helps you make this quilt in what will seem like a flash! This technique is fast and fun, and your quilt is sturdy enough for real-life use. Or appliqué traditionally, if you like. See page 210 for fusible appliqué instructions and page 211 for color options.

Finished Size

Quilt: 38" x 38"
Blocks: 64 (3¾" x 3¾")

Materials

100 (4¼") squares
Scraps for appliqué
½ yard binding fabric
1¼ yards backing fabric
Paper-backed fusible web
    (optional)

continued

Quilt by Christine L. Adams of Rockville, Maryland

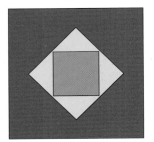 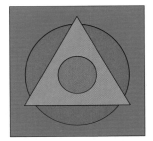 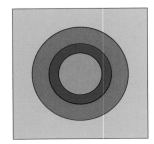

Signs & Symbols Blocks—Make 64.

Choosing Fabrics

For an effective quilt, choose fabrics with a common theme. Christine chose geometrics: stripes, checks, and dots in a rainbow of colors. You might prefer plaids with tone-on-tone prints or stripes alternating with floral prints. Experiment!

You might base your fabric theme on color. Pastels or primary colors are good choices for a child's quilt, while red and green fabrics evoke thoughts of Christmas. See page 211 for more color suggestions.

In addition to Christine's geometric shapes, we've added optional patterns for stars and hearts to give your theme more flexibility.

Manufacturers produce lines of companion fabrics that are ideal for a quilt like this. Buy ⅛ yard of each fabric in the line—and you're instantly coordinated. But it's more challenging to mix and match your own fabrics, looking for the right balance of color, value, and scale.

Cutting

Instructions are for rotary cutting and fusible appliqué. Before cutting, read instructions below and on opposite page to decide whether you prefer fusible or traditional appliqué. Appliqué patterns are on page 212.

1. Following instructions on page 210, trace desired shapes onto paper side of fusible web. Cut out web pieces, leaving small amount of paper around each outline.

2. Fuse web to wrong side of each scrap fabric. Cut out appliqués on drawn line.

Quilt Assembly

1. Set aside 36 (4¼") squares for borders. Fuse appliqués onto 64 squares as desired, mixing different shapes and fabrics.
2. Add finishing to appliqués if desired (see page 210 for finishing suggestions). Christine added topstitching after she joined her

blocks (see Step 1 of "Quilting and Finishing").
3. Lay out appliqué blocks in 8 rows, with 8 blocks in each row (Quilt Assembly Diagram). Arrange blocks to get pleasing balance of color, value, and shape.
4. When satisfied with placement, join blocks in each row.
5. Join rows as shown.
6. Join 8 squares in row for top border. Sew border to top edge of quilt. Repeat for bottom border.

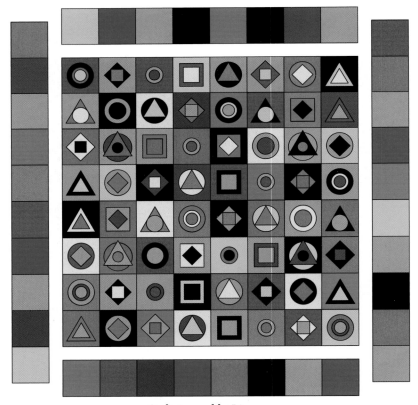

Quilt Assembly Diagram

7. Join 10 squares in a vertical row for each side border. Sew borders to quilt sides.

Quilting and Finishing

1. To topstitch quilt top, Christine used black thread throughout. She outlined each shape, sewing squiggly stitching lines back and forth over seams and around each appliqué. The more wobbly the stitching, the more creative the look will be so don't worry about being too precise. If traditional quilting is desired, mark quilting design on quilt top.

2. Layer backing, batting, and quilt top. Baste. Quilt as desired. On wall hanging shown, machine quilting through all layers is limited to outlining of border blocks. For a bed-size quilt, more quilting is necessary to hold layers together appropriately.

3. Make 4½ yards of 3½"-wide straight-grain binding. Bind quilt.

continued

pinpoints

Cutting Fusible Appliqués

Paper-backed fusible web is a heat-activated adhesive with a temporary paper lining. Heated with a hot iron, fusible web secures shapes to a background fabric, eliminating basting as with traditional appliqué.

Use lightweight web to appliqué quilts or wall hangings. For washable clothing and other items, heavy-duty web might be better. Be sure to read the label for tips on use and washing. Available brands of paper-backed web are HeatnBond, Pellon Wonder-Under, and Aleene's Fusible Web.

Before fusing, always prewash fabrics to remove sizing, which prevents fusible web from bonding with fabric.

Patterns for Fusible Appliqué

Paper-backed web is translucent, so you can lay it directly on a pattern for tracing. This lets you use any printed material as a pattern. Pattern sources include wrapping paper, coloring books, and greeting cards. The kitchen is full of circles and cookie cutters to trace. Even hands and feet are potential patterns. If a tracing isn't the size you want, use a photocopy machine to enlarge or reduce it.

If a shape is not symmetrical (that is, if it must point one way or the other), remember that the finished appliqué is a mirror image of your drawing. If you want the piece to face its original direction, copy the drawing on tracing paper; then darken the image on *both* sides of the tracing paper so you can trace either direction onto the paper-backed web.

Fusing

With a pencil, trace motif onto paper (smooth) side of web (Photo A). Use paper scissors to cut around motif, leaving a small amount of paper around the tracing.

Place adhesive (rough) side of web on *wrong* side of appliqué fabric. Following package instructions, use a dry iron to fuse web to fabric (Photo B). Do not overheat. Some manufacturers recommend a pressing cloth between iron and appliqué to avoid getting sticky fibers on iron.

Let fabric cool. Cut out motif on drawn line. If desired, use pinking shears for a jagged edge.

Peel off paper backing (Photo C). If backing is difficult to remove, use a needle or pin to loosen one corner.

Position appliqué on background fabric. Be sure of placement before you fuse, following manufacturer's instructions. If you have several layers of appliqué, lightly press each piece in place. When all layers are correctly positioned, fuse them together with more heat (Photo D).

Finishing Edges

Fusible web holds appliqués in place through many washings, but inevitably fraying will occur, especially on a garment or quilt that is used daily. For best results, finish the appliqué edges.

Topstitching by machine is an easy solution. Christine Adams used contrasting thread and a deliberately erratic stitch for *Signs & Symbols*. Topstitching might use a matching thread or invisible monofilament to closely outline the shape with a straight or zigzag machine stitch.

A machine satin stitch puts a ridge of tight stitches around each piece, giving the shape strong definition. But be warned: Machine appliqué requires skill in sewing smooth corners, points, and curves.

Buttonhole stitch (also known as blanket stitch) can be worked by hand or machine on appliqué edges.

A finish used on garments is washable fabric paint, available at crafts stores in squeeze tubes that put a thin line of paint around appliqués.

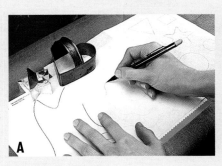

Color Variations

Color choices, as much as fabric patterns, determine the personality of a quilt.
Here are some suggestions for *Signs & Symbols* of a different tone.

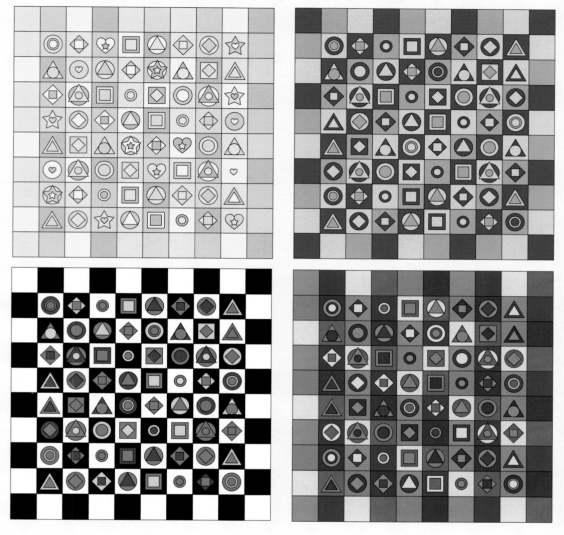

Size Variations*

	Twin	Full	Queen	King
Finished size *	60" x 96"	78" x 96"	84" x 102"	102" x 102"
Appliquéd blocks *	112	154	180	225
Blocks set	8 x 14	11 x 14	12 x 15	15 x 15
Yardage Required				
6½" squares *	160	206	242	289
Binding fabric	1 yard	1 yard	1⅛ yards	1⅛ yards
108"-wide backing fabric	2 yards	2⅜ yards	2½ yards	3 yards

* *Note:* To maintain appropriate scale, a larger block is desirable for bed-size quilts. For these sizes, start with a 6½" base square (finished size 6"). On a photocopy machine, enlarge appliqué patterns 160%.

continued

Geometric Patterns

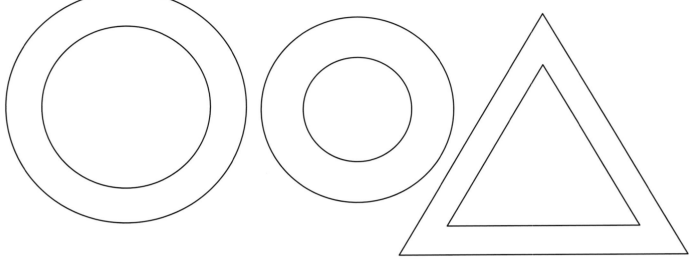

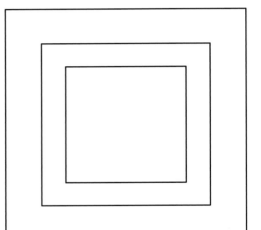

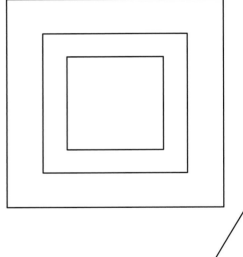

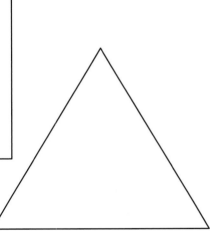

Optional Patterns

WASATCH MEMORIES

Quilt by Bobbi Finley of San Jose, California

W hen she moved to California, Bobbi Finley missed the change of seasons. When autumn came without a show of colorful leaves, Bobbi decided to make an autumn leaf quilt. From a collection of glowing fabrics, Bobbi pieced an original block based on the traditional Drunkard's Path. The quilt reminds her of happy times at her former home near Utah's Wasatch Mountains.

Finished Size
Quilt: 64" x 64"
Blocks: 64 (6" x 6")

Materials
64 (10") squares leaf prints
2½ yards dark brown
¾ yard light brown print for vine
¾ yard gold print for vine leaves
¾ yard rust print for narrow borders
¾ yard binding fabric
4 yards backing fabric

continued

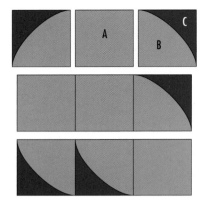

Block Assembly Diagram

Cutting

Make templates of patterns on opposite page. Cut pieces in order listed to get best use of yardage.

From each *leaf print*
• 4 (2½") A squares.
• 5 of Pattern B.

From dark brown
• 2 (6½" x 64") lengthwise border strips.
• 2 (6½" x 52") lengthwise border strips.
• 320 of Pattern C.

From gold print
• 27 of Pattern F.
• 21 of Pattern E.
• 20 of Pattern D.

From rust print
• 16 (1½" x 42") strips.

Block Assembly

1. For each block, select a set of 4 As and 5 Bs.
2. Sew 1 brown C piece to each B.
3. Join units in a row as shown (Block Assembly Diagram). Join rows to complete block.
4. Make 64 blocks.

Quilt Assembly

1. Lay out blocks in 8 horizontal rows, with 8 blocks in each row. Referring to photo, turn blocks in top 4 rows up and blocks in bottom 4 rows down.
2. When satisfied with block placement, join blocks in each row. Then join rows.

Borders

1. Join 2 rust print strips end to end to make each border strip. Sew 2 border strips to quilt sides; then trim excess fabric from strip. Join 2 border strips to top and bottom edges of quilt. Press seam allowances toward borders.
2. Sew longer dark brown strips to quilt sides; then sew remaining strips to top and bottom edges.
3. Repeat Step 1 to join outer rust print border strips to quilt.
4. From light brown print, make 7½ yards of 1¼"-wide continuous bias. Fold bias in thirds to make ³⁄₈"-wide vine; press.
5. From continuous bias strip, cut 27 (3"-long) stems, 21 (3¾"-long) stems, and 20 (4½"-long) stems. Set stems aside.
6. Referring to photo below, pin remaining length of bias to brown border for vine. Pin leaves and stems in place, matching 3"-long stems with F leaves, 3¾"-long stems with Es, and 4½"-long stems with Ds.
7. When satisfied with placement, appliqué leaves, stems, and vine in place.

Quilting and Finishing

1. Mark quilt top with desired quilting designs. Quilt shown is outline-quilted, and veins are quilted in pieced leaves.
2. Layer backing, batting, and quilt top. Baste. Quilt as desired.
3. Make 7¼ yards of continuous bias or straight-grain binding. Bind quilt edges.

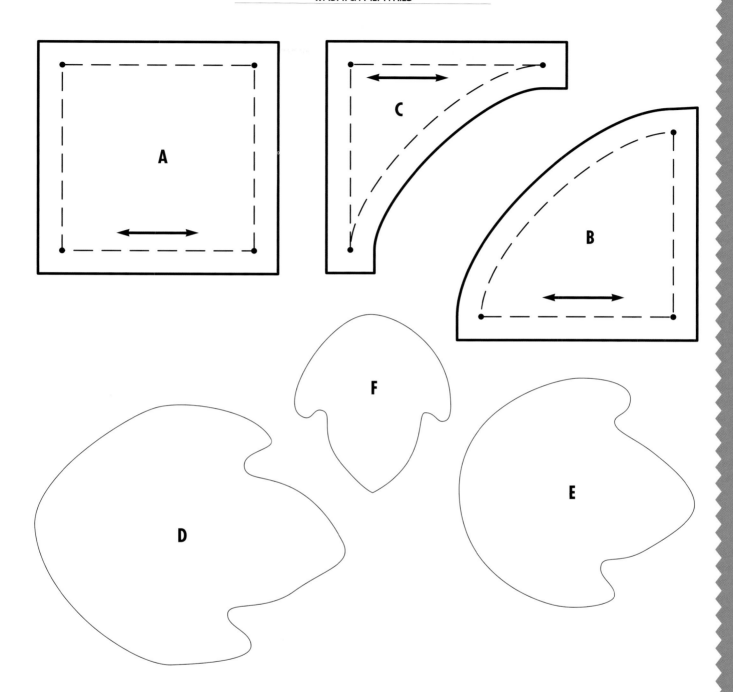

Size Variations

The quilt shown fits a twin-size bed. However, the pattern is easily adapted to fit any bed. Use the chart below as a starting point. All finished sizes assume that the border widths are the same (6¼" wide). You can make the quilt larger with wider borders.

	Wall/Crib	Double	Queen	King
Finished size	48½" x 48½"	72½" x 84½"	84½" x 84½"	96½" x 96½"
Number of blocks	36	120	144	196
Blocks set	6 x 6	10 x 12	12 x 12	14 x 14

POSTAGE STAMP

Vintage quilt from the Oxmoor House collection; circa 1940, quiltmaker unknown

Postage Stamp quilts were all the rage during the Depression, when thrifty homemakers put every scrap to good use—even pieces no bigger than a postage stamp. The pretty pastels of this vintage quilt are typical of that period. Let this quilt inspire you to use today's exciting reproduction fabrics to create a quilt that looks complicated but is really easy to sew with our rotary cutting and quick-piecing instructions.

Finished Size
Quilt: 76½" x 91½"
Blocks: 50 (10½" x 10½")

Materials
3 yards white
1¾ yards blue solid
1¾ yards pink solid
1½ yards green solid
⅛ yard yellow solid
⅛ yard *each* 15 blue prints
⅛ yard *each* 15 pink prints
⅞ yard binding fabric
5½ yards backing fabric

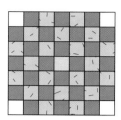

Block 1—Make 15.

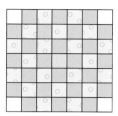

Block 2—Make 15.

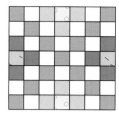

Block 3—Make 20.

Cutting

Instructions are for rotary cutting and quick piecing. Cut all strips on crosswise grain. Cut pieces in order listed to get best use of yardage.

From white
• 32 (2"-wide) strips for strip sets.
• 4 (3⅜"-wide) strips. From these, cut 39 (3⅜") squares. Cut squares in half diagonally to get 154 edge triangles.
• 2 (2⅜"-wide) squares. Cut squares in half diagonally to get 4 corner triangles.

From blue
• 29 (2"-wide) strips for strip sets.

From pink
• 29 (2"-wide) strips for strip sets.

From green
• 23 (2"-wide) strips. From 4 strips, cut 86 (2") squares for Block 3 and edge blocks.

From yellow
• 30 (2") squares for block centers.

From each print fabric
• 2 (2"-wide) strips for strip sets.

Blocks 1 and 2

1. From 1 blue print strip, cut 2 (8") lengths. Cut matching length of blue solid. Join strips as shown to make 1 Strip Set A (Strip Set A Diagram). Press seam allowances toward solid fabric. Cut strip set into 4 (2"-wide) segments.
2. From same blue solid strip, cut 2 (16") lengths. Cut matching length of same blue print used for Strip Set A. Join strips as shown to make 1 Strip Set B (Strip Set B Diagram). Press seam allowances toward solid fabric. Cut strip set into 8 (2"-wide) segments.

3. Cut 1 (16") length from each of white, solid blue, and same blue print strips. Join strips to make 1 Strip Set C (Strip Set C Diagram). Press seam allowances toward blue solid. Cut 8 (2"-wide) segments from strip set as shown.
4. Join 1 each of segments A, B, and C to make a nine-patch (Diagram A). Make 4 nine-patch units.
5. Lay out nine-patches with white square in each outer corner (Block 1

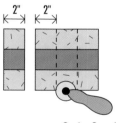

Strip Set A

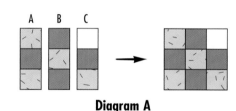

Strip Set B

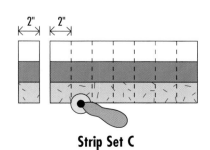

Strip Set C

Assembly Diagram). Add yellow square and remaining 4 B units. Join units in 3 horizontal rows. Join rows to complete Block 1.
6. Repeat steps 1–5 to make 15 of Block 1. Pin 4 extra C units to each block as each block is completed.
7. Make 15 of Block 2 in the same manner, using pink and pink print strips.

continued

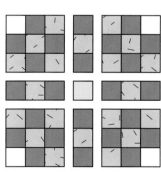

Diagram A

Block 1 Assembly Diagram

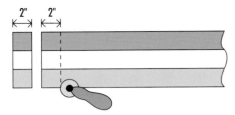

Strip Set D—Make 6.

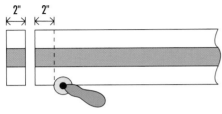

Strip Set E—Make 5.

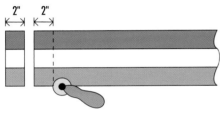

Strip Set F—Make 6.

8. Lay out blocks in diagonal rows as shown (Quilt Assembly Diagram), alternating blue and pink blocks. Each block should have extra C units, which will be used to make adjacent Block 3s.

Block 3

1. Make 5 each of strip sets D, E, and F as shown (Strip Set Diagrams). In each strip set, press seam allowances away from white.
2. Cut 98 (2"-wide) segments from each strip set.
3. Join 1 each of segments D, E, and F to make a nine-patch (Diagram B). Make 98 nine-patches. Set aside 18 for edge blocks.

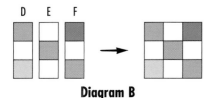

Diagram B

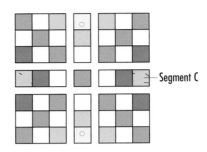

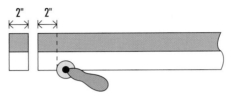

— Segment C

Block 3 Assembly Diagram

Strip Set G—Make 2.

4. Assemble 1 block at a time, adding each block to quilt layout as it is completed. For first block, lay out 4 nine-patches and 1 green square (Block 3 Assembly Diagram). Between these, place C segments (2 blue, 2 pink) from adjacent blocks. Join units in 3 rows; then join rows to complete Block 3.
5. Make 20 of Block 3.

Edge Blocks

1. Make 1 more Strip Set D and 1 more Strip Set F. Press seam allowances away from white. Cut 22 (2"-wide) segments of each strip set.
2. Make 2 of Strip Set G (Strip Set G Diagram). Press seam allowances toward green. Cut these into 44 (2"-wide) segments.

Diagram C

3. For blue units, select 1 each of segments G and F, 1 green square, and 2 white triangles. Sew triangles to green squares (Diagram C); press seam allowances toward green. Join rows to complete unit. Make 22 blue units; then use D segments to make 22 pink units in same manner. Set aside 4 of each color for corner blocks.
4. Join white triangles to 1 side of each remaining green square (Diagram D); press seam allowances toward green. Set aside 4 units for corner blocks.

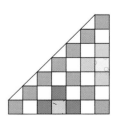

Diagram D

5. Assemble 1 block at a time, adding each block to quilt layout as it is completed. For first block, lay out 1 each of pink and blue edge units, pink/blue nine-patch, green/white triangle unit, and white edge triangle (Edge Block Assembly Diagram). Add C segments from adjacent blocks as shown. Join segments in rows; then join rows to complete edge block.
6. Make 9 edge blocks as shown, adding each to quilt layout in appropriate position. Then make 9 more blocks, reversing positions of pink and blue.

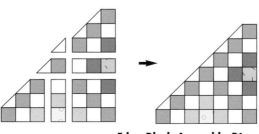

Edge Block Assembly Diagram

Quilt Assembly Diagram

Corner Blocks

1. Join white triangles to the opposite sides of each remaining green/white triangle unit; then join the corner triangle to the top (Diagram E). Make 4 units.

Diagram E

2. Assemble 1 corner at a time. For each corner, lay out 2 matching edge units and 1 corner unit (Corner Block Assembly Diagram). Add C segment from adjacent block as shown. Join units to complete corner block. Make 2 blue corners and 2 pink corners.

Quilt Assembly

1. Join the blocks in diagonal rows as shown above (Quilt Assembly Diagram).
2. Add 1 white triangle to each row end.
3. Join rows, matching seam lines carefully.

Quilting and Finishing

1. Mark quilting design as desired. Quilt has straight lines of quilting that make X through each square.
2. Layer backing, batting, and quilt top. Baste. Quilt as desired.
3. Make 10 yards continuous bias or straight-grain binding. Bind edges.

Corner Block Assembly Diagram

PETRONELLA'S GARDEN

Quilt by Ruth R. Easley of Roswell, Georgia

Ruth Easley created this quilt to showcase 10 blocks she won in her guild's block exchange, plus additional blocks that she made. In a block exchange, each person makes a block in a set color scheme; then one participant wins all the blocks in a drawing.

Finished Size
Quilt: 70" x 82"
Blocks: 12 (10" x 10") flowers
       10 (9¼" x 10") flowers
       1 (20" x 20") center

Materials
30 (6" x 10") scraps for flowers
22 (7") squares assorted green
   scraps for stems and leaves
1 (10") square dark green
½ yard yellow
4 yards white or muslin
2¾ yards green (includes binding)
4½ yards backing fabric

Cutting

Cut all strips on crosswise grain except as noted. Make templates of patterns A–F on pages 222 and 224. Cut pieces in order listed to get best use of yardage.

From each flower print
- 1 of Pattern B for center block.
- 7 or 8 of Pattern E to get a total of 220 flower petals.

From each 7" green square
- 1 (1" x 8½") bias strip for flower stem.
- 2 of Pattern D.

From dark green
- 3 (1¼" x 12") bias strips for center block flower stems.
- 6 of Pattern A for center block.

From yellow
- 3 of Pattern C for center block.
- 22 of Pattern F for flower blocks.

From white
- 4 (7½"-wide) center border strips.
- 2 (22") squares. Cut squares in half diagonally to get 4 corner triangles.
- 1 (20½") square for center block.
- 6 (10½"-wide) strips. From these, cut 12 (10½") squares and 10 (9¾" x 10½") pieces for flower blocks.

From green
- 1 (10½"-wide) strip. From this, cut 4 (2½" x 10½") X strips and 14 (2⅜" x 10½") sashing strips.
- 4 (2½" x 72") lengthwise strips. From these, cut 4 (2½" x 44") medallion border strips and 4 (2½" x 26") strips for center block.
- 2 (2½" x 47") lengthwise strips for inner borders.
- 6 (2½" x 84") lengthwise strips for outer borders and inner borders.
- 4 (2½" x 84") lengthwise strips for straight-grain binding.

Center Block—Make 1.

Flower Block—Make 12 (10½" x 10½") blocks and 10 (9¾" x 10½") blocks.

Block Assembly

1. Fold 20½" white square in quarters diagonally. Finger-press creases to make appliqué placement guidelines.
2. On each 12" bias strip, fold ¼" to wrong side at 1 end; then fold in ¼" on each long edge. Press.
3. Select 10 B petals for each center flower. Join straight edges of petals to make 1 flower circle.
4. Appliqué 1 C at center of each flower, covering B raw edges.
5. Pin 3 flowers, stems, and 6 A leaves on white square (Center Block Diagram). Tuck unfinished edge of each stem under its flower. When satisfied with placement, appliqué pieces in place.

6. Join 10 E petals in circle for each flower block. Appliqué 1 F over center of each flower. Make 22 flowers.
7. Fold each 10½" white square in quarters diagonally and finger-press. Prepare 8½" bias stem as before and pin the stem, 2 D leaves, and the flower in place (Flower Block Diagram). When satisfied with the placement, appliqué the pieces in place. Make 12 (10½") Flower Blocks.
8. Make 10 (9¾" x 10½") flower blocks in same manner, designating 1 (10½") edge of each piece as top of block.

Quilt Assembly

1. Fold 26"- and 44"-long green strips in half to find centers. Repeat for 7½"-wide white strips. Matching centers, sew long and short green strips to opposite edges of each white strip.
2. Center combined strip on each edge of center block. Sew strips to block and miter corners.
3. Trim corners of center unit as shown (Trimming Diagram). Discard cut portions.

continued

3⅝"   3⅝"

Center Block

9⅜"

9⅜"

Trimming Diagram

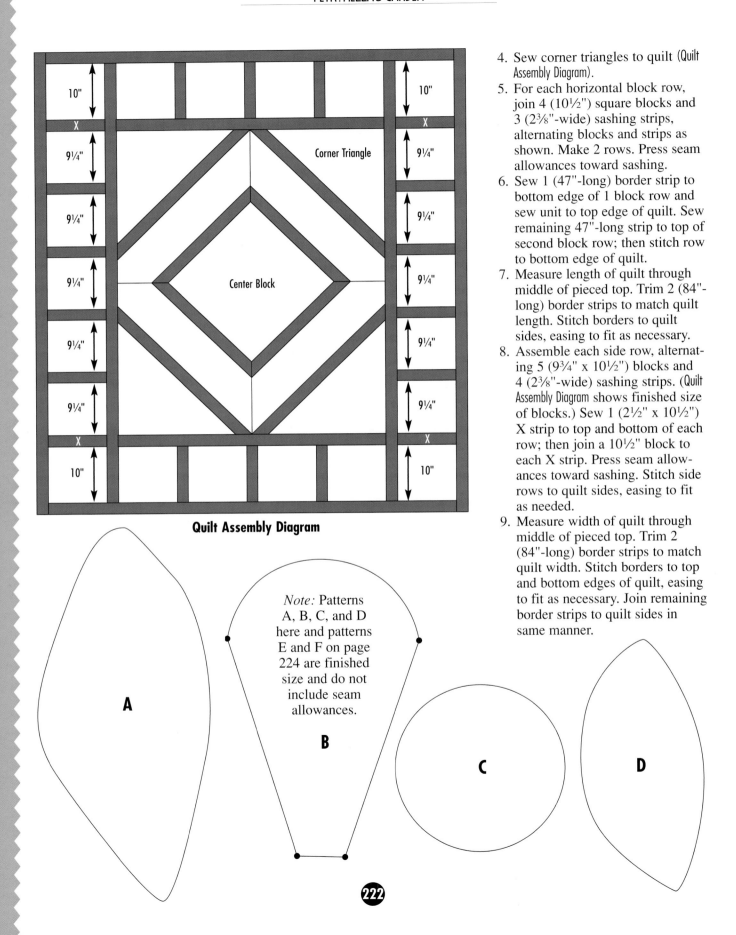

Quilt Assembly Diagram

Note: Patterns A, B, C, and D here and patterns E and F on page 224 are finished size and do not include seam allowances.

4. Sew corner triangles to quilt (Quilt Assembly Diagram).

5. For each horizontal block row, join 4 (10½") square blocks and 3 (2⅜"-wide) sashing strips, alternating blocks and strips as shown. Make 2 rows. Press seam allowances toward sashing.

6. Sew 1 (47"-long) border strip to bottom edge of 1 block row and sew unit to top edge of quilt. Sew remaining 47"-long strip to top of second block row; then stitch row to bottom edge of quilt.

7. Measure length of quilt through middle of pieced top. Trim 2 (84"-long) border strips to match quilt length. Stitch borders to quilt sides, easing to fit as necessary.

8. Assemble each side row, alternating 5 (9¾" x 10½") blocks and 4 (2⅜"-wide) sashing strips. (Quilt Assembly Diagram shows finished size of blocks.) Sew 1 (2½" x 10½") X strip to top and bottom of each row; then join a 10½" block to each X strip. Press seam allowances toward sashing. Stitch side rows to quilt sides, easing to fit as needed.

9. Measure width of quilt through middle of pieced top. Trim 2 (84"-long) border strips to match quilt width. Stitch borders to top and bottom edges of quilt, easing to fit as necessary. Join remaining border strips to quilt sides in same manner.

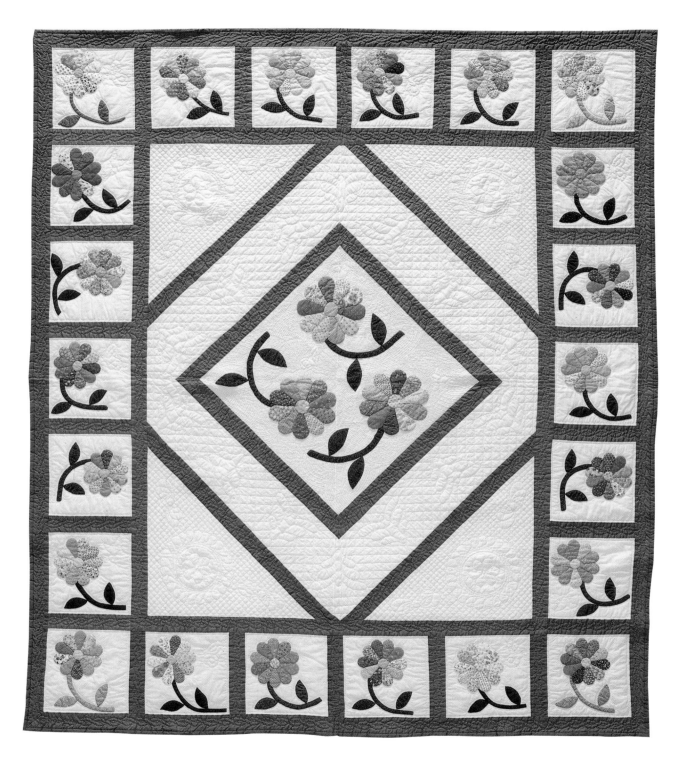

Quilting and Finishing

1. Mark quilt top with desired quilting design. Quilt shown has outline quilting around flower petals, leaves, stems, and block seams, plus stipple quilting in background of center block. Patterns for medallion border design, corner feather wreath, and bow are on page 224. Cross-hatching in border is 1½"-wide and ¾"-wide in corner triangles.

2. Layer backing, batting, and quilt top. Baste. Quilt as desired.

3. From remaining green strips, make 8⅝ yards of straight-grain binding. Bind quilt edges.

continued

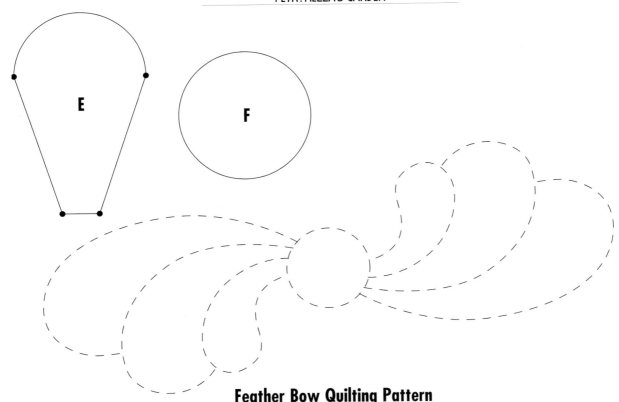

Feather Bow Quilting Pattern

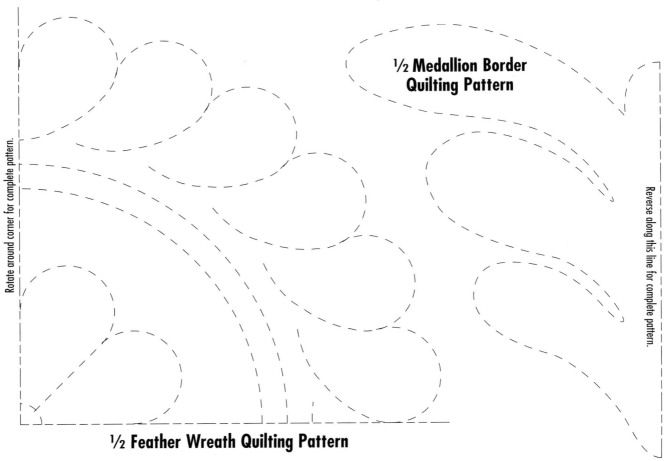

**½ Medallion Border
Quilting Pattern**

Rotate around corner for complete pattern.

Reverse along this line for complete pattern.

½ Feather Wreath Quilting Pattern

PINE BURR

Marion Watchinski loves neatly matched seams and sharply sewn points but found this block intimidating until she discovered foundation piecing. Our instructions show you how to quick-piece this classic quilt block. If you want to try foundation piecing, a good reference is www.planetpatchwork.com/fndpiece.htm.

Finished Size

Quilt: 86" x 98"
Blocks: 42 (12" x 12")

Materials

42 (9" x 22") fat eighths light prints for blocks
42 (18" x 22") fat quarters dark prints for blocks
7½ yards dark green print (includes binding)
2⅝ yards 90"-wide backing fabric

continued

Quilt by Marion Roach Watchinski of Overland Park, Kansas

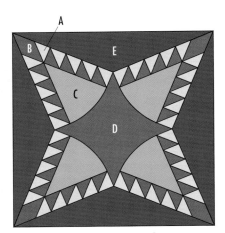

Pine Burr Block — Make 42.

Cutting

Instructions are for rotary cutting and quick piecing, except as noted. Make templates for patterns B, C, D, and E on pages 228 and 229. Patterns A and F are provided if you prefer traditional piecing. Cut all strips on crosswise grain except as noted. Cut pieces in order listed to get best use of yardage.

From each *light print*
- 3 (1⅞" x 22") strips for quick-pieced A units.
- 4 (1⅞") squares. Cut squares in half diagonally to get 8 A triangles.

From each *dark print*
- 3 (1⅞" x 22") strips for quick-pieced A units.
- 4 of Pattern B.
- 1 of Pattern D.
- 4 of Pattern C.

From remaining dark prints
- 26 (3⅞" x 7¾") rectangles for border triangle-squares (F).

From dark green
- Set aside ⅞ yard for binding.
- 12 (13"-wide) strips. From these, cut 168 of Pattern E, placing straight edge of pattern on 13" length.
- 6 (3⅞"-wide) strips. From these, cut 26 (3⅞" x 7¾") pieces for border triangle-squares (F).
- 16 (2½"-wide) strips for borders.
- 1 (7½"-wide) strip. From this, cut 4 (7½") border squares.

Block Assembly

Each block has 32 A triangle-squares, 8 additional light A triangles, 4 B diamonds, 4 Cs, 1 D, and 4 Es (Pine Burr Block Diagram). All pieces in a group are same fabric. In most blocks, dark As, Bs, and D match.

1. Choose 1 (1⅞"-wide) light strip for triangle-squares. On wrong side of strip, mark 16 (1⅞") squares (Diagram A). Draw diagonal line through each square as shown.

Diagram A

2. With right sides facing, match light strip with 1 dark strip. Stitch ¼" seam on *both* sides of each diagonal line. Cut units apart on all drawn lines to get 32 A triangle-square units. Press seam allowances toward dark fabric.

3. Join 4 A units in row. Add 1 A triangle to end of row (Diagram B). Sew row to side of 1 C.

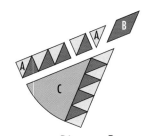

Diagram B

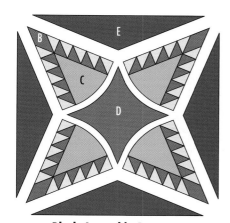

Block Assembly Diagram

4. Make another row of A units, orienting triangles as shown. Add B to end of row; then sew row to opposite side of C. Make 4 matching quadrants for each block.
5. Stitch quadrants to curved edges of piece D (Block Assembly Diagram).
6. Add 4 Es to complete block. Make 42 Pine Burr blocks.

Quilt Assembly

1. Lay out blocks in 7 horizontal rows, with 6 blocks in each row (Quilt Assembly Diagram). Arrange blocks to get pleasing balance of color and value. When satisfied with block placement, join blocks in each row.
2. Join the rows.

Borders

1. On wrong side of each green 3⅞" x 7¾" rectangle, mark 2 (3⅞") squares. Draw diagonal line through each square as before.
2. With right sides facing, match each green rectangle with 1 dark print rectangle. Stitch, cut, and press as before to make 104 F triangle-square units.
3. Join 2 (2½"-wide) green strips end to end to make 8 border strips.
4. Measure length of quilt through middle of pieced top. Then trim 4 strips to match quilt length for side borders. Measure the width

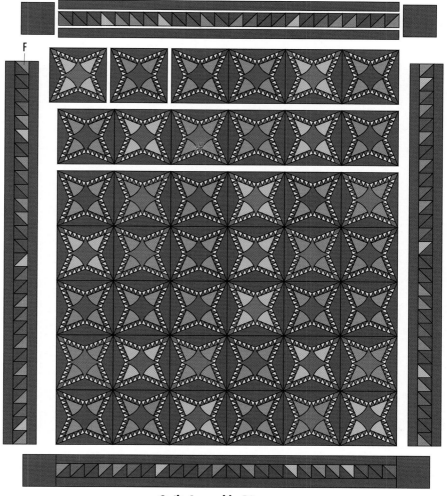

Quilt Assembly Diagram

of the quilt through middle and trim the remaining 4 strips to match width.
5. Join 28 F triangle-squares in row for each side border, changing direction of triangles mid-row as shown (Quilt Assembly Diagram). Sew trimmed border strips to both sides of F rows, easing to fit as needed. Press seam allowances toward border strips.
6. Stitch side borders to quilt sides, easing to fit.
7. For top and bottom borders, join 24 F triangle-squares in row, changing direction of triangles mid-row as shown. Sew remaining border strips to both sides of

24-unit F rows, easing to fit as needed. Press seam allowances toward border strips.
8. Add 1 (7½") green square to each end of top and bottom borders. Stitch borders to top and bottom edges of quilt.

Quilting and Finishing

1. Mark quilting design as desired. Quilt has concentric circles centered on each block intersection.
2. Layer backing, batting, and quilt top. Baste. Quilt as desired.
3. Make 10½ yards of continuous straight-grain or bias binding. Bind quilt edges.

continued

227

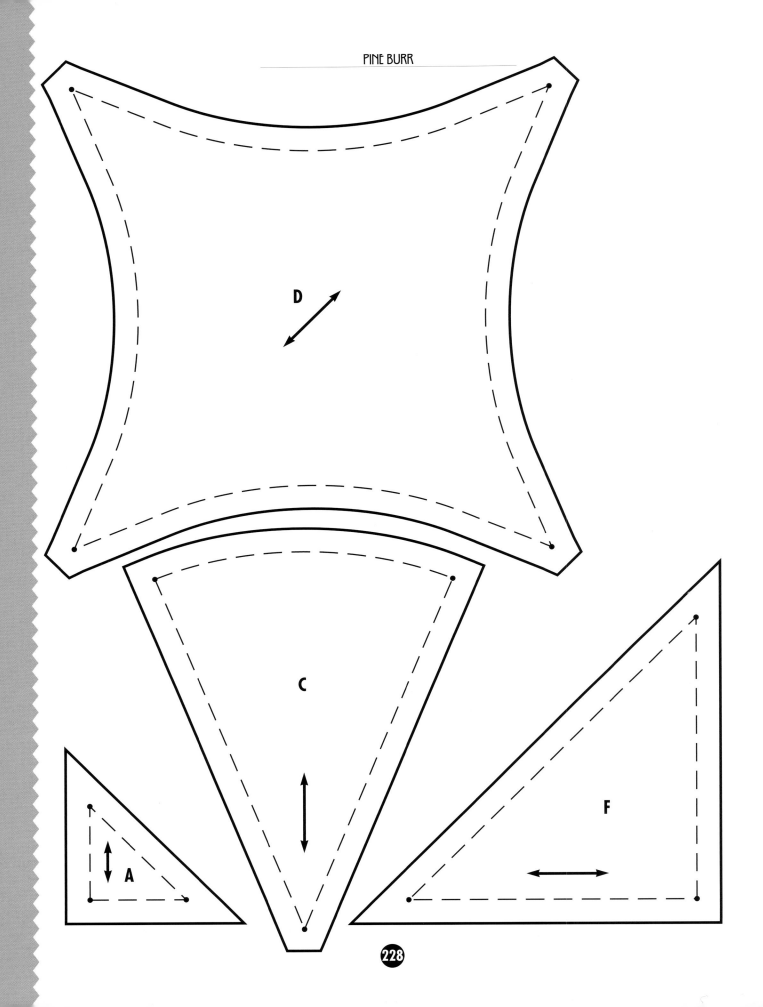

D

C

A

F

Color Variations

Marion Watchinski used dark fabrics to capture the look of a nineteenth-century quilt. You can create your own color scheme in rainbow brights or pretty pastels.

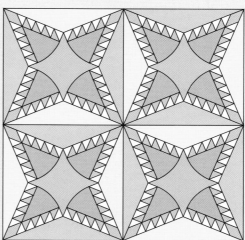

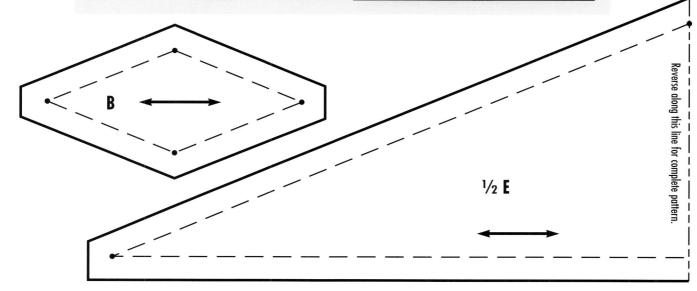

B

½ E

Reverse along this line for complete pattern.

STREAK OF LIGHTNING

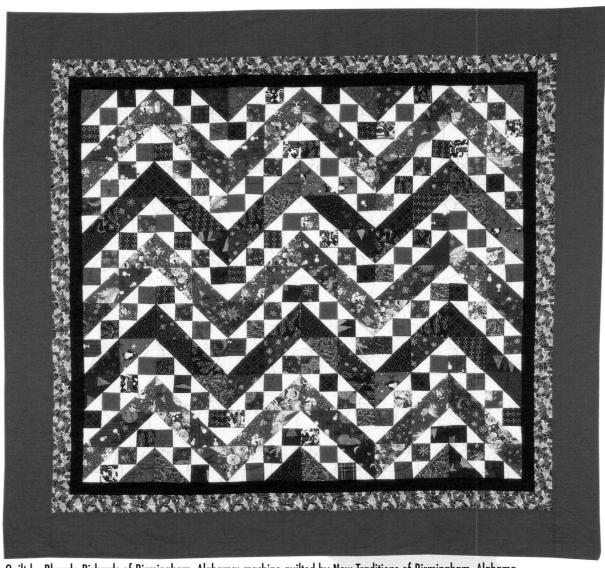

Quilt by Rhonda Richards of Birmingham, Alabama; machine-quilted by New Traditions of Birmingham, Alabama

Believe it or not, you don't need to cut any triangles to make this quilt. Rhonda Richards used a neat quick-piecing technique developed by Sally Schneider. It's an easy way to turn out a lot of blocks in no time. Rhonda made her quilt with cheery Christmas fabrics, but you can use any theme or color scheme to piece this striking design.

Finished Size
Quilt: 73" x 78"
Blocks: 132 (4" x 4")

Materials
11 (18" x 22") fat quarters dark prints
1⅜ yards white or muslin
½ yard dark border fabric
¾ yard print border fabric
2⅛ yards outer border fabric
   (includes binding) *
4½ yards backing fabric
* *Note:* Excess fabric can replace
1 or more fat quarters, if desired.

Cutting

Instructions are for rotary cutting and quick piecing. Cut strips on crosswise grain except as noted.

From outer border fabric
- 4 (5" x 76") lengthwise strips.
- 5 (2½" x 76") strips for binding.

Note: Use remaining fabric for piecing, if desired.

From each dark fat quarter
- 2 (3" x 18") strips. From these, cut 12 (3") squares to get a total of 132 A squares.
- 2 (6½" x 18") strips. From these, cut 6 (5½" x 6½") C pieces to get a total of 66 Cs.

From white
- 10 (4"-wide) strips. From these, cut 132 (3" x 4") B pieces.

Block Assembly

1. Sew each A square to 1 end of each B piece.

2. Join A/B units in pairs, placing A squares at opposite ends as shown.

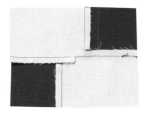

3. Turn block over. Clip seam allowance between dark squares. Then press seam allowances in opposite directions.

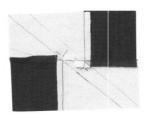

4. Make template of triangle pattern on page 232, drawing square within triangle as shown. With template on *wrong* side of block, align lines of square with square A. Mark diagonal line with pencil. Move template to opposite corner of block and draw another diagonal line.

5. With right sides facing, match each marked block with 1 (5½" x 6½") C piece. Stitch on both drawn lines. Cut block in half between sewn lines to get 2 finished blocks.

6. Open each block and then press the seam allowance toward the C triangle.
7. Make 132 blocks.

Quilt Assembly

1. Refer to photo to lay out blocks in 11 horizontal rows, with 12 blocks in each row. Turn blocks as needed to achieve zigzag design.
2. When satisfied with placement, join blocks in each row.
3. Join the rows.

Borders

1. From dark fabric for first border, cut 8 (2"-wide) strips. Join 2 strips end to end to make border for each edge of quilt.
2. Measure width of quilt through middle of pieced top. Trim 2 border strips to this measurement. Stitch border strips to top and bottom edges of quilt, easing to fit as necessary.
3. Measure length of quilt through middle of pieced top, including top and bottom borders. Trim remaining border strips to match length. Stitch border strips to quilt sides.
4. From print border fabric, cut 8 (3"-wide) strips. Join 2 strips end to end to make each border strip. Repeat steps 2 and 3 to add print borders to edges of quilt.
5. Add outer border strips in same manner.

Quilting and Finishing

1. Mark the pieced top with the desired quilting design. The quilt shown is commercially machine-quilted.
2. Layer backing, batting, and quilt top. Baste. Then quilt as desired.
3. Make 8⅝ yards of straight-grain binding from reserved border fabric. Bind quilt edges.

continued

Color and Set Variations

You can turn this versatile block to create different sets. Here are two examples: The Jewel Box set (left), made by Emily Parrish, has 180 blocks. Kelly Davis made the Barn Raising set (right) with 196 blocks, offsetting with red and green diagonal rows in opposite corners. These quilts were made in a class led by Marge LaBenne of Tucker, Georgia.

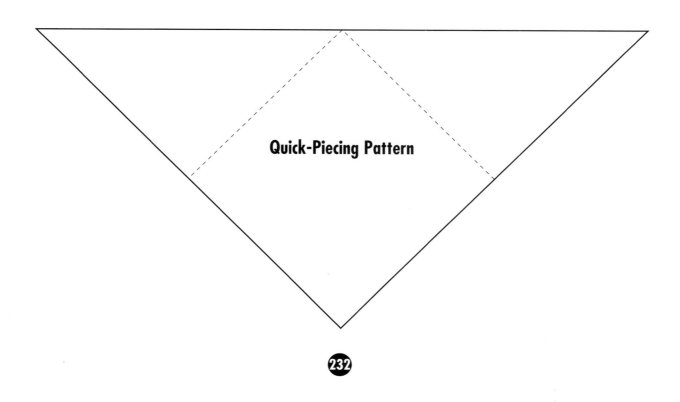

Quick-Piecing Pattern

SPRING BLOSSOMS

Pastels aplenty make this quilt springtime fresh. The block, a variation of the classic Ohio Star, is the result of a block exchange, a swap in which each participant makes blocks for her friends. Winnie Fleming's request for pastel fabrics produced these lovely blocks. Since everyone's fabric choices are different, no two blocks are the same.

Finished Size
Quilt: 67" x 85"
Blocks: 48 (9" x 9")

Materials
48 (4" x 8") print scraps
48 (9" x 14") print scraps
½ yard each of 8 white-on-white
    print fabrics
1¼ yards inner border fabric
    (includes binding)
2½ yards outer border fabric
5⅛ yards backing fabric

continued

Quilt by Winnie S. Fleming of Friendswood, Texas; machine-quilted by Lenel Walsh

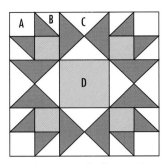

Spring Blossoms Block—Make 48.

Cutting

Instructions are for rotary cutting and quick piecing. Before cutting, read the block instructions and decide whether you prefer quick piecing or traditional piecing. For traditional methods, use the patterns on page 235.

From each 4" x 8" print fabric
• 4 (2") A squares.
• 1 (3½") D square.

From each 9" x 14" print fabric
• 1 (7") square for B triangle-squares.
• 2 (4¼") squares for hourglass units.

From each white-on-white fabric
• 6 (7") squares for B triangle-squares.
• 12 (4¼") squares for hourglass units.
• 24 (2") A squares.

From inner border fabric
• 8 (2"-wide) crosswise strips.

From outer border fabric
• 4 (5½"-wide) lengthwise strips.

Block Assembly

1. For each block, select 1 each of 9" x 14" and 4" x 8" print scraps. From same white fabric, select 1 (7") square, 2 (4¼") squares, and 4 A squares.

2. On wrong side of 7" white square, draw a 2-square by 2-square grid of 2⅜" squares (Diagram A). Mark diagonal lines through centers of squares as shown. (Red lines show first continuous stitching path; blue lines show second path.)

3. With right sides facing, match marked square with 7" print square. Stitch on both sides of diagonal lines, pivoting at grid

corners as shown. Press stitching. Cut on all drawn lines to get 8 B triangle-squares. Press seam allowances toward print fabric.

4. Referring to instructions on page 236, use 4¼" squares to make 4 C Hourglass triangle-squares.

5. For each corner unit, select 2 B triangle-squares and 1 A square each of white and print fabrics. Sew triangle-squares to A squares as shown (Diagram B). Join to make a four-patch corner unit. Make 4 corner units for the block.

6. Arrange corner units, Hourglass units, and D square in 3 rows as shown (Block Assembly Diagram). Join units in each row; then join rows to complete block.

7. Make 48 blocks. In 24 blocks, press seam allowances toward corner units; in remaining 24 blocks, press seam allowances away from corner units. This results in offset seam allowances when you join blocks in rows.

Quilt Assembly

1. Lay out blocks in 8 horizontal rows, with 6 blocks in each row

(Row Assembly Diagram). Arrange the blocks to achieve pleasing balance of color and value.

2. When satisfied with placement, join blocks in each row.

3. Referring to photo on page 233, join rows.

Borders

1. Join 2 strips of inner border fabric end to end to make border strip for each side of quilt.

2. Measure each quilt edge through the middle of the pieced top; mark the borders. Sew inner and outer borders to quilt edges and miter corners.

Quilting and Finishing

1. Mark quilting design on quilt top as desired. Quilt shown is machine-quilted with meandering pattern of stipple quilting all over quilt surface.

2. Layer backing, batting, and quilt top. Baste. Quilt as desired.

3. Use remaining inner border fabric to make 9 yards of bias or straight-grain binding. Bind quilt edges.

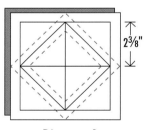

Diagram A

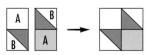

Diagram B

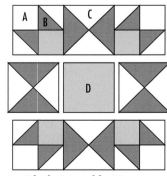

Block Assembly Diagram

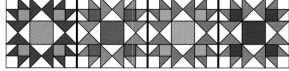

Row Assembly Diagram

Size Variations

	Full	Queen	King
Finished size	76" x 94"	85" x 103"	103" x 103"
Number of blocks	63	80	100
Blocks set	7 x 9	8 x 10	10 x 10
Yardage Required			
4" x 8" prints	63	80	100
9" x 14" prints	63	80	100
½ yards of white	11	14	17
Inner border fabric	1¼ yards	1⅜ yards	1½ yards
Outer border fabric	2¾ yards	3 yards	3 yards
Backing fabric	5⅝ yards	6 yards	9¼ yards

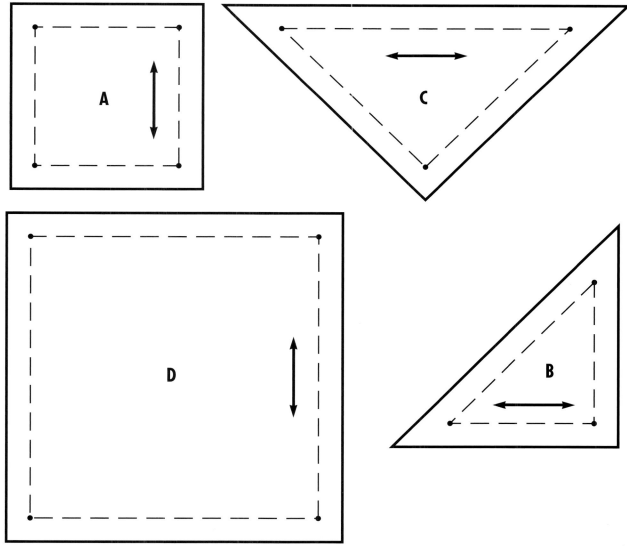

continued

Quick-Piecing Hourglass Units

A patchwork square made up of four right-triangles is sometimes called an Hourglass block (or unit of a block). Traditionally, you would cut four triangles and sew them together to make a square. But if you need several units with the same two-fabric combination, it's easier, faster, and more accurate to quick-piece the blocks as described here.

These instructions are tailored to *Spring Blossoms,* but the technique can be applied to any patchwork that calls for Hourglass units or blocks.

There are two points to remember when you use this technique:
• Always start with fabric squares that are 1¼" larger than the desired *finished* size of the unit.
• You get *two* Hourglass units from each pair of fabric squares.

1. For *Spring Blossoms,* use 4¼" squares of white and print fabrics to make Hourglass units.
2. On wrong side of each white square, draw diagonal line from corner to corner. With right sides facing, match marked square with square of scrap fabric.
3. Stitch ¼" seam on *both* sides of diagonal line (Diagram A). Press.
4. Cut units apart on drawn line between stitching (Diagram B). Press the units open, pressing seam allowance toward scrap fabric. You will have 2 triangle-squares (Diagram C).
5. On wrong side of 1 triangle-square, draw line from corner of white triangle to corner of scrap triangle. Then match both triangle-squares *with contrasting fabrics*

facing and top marked unit.
6. Stitch ¼" seam on *both* sides of marked line (Diagram D).
7. Cut units apart between stitching lines as before (Diagram E). Press both squares open to get 2 Hourglass units (Diagram F).

In this example, sewn units now measure 3½" square (including seam allowances). When sewn into *Spring Blossoms* block, finished unit will be 3".

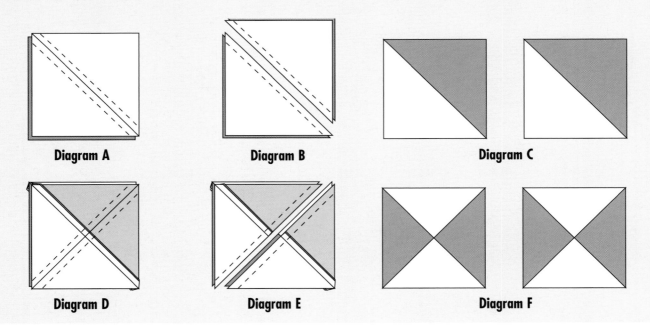

Diagram A   **Diagram B**   **Diagram C**

Diagram D   **Diagram E**   **Diagram F**

WREATH IN THE WINDOW

Group quilts are great fun, and a real plus for busy people," says Mary Lou Watson, one of seven women who call themselves Pieceful Scrappers. Even a big quilt like this one required each member to make just eight blocks. The group meets weekly to spend many a productive hour quilting (and chatting) around a large frame.

The Scrappers created the effect of Attic Windows by using two cream tone-on-tone prints, one slightly darker than the other, for the outer pieces of the block. The scrap fabrics coordinate with the border fabric, a floral print that was chosen with the thought that corner miters would be easy. According to Mary Lou, "We were wrong, but we did it anyway!"

Finished Size

Quilt: 98½" x 108½" *
Blocks: 56 (12" x 12")
* *Note:* This quilt fits a king-size bed. For a 86½" x 98½" queen-size quilt, make 42 blocks, set 6 across and 7 down.

Materials

3⅜ yards muslin
3¼ yards border fabric (includes binding)
2 yards each of 2 beige/tan tone-on-tone prints
½ yard inner border fabric
166 (5" x 9") scraps
8¾ yards backing fabric

continued

Quilt by the Pieceful Scrappers of Toronto, Canada

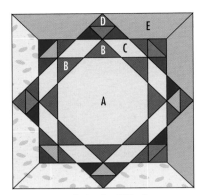

**Wreath in the Window
Block—Make 56.**

Cutting

Make templates for patterns C and E on opposite page. All other instructions are for rotary cutting and quick piecing. Cut all strips on crosswise grain. Cut pieces in order listed to get best use of yardage.

From muslin

• 56 (6½") A squares.
• 28 (1¾"-wide) strips. From these, cut 448 of Pattern C.

From each beige/tan print

• 224 of Pattern E.

From inner border fabric

• 12 (1¼"-wide) strips. Add remaining fabric to scraps.

From scraps

• Set aside 56 scraps for block's inner circle (wreath). From remainder, cut 896 (2⅛") squares. Cut each square in half diagonally to get 1,792 D triangles.

Block Assembly

1. For each block, select 1 A, 8 Cs, 4 Es of each beige/tan fabric, 32 Ds, and 1 (5" x 9") scrap.

2. From scrap, cut 1 (3¾") square. Cut this in quarters diagonally to get 4 B triangles. From remaining scrap, cut 4 (2¼") squares.

3. See page 304 for instructions on diagonal-corner technique. Sew B squares to 4 corners of A square (Diagram A). Press seam allowances toward A.

4. Sew C diamonds to sides of each B triangle (Diagram B). Press seam allowances toward Cs. Make 4 B/C units.

5. Select 4 D triangles. Join 2 triangles to make square; then add 2 more triangles to adjacent sides of square as shown (Diagram C). Make 8 D units.

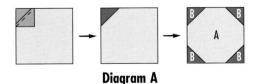

Diagram A

Diagram B

Diagram C

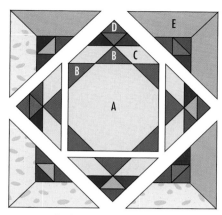

Block Assembly Diagram

Quilt Assembly

1. Referring to photo, lay out blocks in 8 horizontal rows of 7 blocks each. All blocks are positioned in same manner, not turned, so adjacent E pieces are always contrasting fabrics.
2. When satisfied with the placement of the blocks, join the blocks in rows.
3. Join the rows to complete the quilt center.

Borders

1. Cut 4 (6"-wide) lengthwise strips from outer border fabric. Set aside remainder for binding.
2. Join inner border strips end to end to get 4 (115"-long) strips. Sew 1 inner border strip to 1 edge of each outer border, matching center points.
3. Sew the borders to the quilt, mitering the corners.

Quilting and Finishing

1. Mark the pieced top with the desired quilting design. The quilt shown is outline-quilted with a floral design quilted in the center of each block and a lover's knot quilted in the X formed by E pieces where the blocks meet.
2. Layer backing, batting, and quilt top. Then baste together. Quilt as desired.
3. Make 11¾ yards of continuous bias or straight-grain binding. Bind quilt edges.

6. Sew 1 D unit to top of each B/C unit (Block Assembly Diagram). Sew 2 joined units to opposite sides of A/B square as shown. Press. Sew 2 units to remaining sides of A/B.
7. To make corner units, sew 2 Es to adjacent sides of each remaining D unit, mitering corners as shown (Corner Unit Diagram). Select Es carefully, referring to block diagrams for correct placement of beige/tan fabrics. Press seam allowances toward Es.
8. Sew corner units to block as shown to complete block. Make 56 blocks.

Corner Unit

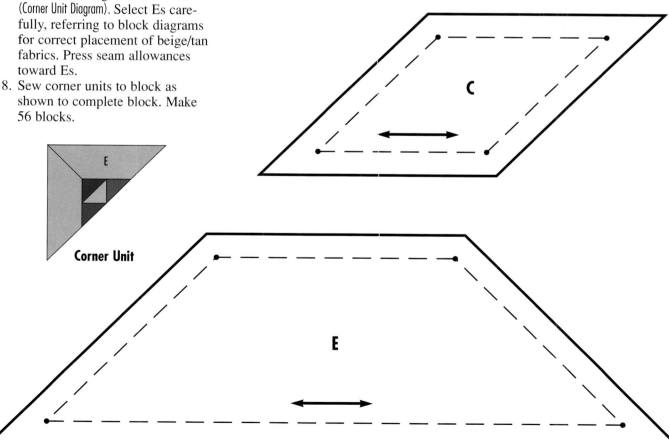

MILKY WAY

Quilt by Mary Radke of Yorkville, Illinois

Tessellating patterns like this one are fun and interesting to sew. *Tessellated* means tiled, or interlocking. Though you see a galaxy of stars in the finished quilt, there is no star block. The stars appear only after you join units together.

Finished Size
Quilt: 28" x 28"

Materials
6 (1½" x 21") strips light plaids
9 (2⅞" x 21") strips light plaids
3 (1½" x 21") strips gold plaid
3 (1½" x 21") strips olive plaid
10 (2⅞" x 21") strips medium and dark plaids
4 (1½" x 42") strips dark plaid for inner borders
¼ yard binding fabric
1 yard backing fabric

Cutting
Cut pieces in order listed to get best use of yardage.
From 2⅞"-wide light strips
• 54 (2⅞") squares. Cut squares in half diagonally to get 108 triangles.
• 12 (2½") squares for light star centers.
From medium and dark strips
• 54 (2⅞") squares. Cut squares in half diagonally to get 108 triangles.
• 17 (2½") squares.

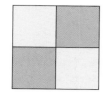

Four-Patch Diagram

Strip Set Diagram

1½"   1½"

Four-Patch Assembly

1. Join 1½"-wide light plaid strips and gold strips in pairs to make 3 strip sets (Strip Set Diagram). Make 3 more strip sets with olive fabric. Press the seam allowances toward dark fabrics.
2. From each strip set, cut 12 (1½"-wide) segments.
3. Join the matching segments to make 36 four-patch units (Four-Patch Diagram).

Quilt Assembly

1. Join light and dark triangles in pairs to make 108 triangle-squares. Press seam allowances toward darker fabrics.
2. Lay out four-patch units, triangle-squares, and 2½" squares in 11 rows as shown (Row Assembly Diagram). Match 4 triangle-square units with the same dark color to form the stars when the rows are joined.
3. Join the units in each row. Press the seam allowances in opposite directions from row to row. Join the rows.

Borders

1. Trim 2 (1½"-wide) border strips to match quilt length. Join strips to quilt sides. Press seam allowances toward borders.
2. Trim the remaining border strips to match the quilt width. Sew the strips to the top and bottom edges of the quilt.

3. For outer borders, join triangle-squares in 4 rows with 12 units in each row. Join 2 rows to quilt sides. Press seam allowances toward inner border.
4. Join remaining 2½" medium/dark squares to ends of remaining borders. Join these to top and bottom edges of quilt.

Quilting and Finishing

1. Mark quilt top with desired quilting design. Quilt shown was hand-quilted in a diagonal grid.
2. Layer backing, batting, and quilt top. Baste together. Then quilt as desired.
3. Make 3½ yards of straight-grain binding. Bind quilt edges.

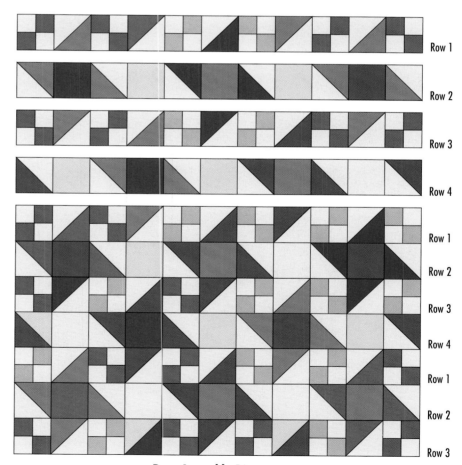

Row 1
Row 2
Row 3
Row 4
Row 1
Row 2
Row 3
Row 4
Row 1
Row 2
Row 3

Row Assembly Diagram

ROSEMARY'S BUTTERFLIES

Quilt by Rosemary Youngs of Walker, Michigan

Rosemary Youngs collected the 1930s vintage fabrics for this quilt at an estate sale. The fabrics remind Rosemary of "quilts my grandmothers would have made if they'd been quilters." Rosemary began her block design with a traditional tulip pattern in the center and then added butterflies for balance. *Rosemary's Butterflies* is her first appliqué quilt, made for daughter Amy. "I know she will always cherish and love it," Rosemary says, "and that's what quilts are for!"

Finished Size
Quilt: 77" x 77"
Blocks: 9 (19" x 19")

Materials
36 (4½" x 6½") pastel print scraps
5⅝ yards white (includes binding)
1¼ yards green
⅛ yard pink
⅛ yard blue
4¾ yards backing
¼"-wide bias pressing bar (optional)
Freezer paper

Cutting

Cut all strips on crosswise grain except as noted. Make templates of A–G on page 245. Cut pieces in order listed to get best use of yardage.

From each pastel scrap
• 1 of Pattern A.

From white
• 2 (10½" x 80") and 2 (10½" x 60") lengthwise border strips.
• 9 (19½") squares.
• 2 (19") squares for binding.

From green
• 1 (15") square for bias vines.
• 7 (2"-wide) strips. From these, cut 68 of Pattern D, 13 of Pattern E, and 16 of Pattern G.
• 44 of Pattern C.

From pink
• 2 (2¼"-wide) strips. From these, cut 20 of Pattern B and 8 of Pattern F.

From blue
• 2 (2¼"-wide) strips. From these, cut 24 of Pattern B and 8 of Pattern F.

Block Assembly

1. Cut 1 (14") square of freezer paper. Fold paper in quarters. Use ruler and pencil to draw quarter-circle with 7" radius on paper. Cut on drawn line through all 4 layers. Unfold to get pattern for 14"-diameter circle.
2. Fold each white fabric square into quarters horizontally, vertically, and diagonally (Diagram A). Crease folds for placement guidelines.
3. Center circle pattern on fabric. Lightly trace perimeter of circle on fabric. Remove pattern. Mark second circle ¼" outside first. Mark all squares in same manner.
4. Position 1 E at center of each block. Then place 4 Cs and 4 Ds, aligning pieces with creased placement guides (¼ Block Appliqué Placement Diagram). Insert 4 blue Bs under C pieces (or 4 pink Bs in 4 blocks). Align scrap butterflies on marked circles at diagonal placement lines as shown.

Butterflies Block—Make 9.

5. When satisfied with placement of pieces on each block, appliqué pieces in alphabetical order.
6. Make 5 blocks with blue B pieces and 4 blocks with pink B pieces.

Quilt Assembly

1. Referring to photo on page 244, lay out blocks in 3 horizontal rows of 3 blocks each. Alternate blocks with blue B pieces and pink Bs as shown.

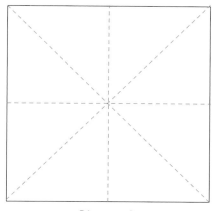

Diagram A

2. Join the blocks in each row.
3. Join the rows.

Borders

1. From green square, cut 16 (¾"-wide) bias strips. Trim 8 strips to 6¼" long and 8 strips to 9" long. Fold and press each strip in thirds (use bias pressing bar, if desired) to get ¼"-wide vine pieces.

continued

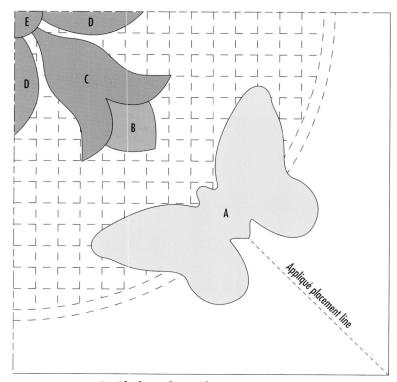

¼ Block Appliqué Placement Diagram

2. Fold each border strip in half to find center. Position 1 E on each border at this point, 2" from 1 long edge. Position Cs on both sides of E (½ Border Appliqué Placement Diagram). Place short vine strips; then place longer strips, adding Ds, Gs, and Fs as shown.

3. When satisfied with placement of appliqué pieces, stitch vines in place. Then appliqué remaining pieces in alphabetical order.

4. Measure width of the quilt through middle of pieced top. Trim 2 (60") border strips to this measurement, measuring from center of border strip. Stitch borders to top and bottom edges of quilt, easing to fit as needed.

5. Measure length of the quilt through middle of pieced top. Trim remaining borders to this length, measuring from center of border strip. Sew border strips to quilt sides.

Quilting and Finishing

1. Mark quilt top with desired quilting design. Quilt shown is hand-quilted with ½" crosshatch pattern quilted inside marked circles. Pattern for plume quilted in block corners is on opposite page.

The borders are quilted in lines spaced ½" apart.

2. Layer backing, batting, and quilt top. Baste. Outline-quilt around all appliqué pieces. Quilt circles on marked lines. Add additional quilting as marked or as desired.

3. Make 8¾ yards of continuous bias or straight-grain binding. Bind quilt edges.

Reverse along this line.

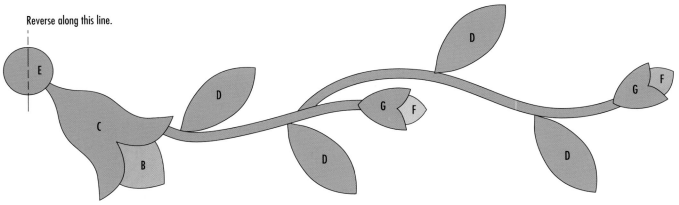

½ Border Appliqué Placement Diagram (40% of actual size)

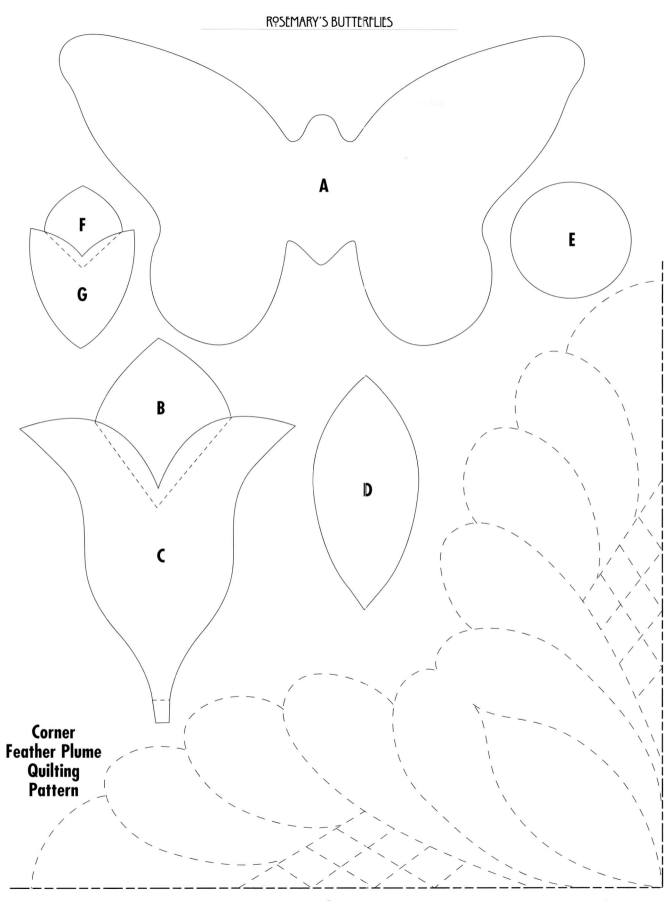

**Corner
Feather Plume
Quilting
Pattern**

MOON & STAR WHIMSY

Quilt by Marion Roach Watchinski of Overland Park, Kansas

Heavenly bodies flicker to life in this interesting quilt. Full moons, half-moons, and over-size stars are framed by a border of Marion Watchinski's original design.

Finished Size
Quilt: 78" x 92½"
Blocks: 20 (14½" x 14½")

Materials
10 (⅜-yard) pieces or scraps for appliqué
5¼ yards cream background print *
1 yard brown for bias border
1 yard binding fabric
5½ yards backing fabric
* *Note:* If prewashed fabric is not full 45" wide, you may need an additional 1½ yards to cut blocks.

Cutting
See page 307 for tips on cutting pieces of appliqué. Trace all 4 sections of Pattern A on pages 248 and 249 to make complete full moon template. Make star and half-moon templates from patterns on opposite page.
From cream background fabric
• 4 (10½" x 80") lengthwise border strips.
• 20 (15") squares for blocks.
From bias border and binding fabrics
• 1 (30") square of each.
Note: Add remaining fabric to scraps for appliqué.
From scrap fabrics
• 20 full moons
• 36 stars
• 22 half-moons.

Moon & Star Block—Make 20.

Appliqué Block Assembly

See page 307 for tips on preparing moons and stars for appliqué.

1. Center 1 full moon on each cream square. Referring to photo, vary position of moons. Appliqué.
2. Position 1 star in open circle of each full moon. Appliqué.

Quilt Assembly

1. Lay out blocks in 5 horizontal rows, with 4 blocks in each row, turning blocks as desired.

2. When satisfied with placement, join blocks in each row.
3. Join the rows.

Borders

1. Measure quilt from top to bottom through middle. Trim 2 border strips to match length. Sew these borders to quilt sides. Press seam allowances toward borders.
2. Measure quilt from side to side through middle. Trim remaining borders to match quilt width.

Sew borders to top and bottom edges of quilt. Press seam allowances toward borders.
3. Fold quilt in half to find center. Use pin to mark center on outer edge of each border.
4. Using reserved brown square, make 7½ yards of 2½"-wide continuous bias binding.

continued

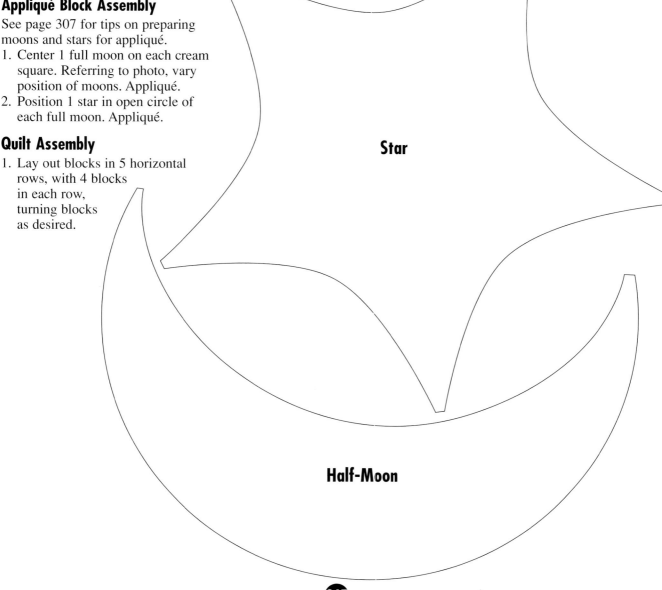

Star

Half-Moon

5. With wrong sides facing, fold bias strips in half lengthwise. Stitch ¼" seam through both layers. Press seam allowance open, centering seam on 1 side of strip.

6. Fold bias strip in 8 equal lengths; mark each eighth with pin.

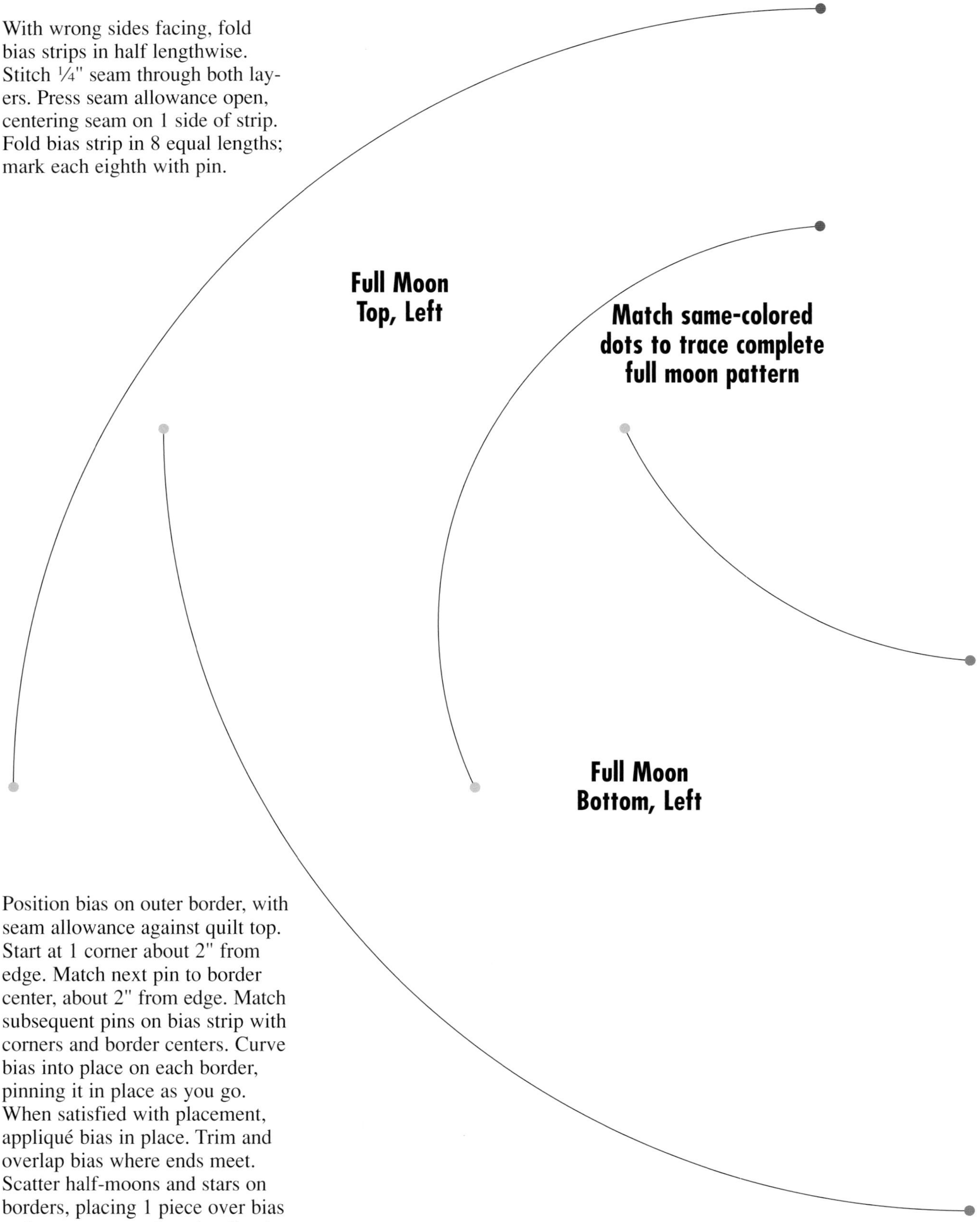

**Full Moon
Top, Left**

**Match same-colored
dots to trace complete
full moon pattern**

**Full Moon
Bottom, Left**

7. Position bias on outer border, with seam allowance against quilt top. Start at 1 corner about 2" from edge. Match next pin to border center, about 2" from edge. Match subsequent pins on bias strip with corners and border centers. Curve bias into place on each border, pinning it in place as you go.

8. When satisfied with placement, appliqué bias in place. Trim and overlap bias where ends meet.

9. Scatter half-moons and stars on borders, placing 1 piece over bias ends to cover overlap. Appliqué.

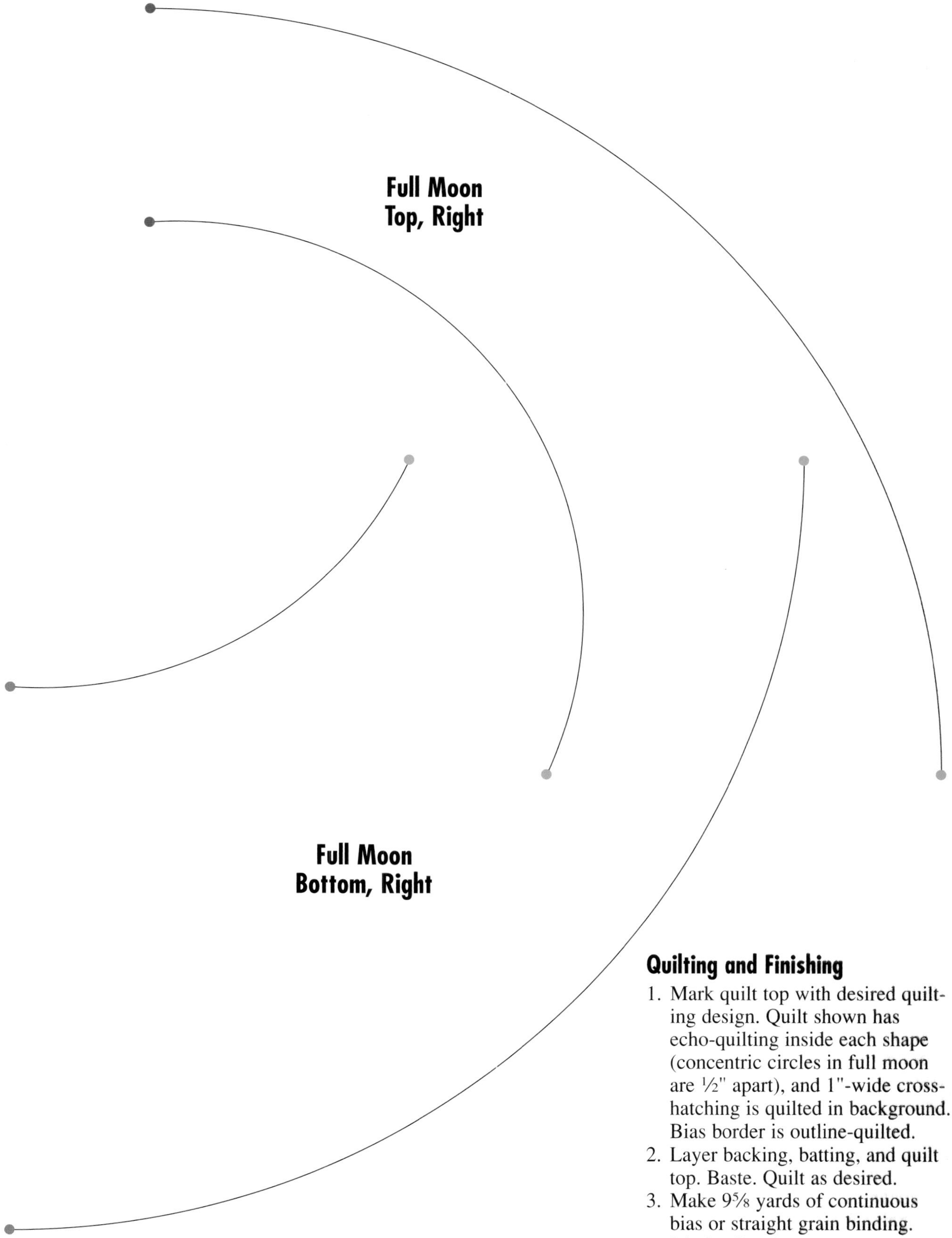

**Full Moon
Top, Right**

**Full Moon
Bottom, Right**

Quilting and Finishing

1. Mark quilt top with desired quilting design. Quilt shown has echo-quilting inside each shape (concentric circles in full moon are ½" apart), and 1"-wide cross-hatching is quilted in background. Bias border is outline-quilted.
2. Layer backing, batting, and quilt top. Baste. Quilt as desired.
3. Make 9⅝ yards of continuous bias or straight grain binding. Bind quilt edges.

HUNTER'S STAR

Quilt by Robin Miller Brower of Hayden, Alabama; owned by Jimm Brower

How do you turn one block into another? With quick-piecing techniques and clever placement, Robin Brower's Indian Arrowhead blocks become a variation of the traditional Hunter's Star. Instead of cutting and piecing tricky diamonds, this method uses only squares and rectangles.

Finished Size
Quilt: 76" x 92"
Blocks: 80 (8" x 8")

Materials
¼ yard *each* of 27 scrap fabrics
5 yards muslin
⅞ yard binding fabric
5½ yards backing fabric

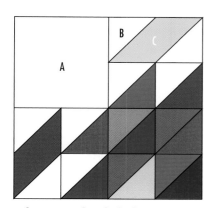

Indian Arrowhead Block—Make 80.

Cutting

Instructions are for rotary cutting and quick piecing. Before cutting, read block instructions and decide whether you prefer quick piecing or traditional piecing. For traditional cutting, use patterns on page 253.

From scrap fabrics
• 60 (8" x 14") pieces for B triangle-squares.
• 160 (2½" x 4½") C pieces.

From muslin
• 4 (6½" x 85") lengthwise strips for borders.
• 20 (8" x 14") pieces for B triangle-squares.
• 80 (4½") A squares.
• 160 (2½") B squares.

Block Assembly

1. On wrong side of 1 (8" x 14") muslin piece, draw a 2-square by 4-square grid of 2⅞" squares (Diagram A). Mark diagonal lines through squares as shown.
2. With right sides facing, match marked fabric piece with scrap fabric. Starting at middle of 1 side, stitch on both sides of diagonal lines, pivoting at grid corners. (Red lines on diagram show 1 continuous stitching line; blue lines show second line.) Press. Cut on all drawn lines to get 16 triangle-squares from grid.

3. Following steps 1 and 2, stitch 20 muslin/scrap grids to get total of 320 muslin/scrap triangle-squares. Follow the same steps to stitch 20 scrap/scrap grids to get a total of 320 scrap/scrap triangle-squares. Press seam allowances toward darker fabric.
4. Referring to page 304, use the diagonal-corner technique to sew 2 (2½") muslin B squares to 1 C (Diagram B). Or sew B triangles to C traditionally. Make 80 B/C units as shown; then reverse direction of diagonal seams to make another 80 B/C units. Press seam allowances toward Cs.
5. Join 2 muslin/scrap triangle-squares, sewing the colored side of first to muslin side of second

(Diagram C). Join pair to 1 B/C unit as shown. Make 160 units.
6. Join scrap/scrap triangle-squares in pairs (Diagram D) and then join pairs to make 1 four-patch. Make 80 four-patch units as shown.
7. For each block, select 1 A square, 2 B/C units, and 1 scrap triangle-square unit (Block Assembly Diagram). Join the units in 2 rows as shown; then join the rows to complete the block. Make 80 blocks. Lay out the blocks in rows as you finish each block (Row Assembly Diagram, page 252). To make the stars come out, you'll want to select matching B/C units for the adjoining block(s).

continued

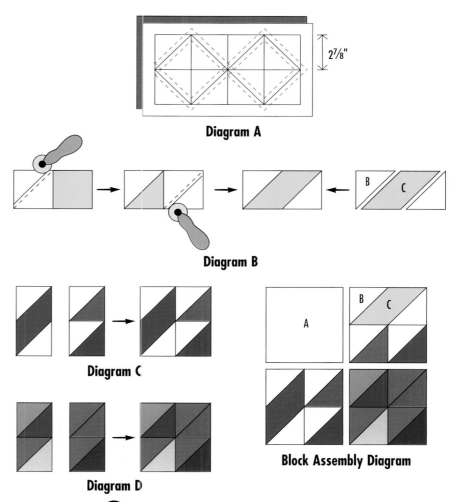

Diagram A

Diagram B

Diagram C

Diagram D

Block Assembly Diagram

Quilt Assembly

1. Lay out blocks in 10 horizontal rows, with 8 blocks in each row (Row Assembly Diagram). Referring to diagram and photo on page 250, turn blocks to achieve star pattern.
2. When satisfied with placement, join blocks in each row.
3. Referring to photo, join rows.

Borders

1. Measure from top to bottom through middle of pieced top. Trim 2 border strips to match length. Sew borders to quilt sides.
2. Measure quilt from side to side through middle of pieced top.

Trim remaining border strips to match width. Sew borders to top and bottom edges of quilt.

Quilting and Finishing

1. Mark quilting design on quilt top as desired. Quilt shown is outline-quilted with stencil design quilted in muslin part of each block. Leaf and vine pattern is quilted in borders.
2. Layer backing, batting, and quilt top. Baste. Quilt as desired.
3. Use remaining inner border fabric to make 9¾ yards of bias or straight-grain binding. Bind quilt edges.

Row 1—Make 5.

Row 2—Make 5.

Row Assembly Diagram

Size Variations

	Twin	Queen/King
Finished size	60" x 92"	92" x 92"
Number of blocks	60	100
Blocks set	6 x 10	10 x 10
Yardage Required		
¼-yard scraps	19	31
Muslin	4¾ yards	6¾ yards
Binding fabric	¾ yard	1 yard
Backing fabric	5½ yards	8¼ yards

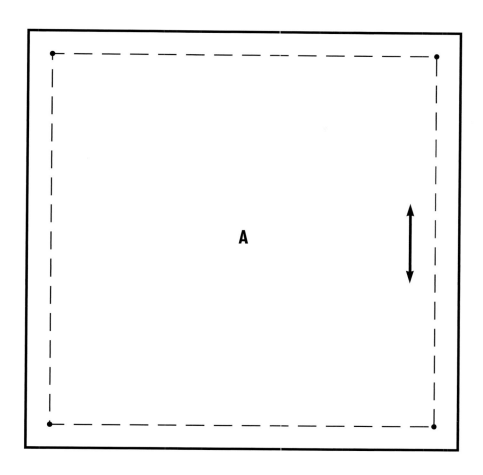

A

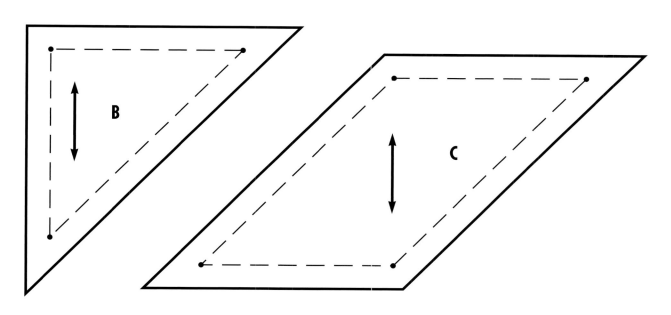

B

C

NIGHT & NOON STARS

Quilt by Winnie S. Fleming of Friendswood, Texas

Winnie Fleming likes to put a new spin on traditional designs. Using strong colors and a black background, she made a dramatic contemporary quilt. The blocks are set so that they form a field of bright stars in a dark sky.

Finished Size

Quilt: 51" x 60"
Blocks: 20 (9" x 9")

Materials

14 (8½") squares tone-on-tone prints for blocks and border
10 (18" x 22") fat quarters bright prints
3 yards black (includes binding)
3¼ yards backing fabric

Cutting

Instructions are for rotary cutting and quick piecing. Cut strips on crosswise grain except as noted. Cut in order listed for best use of yardage.

From tone-on-tone squares
• 56 (4¼") squares. Cut each square in quarters diagonally to get 224 B triangles (160 for blocks, 62 for border, and 2 extra).

From each bright print
• 6 (1⅝" x 18") strips for strip sets.
• 2 (4¾") A squares for star centers.
• 6 or 7 (1½") squares to get a total of 66 C squares for border.

From black
• 8 (3½" x 58") lengthwise strips for borders.
• 3 (15" x 18") pieces, cut from length left over from borders. From these, cut 27 (1⅝" x 18") strips for Strip Set 2.
• 1 (25") square for binding.
• 2 (4¼") strips. From these, cut 20 (4¼") squares. Cut each square in quarters diagonally to get 80 B triangles.
• 2 (2¾") strips. From these and scrap, cut 33 (2¾") squares. Cut each square in quarters diagonally to get 132 D triangles for border.

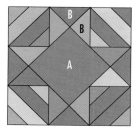

Night & Noon Block—Make 20.

Block Assembly

1. For Strip Set 1, join 2 (1⅝")
colored strips. Press seam allowances toward darker fabric. Make
16 of Strip Set 1.

2. Place 1 strip set on cutting mat.
Measure 2¾" from top right corner (reverse directions if you're
left-handed). Make diagonal cut
from this point to bottom right
corner (Strip Set 1 Diagram). Measure
5½" along bottom edge. Make
second cut from this point to top
edge to get first triangle. Continue
cutting in this manner to get 5
triangles from each strip set.

3. For Strip Set 2, join each remaining colored strip to black strip.
Make 27 strip sets. Press seam
allowances toward black.

4. Cut triangles in same manner as
for Strip Set 1, cutting 3 black-
bottomed triangles from each
strip set (Strip Set 2 Diagram). Discard
alternate triangles.

5. Join each black-bottomed triangle
to colored triangle to make each
corner unit (Diagram A). Make 80
corner units, 4 for each block.

continued

Diagram A

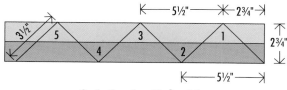

Strip Set 1—Make 16.

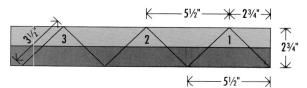

Strip Set 2—Make 27.

Color Variations

Winnie's Night & Noon blocks
twinkle in a midnight field. If you
prefer a daytime look, your quilt
can represent the rosy colors of
dawn or the glow of an autumn
sunset. Or forget the time of
day and just use any color combination you like. These illustrations
give you some idea of the many
quilts you can make with these
handsome blocks.

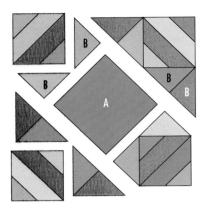

Block Assembly Diagram

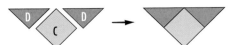

Diagram B

Diagram C

6. Sew each black B triangle to bright B to make 1 Star Point Unit (Block Assembly Diagram). Make 40 Star Point Units with black triangle on right and 40 units with black triangle on left. Press seam allowances toward black.

7. For each block, select 4 Star Point units, 1 A square, 4 B triangles, and 4 corner units (Block Assembly Diagram). Join Bs to adjacent sides of 2 corner units as shown; sew these to opposite sides of A.

8. Sew Star Point units to adjacent sides of remaining corner units. Sew these to remaining sides of A to complete block.

9. Make 20 blocks.

Quilt Assembly

1. Lay out blocks in 5 horizontal rows, with 4 blocks in each row (Quilt Assembly Diagram).
2. Join blocks in each row.
3. Join the rows.

Borders

1. Measure length of quilt through middle of pieced top. Trim 2 border strips to match quilt length. Stitch borders to quilt sides, easing to fit as needed.
2. Measure width of quilt through middle of pieced top. Trim 2 border strips to match width. Sew borders to top and bottom edges of quilt, easing to fit as needed.

3. Sew black D triangles to adjacent sides of each 1½" C (Diagram B). Press seam allowances toward Ds. Piece 66 C/D units as shown.

4. For top border, join 14 Bs and 15 C/D units in a row (Diagram C). Sew border to top edge of quilt (Quilt Assembly Diagram). Make bottom border in same manner.

5. Join 17 Bs and 18 C/D units in row to make each side border. Sew borders to quilt sides. Miter border corners.

6. Repeat steps 1 and 2 to add outer black borders.

Quilting and Finishing

1. Mark quilt top with desired quilting design. Quilt shown is machine-quilted in-the-ditch with floral motif quilted in star centers and wave pattern in black borders.

2. Layer backing, batting, and quilt top. Baste layers together. Then follow marked lines to quilt as desired.

3. From 25" black square, make 6⅜ yards of continuous bias or straight-grain binding. Bind quilt edges.

Quilt Assembly Diagram

BEAR'S PAW

Quick piecing makes triangle-squares easy to sew. This quilt has lots of them, including a sawtooth border. Bear's Paw block has many variations and names, including Duck's Foot in the Mud, Hand of Friendship, Small Hand, Cat's Paw, and Illinois Turkey Track.

Finished Size
Quilt: 67" x 83"
Blocks: 12 (14" x 14")

Materials
6 (12½" x 18") green prints
6 (12½" x 18") red prints
13 (12½" x 18") tone-on-tone background prints
1 (12½" x 18") piece green solid fabric
1½ yards red solid fabric (includes binding)
2¼ yards print fabric for border
5 yards backing fabric

Cutting
Instructions are for rotary cutting and quick piecing. Before cutting, read the block instructions and decide whether you prefer quick piecing or traditional piecing. For traditional cutting, use the patterns on page 259.
From each green print
• 1 (7½" x 18") for triangle-squares.
• 8 (4½") B squares.
From each red print
• 1 (7½" x 18") for triangle-squares.
• 8 (4½") B squares.
From each of 12 background prints
• 1 (7½" x 18") for triangle-squares.
• 8 (2½") C squares.
• 8 (2½" x 6½") D rectangles.
From green solid
• 1 (7½" x 18") for triangle-squares.
• 8 (2½") C squares.

Quilt by Winnie S. Fleming of Friendswood, Texas

From red solid
• 8 (2½" x 39") crosswise strips for middle border.
• 8 (2½") C squares.
From border fabric
• 4 (5" x 76") lengthwise strips.
• 4 (2½" x 65") lengthwise strips.

continued

257

Block Assembly

1. On wrong side of each 7½" x 18" background piece, draw a 2-square by 6-square grid of 2⅞" squares (Diagram A). Mark diagonal lines through squares as shown.
2. With right sides facing, match 1 marked piece with 1 red or green piece. Starting at middle of 1 side, stitch on both sides of diagonal lines, pivoting at grid corners as shown. (Red lines in diagram show first continuous stitching path; blue lines show second path.) Press stitching. Cut on all drawn lines to get 24 triangle-squares from each grid. Stitch 13 grids to get 312 triangle-squares. Press seam allowances toward dark fabric.
3. For each block, find 16 matching triangle-squares, 4 C squares and 4 Ds of matching background fabric, 4 matching B squares, and 1 C square of contrasting print fabric.
4. Match 1 solid red or solid green C square with pieces for each block as desired.
5. For 1 block, join triangle-squares in 8 pairs as shown, always sewing print fabric to background fabric (Block Assembly Diagram). Sew 1 pair to 1 B square as shown. Join C background square to remaining pair; then join 3-square strip to adjacent side of B. Press seam allowances toward B. Make 4 units in this manner.
6. Join 2 units to opposite sides of 2 D pieces as shown. Press seam allowances toward D.
7. Sew remaining Ds to opposite sides of solid-colored C square. Press seam allowances toward Ds.
8. Join rows to complete block.
9. Make 12 blocks. Set 96 triangle-squares aside for border.

Quilt Assembly

1. Alternating red and green blocks, lay out in 4 horizontal rows of 3 blocks each (Row Assembly Diagram). When satisfied with placement, join blocks in each row.
2. For sashing row, join 3 sashing strips and 2 sashing squares as shown. Make 3 sashing rows, placing red and green sashing squares as desired.
3. Join rows, alternating block rows and sashing rows.

Borders

1. Measure quilt from top to bottom; trim 2 inner borders to match length. Sew to sides.
2. Measure quilt from side to side and trim remaining borders to match quilt width. Sew borders to top and bottom edges of quilt.
3. Join 2 red strips end to end for each middle border. Repeat steps 1 and 2 to measure quilt, trim borders to fit, and sew borders to edges of quilt.
4. Use 1 (7½" x 18") solid green piece and remaining background fabric to stitch another grid of 24 triangle-squares. From scraps, cut

2 (2⅞") squares each of background fabric and print border fabric. Cut squares in half to get 4 A triangles. Join background triangle to print triangle to make 4 triangle-squares. You should have 124 triangle-squares for sawtooth border.
5. Select 34 triangle-squares for each side border. Join squares in vertical row, sewing background fabric triangle to print triangle and changing direction in middle (see photo on page 257). Sew borders to sides, easing as necessary.
6. For top border, join 26 triangle-squares in a horizontal row, again changing direction in middle of row. Add 1 square to each end of row, changing position of end squares as shown in photo. Sew row to top edge of quilt, easing as needed. Repeat for bottom border.
7. Measure length of quilt. Trim and sew outer borders to quilt.

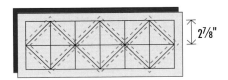

Diagram A

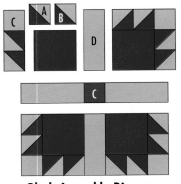

Block Assembly Diagram

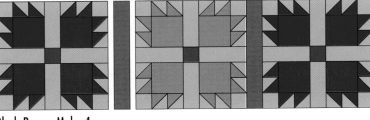

Block Row—Make 4.

Sashing Row—Make 3.

Row Assembly Diagram

Quilting and Finishing

1. Mark quilting design on quilt top as desired. Quilt shown has diagonal lines quilted in blocks and borders.
2. Layer backing, batting, and quilt top. Baste together. Then quilt as desired.
3. Use remaining solid red fabric to make 9 yards of bias or straight-grain binding. Bind quilt edges.

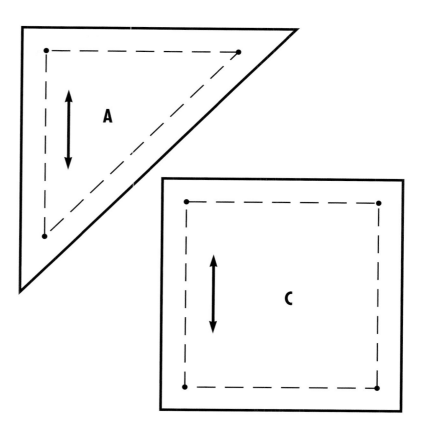

A

C

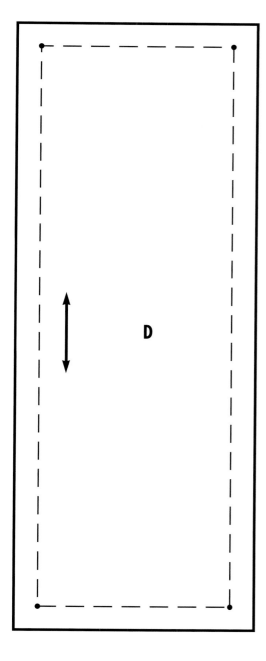

D

B

Size Variations

	Full/Queen	King
Finished size	83" x 99"	99" x 99"
Number of blocks	20	25
Blocks set	4 x 5	5 x 5
Number of		
Sashing strips	31	40
Sashing squares	12	16
Triangle-squares for border	160	176
Yardage Required		
Green prints	10	13
Red prints	10	12
Background prints	20	25
Solid green fabric	10 (2½") squares	12 (2½") squares
Solid red fabric	1½ yards	1½ yards
Print border fabric	2⅝ yards	2⅞ yards
108"-wide backing fabric	2½ yards	3 yards

BLUEPRINTS

Quilt by Karen Kratz-Miller of Cincinnati, Ohio

Piece this village full of cheery houses—and you'll be a great "homemaker"! Karen Kratz-Miller chose hues of yellow and rust to put a warm glow in the windows and door of each house of blues.

Finished Size
Quilt: 70" x 89"
Blocks: 48 (8" x 8")
        Schoolhouse blocks
        4 (5¼" x 5¼")
        Log Cabin blocks

Materials
For Schoolhouse Blocks:
96 (4" x 5½") blue scraps
48 (4" x 8") blue scraps
80 (1½" x 22") blue strips
28 (1½" x 22") yellow and/or
    rust strips

For Log Cabin blocks:
4 (1¼") squares rust
4 (1¼" x 22") dark blue strips
4 (1¼" x 22") light blue strips

13 (1" x 22") rust strips for
    inner border
60 (2" x 42") dark blue strips
    for sashing
¼ yard light blue fabric for
    sashing squares
⅞ yard navy fabric for binding
5½ yards backing fabric or
    2¾ yards 90"-wide muslin

Cutting
Make templates for patterns A, B, and C on pages 262 and 263. (See page 302 for tips on making and using templates. You'll find piecing easier if you mark pivot points on these pieces.) All other pieces are rotary cut.

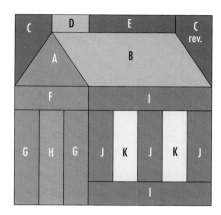

Schoolhouse Block—Make 34.

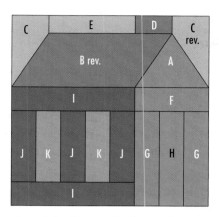

Rev. Schoolhouse Block—Make 14.

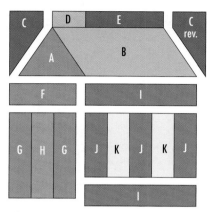

Schoolhouse Block Assembly Diagram

This quilt has many pieces of similar size. Store cut pieces in zip-top plastic bags that are labeled with identifying letters.

From 4" x 5½" blue scrap fabrics
• 48 of Pattern A.
• 48 of Pattern C.
• 48 of Pattern C reversed.
• 48 (1¼" x 4") E pieces.
Note: Cs and E for each block are usually cut from same fabric.

From 4" x 8" blue scrap fabrics
• 34 of Pattern B.
• 14 of Pattern B reversed.
• 48 (1¼" x 2") D pieces.

From 1½" x 22" blue strips
• 192 (1½" x 3½") pieces for F and J.
• 96 (1½" x 4½") G pieces.
• 96 (1½" x 5½") I pieces.

From rust and/or yellow strips
• 48 (1½" x 4½") H pieces.
• 96 (1½" x 3½") K pieces.

From dark blue strips
• 110 (2" x 8½") sashing strips.
• 368 (2" x 4") border strips.

From light blue
• 63 (2") sashing squares.

Schoolhouse Block Assembly

In quilt shown, 34 houses have the door on left side, and 14 blocks have door on the right. (See block diagrams.) The only difference in the construction is B piece in 14 reversed blocks.

1. For each block, select 1 each of pieces A, B, C, C rev., D, E, F, and H. Select 2 each of pieces G, I, and K, and 3 Js (Block Diagrams).
2. For roof section, join D to E; then join D/E to top of B (Schoolhouse Block Assembly Diagram). Join A to B, being careful not to sew into seam allowance at top of A. Press the seam allowance toward B.
3. To set in C, first sew short side of C to D, stopping at pivot point, and backstitch. Reposition C to align diagonal edge with A. Starting with backstitch at pivot point, continue seam to end of A/C.
4. Set in C rev. on opposite side in same manner.
5. For door, join Gs to both sides of H. Join F at top of unit. Press seam allowance away from F.

6. For windows section, join Js and Ks in row as shown. Press seam allowances toward Js. Add 2 I pieces to top and bottom edges of unit. Press seam allowances toward I pieces.
7. Join door and windows sections.
8. Join roof section to door/window section to complete block.
9. Make 34 Schoolhouse blocks and 14 reversed blocks.

Quilt Assembly

1. Lay out Schoolhouse blocks in 8 horizontal rows, with 6 blocks in each row (Row Assembly Diagram). Position sashing strips between blocks and at row ends as shown. When satisfied with placement, join blocks and sashing in each row. Press seam allowances toward sashing.
2. Lay out remaining sashing strips in 9 horizontal rows, with 6 strips in each row and 7 light blue squares at row ends and between strips as shown. Join strips and squares in each row. Press seam allowances toward sashing.
3. Lay out all the rows, alternating sashing rows and block rows as shown in photo. Join rows.

continued

Row Assembly Diagram

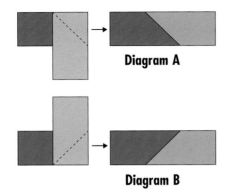

Diagram A

Diagram B

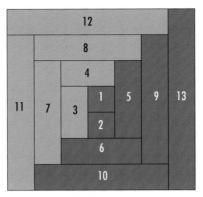

Log Cabin Block Diagram

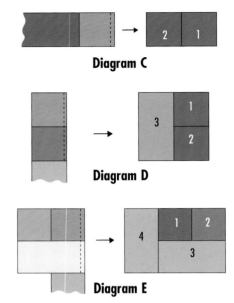

Diagram C

Diagram D

Diagram E

Adding Borders

1. Measure quilt from top to bottom through the middle of the pieced top. For each inner side border, join the rust strips to achieve needed length. Join the borders to quilt sides.
2. Measure quilt from side to side through middle; join rust strips to match width. Join border to quilt top. Repeat for bottom border.
3. To make each unit for pieced border, select 2 (2" x 4") strips. See page 305 for instructions on sewing diagonal ends. Make 92 units with seams going 1 way (Diagram A) and another 92 units with seams going in opposite direction (Diagram B). Cut each unit down to 5¾" long, trimming equally from each end of unit.
4. Join 52 pieced units for each side border, mixing the seam directions. Join side borders to quilt. (If pieced border

doesn't fit precisely, add or subtract strips as needed.) Press seam allowances toward inner border.
5. Join 40 pieced units each for top and bottom borders. Set aside.

Log Cabin Block Assembly

To complete the house theme, corners of top and bottom borders are traditional Log Cabin blocks.
1. Log 1 is 1¼" square of rust fabric (Log Cabin Block Diagram). For Log 2, select 1 strip of dark blue fabric. With right sides facing, stitch end of strip to square (Diagram C). Trim strip even with square and press.
2. With right sides facing, match 1 light strip to long edge of joined squares and stitch (Diagram D). Trim Log 3 even with bottom of unit as before and press.
3. Turn unit so that Log 3 is at the bottom. With right sides facing,

match another light strip to the edge of logs 1 and 3, and stitch (Diagram E). Trim Log 4 even with bottom of unit and press.
4. Continue adding light and dark logs in this manner until you have 3 logs on all sides of center square (Log Cabin Block Diagram). Always press seam allowances toward newest log; then rotate unit to put new log at bottom to add next strip. Make 4 blocks in this manner.
5. Join 1 Log Cabin block to each end of top border. Join border to top edge of quilt, easing as needed to fit. Repeat for bottom border.

Quilting and Finishing

1. Mark quilting design on the quilt top as desired. On quilt shown, blocks are quilted differently with horizontal, vertical, and diagonal lines that echo patchwork shapes and extend into sashing and borders. Outline quilting is a good alternative, if desired.
2. Layer backing, batting, and quilt top. Baste. Quilt as desired.
3. From navy fabric, make 9¼ yards of straight-grain or bias binding. Bind quilt edges.

A

Color Variations

Every neighborhood has its own style. These ideas may inspire a subdivision of a different stripe.

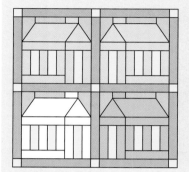
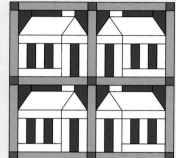
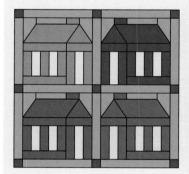

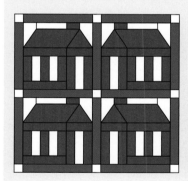
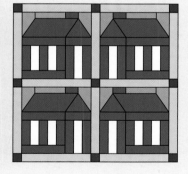
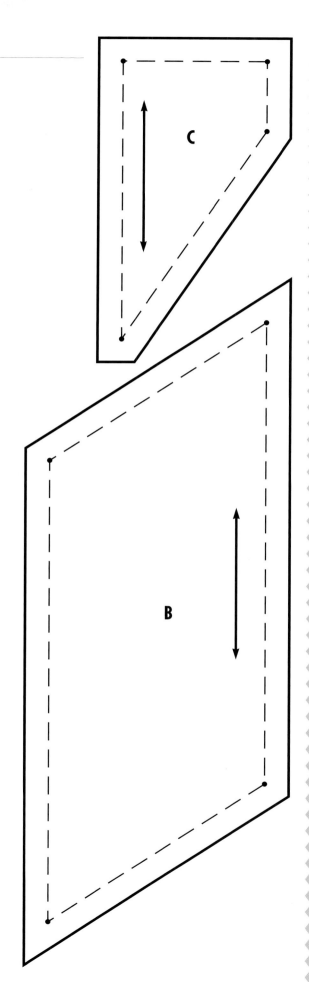

OLD THYME CHAIN & STAR

Quilt by Darlene K. Orton of Salina, Kansas

Darlene Orton says she fell in love with this quilt the minute she saw it in *New Jersey Quilts,* published in 1992 by the Heritage Quilt Project of New Jersey, which documented New Jersey's quilt history. Darlene wanted to make her own version of the 1840s-era quilt, staying true to the colors and fabrics of the period. "The patterns were easy," says Darlene. "The challenge was finding enough of the right fabrics." Of course, that's also the *fun* part.

Finished Size

Quilt: 106½" x 121½"
Blocks: 195 (7½" x 7½")

Materials

49 (6" x 22") strips for stars *
188 (2" x 22") strips assorted fabrics
    (red, pink, brown, and blue) *
½ yard red for stars and bows
1½ yards red print for swags
7¾ yards muslin
1 yard binding fabric
9½ yards backing fabric
* *Note:* 25 (18" x 22") fat quarters
are sufficient to cut all strips.

Cutting

Instructions are for rotary cutting.
Cut all strips on crosswise grain
except as noted. Cut pieces in order
listed to get best use of yardage.
From each *star fabric*
• 6 (2¾") squares. Cut each square
  in quarters diagonally to get 24 B
  triangles, 12 for each of 2 blocks.
• 10 (2") squares. Set aside 2 squares
  for star centers (A) and 8 squares
  for block corners (D) for 2 blocks.
From assorted fabric strips
• 97 sets of 4 matched 2" D squares.
• 97 sets of 8 matched 2" E squares.
• 97 sets of 4 matched 2" F squares.
• 97 sets of 4 matched 2" G squares.
• 97 assorted 2" H squares.
Note: To keep track of which sets
are which, we recommend putting

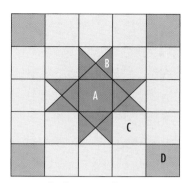

Block 1—Make 98.

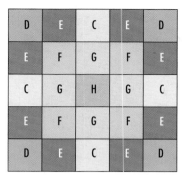

Block 2—Make 97.

cut sets in labeled zip-top plastic bags. Then when you need 4 Ds, for example, you can just reach in and find any 4 squares that match.

From red
- 36 stars.
- 4 bows (4 each of X and Y).

From red print
- 22 of side swags.
- 18 top/bottom swags.

From muslin
- 73 (2"-wide) strips. From these, cut 1,533 (2") C squares.
- 4 (5" x 126") lengthwise border strips. Remaining fabric should be approximately 23" wide. Make next 2 cuts from this length.
- 14 (3¼"-wide) strips. From these, cut 98 (3¼") squares. Cut each square in quarters diagonally to get 392 B triangles for star points.
- 39 (2"-wide) strips. From these, cut another 423 (2") C squares to get a total of 1,956 squares.

Block 1 Assembly

1. For 1 block, choose 1 A square and 12 B triangles of same fabric,

4 muslin B triangles, 16 muslin C squares, and 4 print D squares.

2. Join 1 muslin B and 1 print B (Diagram A). Press seam allowances toward print fabric. Join 2 print Bs as shown. Join pairs to complete 1 star point unit. Make 4 units for each block.

Diagram A

3. Lay out squares and star point units in 5 rows (Block 1 Assembly Diagram). Join squares in each

row; then join rows to complete block. Press all the row seam allowances in same direction.

4. Make 98 of Block 1.

Block 2 Assembly

1. For each block, choose 4 muslin C squares and 1 set each of D, E, F, G, and H squares. Lay out squares in 5 rows (Block 2 Assembly Diagram).
2. Join squares in each row.
3. Join rows to complete block. Press all row seam allowances in same direction.
4. Make 97 of Block 2.

Quilt Assembly

1. Lay out blocks in 15 horizontal rows, with 13 blocks in each row. For Row 1 and all odd-numbered rows, start with a star block and alternate blocks as shown (Row Assembly Diagram). For Row 2 and all even-numbered rows, start with

continued

Block 1 Assembly Diagram

Block 2 Assembly Diagram

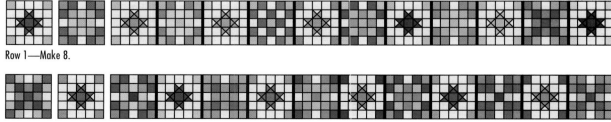

Row 1—Make 8.

Row 2—Make 7.

Row Assembly Diagram

Block 2. Turn adjacent blocks as needed to offset seam allowances.
2. Join the blocks in each row. Then join the rows.
3. Sew 1 border strip to each side of the quilt, centering each strip. Miter corners.
4. Pin 9 swags and 8 stars each on top and bottom borders. Pin 11 swags and 10 stars on each side border and bows at border corners at mitered seam. When satisfied with placement, appliqué.

Quilting and Finishing

1. Mark quilt top with desired quilting design. Quilt shown is quilted in-the-ditch around each star, around muslin surrounding each star, and diagonally through each chain square. Echo quilting surrounds each swag to fill border.
2. Layer backing, batting, and quilt top. Baste. Quilt as desired.
3. Make 13 yards of continuous straight-grain or bias binding. Bind quilt edges.

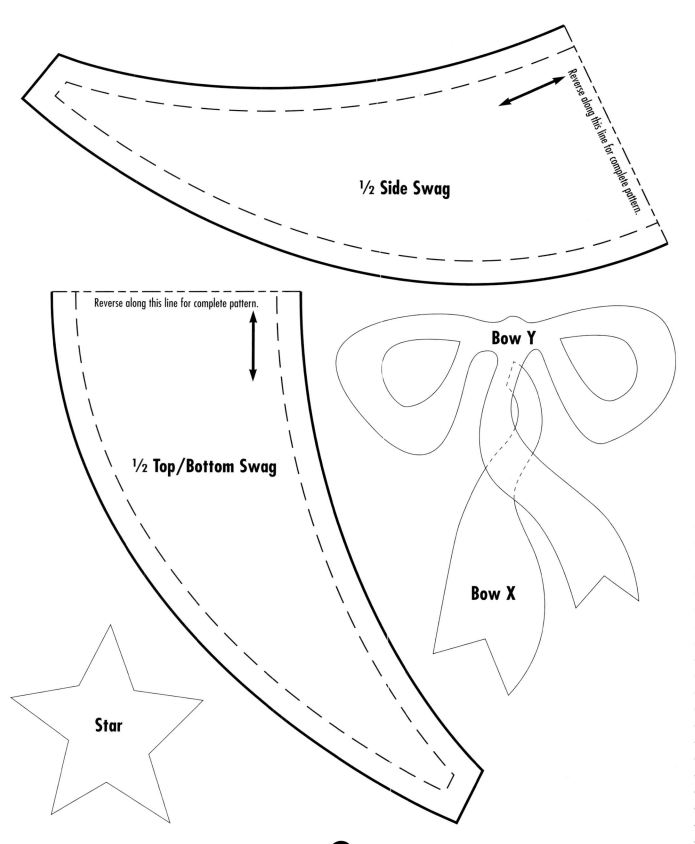

½ Side Swag

Reverse along this line for complete pattern.

Reverse along this line for complete pattern.

½ Top/Bottom Swag

Bow Y

Bow X

Star

STARS WITH FLAIR

Quilt by Christine Kennedy of Oak Ridge, Tennessee

Bias appliqué around the points of these stars gives this quilt an unusual flair, so Christine Kennedy named her original design *Stars with Flair*. The colors in the floral fabric set the tone for a coordinating background fabric and scraps. Christine hand-pieced her award-winning quilt, but we offer you a quick-piecing option.

Finished Size

Quilt: 78" x 95"
Blocks: 20 (17" x 17")

Materials

40 (⅛-yard) pieces coordinating scrap fabrics
5 yards floral print (includes binding)
4 yards pale pink tone-on-tone print
5¾ yards backing fabric

Cutting

Instructions are for rotary cutting and quick piecing. Cut all strips on crosswise grain except border strips as noted. For traditional cutting and piecing, use patterns on pages 271 and 272. Cut pieces in order listed to get best use of yardage.

Star Block—Make 20.

From each *scrap fabric*
- 3 (1⅜"-wide) strips. From these, cut 6 (1⅜" x 20") strips for strip sets. Divide these into 20 sets (1 for each star block), selecting 3 strips each of 4 coordinating fabrics for each for set.

From floral print
- 4 (1½" x 94") inner border strips.
- 3 (31") squares for bias appliqué.
- 1 (31") square for binding.
- 36 (1⅜"-wide) strips. From these and narrow length left from previous cuts, cut 100 (1⅜" x 20") strips for strip sets.

From pink
- 1 (2¾-yard) length. From this, cut 2 (4½" x 99") lengthwise strips for side outer borders and 2 (4½" x 84") strips for top and bottom outer borders. Use leftovers from this piece for next 2 steps.
- 20 (8⅜") squares. Cut each square in quarters diagonally to get 80 C triangles.
- 80 (5½") B squares.

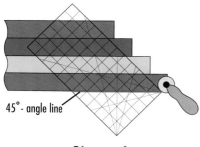

45°- angle line

Diagram A

Block Assembly

1. For each star, select 1 set of scrap strips and 5 strips of floral print. Floral print is Fabric 1 throughout (see Strip Set Diagrams). Designate each scrap fabric as fabric 2, 3, 4, or 5.
2. Select 2 floral print strips and 1 each of fabrics 2 and 3. Starting with floral print, join strips as shown (Strip Set 1 Diagram). Instead of matching ends of each new strip, offset each strip about 1½" (this allows you to get more cuts per strip set, reducing waste).
3. Make 1 each of strips sets 2, 3, and 4 in same manner, positioning scrap fabrics consistently as shown. Press seam allowances in strip sets 1 and 3 toward bottom strip and seam allowances in sets 2 and 4 toward top strip.
4. Lay Strip Set 1 on cutting mat with uneven end to your right (if you're left-handed, reverse directions throughout). Position acrylic ruler over strip set, aligning 45°-angle line with bottom edge of strip set (Diagram A). Trim uneven ends as shown.
5. Turn strip set upside down to continue cutting (Diagram B). Measuring from cut edge, measure 8 (1⅜"-wide) diagonal segments, 1 for each star point. Cut all strip sets in same manner. You should have 1 Fabric 5 strip left over.
6. For each star point, select 1 segment from each strip set. Join these in numerical order (Diagram C), offsetting adjacent segments to match seams correctly. Make 8 diamond-shaped star points.

continued

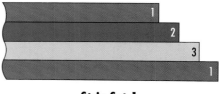

Strip Set 1

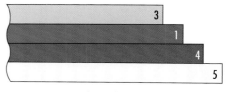

Strip Set 2

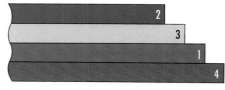

Strip Set 3

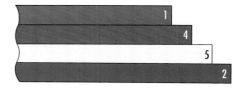

Strip Set 4

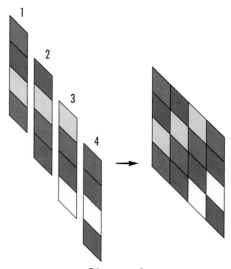

1⅜"

Diagram B

Diagram C

Block Assembly Diagram

7. Join 4 pairs of diamonds, matching seam lines carefully (Block Assembly Diagram). To allow for set-in Bs and Cs, be sure to leave ¼" unstitched at beginning and end of each seam. Join pairs in same manner to make 2 half-star units. Join halves to complete star.

8. Cut 31" floral print square in half diagonally (see below). Measuring from the cut edges, cut 1"-wide bias strips. Cut these down to 7" lengths. You need 16 (7") bias strips for each block (total of 320). Fold under ¼" on both long edges of each strip and then press. (Set aside the remainder for the border.)

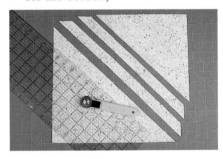

9. Lightly trace bias placement lines (on patterns B and C) on 4 B squares and 4 C triangles. Appliqué bias strips in place, trimming ends of bias even with edges of each piece.

10. Set in Bs and Cs as shown to complete each block, sewing bias ends into each seam (Block Assembly Diagram). Make 20 blocks.

Quilt Assembly

1. Lay out blocks in 5 horizontal rows, with 4 blocks in each row. When satisfied with block placement, join blocks in each row.
2. Join the rows.

Borders

1. From remainder of floral print bias fabric, cut 72 (7"-long) bias strips.
2. Trace bias placement lines from Border Quilting Pattern to each pink border strip, leaving at least 2" of extra fabric at ends of each border strip. Appliqué 20 bias strips on each of 2 side borders and 16 bias strips each on top and bottom borders, trimming ends of bias even with border edges.
3. Matching centers, stitch the inner border strip to the bottom edge of each pink border strip.
4. Matching centers of border strips with middle point of each side, sew borders to each side of quilt and miter corners.

Quilting and Finishing

1. Mark quilt top with desired quilting patterns. Patterns for quilting designs in B squares, C triangles, and outer border are opposite and on page 272.

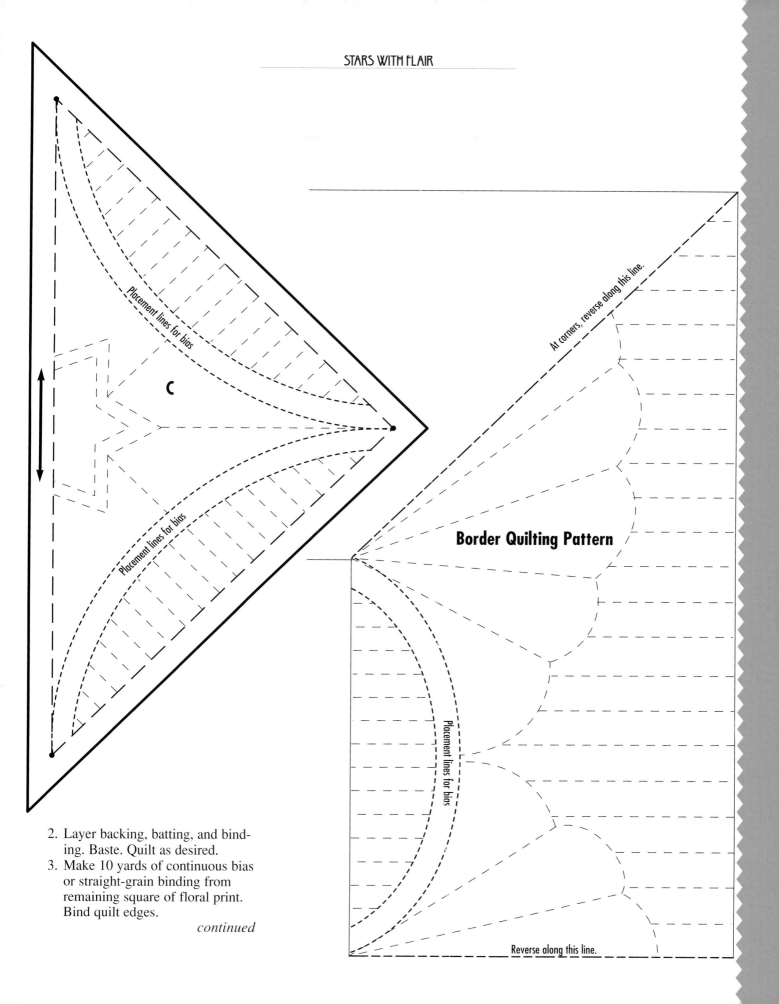

C

Placement lines for bias

Placement lines for bias

Border Quilting Pattern

At corners, reverse along this line.

Placement lines for bias

Reverse along this line.

2. Layer backing, batting, and binding. Baste. Quilt as desired.
3. Make 10 yards of continuous bias or straight-grain binding from remaining square of floral print. Bind quilt edges.

continued

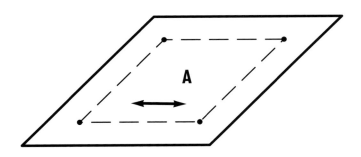

A

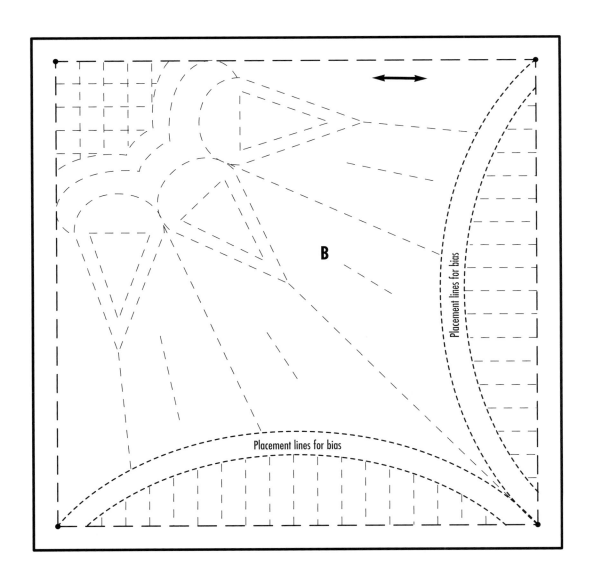

B

Placement lines for bias

Placement lines for bias

RAILROAD CROSSING

This modern-day interpretation of a nineteenth-century classic captures the excitement of old Amish quilts with the simplicity of bright, solid colors against an inky background. Quick-piecing techniques are a bonus that make the quilt fun and easy to sew. Put your own stamp on this design by mixing prints with solids. Or turn the look around and make a soft, pastel version.

Finished Size

Quilt: 70" x 90"
Blocks: 12 (17" x 17")

Materials

60 (7" x 17") solid-colored scrap fabrics, ranging in value from light to medium/dark
4½ yards black fabric (includes binding)
1 yard pale blue fabric for stars and inner border
5½ yards backing fabric

continued

Quilt by Winnie S. Fleming of Friendswood, Texas; hand-quilted by Evelyn Anthony

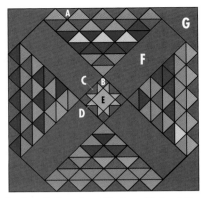

Railroad Crossing Block—Make 12.

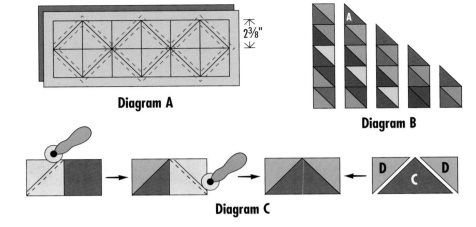

Diagram A

Diagram B

Diagram C

Cutting

Instructions are for rotary cutting and quick piecing. Before cutting, read block instructions and decide whether you prefer traditional or quick piecing. For traditional cutting, use patterns on page 276. Cut strips on crosswise grain except as noted.

From black

- 4 (5¼" x 86") lengthwise strips for outer border. Use 21"-wide strip for next 3 cuts.
- 3 (3⅜" x 21") strips. From these, cut 48 (3⅜") squares. Cut each square in quarters diagonally to get 192 A triangles.
- 12 (1¼" x 21") strips. From these, cut 72 (1¼" x 2") C pieces and 72 (1¼") B squares.
- 3 (5⅛" x 21") strips. From these, cut 24 (5⅛") squares. Cut each square in half diagonally to get 48 G triangles.
- 17 (3½"-wide) strips. From these (and scraps from previous cuts, if necessary), cut 17 (17½"-long) strips for sashing and 48 (8"-long) F strips.

From pale blue

- 5 (1¼"-wide) strips. From these, cut 144 (1¼") D squares.
- 1 (2"-wide) strip. From this, cut 18 (2") E squares.
- 8 (2"-wide) strips for inner border.

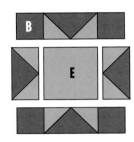

Diagram D

Block Assembly Diagram

Block Assembly

1. On wrong side of each light scrap fabric, draw a 2-square by 6-square grid of 2⅜" squares (Diagram A). Mark diagonal lines through squares.

2. With right sides facing, match marked piece with medium/dark fabric. Starting at middle of 1 side, stitch on both sides of diagonal lines, pivoting at grid corners as shown. (Red lines on diagram show 1 continuous stitching line; blue lines show second line.) Press stitching. Cut on all drawn lines to get 24 triangle-squares from grid. Stitch 30 grids for total of 720 triangle-squares. Press seam allowances toward darker fabric.

3. Each block has 4 quadrants of triangle-squares. To keep fabric placement random, assemble all quadrants before assembling blocks. For each quadrant, choose 15 triangle-squares and 4 A triangles. You can select triangle-squares randomly, but quilt shown has matching (more or less) triangle-squares in rows across quadrant (see photo on page 273). Join A triangles and triangle-squares in rows as shown (Diagram B); then join rows to complete quadrant. Make 48 quadrants and set aside.

4. Referring to page 304, use diagonal-corner technique to sew 2 D squares to each C (Diagram C). Or sew D triangles to C traditionally as shown. Make 4 C/D units for each star, total of 72. Press seams toward Ds.

5. For each star, select 4 Bs, 4 C/D units, and 1 E square. Join units in rows as shown (Diagram D). Press

seam allowances away from C/D units. Join rows to complete star. Make 18 star units, 12 for blocks and 6 for sashing.

6. For each block, select 1 star unit and 4 each of F, G, and triangle-square quadrants. Join quadrants to sides of 2 F strips as shown (Block Assembly Diagram). Join remaining Fs to opposite sides of star. Press seam allowances toward Fs. Join 3 sections; then add G triangles to corners to complete block.
7. Make 12 blocks.

Block Row—Make 4.

Sashing Row—Make 3.

Row Assembly Diagram

Quilt Assembly

1. Lay out blocks in 4 horizontal rows, with 3 blocks in each row (Row Assembly Diagram), placing a sashing strip between blocks. Arrange blocks to achieve pleasing balance of color and value.
2. When satisfied with placement, join blocks in each row.
3. For sashing row, join 3 sashing strips and 2 star units as shown. Make 3 sashing rows.
4. Join rows, alternating block rows and sashing rows.

Borders

1. Join 2 inner border strips end to end to make each border strip.
2. Measure quilt from top to bottom through middle of pieced top and then trim 2 borders to match length. Sew the borders to the quilt sides.
3. Measure quilt from side to side through middle and trim remaining borders to match quilt width. Sew borders to top and bottom edges of quilt.

4. Repeat steps 2 and 3 to measure quilt, trim black outer borders to fit, and sew borders to quilt.

Quilting and Finishing

1. Mark quilting design as desired. Quilt has outline quilting in blocks and cable in sashing and borders.
2. Layer backing, batting, and quilt top. Baste. Quilt as desired.
3. Use remaining black to make 9¼ yards of bias or straight-grain binding. Bind edges.

continued

Size Variations*

	Queen	King
Finished size	90" x 90"	110" x 110"
Number of blocks	16	25
Blocks set	4 x 4	5 x 5
Number of		
Sashing strips	24	40
Stars	25	41
Yardage Required		
7" x 17" scraps	80	126
Blue fabric	1 yard	1⅜ yards
Black fabric	6½ yards	9¼ yards
Backing fabric	2¾ yards	3¼ yards
	(108" wide)	(120" wide)

* *Note:* The size of this block makes a full-size variation impractical.

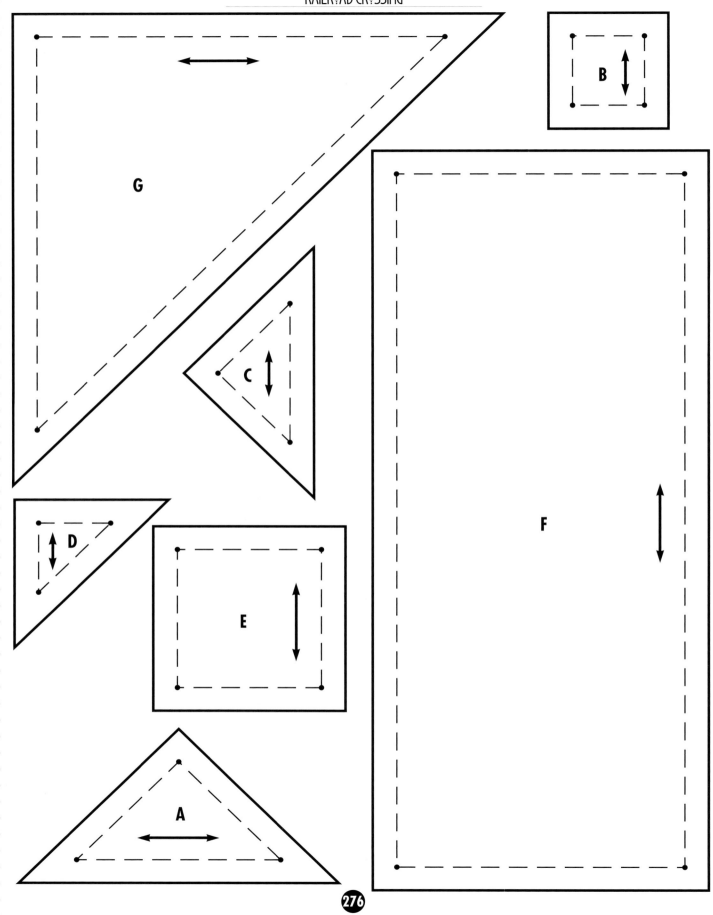

CHURN DASH

Quilt by Mary Carole Sternitzky Knapp of Garfield, Arkansas

This block is also known as Shoo-fly, Monkey Wrench, or Hole in the Barn Door. By any name, this quilt is just as intriguing. Blocks seem to appear within blocks—and how does it all go together? Clever sashing does the trick, along with a slap of quick-pieced triangle-squares and a dash of strip piecing.

Finished Size
Quilt: 42½" x 42½"
Blocks: 24 (6" x 6")

Materials
12 (⅜-yard) pieces dark prints or equivalent scraps
12 (⅜-yard) pieces light/medium prints or equivalent scraps
24 (2½") squares light prints for block centers
¼ yard red print for sashing squares
⅝ yard binding fabric
1⅜ yards backing fabric

continued

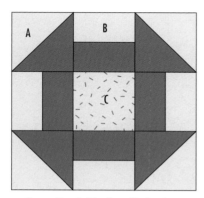

Churn Dash Block—Make 24.

Cutting

Instructions are for rotary cutting and quick piecing. Cut pieces in order listed to make best use of yardage.
From each dark print

• 1 (7½") square for block triangle-squares.
• 1 (1½" x 34") strip for sashing strip sets.
• 2 (1½" x 10") strips for blocks.
• 1 (2⅞") square for border units.

From light/medium prints

• 12 (7½") squares for block triangle-squares.
• 9 (1½" x 34") strips for sashing strip sets.
• 24 (1½" x 10") strips for blocks.
• 8 (2⅞") squares for border units.
• 14 (4") squares. Cut each square in quarters diagonally to get 56 D triangles for sashing.
• 64 (2½") C squares for sashing.
• 2 (2¼") squares. Cut squares in half diagonally to get 4 E corner triangles.

From red print

• 2 (2½") C squares.

Block Assembly

See page 306 for illustrated step-by-step instructions for quick-pieced triangle-squares. See page 303 for tips on strip piecing.

1. On wrong side of each light 7½" square, draw a 2-square by 2-square grid of 2⅞" squares (Diagram A). Draw diagonal lines through center of each square as shown.

2. With right sides facing, match each marked square with a dark square.
3. Stitch on both sides of diagonal lines as shown. (Red lines on diagram show first continuous stitching path; blue lines show second continuous path.)
4. Cut on drawn lines to separate triangle-squares. Cut 8 A triangle-squares from each grid. Press the seam allowances toward darker fabric.
5. Sort pairs of light and dark 1½" x 10" strips, matching same fabrics as for triangle-squares.
6. Join strips (Diagram B). Press; then cut 4 (2½"-wide) B segments from each strip set as shown.
7. For each block, select 4 matching A triangle-squares, 4 B units, and 1 C square. Lay out units in 3 horizontal rows (Block Assembly Diagram). Join the units in each row. Press the seam allowances away from B units. Join the rows to complete the block.
8. Make 24 blocks.

Sashing Units

1. Select 9 dark 1½" x 34" strips and 9 matching light strips. (Discard 3 extra dark strips.) Join the dark and light strips in pairs as shown (Strip Set Diagram). Make

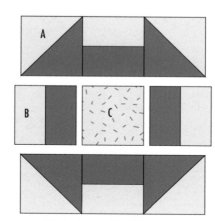

Block Assembly Diagram

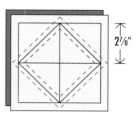

Diagram A

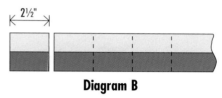

Diagram B

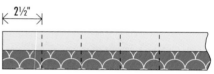

Strip Set Diagram

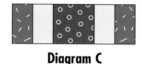

Diagram C

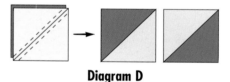

Diagram D

9 of the strip sets. Press the seam allowances toward the dark fabrics.
2. From these strip sets, cut 300 (2½"-wide) B sashing segments.
3. Sew matching B units to the opposite sides of each red print C square (Diagram C). Press the seam allowances toward square. Make 25 Sashing Units.
4. On wrong side of each 2⅞" light square, draw a diagonal line (Diagram D). With right sides facing, match light and dark squares. Stitch on both sides of the diagonal line. Cut 2 triangle-squares apart on drawn line. Make 16 A triangle-squares.

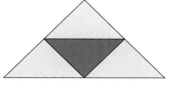

Border Unit—Make 16.

5. Sew 2 D triangles to sides of each triangle-square (Border Unit Diagram). Press seam allowances toward triangles. Make 16 Border Units.

Quilt Assembly

Following Quilt Assembly Diagram, lay out blocks and sashing units in diagonal rows on a clean floor or large table. Start laying out units from bottom left corner of quilt. Do not join units until all rows are laid out and you are satisfied with placement.

1. For Row 1, select 2 Border Units. Between these units, line up 1 each of units B, C, and E as shown.
2. For Row 2, select 1 Sashing Unit with fabrics that match B unit in Row 1. Stack C squares and D triangles at both ends of Sashing Unit as shown.
3. For Row 3, select any 2 blocks, 2 Border Units, 3 C squares, 2 D triangles, and 4 B units (1 of which matches fabrics in Row 2 Sashing Unit). Lay out the units as shown.
4. Continue selecting units for each row as shown, being careful to match adjacent Bs and Sashing Units that make secondary blocks when rows are joined.
5. When units are laid out for rows 1–8, stand back and take stock of your layout. Change color placement as desired. Row 8 is center row of quilt—to continue with top half of quilt, turn diagram around and work out from Row 8 toward the upper right corner of the quilt.
6. Check position of all units. When satisfied with placement, join units in each row.
7. Lay out the rows again to check position. (It's important for everything to be in positioned correctly for design to work.) Make any changes needed and then join rows.

Quilting and Finishing

1. Mark quilting design on pieced top as desired. Quilt shown is outline-quilted.
2. Layer the backing, batting, and quilt top. Baste together. Quilt as desired.
3. Make 5 yards of straight-grain or bias binding. Then bind the quilt edges.

Quilt Assembly Diagram

Border Unit

CABIN IN THE WOODS

Quilt by Bette Haddon of New Port Richey, Florida

Whether you see this bucolic setting as cabins in the country or a suburban subdivision, you can customize a patchwork neighborhood to suit your fancy. A consistent sky fabric unifies these fun, scrappy blocks.

Finished Size

Quilt: 82" x 92"
Blocks: 27 (10" x 10") cabin blocks
       58 (5" x 10") tree blocks

Materials

2⅜ yards sky fabric
3 (6"-wide) green print strips
8 (5½"-wide) green print strips
25 (1½"-wide) green print strips
4 (1½"-wide) brown print strips
7 (13" x 16") gold print scraps
11 (1½" x 22") gold print strips
27 (6" x 12") red print scraps
32 (1½" x 22") red print strips
⅞ yard binding fabric
2¾ yards 90"-wide backing fabric

280

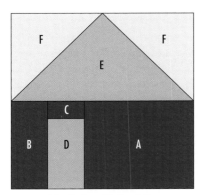

Block 1—Make 15.

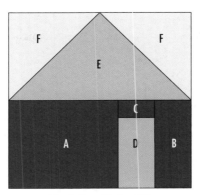

Block 2—Make 12.

Strip Set Diagram

Cutting

Instructions are for rotary cutting and quick piecing. Make templates of patterns J, K, M, and N on pages 282 and 283. Cut all strips on crosswise grain except as noted and in order listed to get best use of yardage.

From sky fabric
- 4 (5⅞"-wide) strips. From these, cut 27 (5⅞") squares. Cut each square in half diagonally to get 54 F triangles.
- 8 (2½"-wide) strips for Strip Set.
- 6 (4"-wide) strips. From these, cut 14 of Pattern J and 14 of Pattern J reversed.
- 2 (5½"-wide) strips. From these and remaining scraps, cut 4 (5½") L squares, 14 (2½" x 5½") I pieces, 4 of Pattern N, and 4 of Pattern N reversed.

From 6"-wide green print strips
- 14 of Pattern K.

From 5½"-wide green print strips
- 26 (5½" x 7½") G pieces.
- 14 (5½" x 6½") H pieces.
- 4 of Pattern M.

From each gold print scrap fabric
- 1 (1½" x 16") strip for border.
- 1 (11¼") square. Cut each square in quarters diagonally to get a total of 27 E triangles (and 1 extra).
- 4 (2½" x 4½") D pieces (includes 1 extra).

From each red print scrap fabric
- 1 (5½" x 6½") A piece.
- 1 (2½" x 5½") B piece.
- 1 (1½" x 2½") C piece.

House Block Assembly

1. Sew F triangles to both short legs of each E triangle (Block 1 Diagram). Press seam allowances toward Fs.
2. Join C piece to top edge of each D piece. Press seam allowances toward C.
3. For Block 1, sew A piece to right edge of C/D. Then sew B to left edge. Press seam allowances toward A and B.
4. Join E/F unit to top of each A/B/C/D unit to complete block. Make 15 of Block 1.
5. For Block 2, reverse position of A and B pieces (Block 2 Diagram). Complete block in same manner as for Block 1. Make 12 of Block 2.

Tree Block Assembly

Refer to Block Diagrams throughout.
1. Sew 2 (2½"-wide) sky fabric strips to both sides of each brown strip

for 4 strip sets (Strip Set Diagram). Press seam allowances toward brown.
2. From strip sets, cut 26 (3½"-wide) tree trunk segments for Block 3. Sew 1 G piece to top edge of each segment to complete block. Make 26 of Block 3.
3. For Block 4, sew I sky piece to each H piece. Press seam allowance toward H. Then cut 28 (2½"-wide) trunk segments from strip set. Sew 14 segments to bottom of each H to make 14 of Block 4. (Use remaining segments for Block 5.)
4. For Block 5, sew J and J rev. pieces to both sides of each K piece. Press seam allowances toward Js. Sew 1 trunk segment to bottom of each J/K unit to make 14 of Block 5.
5. Sew N and N rev. pieces to both sides of each M piece. Press the seam allowances toward Ns. Sew 1 L piece to the top edge of tree. From the remainder of strip set, cut 4 (1½"-wide) segments. Sew these to bottom edge of M/N units to complete 4 of Block 6.

continued

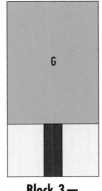

Block 3—Make 26.

Block 4—Make 14.

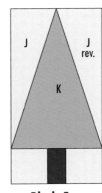

Block 5—Make 14.

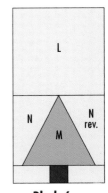

Block 6—Make 4.

Quilt Assembly Diagram

Quilt Assembly

1. Lay out blocks in 8 horizontal rows (Quilt Assembly Diagram). When satisfied with placement, join blocks in each row. Press seam allowances toward tree blocks.
2. Join rows to complete quilt center.

Borders

1. Cut 1½"-wide gold strips into pieces of varying lengths.
2. Join gold strips end to end to make 2 pieced border strips 96" long and 2 pieced border strips 86" long. In same manner, make 4 red borders of each length and 6 green borders of each length.
3. For each side border, join 1 gold, 2 red, and 3 green 96"-long strips. Join 86"-long strips in same manner for top and bottom borders.
4. Sew borders to quilt edges, with gold strip against edge of quilt center, and miter corners. Press seam allowances toward borders.

Quilting and Finishing

1. Mark quilting design on quilt top as desired. Layer backing, batting, and quilt top. Baste.
2. Quilt 1" crosshatch pattern across entire quilt or quilt as desired.
3. Make 10 yards of bias or straight-grain binding. Bind quilt edges.

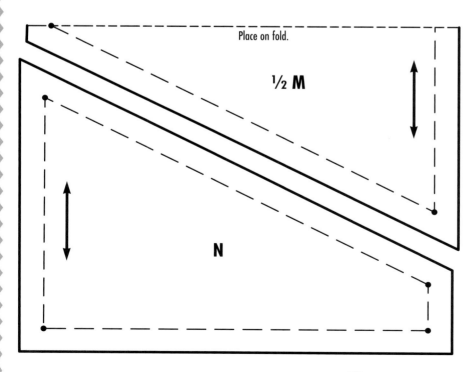

Place on fold.

½ M

N

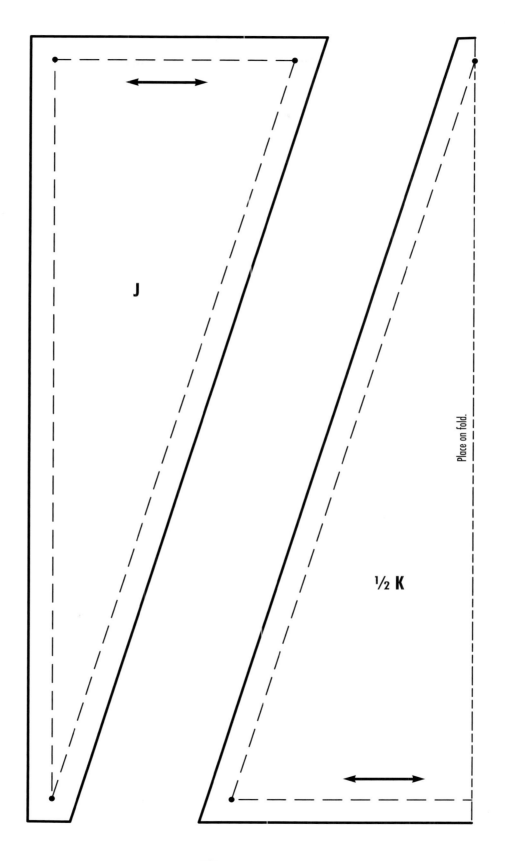

J

½ K

Place on fold.

STARS & CROSSES

Quilt by Linda Esslinger Winter of Holdrege, Nebraska

This quilt reminds Linda Winter of her great aunt, Alma Esslinger. Linda used feedsacks that belonged to Alma to make a quilt in her aunt's memory. "I quilted a rose trellis in the borders," says Linda, "because my aunt had beautiful rose gardens."

The stars you see in this quilt appear only when the pieced cross blocks are joined. If you don't have a collection of authentic feedsacks, reproduction prints work just as well.

Finished Size
Quilt: 101" x 101"
Blocks: 36 (14" x 14")

Materials
20 (9" x 22") fat eighths medium and dark prints
14 fat eighths light prints
6¼ yards white or muslin
2 yards pink print for outer border and binding
½ yard blue print for inner border
3 yards 108"-wide backing fabric

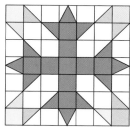

Cross Block—Make 20.

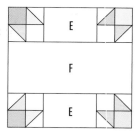

Setting Block—Make 16.

Corner Unit Diagram

Cutting

Cut all strips on crosswise grain except as noted. Make templates for patterns B and C on page 286. Instructions are given for rotary cutting; make templates of patterns A and D for traditional cutting. Cut pieces in order listed to get most efficient use of yardage.

From each medium/dark fabric
• 9 (2½") A squares.
• 4 of Pattern B.
• 4 (2⅞") squares. Cut squares in half diagonally to get 8 D triangles.
Note: You will have 20 A/B/D sets, 1 for each block. Add remaining fabric to lights for additional patches.
From light fabrics and leftover mediums
• 28 (2⅞" x 22") strips. From these, cut 196 (2⅞") squares. Cut squares in half diagonally to get 392 D triangles.
• 25 (2½" x 22") strips. From these, cut 196 (2½") A squares.
From white
• 10 (6½"-wide) strips. From these, cut 16 (6½" x 14½") F pieces and 56 (4½" x 6½") E pieces.
• 28 (2½"-wide) strips. From these, cut 436 (2½") A squares.
• 80 of Pattern C.
• 80 of Pattern C reversed.
• 19 (2⅞"-wide) strips. Cut strips into 276 (2⅞") squares. Cut squares in half diagonally to get 552 D triangles.
From blue print
• 10 (1½"-wide) strips.
From pink print
• 10 (4"-wide) strips.
• 11 (2½"-wide) strips for binding.

Cross Block Assembly

Refer to Cross Block Assembly Diagram throughout.
1. Select 1 block set of A/B/D pieces. Join 5 print A squares and 4 white A squares to make a nine-patch unit (Nine-Patch Diagram).

Nine-Patch Diagram

2. Join 1 C and 1 C rev. to B (Point Unit Diagram). Press seam allowances toward Cs.
3. For each Side Unit, join print D triangles and white Ds to make 2 triangle-square units (Side Unit Diagram). Sew these to opposite

Point Unit Diagram   **Side Unit Diagram**

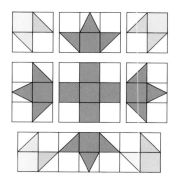

Cross Block Assembly Diagram

sides of print A square, positioning triangles as shown. Sew 2 white A squares to the sides of Point Unit. Join the rows to complete Side Unit. Make 4 units for each block.
4. For each Corner Unit, make 2 triangle-square units, using white Ds and light print Ds (Corner Unit Diagram). Join these to 1 light print A square and 1 white A as shown. Make 4 Corner Units.
5. Join 4 Side Units, nine-patch, and 4 Corner Units to make 1 block.
6. Make 20 blocks, using set of print A/B/D pieces for each block.

Setting Block Assembly

Refer to Setting Block Assembly Diagram throughout.
1. Make 64 more Corner Units for Setting Blocks.
2. Select 4 units for each block. Sew 2 Corner Units to opposite ends of 2 E pieces. Press seam allowances toward E.
3. Sew corner rows to 1 F to complete block. Press seam allowances toward F.
4. Make 16 Setting Blocks.

continued

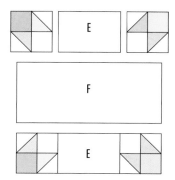

Setting Block Assembly Diagram

Border Unit Assembly

Make 52 Corner Units as before. Join 1 unit to each end of 1 E (Border Unit Assembly Diagram). Make 24 Border Units. Remaining 4 Corner Units will be border corners.

Border Unit Assembly Diagram

Quilt Assembly

Refer to Quilt Assembly Diagram throughout.

1. Lay out blocks in 6 horizontal rows of 6 blocks each, alternating Cross Blocks and Setting Blocks as shown. Rearrange blocks until you achieve pleasing balance of color and value. Then join blocks in each row. Press seam allowances toward Setting Blocks.
2. Join rows to complete quilt center.
3. Join 2 rows of Border Units, with 6 units in each row. Sew 1 strip to each quilt side, matching seams. Make 2 more rows of Border Units, adding Corner Units to row ends. Add rows to top and bottom of quilt, matching seams.

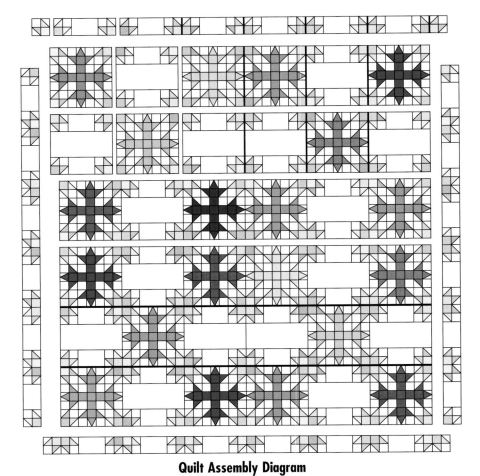

Quilt Assembly Diagram

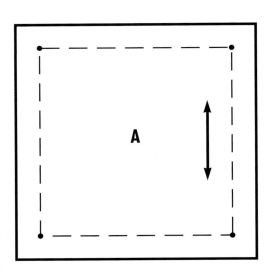

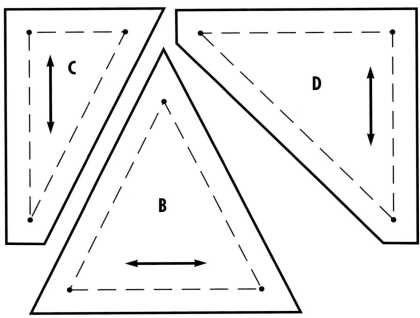

Borders

1. Cut 2 blue border strips in half. Join 2 strips plus 1 half strip to make border for each quilt side.
2. Measuring through middle of quilt, measure quilt from top to bottom. Trim 2 borders to match length. Sew strips to quilt sides.
3. Measure the width of the quilt.

Trim the remaining 2 borders to fit and then sew to the top and bottom edges.
4. Sew pink outer borders to quilt top in same manner.

Quilting and Finishing

1. Mark the quilting designs on the quilt top as desired. The quilt shown is outline-quilted, and the background is filled with a diagonal grid pattern.
2. Layer backing, batting, and quilt top. Baste together. Then quilt as desired.
3. Join pink strips into 1 continuous piece for straight-grain binding. Bind quilt edges.

PYRAMIDS

Quilt by Lyn D. Johnson of Columbia, South Carolina

A skillful blend of hue and value, this easy-to-sew quilt contrasts busy prints with subtle tone-on-tone fabrics in each triangular block. To expand your fabric selection, exchange scraps with friends. It's fun—and you can all make quilts together.

Finished Size

Quilt: 85½" x 93¼"
Blocks: 88 (9⅞" x 11⅞")
Half-blocks: 16 (8" x 11⅞")

Materials

16 (4" x 14") or equivalent
    scraps *each* of gold and
    purple fabrics
11 (4" x 14") or equivalent
    scraps *each* of brown and
    beige fabrics
30 (4" x 14") or equivalent
    scraps of blue fabrics
44 (4" x 14") or equivalent
    scraps of green fabrics
36 (4" x 14") or equivalent
    scraps of red/pink fabrics
2¾ yards black miniprint
8 yards backing fabric or
    3 yards 90"-wide backing
Note: Divide scraps evenly
between prints and tone-on-
tone fabrics, with a range
of light, medium, and dark
values in each color group.
See "Sorting Fabrics" for
more information.

288

Sorting Fabrics

To achieve the look of Lyn Johnson's quilt, sort fabrics by color, value, and texture. Each block is a combination of multicolored prints and tone-on-tone fabrics. For each dark block, make corresponding light block of same color family.

Start by sorting fabrics into color families: blue, green, gold, brown, red, and purple. Some fabrics could fit more than 1 group. For example, is teal a blue or a green? If you have enough blue-green fabrics, make that new color family. If you have only a few, mix them into both groups.

Next, sort each color family into lights and darks. Most fabrics clearly fall into 1 group or another. Mediums can go in either group because these adapt to lightness or darkness of surrounding fabrics.

Lastly, sort for texture. Separate each group into large or multicolored prints and tone-on-tone fabrics.

When you've finished sorting, you should have at least 24 distinct fabric groups. (Use zip-top bags or plastic boxes to keep them sorted.) Cutting instructions below list how many triangles to cut from each group.

Cutting

For traditional cutting, use patterns A, B, and C on page 291 to make templates. For rotary cutting, align 60° angles on rotary-cutting ruler with bottom edge of 4"-wide strip to cut equilateral triangles (Diagrams A and B).

From prints
- 48 As, 5 Bs, and 4 Bs reversed of brown.
- 48 As, 4 Bs, and 5 Bs reversed of beige/light brown.
- 58 As of dark blue.
- 56 As of light blue.
- 72 As each of dark green and light green.

- 72 As, 4 Bs, and 5 Bs reversed of dark red/red-violet.
- 72 As, 4 Bs, and 4 Bs reversed of pink (light red).
- 30 As of dark purple.
- 24 As each of light purple, dark gold and yellow (light gold).

From tone-on-tone fabrics
- 25 As, 2 Bs, and 2 Bs reversed of brown.
- 23 As, 2 Bs, and 2 Bs reversed of beige.
- 34 As of dark blue.
- 31 As, 1 B, and 1 B reversed of light blue.
- 46 As and 1 B of dark green.
- 44 As of light green.
- 47 As, 2 Bs, and 2 Bs reversed of dark red/red-violet.
- 42 As, 2 Bs, and 2 Bs reversed of pink.
- 19 As and 1 B reversed of dark purple.
- 22 As of light purple.
- 23 As and 1 B of dark gold.
- 19 As of yellow.

Diagram A

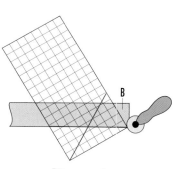

Diagram B

Block Assembly

1. For 1 block, select 6 print triangles and 3 tone-on-tone triangles of same color and value.
2. Join print triangles in 2 rows of 3 triangles each as shown (Diagram C). Join the rows.

Diagram C

3. Sew tone-on-tone triangles to 3 sides of center unit to complete block as shown (Diagram D). Press.

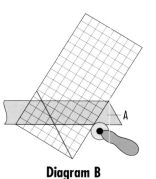

Diagram D

4. In this manner, make 4 blocks each of dark purple, light purple, gold, and yellow; 6 blocks each of brown and beige; 8 blocks each of dark blue and light blue; 12 blocks each of dark green and light green; and 10 blocks each of red and pink.
5. Make half-blocks in same manner. Make 4 each of red or red-violet, pink, brown, and beige. Make half of each set with 2 Bs and 1 B rev. (Diagram E, left); make second pair of half-blocks with 1 B and 2 Bs rev. (Diagram E, right).

continued

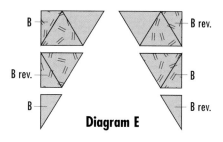

Diagram E

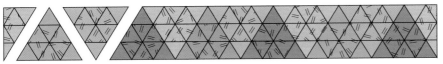

Row 1—Make 2.

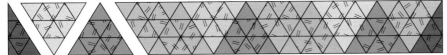

Row 2—Make 2.

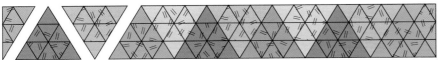

Row 3—Make 2.

Row 4—Make 2.

Row Assembly Diagram

Quilt Assembly

Refer to photo on page 288 and Row Assembly Diagram throughout.

1. For Row 1, select 2 blocks each of dark blue and pink, 3 blocks each of dark green and beige, 1 dark purple block, and 2 pink half-blocks. Starting with half-block at left side, join blocks as shown. Make 2 of Row 1.

2. For Row 2, select 2 blocks each of gold and light blue, 3 blocks each of light green and red, 1 light purple block, and 2 brown half-blocks. Join blocks as shown. Make 2 of Row 2.

3. For Row 3, select 2 blocks each of dark blue and yellow, 3 blocks each of dark green and pink, 1 dark purple block, and 2 beige half-blocks. Join blocks as shown. Make 2 of Row 3.

4. For Row 4, select 2 blocks each of light blue and red, 3 blocks each of light green and brown, 1 light purple block, and 2 red half-blocks. Join blocks as shown. Make 2 of Row 4.

5. Join rows 1-2-3-4. Assemble second set of rows 1-2-3-4. Join Row 4 of first set to Row 1 of second set.

Borders

1. From black fabric, cut 8 (2½"-wide) lengthwise strips. Set aside 4 strips for outer border. Measure quilt through middle of pieced top and trim remaining strips for inner border. Sew the border strips to the quilt edges with square corners.

2. For the middle border, join the remaining A triangles in 14 groups of 5, consisting of 2 lights and 3 darks per group (Diagram F). Then make 8 units with B triangles for the corners (Diagram G) and make 4 nine-triangle units with 4 lights and 5 darks (Diagram H).

3. From black fabric, cut 22 A triangles and 4 (3¾") C squares.

4. For the top border, select any 5 five-triangle units, 2 corner units, and 6 black As. Referring to the photo on page 288, lay out the units in a row, with the black triangles between the units and the dark fabrics at the bottom. When satisfied with the placement, join the units. Sew the border to the top edge of the quilt, easing as necessary.

5. Make the bottom border in the same manner.

6. For each side border, join 2 nine-triangle units, 2 five-triangle units, 2 corner units, and 5 black triangles as shown. Sew black squares to border ends. Sew the borders to the quilt sides, easing as necessary.

7. For outer border, measure and trim remaining black strips to quilt edges. Sew borders to quilt with square corners.

Quilting and Finishing

1. Mark quilting design on quilt top as desired. Quilt shown has echo quilting in each block and half-block (see Quilting Pattern on opposite page). Black borders on quilt are outline-quilted.

2. Layer backing, batting, and quilt top. Baste together. Then quilt as desired.

3. Use remaining black fabric to make 10 yards of bias or straight-grain binding. Then bind the quilt edges.

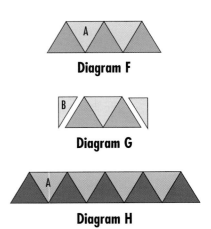

Diagram F

Diagram G

Diagram H

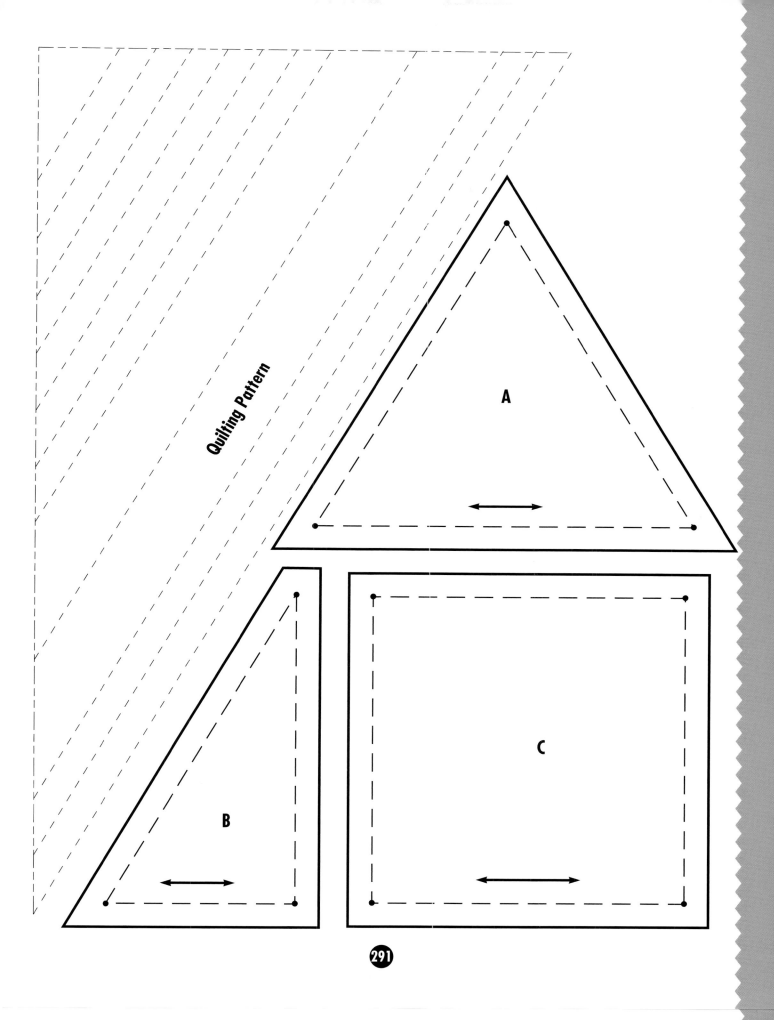

Quilting Pattern

A

B

C

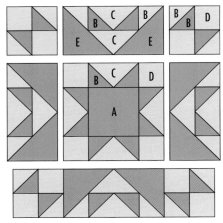

Block Assembly Diagram

Quilt Assembly

1. Sew 1 green sashing strip to both sides of each pink/orange sashing strip (Diagram D). Make 17 strip sets. Press all seam allowances toward green.

2. Cut 3 (12½"-wide) segments from each strip set to get total of 49 segments.

3. Lay out the blocks in 5 horizontal rows, with 4 blocks in each row (Row Assembly Diagram). Arrange the blocks to achieve a pleasing balance of color and pattern. Then place the sashing units between the blocks and at both ends of each row.

4. Lay out remaining sashing units in 6 rows at top, bottom, and between block rows, alternating sashing units with small star blocks (Row Assembly Diagram).

5. When satisfied with the placement of blocks, join blocks and sashing in each row. Press the seam allowances toward sashing units in all rows.

6. Then join the rows, alternating the sashing rows and the block rows.

Borders

1. Measure the length of the pieced top through middle. Trim 2 border strips to match length. Sew the borders to the sides, easing to fit. Press the seam allowances toward borders.

2. Measure width of top through middle, including side borders. Trim remaining borders to match width. Sew to top and bottom edges, easing to fit. Press seam allowances toward borders.

Quilting and Finishing

1. Layer backing, batting, and quilt top. Baste.

2. Quilt as desired. Quilt is outline-quilted with variegated embroidery floss; diagonal lines extend into sashing and borders.

3. Make 9¼ yards of straight-grain or bias binding from reserved fabric. Bind quilt edges.

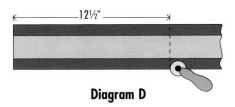

Diagram D

Sashing Row—Make 6.

Block Row—Make 5.

Row Assembly Diagram

294

continued

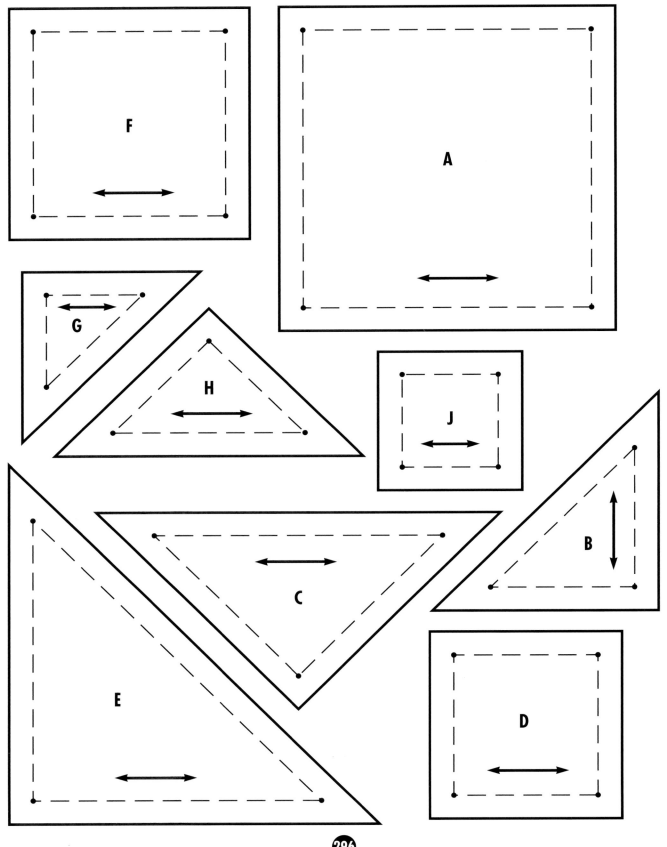

STEP-BY-STEP GUIDE TO QUILTMAKING

The following pages reveal the basics of
making quilts, with step-by-step photos and
easy-to-follow illustrations. Just take one step at
a time, and you'll find quiltmaking engrossing,
fulfilling, and a joy for life.

FABRIC PREPARATION

Lightweight 100% cotton fabric is the best choice for quilts. Sturdy and durable, cotton is neither stretchy nor tightly woven and takes a crease well, so seams are easy to press. When you use good quality fabrics, your quilt looks nice and lasts a long time.

Selecting Fabrics

Choosing fabrics seems to bring out insecurities in many quiltmakers. Will my quilt look as good as the one in the picture? If I change the color to blue, will my quilt look as nice as the green one?

Trust your instincts. There are no right or wrong choices, nor are there any hard-and-fast rules governing fabric selection. Go with fabrics you like. You can ask for help from family and friends, but the final choice should be yours.

Work with the staff at your local quilt shop. Take down half the bolts in the store, if necessary, to try different combinations. Group your choices on a table and then—and this is important—step back at least 8 feet and *squint*. This gives you a preview of the mix of value and texture. If a fabric looks out of place, replace it and try again ... and again ... and again, until you're satisfied.

Prewashing

Conventional wisdom is to wash, dry, and iron fabrics before cutting to eliminate the center crease, excess dye, and sizing. However, many quilters skip this step because they like working with the crispness of unwashed fabric. If you decide not to prewash, you risk bleeding of dyes and/or random shrinkage when the completed quilt is washed.

To prewash fabric, use the same washer and detergent that you'll use to wash the finish quilt. Wash light and dark colors separately in warm water. Use a mild detergent or Orvus Paste (a mild soap available at many quilt shops).

If repeated rinsing doesn't stop the bleeding, don't use that fabric—the bleeding may never stop and could ruin your quilt the first time you wash it. Take the fabric back to the store and *complain!*

Test for colorfastness. Thanks to the improved dyes and processes, bleeding isn't the problem it was in grandmother's time. If you want to skip prewashing, cut a small piece of each fabric and rinse each separately in the sink, adding a clean scrap of white fabric. If any scrap becomes stained with dye, you should definitely prewash. If all scraps remain white, the odds are good—but not guaranteed—that the dyes won't run.

Dry and press. Dry prewashed fabrics in the dryer at medium or permanent-press setting until they're just damp. Then press them dry. It's important to iron out all creases and folds so that you'll have smooth, straight fabrics with which to work.

Grain Lines

The interwoven lengthwise and crosswise threads of a fabric are grain lines. Think about grain direction before you cut. Cotton fabric can be stable or stretchy, depending on how it is cut.

Selvage. The lengthwise finished edges of uncut fabric are selvages (Grain Diagram). These edges are more tightly woven than the body of the fabric. Always trim the selvage from the ends of a strip before cutting quilt pieces.

Straight grain. Lengthwise grain, parallel to the selvage, has the least give. Long strips for sashing and borders, which must retain their shape over time, are best cut lengthwise for stability.

Crosswise grain, perpendicular to the selvage, has more give. For most patchwork pieces, strips are cut on the crosswise grain, but either direction is acceptable.

Bias. True bias is at a 45° angle to the selvages, on the diagonal between lengthwise and crosswise grains (Grain Diagram). Bias-cut fabric has the most stretch. When you cut a triangle, at least one edge of it is bias. Handle bias edges carefully, as they can easily stretch out of shape, warping the patchwork.

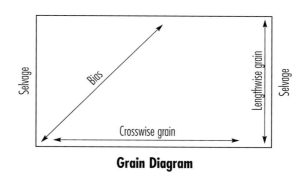

Grain Diagram

BEDCOVER SIZE VARIATIONS

We give instructions for each quilt project in one size. When possible, we include bonus size information. Even so, you might want to make adjustments to suit a quilt intended for a particular bed. Consider the quilt's design, the bed's size and style, and your own preferences.

Lap quilts, doll quilts, wall hangings, or quilts "just for show" can be any size you like.

Getting a Good Fit

The bed style will influence a quilt's finished size. For example, a quilt made for a four-poster bed needs more length and width than one made for a contemporary platform-style bed.

On most beds, a quilt's length and width is also affected by whether you use a dust ruffle or whether you let the quilt hang past the box spring or even to the floor. Also consider the bed's height and if you want to tuck pillows underneath or prefer to let the quilt lie flat at the top of the bed.

Standard Sizes

Once you choose the look you want, refer to the chart below to find the mattress size and dimensions of the corresponding style of bedcover.

Comforters. Most comforters cover the mattress but not the box spring and do not allow for a pillow tuck. Treat comforter dimensions as minimum standards if you want to use your quilt with a dust ruffle and decorative pillows.

Bedspreads. A bedspread covers the bed, falls almost to the floor, and allows for a pillow tuck. These sizes are maximum proportions, assuming the top of the mattress is a standard 20" from the floor.

Custom calculations. The information in the chart below gives average dimensions for four popular bed sizes. These dimensions include a 12" drop on three sizes and 8" for a pillow tuck. If your needs differ, here's how to calculate the best finished size for your quilt:

Start with the mattress dimensions. If you want a pillow tuck, add 8" to 10" to the length.

To determine the length of the drop, measure from the top of your mattress to just below the top of the dust ruffle, all the way to the floor, or to some desired point in between. For most quilts, you'll add the measurement for one drop to the length and two drops to the width of the quilt's finished size.

Example: Let's figure the size of a quilt for a queen-size bed. For this example, we'll assume a 12" drop is wanted, but no extra is needed for a pillow tuck.

We know a queen-size mattress measures 60" x 80". To figure the desired width of your quilt, add the 12" drop twice to the width of the mattress: 60" + 12" + 12" = 84". To figure the quilt's desired length, add the 12" drop to the length of the mattress: 80" + 12" = 92".

Finally, remember that these calculated dimensions (and sizes given with instructions) are mathematical calculations. The finished size of your quilt will vary slightly with the effects of sewing and quilting.

Adapting a Design to Fit

If the quilt you plan to make is not the size you want, there are several ways to adapt the design.

To make a smaller quilt, you can choose to omit a row of blocks, set the blocks without sashing, and/or eliminate a border.

To make a quilt larger, add rows of blocks, sashing, and/or multiple borders. Each addition requires extra yardage, which you should estimate before you buy fabric.

	Standard Mattress Size*	Comforter Size	Bedspread Size	Our Average Quilt Size**
Twin	38" x 75"	58" x 86"	80" x 108"	62" x 95"
Full	53" x 75"	73" x 86"	96" x 108"	77" x 95"
Queen	60" x 80"	80" x 88"	102" x 108"	84" x 100"
King	76" x 80"	96" x 96"	120" x 120"	100" x 100"

Standards for spring mattresses; waterbeds may vary.   **Includes 12" drop at end and sides, as well as 8" for pillow tuck.*

ROTARY CUTTING

Rotary cutting is fast because you measure and cut with one stroke, skipping steps of making templates and marking fabric. It's also accurate because the fabric stays flat as you cut, instead of being raised by a scissor blade. If rotary cutting is new to you, use these instructions to practice on scraps. Rotary cutting may seem strange at first, but give it a try—you'll love it!

Rotary cutting usually begins with cutting fabric strips that are then cut into smaller pieces. Unless specified otherwise, cut strips crosswise, from selvage to selvage.

Instructions specify the number and width of strips needed, as well the size and quantity of pieces to cut from these strips. *Seam allowances are included in measurements given for all strips and pieces.*

A rotary cutter is fun to use, but it is very sharp and should be handled with caution. Carelessness can result in cutting yourself, other people, or objects that you had no intention of slicing. Always keep the safety guard in place on the cutter until you're ready to use it. In use or in storage, keep the cutter out of reach of children.

1 Cutters, mats, and rulers (right) come in many sizes and styles. Choose a cutter that is comfortable to hold. Change the blade when it becomes dull. The most useful cutting mat is 24" x 36", but you may also want a smaller one to use when cutting scraps.

Rotary-cutting rulers are made of thick, transparent acrylic. Select rulers that are marked in increments of 1", ¼", and ⅛". A 45°-angle line is also useful. Rulers are available in many sizes and shapes. The most popular rulers are 6" x 24" for cutting long strips, a 12" square, and a 6" x 12" for small cuts.

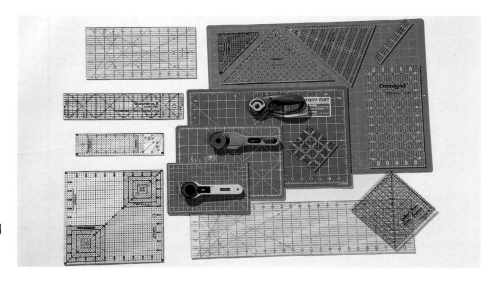

2 To cut straight strips, you must square up an edge. Start by folding the fabric in half, matching selvages. Fold again, aligning the selvage with the first fold to make 4 layers. Let the yardage extend to the right, leaving the end to be cut on the mat. (Reverse directions if you are left-handed.)

3 Align the edge of a large square ruler with the bottom fold. The left edge of the square should be about 1" from the rough edge of the fabric. Butt a long ruler against the left side of the square, overlapping top and bottom fabric edges. Remove the square, keeping the long ruler in place.

4 **Holding the long ruler** still with your left hand, place the cutter blade against the ruler at the bottom of the mat. Begin rolling the cutter before it meets the fabric, moving it away from you. Use firm, even pressure, keeping the ruler stable and the blade against the ruler. Do not lift the cutter until it cuts the opposite fabric edge.

5 **To measure the strip width,** place the ruler on the left edge of the fabric. Carefully align the desired measurement on the ruler with the fabric, checking the ruler line from top to bottom of the fabric. Cut, holding the ruler firmly in place. A sharp blade cuts easily through 4 layers of fabric.

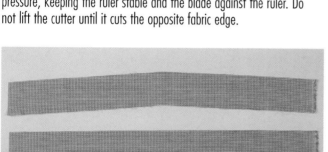

6 **Check cut strips.** If the fabric edge is not squared up properly, the strip will bow in the middle (above.) If necessary, square up the fabric edge again and cut another strip. When satisfied with cut strips, rotary-cut ½" from the strip ends to remove selvages.

7 **To cut squares and rectangles** from a strip, align the desired measurement on the ruler with the end of the strip. Check the ruler alignment from top to bottom as well as side to side to be sure the ruler is straight. When satisfied with the ruler alignment, cut.

8 **For right triangles,** instructions may say to cut a square in half or in quarters diagonally. This works with rectangles, too. The edges of the square or rectangle are straight grain, so the triangle's diagonal edge, from the inside of the square, is bias. Handle this edge with care to keep the fabric from stretching as you work with it.

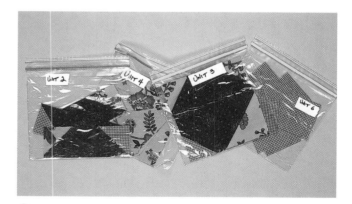

9 **Keep cut pieces** and sewn units neatly stored in zip-top plastic bags labeled with the appropriate unit number or letter. If the sewing takes several weeks, your pieces won't get lost, mixed up, or dirty each time you move them on or off your worktable. Remove 1 piece at a time as you work.

CUTTING WITH TEMPLATES

A template is a duplication of a printed pattern that you use to trace a shape onto fabric. Use templates to accurately mark curves and complex shapes. For straight-sided shapes, it is a matter of preference whether you use templates or a rotary cutter and ruler.

All patterns in this book are full size. Appliqué patterns do not include seam allowances. Patterns for pieced blocks show the seam line (dashed) and the cutting line (solid). To make a template from dimensions given for rotary cutting, use a ruler to draw a pattern onto graph paper or template material.

We recommend using template plastic, which is easy to cut and can be used repeatedly without fraying or cracking. Best of all, the transparency of the plastic lets you trace a pattern directly onto it. Plastic templates are more reliable than those made of cardboard or sandpaper.

To check the accuracy of your templates, cut and piece a test block before cutting pieces for a whole quilt.

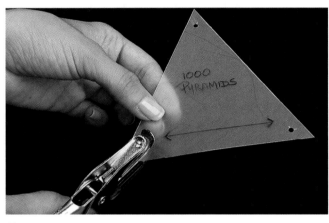

1 Trace the pattern onto plastic, using a ruler to draw straight lines. If desired, punch ¹⁄₁₆"-diameter holes at the corners of the template's seam line to enable you to mark pivot points. (See page 67 for a hole-punch source.)

2 For piecing, trace around the template on the wrong side of the fabric. For symmetrical pieces, such as squares and most right triangles, it doesn't matter whether the template is faceup or facedown. If the template is not symmetrical, always place it facedown on the wrong side of the fabric. Use common lines for efficient cutting.

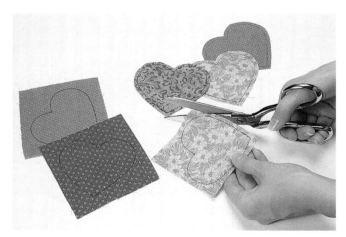

3 For appliqué, trace template on right side of fabric. (A lightly drawn line disappears into the seam allowance fold when the piece is stitched onto the background fabric.) Position tracings at least ½" apart so that you can add seam allowances when cutting each piece.

4 A window template provides the guidance of a drawn seam line, which is useful for sewing a set-in seam. When traced on the right side of the fabric, a window template can also help you center specific motifs with accuracy.

MACHINE-PIECING BASICS

A consistent ¼" seam allowance is essential for accurate piecing. If each seam varies by the tiniest bit, the difference multiplies greatly by the time a block is complete. Be sure your sewing machine is in good order and that you can sew a precise ¼" seam allowance.

On some machines, you can position the needle to sew a ¼" seam. Or use a presser foot that measures ¼" from the needle to the outside edge of the toe. If neither option is available, make a seam guide as described under Photo 1.

To test your seam allowance, cut three 1½" fabric squares and join them in a row. Press the seams and then measure the strip. If it's not precisely 3½" long, try again with a deeper or shallower seam allowance.

Set your sewing machine to 12 to 14 stitches per inch. Use 100% cotton or cotton/polyester sewing thread.

With right sides facing, sew each seam from cut edge to cut edge of the fabric. It is not necessary to backstitch, because most seams are crossed and held by another.

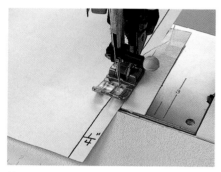

1 Use a ruler and a sharp pencil to draw a line ¼" from the edge of a piece of paper. Lower the machine needle onto the drawn line, drop the foot, and adjust the paper to parallel the foot. Lay masking tape on the throat plate at the edge of the paper. Sew a seam to test the guide. If seam allowances get wider or narrower, the tape is not straight.

2 When you piece triangles with other units, seams should cross in an X on the back. When these units are joined, the joining seam should go precisely through the center of the X so that the triangle will have a nice sharp point on the right side.

3 To press, use an up-and-down motion. (Sliding the iron can push seams out of shape.) Press the seam flat on the right side. On the wrong side, press seam allowances to 1 side, not open as in dressmaking. Press seam allowances in opposite directions so that they offset where seams meet. If possible, press seam allowances toward the darker fabric.

4 Use pins to match seam lines. With right sides facing, align opposing seams, nesting seam allowances. On the top piece, push a pin through the seam line ¼" from the edge. Then push the pin through the bottom seam and set it. Pin all matching seams; then stitch the joining seam, removing pins as you sew.

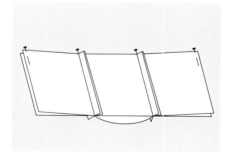

5 Sometimes a pair of units that should match are slightly different. To join these units, pin-match seams and sew with the shorter piece on top. The feed dogs will ease the fullness of the bottom piece. If units are too different to ease, resew the piece that varies most from the desired size.

6 Chain piecing is an efficient way to sew many units in 1 operation, saving time and thread. Sew 1 unit as usual but do not clip the thread at the seam end or lift the foot. Feed in the next unit on the heels of the first and continue. Sew as many units as you like on a chain. Clip units apart as you press.

QUICK-PIECING TECHNIQUES

The three methods explained here are uniquely suited to machine sewing. Combined with rotary cutting, they reduce cutting and sewing time without sacrificing results. Before starting your project quilt, practice any required technique that is new to you. You'll love how quickly and easily the pieces come together.

Diagonal corners. These turn squares into sewn triangles with just a stitch and a snip. This technique is particularly helpful if the corner triangle is very small because it's easier to cut and handle a square than a small triangle. By sewing squares to squares, you don't have to guess where seam allowances meet, which can be difficult with triangles.

Project instructions give the size of the fabric pieces needed. The base fabric can be either a square or a rectangle, but the contrasting corner always starts out as a square.

Diagonal ends. These ends are sewn in a similar manner as diagonal corners. This method joins two rectangles on the diagonal without your having to measure and cut a trapezoid.

Strip piecing. This method requires you to join multiple strips of different fabrics to make a strip set. From these, you cut segments that become units of patchwork. Project directions specify how to cut strips, and each strip set is illustrated. This is a fast and accurate technique because you sew and press the strip set *before* you cut the individual units.

Diagonal Corners

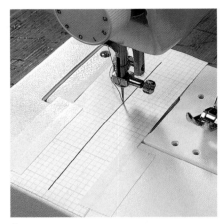

1 Make a seam guide that will help you sew diagonal lines without having to mark the fabric beforehand. Draw a straight line on graph paper. Lower the needle onto the line. (Remove the foot if necessary for a good viewpoint.) Use a ruler to confirm that the drawn line is in line with the needle. Tape the paper in place; then trim it as needed to clear the needle and feed dogs.

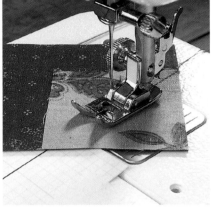

2 Match the small square to 1 corner of the base fabric, with right sides facing. Align the top tip of the small square with the needle and the bottom tip with the seam guide. Stitch a diagonal seam from tip to tip, always keeping the bottom tip of the small square in line with the seam guide. If desired, you can chain-stitch a number of diagonal corners before you stop to press and clip.

3 Press the small square in half at the seam line.

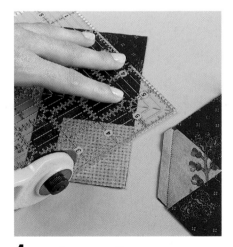

4 Trim the seam allowance to ¼". Repeat the procedure as needed to add a corner to 2, 3, or all 4 corners of the base fabric. This technique is the same when you add a diagonal corner to a strip set or a diagonal end: Treat the base fabric as a single unit, even if it is already pieced.

Diagonal Ends

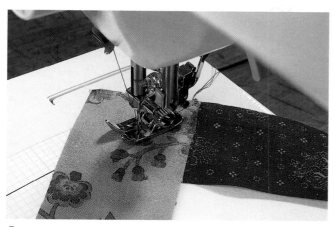

1 **Position rectangles** perpendicular to each other, with right sides facing and corners to be sewn matching. Before you sew, pin on the stitching line and check the right side to be sure that the line is angled in the desired direction.

Leading with the top edge, sew a diagonal seam to the corner of the bottom rectangle, keeping that corner in line with your stitching guide.

2 **Check the right side** to see that the seam is angled correctly. Then press the seam and trim the excess fabric from the seam allowance.

As noted in Step 1, the direction of the seam makes a difference. Make mirror-image units with this in mind. Or you can put different ends on the same strip, as shown above.

Strip Piecing

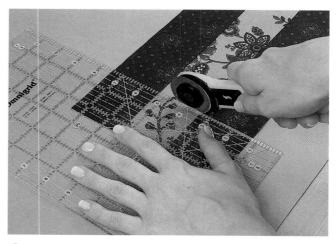

1 **To make a strip set,** match each pair of strips, with right sides facing. Sew through both layers along 1 long edge. As you add strips to the set, sew each new seam in the opposite direction.

2 **When a strip set** is assembled and pressed, you will be directed to cut it into segments. Use a ruler to measure; then make appropriate crosswise cuts to get individual segments.

QUICK-PIECED TRIANGLE-SQUARES

Many patchwork designs are made by joining contrasting triangles to make triangle-squares. These can consist of two or four contrasting right triangles.

Cutting and sewing triangles pose unique problems for quilters. These quick-piecing techniques eliminate those difficulties and enable you to create many presewn units with one process—a real time-saver.

These instructions use a grid method. A grid is marked on the fabric and then stitched as described below.

Cutting instructions specify two fabric rectangles for each grid. We recommend that you spray both pieces with spray starch to keep the fabric from distorting during marking and stitching. For marking, use a see-through ruler and a fine-tipped fabric pen—a pencil can drag on the material, making an inaccurate line and stretching the fabric. Accuracy is important in every step. If your marking, cutting, sewing, and pressing are not precise, then your triangle-squares may be lopsided or the wrong size.

Two-Triangle Squares

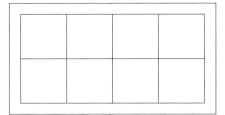 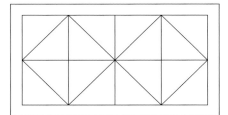 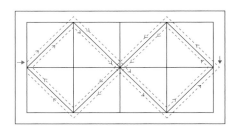

1 For our example, let's say the project instructions call for a 2-square x 4-square grid of $2\frac{7}{8}$" squares. This describes a grid of 8 squares, drawn 2 down and 4 across.

Draw the grid on the wrong side of the lighter fabric. The fabric size specified allows a margin of about 1" around the grid. Align the ruler parallel to 1 long edge of the fabric, 1" from the edge, and draw the first line.

Draw another line exactly $2\frac{7}{8}$" below the first. Continue in this manner, using ruler markings to position each line. Take care that lines are accurately parallel and/or perpendicular.

2 When the grid is completely drawn, draw a diagonal line through each square. Alternate direction of diagonals in adjacent squares. Project instructions will illustrate this final version of the grid.

In this example, we're working toward a desired finished triangle-square of 2" square. The grid squares are drawn $\frac{7}{8}$" larger than the finished size. After the grid is sewn, the cut and pressed square will be $\frac{1}{2}$" larger than the finished size, or $2\frac{1}{2}$".

3 Match edges of the 2 fabric pieces, with right sides facing. Start near the left corner of the grid (red arrow, above). Stitch $\frac{1}{4}$" from the diagonals, as indicated by the red line. At the end of 1 line, stitch into the margin as shown. Keep the needle down, raise the foot, and pivot the fabric to stitch the next line. When you return to the start, you will have sewn 1 side of all diagonal lines.

Begin again at another point (blue arrow). Stitch on the opposite side of all diagonal lines. When the grid is completely stitched, press the fabric to smooth the stitching.

4 Rotary-cut on all drawn lines to separate the triangle-squares. Each grid square yields 2 triangle-squares, so our example will produce 16 units.

5 Press each triangle-square open, pressing the seam allowance toward the darker fabric. Carefully trim points (sometimes called "dog ears") from ends of each seam allowance.

TRADITIONAL APPLIQUÉ

Appliqué is the process of sewing pieces onto a background to create a fabric picture. The edges of appliqué pieces are turned under and sewn to the background by hand or machine.

For hand appliqué, the edges of each piece must be turned under by hand. You can avoid this with some machine techniques. Usually, however, machine appliqué is accomplished by preparing pieces in the same manner and using a topstitch or blindhem stitch to secure them to the background.

For traditional hand appliqué, follow steps 1 and 2 at right. See page 302, Step 3, for tips on making templates and cutting appliqué pieces. Some quiltmakers find it easier to turn edges under with freezer-paper templates as described below.

1 For traditional hand appliqué, use the drawn line as a guide to turn under seam allowances on each piece. Do not turn under an edge that will be covered by another piece. Hand-baste seam allowances. (You can eliminate basting, if you prefer, and rely on rolling the edge under with the tip of your needle as you sew each piece in place. This is called needle-turned appliqué.) Pin appliqué pieces in place on the background fabric.

2 Slipstitch around each piece, using thread that matches the appliqué fabric. (We used contrasting thread for photography purposes only.) Pull the needle through the background and catch a few threads of fabric on the fold of the appliqué. Reinsert the needle into the background and bring the needle up through the appliqué for the next stitch. Make close, tiny stitches that do not show on the right side of the work. Remove basting and press.

FREEZER-PAPER APPLIQUÉ

When working with freezer paper, the finished appliqué is a mirror image of the pattern. So if the pattern is an irregular shape (not symmetrical), you should first make a pattern from tracing paper so that you can turn it over to trace the shape onto the freezer paper, which will prevent the appliqué from coming out in reverse. Usually, you trace a full-size pattern onto the dull side of freezer paper. Cut out paper templates on the drawn lines.

Use a dry iron at wool setting to press the shiny side of the freezer-paper template to the wrong side of the appliqué fabric. Allow at least ½" between templates for seam allowances.

1 Cut out appliqué pieces, adding ¼" seam allowance around each shape. With small, sharp scissors, snip seam allowance at curves, clipping halfway to paper edge. This allows the seam allowance to spread when turned so that the curve will lie flat.

2 Use your fingers or a cool, dry iron to turn the seam allowances over the edges of the template. Do not turn edges that will be covered by another appliqué piece. Pin and sew pieces in place as described in steps 1 and 2 above.

3 When stitching is complete, turn the work to the wrong side. Cut background fabric from behind the appliqué (see left), leaving scant ¼" seam allowances. Use tweezers to remove the paper pieces.

JOINING BLOCKS

The easiest way to join blocks is in rows, either vertically, horizontally, or diagonally.

Arrange blocks and setting pieces, if any, on a clean floor or on a large table. Identify the pieces in each row and verify the position of each block. This is playtime—moving the blocks around to find the best balance of color and value is great fun. Don't start sewing until you're happy with the placement of each block.

As you join blocks in each row, pick up one block at a time to avoid confusion. Pin-match adjoining seams. Re-press a seam if necessary to offset seam allowances. If you find that some blocks are larger than others, pinning may help determine where easing is required. A blast of steam from the iron may also help fit the blocks together.

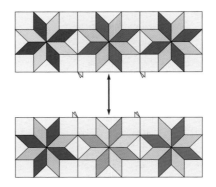

1 Press the seam allowances between blocks in the same direction in each row. From row to row, press them in opposite directions so that seam allowances will offset when the rows are joined.

3 Sashing eliminates questions about pressing joining seams (see right). Assemble rows with sashing strips between blocks, always pressing new seam allowances toward the sashing. If necessary, ease a block to match the length of the sashing strip. Assemble the quilt with rows of sashing between pieced block rows.

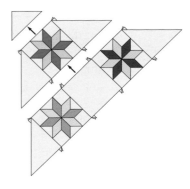

2 In any alternate set, press seam allowances between blocks toward the setting squares or triangles. This creates the least bulk and always results in offset seam allowances when adjacent rows are joined.

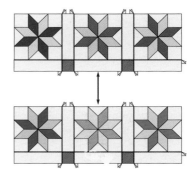

BORDERS

Most quilts have one or more borders that frame the central design. Borders can be plain, pieced, or appliquéd; corners are square or mitered.

The colors, shapes, and proportions of border pieces should complement those in the quilt. The color of an outside border makes that color dominant in the quilt. For example, if a quilt has equal amounts of red, white, and blue, a red border emphasizes red in the pieced design.

Measuring

It's common for one side of a sewn quilt to be a slightly different measurement than the opposite side. Little variables in cutting and piecing add up. Sewing borders of equal length to opposite sides will square up the quilt.

Most cutting instructions include extra length for border strips to allow for piecing variations. Before sewing borders, trim the strips to fit your quilt properly. How you measure, trim, and sew border strips depends on the type of corner you're making.

Square corners. Measure from top to bottom *through the middle* of the quilt, edge to edge (Diagram A). Trim side borders to this length and sew

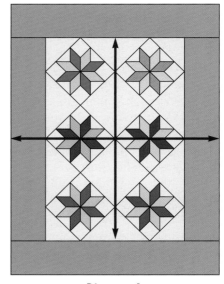

Diagram A

them to the quilt sides. You may need to ease one side of a quilt to fit the border and then stretch the opposite side to fit the same border length. In the end, both sides will be the same measurement.

For top and bottom borders, measure from side to side *through the middle* of the quilt, including side borders. Trim remaining borders to this length and sew them to the quilt.

Mitered corners. The seam of a mitered corner is more subtle than that of a square corner, so it creates the illusion of a continuous line around the quilt. Mitered corners are particularly suitable for striped fabric borders, pieced borders, or multiple plain borders. Sew multiple borders together and treat the resulting striped units as a single border for mitering.

First, measure the quilt's length through the middle (Diagram B). Subtract ½" for seam allowances at the outer edges. Mark the center of each border strip. Working out from the center, measure and mark the determined length on the border strip.

Measure the quilt's width and repeat marking on remaining border strips. Do not trim borders until after corner seam is sewn.

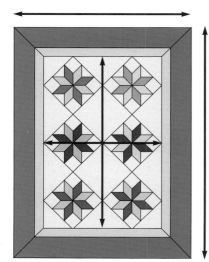

Diagram B

Sewing a Mitered Corner

1 Mark the center and each corner, ¼" from the edge on the wrong side of each quilt side. These marks correspond to marks on each border strip. With right sides facing, pin borders to quilt, matching marked points.

2 Backstitching at both ends, sew the border seam from match point to match point, easing as needed. Join remaining borders in the same manner. (We've used contrasting thread for photography only.)

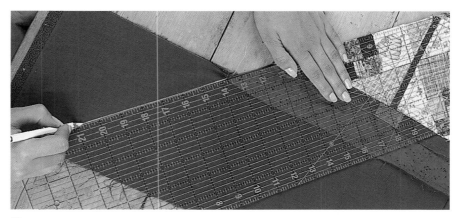

3 Fold the quilt at 1 corner to align adjacent borders, with right sides together. Align the ruler with the fold of the quilt. Along the edge of the ruler (which is at a 45° angle to the border), draw a line from the corner of the seam to the outside edge. This is the sewing line for the miter.

4 Beginning with a backstitch at the inside corner, stitch on the marked line to the outside edge. Check the right side to see that the seam lies flat and that stripes match. When satisfied with mitered seam, trim excess fabric to a ¼" seam allowance.

5 Press the mitered seam open or to 1 side, as you prefer, so that the interior portion of the quilt lies flat. Then press the seam on the right side of the quilt.

MARKING A QUILTING DESIGN

The quilting design is an important part of any quilt, so choose it with care. Stitching together the layers of your quilt creates shadows and depths that bring the quilt to life, so you should make the design really count.

Most quilters mark a quilting design on the quilt top before it is layered and basted. To do this, you need marking pencils; a long ruler or yardstick; stencils for quilting motifs; and a smooth, hard surface on which to work. Press the quilt top before you begin.

To find a stencil for a quilting design, check your local quilt shop or mail-order catalogs for a design that suits your quilt. Or if you know what kind of design you want, make your own stencil.

Testing Markers

Before using any marker, test it on scraps to be sure that the marks will wash out. Don't use a lead pencil just because that's what your grandmother used. There are many pencils and markers on the market today that are designed to wash out. No matter which marking tool you decide to use, remember that lightly drawn lines are easier to remove than heavy ones.

Marking a Grid

Many quilts feature a grid of squares or diamonds as a quilting design in the background areas of the quilt. Use a ruler to mark a grid, starting at one border seam and working toward the opposite edge. Mark parallel lines, spacing them as desired (usually 1" apart), until background areas are marked as desired.

Stencils

1 To transfer a design onto the quilt top, position the precut stencil on the quilt fabric and mark through the openings in the stencil with an appropriate marker. Connect the lines of the design after removing the stencil.

2 To make a stencil, trace a design onto freezer paper or template plastic. Use a craft knife to cut little slots along the lines of the design. Place the stencil on the fabric and mark in each slot.

Quilting Without Marking

Some quilts are quilted in-the-ditch (right in the seams) or outline-quilted (¼" from the seam line). These methods do not require marking.

If you are machine-quilting, use the edge of your presser foot and the seam line as guides for outline quilting. If you are hand-quilting, use narrow drafting tape as a guideline between the seam and quilting line.

Another option is stippling: freestyle, meandering lines of quilting worked closely together to fill open areas. This can be done by hand or by machine, letting your needle go where the mood takes you.

MAKING A BACKING

The backing should be at least 3" larger than the quilt top on all sides. For quilts up to 40" wide, use one length of 45"-wide cotton fabric. For a large quilt, 90"- or 108"-wide fabric is a sensible option that reduces waste. But selection is limited in wide fabrics,

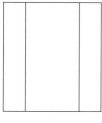

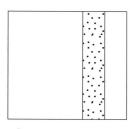

Backing Options Diagrams

so many quilters piece two or three lengths of 45"-wide fabric to make a backing.

Choose a light backing fabric for light-colored quilts because you don't want a dark color peeking through. To feature your stitching, select a plain fabric. If you don't want to showcase your quilting this way, choose a busy print for the backing as camouflage or piece the backing from assorted scraps.

Most backings have two or three seams (Backing Options Diagrams) to avoid having a seam in the center back. (Many experts feel that a center seam augments the creases formed by routine folding of a quilt.) Press seam allowances open.

Creating a scrappy backing is a good way to use up old or leftover fabrics—and make the back almost as much fun as the top. This is how Marion Watchinski got creative with the back of Moon & Star Whimsy *(page 246).*

BATTING

When selecting batting, consider loft, washability, and fiber content. Read the package label to decide if a particular product suits your needs.

Precut batting comes in five sizes. Some stores sell 90"-wide batting by the yard, which might be more practical for your quilt.
Loft. Loft is the thickness of the batt. For a traditional flat look, use low-loft cotton batting. Polyester batting in medium and low lofts are suitable

for most quilts. A thick batting is difficult to quilt, but it's nice for a puffy tied comforter.
Cotton. Cotton batting provides the thin, flat look of an antique quilt. Cotton shrinks slightly when it is washed, giving it that wrinkled look that is characteristic of old quilts, so always wash quilts with cotton batting in cold water to prevent excessive shrinking. Most cotton batting should be closely quilted, with quilting lines no more than 1" apart.
Polyester. Look for the word *bonded* when choosing a polyester batting.

Bonding keeps the loft of the batt uniform and reduces the effects of bearding (migration of loose fibers through the quilt top). Polyester batting is easy to stitch and can be machine washed with little shrinkage. Avoid bonded batts that feel stiff.
Fleece and flannel. Fleece is the thinnest of all low-loft batts. It is recommended for use in clothing, table runners, or wall hangings. A single layer of prewashed cotton flannel is also good for making quilted tablecloths, as it allows the cloth to drape nicely.

LAYERING

A quilt is a three-layer sandwich held together with quilting stitches. Before you layer the quilt top on the batting and backing, unfold the batting and let it "relax" for a few hours.

Lay the backing right side down on a large, flat work surface: a large table, two tables pushed together, or a clean floor. Use masking tape to secure the edges, keeping the backing wrinkle free and slightly taut.

Smooth the batting over the backing and then trim the batting even with the backing. Center the pressed quilt top right side up on the batting. Make sure that the edges of the backing and the quilt top are parallel.

BASTING

Basting the layers together keeps them from shifting during quilting. Baste with a long needle and white sewing thread. (Colored thread can leave an unsightly residue on light fabrics.)

1 Start in the center and baste a line of stitches to each corner, making a large X. Then baste parallel lines 6" to 8" apart. Finish with a line of basting ¼" from each edge of the quilt.

2 Some quilters use nickel-plated safety pins for basting. Pin every 2" to 3". To prevent puckering the backing, don't close pins as you go. When all pins are in place, remove the tape at the edges. Gently tug the backing as you close each pin so that pleats don't form underneath.

QUILTING

Quilting is the process of stitching the layers of a quilt together, by hand or by machine. The choice of hand or machine quilting depends on the design of the quilt, its intended use, and how much time you want to devote to quilting. The techniques differ, but the results of both are functional and attractive.

Hand Quilting

To quilt by hand, you need a quilting hoop or a frame, a thimble, quilting thread (which is heavier than sewing thread), and quilting needles. If you're not used to a thimble, you'll find it necessary to prevent a quilting needle from digging into your fingertip.

Preparation. Put the basted quilt in a hoop or frame. Start with a size 7 or 8 "between," or quilting needle. (As your skill increases, try a shorter between to make smaller stitches. A higher number indicates a shorter needle.) Thread the needle with 18" of quilting thread and make a small knot in the end. (See page 314.)

The stitch. The quilting stitch is a small running stitch that goes through all three layers of the quilt. Stitches should be small (8 to 10 per inch), straight, and evenly spaced. Uniformity is more important than number of stitches per inch. Don't worry if you take only five or six stitches per inch. Concentrate on even and straight; tiny comes with practice.

Knot Diagram

Popping the knot. Insert the needle through the top about 1" from the point where the quilting will start. Slide the needle through the batting, without piercing the backing, and pull it out where the first stitch will be. Pull the thread taut and tug gently until the knot pops through the top and lodges in the batting (Knot Diagram).

If the knot does not pop through, then use your needle to gently separate the fabric threads to let the knot slip through.

Machine Quilting

Choose a small project for your first try at machine quilting because the bulk of a large quilt can be difficult to manage. Plan simple quilting with continuous straight lines. Good choices are outline or in-the-ditch quilting and allover grids. When you are comfortable with machine quilting, try free-motion quilting and more complex designs.

Preparation. To quilt straight lines, use even-feed presser or walking foot. You can machine-quilt without this foot, but the work is easier with it.

Thread the machine with .004 monofilament "invisible" thread or regular sewing thread in a color that coordinates with the quilt. For the bobbin, use sewing thread that matches the backing. Set the stitch length at 8 to 10 stitches per inch. Adjust the tension so that the bobbin thread does not pull to the top.

Roll the sides of the quilt to the middle and then secure the rolls with clips. If you're working on a large quilt, extend your work area by setting up tables to the left and behind the sewing machine to support the quilt while you work. (See page 314.)

Straight lines. Work in long, continuous lines as much as possible. The block seam lines form a grid of long lines across the quilt—quilt these first, starting at the top center and stitching to the opposite edge. Quilt the next line from the bottom to the top. Alternating the direction of the quilting lines helps keep the layers from shifting.

continued

Tying a Quilt

Tying is a fast and easy way to secure the quilt layers. It's best for working with thick batting for puffy comforters. Tying is also fine for polyester batting but not for cotton or silk batts, which require close quilting.

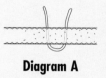

Diagram A

Diagram B

For ties, use pearl cotton, lightweight yarn, floss, or narrow ribbon; these are stable enough to stay tightly tied. You'll also need a sharp needle with an eye large enough to accommodate the tie material. Thread the needle with 6" of thread or yarn. Do not knot the ends. Starting in the center of your basted quilt top, take a small stitch through all three layers. Center a 3"-long tail on each side of the stitch (Diagram A). Tie the tails in a tight double knot (Diagram B). Make a tie at least every 6" across the surface of the quilt. Trim the tails of all knots to a uniform length.

Bind the quilt as described on page 315. If your quilt has thick batting, you'll want to cut wider binding strips.

Hand Quilting

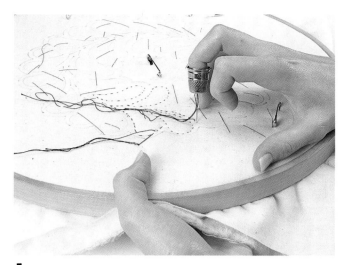

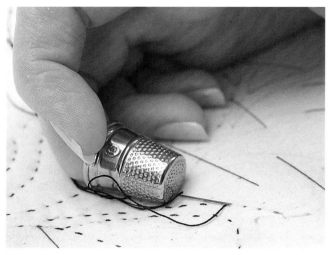

1 **To make a stitch,** first insert the needle straight down. With your other hand under the quilt, feel for the needle point as it pierces the backing. With practice, you'll be able to find the point without pricking your finger.

2 **Roll the needle** to a nearly horizontal position. Use the thumb of your sewing hand and the hand underneath to pinch a tiny hill in the fabric as you push the needle back through. Rock the needle back to an upright position for the next stitch. Load 3 or 4 stitches on the needle before pulling it through. When you have about 6" of thread left, tie a knot in the thread close to the quilt top. Take a back stitch and tug to pop the knot into the batting as you did before (see page 313). Run the thread through the batting and out the top to clip it.

Machine Quilting

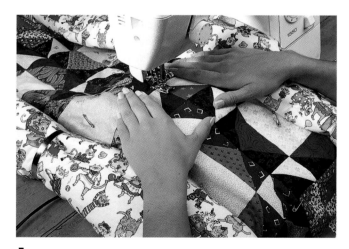

1 **Use your hands** to spread the fabric slightly. Gently push the quilt toward the foot to reduce the drag on the fabric. Quilt vertical lines on half the quilt, unrolling it until you reach the edge. Remove the quilt from the machine and reroll it so that you can quilt the other half. When all vertical lines are done, reroll the quilt in the other direction to quilt horizontal lines in the same manner.

2 **Following a curved design** is a skill that takes practice and patience to master. Start with a small project that is easy to handle. Attach a darning foot or free-motion quilting foot to your machine. Lower the feed dogs or cover them. You control the stitch length by manually moving the fabric.

Place your hands on each side of the foot so that you can maneuver the fabric. To make even stitches, run the machine at a slow, steady speed. Move the fabric smoothly so that the needle follows the design. Do not rotate the quilt; simply move it forward, backward, and side to side.

BINDING

These instructions are for making double-fold binding. Doubled binding is stronger than one layer, so it better protects the edges of the quilt, which get the most wear and are most likely to fray with use and over time.

Cut fabric strips 2" to 2½" wide to make a finished binding ⅜" to ½" wide. Cut wider binding strips when using a thick batting.

Whether to make bias or straight-grain binding is a personal choice. With bias binding, woven threads in the binding fabric crisscross and reinforce the quilt edge. With straight-grain binding, single threads run parallel to the edge of the quilt, making it a weaker binding. But straight-grain binding has the advantages of being easier to make and usually requiring less fabric. When you make double-fold binding, straight-grain binding strips are satisfactory for most quilts.

Follow steps 1–5 to make continuous bias for binding or Step 6 for joining straight-grain strips to get a continuous binding strip. Then follow steps 7–14 to prepare the binding and apply it to the quilt.

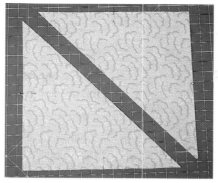

1 To cut bias binding, start with 1 large square. (For example, a 32" square is sufficient to make bias binding for a queen-size quilt.) Center pins at top and bottom edges, with their heads toward the inside of the fabric square. At each side, center a pin with the head toward the outside edge of the square. With the 4 pins in place, cut the square in half diagonally to get 2 triangles.

2 Match edges with pin heads pointed to the outside, with right sides facing. Remove pins and join triangles with a ¼" seam. Press the seam open.

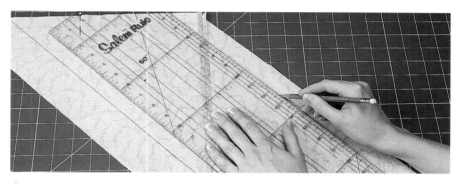

3 Mark cutting lines parallel to the long edges, on the wrong side of the fabric. Space between the lines should be the width of the desired binding strip. For a 2"-wide binding strip, draw lines 2" apart.

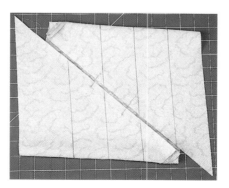

4 Match edges with pin heads pointed to the inside, with right sides facing, offsetting 1 width of binding strip as shown. Join the edges with a ¼" seam to make a tube. Press the seam open.

5 Begin cutting at the extended edge. Follow the drawn lines, rolling the tube around as you cut, until all fabric is cut in a continuous strip.

continued

6 For straight-grain binding, lay 2 crosswise grain strips perpendicular to each other, with right sides facing and then sew a diagonal seam across the corner. Trim the seam allowances and then press them open. Make a continuous strip that is the length specified in project instructions.

7 Press the strip in half along the length of the strip, with wrong sides facing.

8 Position the binding on the front of the quilt top, in the middle of any side, with the edges aligned. Leave about 3" of binding free before the point where you begin.

9 Stitch through all layers with a ¼" seam. Stop stitching ¼" from the quilt corner and backstitch. (Placing a pin at the ¼" point beforehand shows you where to stop.) Remove quilt from the machine.

10 Rotate the quilt a quarter turn. Fold the binding straight up, away from the corner, making a 45°-angle fold.

11 Fold the binding down in line with the next edge, with the top fold even with the raw edge of the previously sewn side. Start stitching at the top edge, sewing through all layers. Stitch all corners in this manner. Stop about 4" from starting point. Choose Step 12 or Step 13 (a and b) to finish.

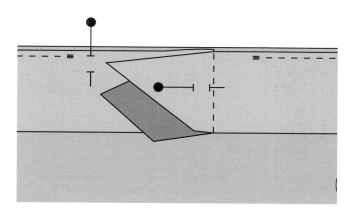

12 **Bring ends** of the binding together, with right sides facing. Hand-baste a seam where ends of the binding strip meet at the quilt surface. Check to see that the seam lies flat; then machine-stitch. Trim seam allowances to ¼" and press open. Stitch unsewn edge of binding to the quilt.

13a **Fold the beginning** 3" tail of binding over itself and pin. Then stitch the end of the binding over it, overlapping the folded section. Continue stitching through all layers to 1" beyond the folded tail. Trim any extra binding.

13b **The beginning fold** conceals the raw end of the binding when it is turned over to the back.

14 **Trim batting** and backing nearly even with the seam allowance, leaving a little extra to fill out the binding. Fold the binding over the seam allowance to the back. Blindstitch folded edge of binding to the backing fabric. Fold a miter into the binding at the back corners.

MAKING A HANGING SLEEVE

Only a sturdy quilt should be hung. If a quilt is fragile, hanging will only hasten its deterioration. Never use nails, staples, or tacks to hang a quilt.

The hanging method most often used is to slip a dowel or curtain rod through a sleeve sewn to the backing. This distributes the weight evenly across the width of the quilt.

To make a sleeve, cut an 8"-wide strip of leftover backing fabric that is the same length as the quilt edge.

1 **Turn under** ½" on each end of the strip; then turn under another ½". Topstitch to hem both ends. With wrong sides facing, fold the fabric in half lengthwise and stitch the long edges together. Press seam allowances open and to the middle of the sleeve.

2 **Center the sleeve** on the quilt 1" below the binding, with its seam against the backing. Hand-sew the sleeve to the quilt through backing and batting along both long edges. For large quilts, make 2 or 3 sleeve sections so you can use more nails to support the dowel.

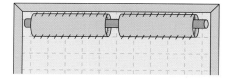

CARE & CLEANING

A quilt's greatest enemies are light and dirt. To keep your quilt in prime condition would mean never using it—but then you'd never get to see it, enjoy it, or share it. You *can* enjoy your quilt and still have it last a lifetime if you treat it with care.

Always shield quilts from direct light and heat, dust, damp, cigarette smoke, and aerosol sprays. The following suggestions for displaying, storing, and cleaning are suitable for most quilts. A museum-quality heirloom or fragile antique may have special needs; if you have such a quilt, get expert advice on its care.

Washing

Wash a quilt only when absolutely necessary. Often, a good airing is all that's needed to freshen a quilt. Vacuuming with a hose removes dust. Dry cleaning is not recommended for quilts because it leaves harmful chemicals in the fabric.

When you must wash a quilt, use a mild soap, such as Ensure or Orvis Paste. These soaps are available at most quilt shops and from mail-order catalogs (see page 320).

If you know that a quilt's fabrics were prewashed and tested for color-fastness, you can wash the quilt as described below. If you don't know, soak a corner of the quilt in luke-warm water for 30 minutes. If the water stays clear, you can be reasonably sure that the dyes will not bleed.

A good soak. If fabrics are prewashed, you can wash your quilt in the washing machine if the machine is large enough to accommodate the quilt. Use cold or lukewarm water and let the machine run through its normal cycles. Never use bleach.

If your quilt is too large for the machine, wash it in the bathtub, letting it soak in warm, soapy water for about 15 minutes. Rinse repeatedly to remove the soap. Squeeze as much water out of the quilt as possible but don't wring or twist it.

Drying. Carefully lift the quilt out of the washer or tub, supporting the weight of the quilt in your arms so that no part of the quilt is pulled or stressed by the weight of the water. Lay the quilt flat between two layers of towels and roll it up to remove as much moisture as possible.

Let the quilt dry flat on the floor. If you want to dry it outside, pick a shady spot on a dry day and place the quilt between sheets to protect it. When the quilt is almost dry—and if it isn't too large—you can put it in the dryer on a cool setting to smooth out wrinkles and fluff it up.

Putting a wet quilt in a clothes dryer is not recommended because heat and agitation can damage fabric and batting.

Fading

All fabrics fade over time. Some fade faster and more drastically than others, and there's no sure way to identify those fabrics beforehand.

However, here is a simple test that is worthwhile if you have time before making a quilt: Cut a 4" square of each fabric. Tape the squares to a sunny window-pane. After 18 days, compare the squares to the remaining yardage. If the squares have all faded to the same degree, you can assume that the finished quilt will keep a uniform appearance as it ages. If one fabric fades more than the others, however, you might want to replace that fabric.

Airing

By changing out the quilt on your bed regularly, you can reduce the damage that exposure causes to any one quilt. Rotate quilts with the change of the seasons, for their own good as well as for a fresh look.

All quilts collect dust. Before you put a quilt away for the season, shake and air it outdoors. A breezy, over-cast day is best if humidity is low. Lay towels on the grass or over a railing; then lay the quilt on the towels. Be sure to protect the quilt from direct sunlight.

Storing

Never store quilts in plastic, which traps moisture and encourages the growth of mildew. Instead, wrap your quilt in a cotton pillowcase or in acid-free tissue paper. Boxes made of acid-free material are also available (see "Mail-Order Resources" on page 320). These materials let air circulate but still protect the quilt from dust and dampness.

Each time you put a quilt away, fold it differently to prevent damage where fibers become cracked and weak. Put crumpled acid-free paper inside each fold to prevent stains and creases from developing along fold lines. If possible, avoid folds altogether by rolling the quilt around a tube covered with a cotton sheet.

Store quilts in a cool, dry place. Winter cold and summer heat make most attics, basements, and garages inappropriate storage areas.

If you keep a quilt on a rack or in a chest, put several layers of muslin or acid-free paper between the quilt and the wood. A quilt should not be in contact with wood for long, as the natural acids in wood will eventually stain the cloth.